Database Design
and
Implementation

PRENTICE HALL
ADVANCES IN COMPUTER SCIENCE SERIES
Editor: Richard P. Brent

Gough & Mohay	*Modula-2: A Second Course in Programming*
Hille	*Data Abstraction and Program Development using Pascal*
	Data Abstraction and Program Development using Modula-2
Rankin	*Computer Graphics Software Construction*
Seberry & Pieprzyk	*Cryptography: Introduction to Computer Security*

Database Design
and
Implementation

L. A. Maciaszek

Department of Computing Science
University of Wollongong

PRENTICE HALL

New York   London   Toronto   Sydney   Tokyo

© 1990 by Prentice Hall of Australia Pty Ltd

Prentice Hall, Inc., *Englewood Cliffs, New Jersey*
Prentice Hall Canada, Inc., *Toronto*
Prentice Hall Hispanoamericana, SA, *Mexico*
Prentice Hall of India Private Ltd, *New Delhi*
Prentice Hall International, Inc., *London*
Prentice Hall of Japan, Inc., *Tokyo*
Prentice Hall of Southeast Asia Pty Ltd, *Singapore*
Editora Prentice Hall do Brasil Ltda, *Rio de Janeiro*

Typeset by
Midnight Express Professional Typesetting Pty Ltd, Cromer, N.S.W.

Printed and bound in Australia by
Impact Printing, Brunswick, Victoria.

1 2 3 4 5 94 93 92 91 90
ISBN 0 7248 0307 6 (paperback)
ISBN 0-13-200015-6 (hardback)

National Library of Australia
Cataloguing-in-Publication Data

Maciaszek, Leszek A.
   Database design and implementation.

   Includes bibliographies and index.
   ISBN 0 7248 0307 6.

   1. Data base design.   I. Title.

005.74

Library of Congress
Cataloguing-in-Publication Data

Maciaszek, Leszek.
   Database design and implementation/Leszek Maciaszek.
     p. cm.
   Includes bibliographies and index.
   ISBN 0-13-200015-6.

   1. Data base design. 2. Data base management. I. Title.

QA76.9.D26M33   1989   89-334435
005.74—dc20   CIP

PRENTICE HALL

A division of Simon & Schuster

To Bożena with love

Contents

Preface

Databases are an essential, if not a dominant, part of computing. Courses in databases assume a central position in undergraduate and graduate computing science curricula and the majority of corporate data processing relies on database technology. Database management is also crucial to a successful and practically viable integration of modern computing principles such as the knowledge-based approach and the object-oriented paradigm. While many books have been written about database management and database theory (including the theory of database design), very few attempts, if any, have been made to provide a pragmatic methodology for the lifecycle of database development. This book aims to provide such a methodology.

OBJECTIVES AND PREREQUISITES

This book is intended for students studying courses in data processing and engineering and for computer professionals.

One objective of this book is to make the methods and techniques of database design and implementation more easily accessible to students of information systems and computer science courses. The book is best suited to graduate and postgraduate courses in databases. It is possible, however, that at educational institutions emphasizing information systems programs, the book could also be used as a principal text for undergraduate database courses. Moreover, it is hoped that the book will be considered as recommended reading for a variety of other computer science courses, in particular in systems analysis and file processing.

A complementary objective of the book is to be useful to people professionally involved in building computer applications which need to be run with a relational Database Management System. This group includes systems analysts and designers, application programmers and database administrators. The book contains numerous practical hints and guidelines supported by detailed examples which are often reproduced from screen dumps taken during sessions with an ORACLE DBMS. An attempt is made to conduct the discussion in terms of the ANSI (American National Standards Institute) relational standard. Whenever the standard is inadequate on technical details, or whenever it does not address some important practical issues, the concepts and solutions available either in ORACLE or in IBM's DB2, or in both, are used to expand on the problem.

The single most important feature of the text is the presentation of an integrated practical methodology for database design. The methodology commences with the analysis and specification of user requirements, derives a conceptual design, then extends

xiii

this to logical and physical designs for relational databases. It then describes the development of application software and concludes by discussing testing and maintenance issues. The methodology uses a wide spectrum of most currently recognized system development methods, such as data flow diagramming, entity-relationship modeling, relational normalization and application generation.

This book assumes that the reader has an appreciation of the capabilities of a modern database system and basic skills in high-level programming. To receive maximum benefit from the text, readers should be familiar with interactive SQL—the principal data language to communicate with a relational DBMS. These prerequisites are not particularly restrictive, and a reader who suspects that immediate study of the book might be tough going, is advised to first read one of the introductory texts on databases, such as *An Introduction to Database Systems* by C. J. Date (1986, Addison-Wesley, 4th ed.).

OVERVIEW

The book is divided into eight chapters and an appendix. The first two chapters establish the background and foundations for the development of a database system. The remaining chapters offer a systematic treatment of successive phases of database design and implementation. The appendix gives a list of Computer-Assisted Software Engineering (CASE) environments useful for database development.

Chapter 1 *Background* addresses some common misconceptions about databases and discusses several crucial issues relevant to database design. Despite its title, Chapter 1 is quite independent of the rest of the material and may be omitted on the first reading of the book.

Chapter 2 *Foundations of Database Design* prepares a reader for a systematic study of the successive design phases. It introduces the concept of the design lifecycle and a few important techniques of database development such as data dictionary, data flow diagrams, entity-relationship model and relational normalization.

Chapter 3 *Requirements Analysis* deals with the analysis and specifications of user requirements. This involves examining the current system and building a problem model. Structured systems analysis techniques, centered around data flow diagramming, are used.

Chapter 4 *Design of Conceptual Structure* discusses the consecutive steps of the second database development phase—conceptualization. This phase is independent of the technical implementation issues, in particular of the DBMS to be used in the implementation. The conceptual design presented in this chapter is based on the Chen's Entity-Relationship Model; however, the Chen's model has been enhanced to provide for a required level of semantic support.

Chapter 5 *Design of Logical Schema* addresses the logical level design of a relational database. The presentation is practically oriented and is placed within the framework of a lifecycle design methodology. The objective is to provide transformation rules whereby a logical schema is derived from a conceptual diagram. Once a first-cut schema is derived, it is subject to formal normalization algorithms (synthesis and decomposition). The normalization is discussed in a rigorous fashion, based on realistic examples to better relate to typical design situations. A highlight of the chapter is the introduction of a graphical representation for a relational schema. This graphical representation is directly convertible to a verbal schema of the database definition (e.g. using SQL's CREATE statements).

Chapter 6 *Design of Physical Schema* examines methods for the physical level design of a relational database. The objective of physical database design is performance. A "good" physical design minimizes the number of input/output (I/O) transfers and makes efficient use of external and virtual storage. In achieving these goals, considerations of concurrency and processing efficiency are involved. Physical database design can be based on an external model of the system's behavior or on an internal model of cost estimates obtained statistically by a DBMS and based on the analysis of "real" query optimizer decisions. Both models are discussed in this chapter and related to storage structures implemented in two DBMSs—the DB2 and ORACLE.

Chapter 7 *Programming User Applications* is about building user applications. Any self-respecting DBMS has its own, usually proprietary, application generator. In ORACLE, the generator is called SQL*Forms. In DB2, an interactive tool (called DB2I) is provided which uses Interactive System Productivity Facility (ISPF) to help develop and execute application programs. Chapter 7 presents the official ANSI standard for the programmatic SQL and uses ORACLE's Pro*C and SQL*Forms to exemplify the application programming and generation.

Chapter 8 *Testing and Maintenance of Database System* covers basic problems and techniques involved in testing and maintenance of a database system. The open architecture of relational DBMSs is helpful in this task. ORACLE database administration and support utilities are used in examples.

ACKNOWLEDGEMENTS

My thanks go to numerous people and organizations. I would like to express my gratitude to Prentice Hall of Australia: to Ted Gannan for initiating and developing contracts for this book and for his knowledgeable control over the contents of the first draft; to Pat Evans for managing a truly professional team at Prentice Hall, and for taking care of the book after Ted was given another offer which was too good to pass up; and to Terri Dodd, Ian MacArthur, Stephen Moore, to the freelance editor Maggie Aldhamland and, most of all, to Fiona Marcar for guiding the book through production and onto the market.

I would like to thank the University of Wollongong (Wollongong, Australia) and, in particular, the Head of the Department of Computing Science, Greg Doherty for hardware/software support and encouragement in my venture. I am grateful to Andersen Consulting of Arthur Andersen & Co. (Chicago, Illinois, USA) and, in particular, to the Director of the Center for Strategic Technology Research, Bruce Johnson, for allowing much of the final editing work on the book to be done using company resources.

I am grateful to friends and colleagues at the University of Wollongong for reading drafts of the project, suggesting improvements, correcting errors, helping over various technical issues and giving advice to my students in the areas where my supervision could not be sufficient. These thanks go to William Bowie, Neil Gray, Phil Herring, Gary Kelly, Warwick Kelly, Stein Krav and, most of all, to Gary Stafford. At this juncture, my gratitude extends also to friends and colleagues at the Academy of Economics in

Wroclaw (Poland) and, in particular, to Zdzislaw Hellwig and Elzbieta Niedzielska for first teaching me the difficult art of writing textbooks.

A special acknowledgement is due to numerous students who took up the challenge of developing software engineering tools for the Intelligent Database Design Kit (IDDK). Some of these tools came very close to production quality—close enough to attract such programming gurus as Gary Stafford and Stein Krav who converted them to commercial products. Many potential errors in this book were avoided by using the IDDK tools in examples and by running appropriate consistency checks (mainly for data flow diagramming, entity-relationship-attribute modeling, and logical schema derivation). Thanks as well to those students who tested and used the IDDK tools in developing full-blown database systems. Their experience and results were invaluable in constructing the case study examples. It is not possible to give a complete list of students who contributed to this book. Special acknowledgements, however, are due to Gerardo Barranquero, Michael Farnan, Wayne Findlay, Jeff Hayward, Mark Hayward, Phil Herring, Sandra Liverani, Stephen Lucas, Kellie Massey, Mark Paine, Phillip Piper, Nicky Plavsic, Peter Roan, Selim Soker and George Zamroz.

I am grateful to Oracle Australia for providing free-of-charge (unless maintenance fees are counted) ORACLE software, worth many tens of thousands of dollars. Apart from the fact that without ORACLE software this project would be unrealistic, hundreds of our graduates would have entered professional life without having the experience and satisfaction of using one of the best, if not the best, database management systems currently on the market. These thanks go mostly to Barry Wong.

All these professional contributions were invaluable in building up ideas. However, the ideas needed to be put on paper and this could not have been done without the loving assistance of those who had to put up with my struggle and metaphysical presence. I thank my wife Bożena for her love, understanding, support and insistence that this book be finished; but also for dragging me off my Macintosh whenever it was all too clear that I could no longer recognize letters on the screen. I thank my daughters, Dominika and Diana, for their interest in what Dad was working on and all the interruptions which, although seemed annoying at the time, might well have protected me from complete madness.

L. A. Maciaszek

Wollongong, New South Wales, Australia
December, 1988
Chicago, Illinois, USA
April, 1989

1

Background

The aim of this chapter is to address some common misconceptions about databases and to discuss several crucial issues relevant to database design. It is an introductory chapter and is complemented by Chapter 2 which offers a more systematic treatment of the foundations of database design. In these two chapters, the emphasis is on breadth rather than depth. An assumption is made that the reader has a basic understanding of database technology.

1.1 FILE SYSTEM VERSUS DATABASE SYSTEM

As a concept, file system is a subset of database system. It is a misnomer to call any simple file system a database system (despite the flexible semantics of the phrase "data base" in English). The whole new branch of computer science called databases developed in response to the shortcomings of file systems which were often called data bases or data banks. In fact, to emphasize the special meaning of the term, the two-word phrase *data base* has been replaced (since the late seventies) by the single word *database*.

A *file* is a data object that resides on an external storage medium such as magnetic disk or tape. It contains a collection of data that is structured according to the requirements of a data processing system. Individual applications (programs) lock one or more files for processing so that other applications requesting the same files cannot run simultaneously.

To achieve a reasonable throughput with a file processing system, there is a tendency to hold some data items in multiple files, thus decreasing the number of files to be locked when running different applications. However, this increases data redundancy in the system and requires extra effort to maintain consistency of the system after updates to redundant data items. Due to the limited cooperation possibilities between files, applications built on a file system are based on file access methods provided by the operating system and on file organizations supported by the programming languages (normally restricted to sequential, indexed-sequential, and relative organizations).

A *database* is a data object that requires a direct access storage medium for processing (magnetic tapes can be used for backup). It has the capability for handling large integrated data structures in a shared multi-user fashion. Physically, that is from the

1

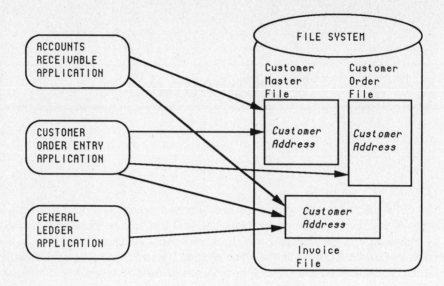

(a) file system

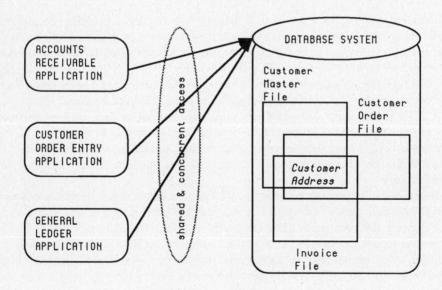

(b) database system

Figure 1.1   File versus database system

viewpoint of the operating system, the database consists of files. However, the data is structured with only limited consideration given to file boundaries. An important motivation in designing database structures is to achieve an extremely flexible level of cooperation (linkages) between small data items, and to minimize redundancy. This is possible due to a fine locking granularity (at the record or even data-item level, rather than at file level). A database system allows concurrent processing, maintains consistency of data (the up-to-date values are available to all users) and supports testing and maintenance (including rapid prototyping as a development strategy for the system).

The database applications need a large software system which runs on top of the operating system and which provides extended file organizations (usually sophisticated multilist and multiattribute-indexing schemes). Such a software is called Database Management System (DBMS). The data structures are defined for an entire database application and are maintained separately from the processes (programs). At run-time, the DBMS is invoked and acts as an intermediary between the programs and the data structures; hence a logical and physical data independence (from programs) is possible.

Figure 1.1 contrasts the file and database system. Suppose that three typical applications and three files have been used for the development of a file system and a database system. The applications are: accounts receivable, customer order entry, and general ledger. The files required by the three applications include: customer master file, customer order file, and invoice file. The data item *Customer Address* is used by all applications. In order to increase the overall throughput of the file system, *Customer Address* is repeated in all three files. This allows for such things as the customer order entry and the general ledger applications to operate simultaneously. In the database system, due to a finer locking granularity, *Customer Address* can be shared by the three applications. Technically speaking, *Customer Address* will be stored in one of the files and the two remaining files will be able to access this data item whenever needed (this is the essence of database design). The user does not have to be aware of where *Customer Address* is stored and will be given the impression of being the exclusive user of this data item. It is the responsibility of a DBMS to enforce, at all times, such an impression on the user. The modification of *Customer Address* does not pose any difficulty, as there is only one copy of this data item in the database.

The following is a list of features that distinguish a database system from a file system (and unless a software system satisfies most of these features, it cannot be considered a database system):

1. multiuser support and concurrent processing;
2. integrated and shared data structures;
3. separation of data definition and data manipulation;
4. logical and physical data independence;
5. support for transaction as a database consistency and recovery unit (a transaction is either successfully completed or rolled back);
6. integrity enforcement (from the entire user community viewpoint);
7. security enforcement (from the individual user viewpoint);
8. interface to data dictionary software (standalone or as a part of the DBMS);
9. built-in application generator or fourth generation language (4GL);
10. built-in restructuring, reorganization, and performance tools;

11. interface to teleprocessing monitor (standalone or as a part of the DBMS);
12. sophisticated physical data structures (multilists, multiattribute indexing, dynamic hashing).

1.2   INFORMATION RETRIEVAL SYSTEM VERSUS DATABASE MANAGEMENT SYSTEM

The demarcation line between Information Retrieval System (IRS) and Database Management System (DBMS) tends to be blurred by superficial similarities; nevertheless the differences are critical. A data object handled by the IRS may be called a database, yet such a database has little in common with the database managed by a DBMS. A generalized DBMS (such as ORACLE, DMS-1100, or dBASE) cannot be satisfactorily applied to typical information retrieval processing and cannot replace, in this role, an IRS (such as STAIRS, MEDLARS, or DIALOG). Moreover, with the prominent exception of IBM's STAIRS, the best-known commercial IRSs are specialized to cater for a particular information retrieval service for a user. This is in contrast to DBMSs which are general-purpose and can be applied to varied data processing systems.

Special features of IRSs, which are not likely to be supported by present DBMSs, include:

1. processing of *unformatted information* (text, pictures, drawings, sound) along with formatted attributes (DBMSs can only easily access formatted data);
2. *fuzzy retrieval* (IRSs attempt to retrieve relevant, rather than matching, information); fuzziness has at least two immediate implementation consequences:
   (a) a highly interactive interface with the user to obtain frequent relevance feedback (i.e. the user's comment on relevance of retrieved information which guides further retrieval);
   (b) probabilistic searches based on fuzzy set theory and which use weights with query and index terms (the weights are used to express the relative importance of a concept within queries and subject keywords);
3. special access methods, such as:
   (a) *multiattribute retrieval* methods, including multiattribute hashing and signature files;
   (b) *inversion* of index terms (which can yield a storage overhead as much as 300 percent greater than the size of user data file);
   (c) *full text scanning* (attractive only when carried out by special purpose hardware or in cooperation with another access method that restricts the scope of retrieval);
4. *automatic indexing* (by a computer program that analyzes text and derives index terms).

In making a comparison between IRS and DBMS, it is important to recognize the existence of different kinds of IRSs, sometimes as different from each other as from any DBMS. Typically, the following systems are categorized as IRSs:

1. *document retrieval systems* (such as library information retrieval);

2. *office information systems* (with significant text retrieval aspects and more dynamic behavior (insertions!) than document retrieval systems);
3. *management information systems* (that also cater for special managerial reports, summaries, averages and projections);
4. *decision support systems* (with strong econometric aspects).

Moreover, *expert* or *question-answering systems* are sometimes considered to be IRSs. These are the systems which use declarative programming and inference rules to deduce information not necessarily stored explicitly in the database. In general, it is more appropriate to classify such systems as DBMSs. Indeed, the most widely used name for such software is an expert database system.

Efforts to incorporate IRS features in DBMSs have more recently resulted in a new class of DBMSs called hypertext systems. *Hypertext systems* take full advantage of the powerful graphics interfaces of modern workstations to represent text, pictures and drawings. Windows and icons on the screen are used to represent objects in the database. The relationships between objects are also graphically visualized on the screen. Mouse, menu bars, pop-up menus, multiple windows, scrolling and scaling are used as techniques for database processing. An example of a sophisticated hypertext system is HyperCard (Apple Macintosh). A Macintosh version of ORACLE DBMS offers a SQL extension to HyperCard called Hyper*SQL.

1.3 MAINFRAME VERSUS MICROCOMPUTER DATABASE SYSTEM

There is just as much difference between a file system and a database system as there is between a *mainframe* and a *microcomputer database system*. Some would go as far as saying that a micro-database is in fact just a file system. However, the development of powerful workstations, together with communications networks to integrate them, must give rise to a reevaluation of the microcomputer's suitability for database applications. Indeed, the special characteristics of contemporary microcomputers have led to rapid successes of a new class of database system—*distributed databases*.

In Section 1.1, we listed twelve features of a database system. We stated also that unless a software system satisfies most of those features, it must not be considered a database system. It comes as no surprise that the first two features from the list are not properly supported in a typical single-user micro-database. These features are:

1. multiuser support and concurrent processing ;
2. integrated and shared data structures.

Support for the following three features is likely to be only rudimentary in a single-user micro-database:

5. support for transaction as a database consistency and recovery unit;
6. integrity enforcement (entire user community viewpoint);
7. security enforcement (individual user viewpoint).

However, current microcomputer DBMSs must make provisions for multiuser *distributed processing* in order to attract corporate users. Whereas individual owners of microcomputers may still be interested only in limited single-user DBMS versions, full-fledged distributed versions of such DBMSs now constitute a real competition to mainframe databases in all but the very large corporate market. At the time of writing, at least three popular DBMSs have attractive state-of-the-art distributed versions—dBASE, INGRES, and ORACLE. It is interesting to note that although the listed DBMSs were originally developed for different-size environments (dBASE for microcomputers (IBM-PC), INGRES for minicomputers (Unix-based) and ORACLE for mainframes (IBM)), the distributed versions of these systems are either based on, or make use of, workstations. It is precisely this convergence of database technology towards workstations that has given rise to the emergence of microcomputer databases in the proper sense of the word.

In short, the real potential of microcomputer DBMSs to support shared distributed systems invalidates attempts to classify such databases as mere file systems (even if they are used by single users for personal applications). In reality, the microcomputer databases of today can not only match the twelve features of a centralized database system, they are most likely to provide the additional benefits of a distributed environment. These benefits include:

1. reliability and availability (if one site fails, another site can assume its tasks);
2. faster processing at lower cost (because of accessing data at local sites);
3. location and replication transparency (the user is not aware at what site the data resides or what data copy (because of necessary redundancy) is accessed);
4. configuration expandability (hardware upgrades do not affect software);
5. nonhomogeneous environment (different DBMSs can be integrated into a common distributed system).

To summarize, at this point in time there is no justification for drawing a strong separation line between microcomputer and mainframe databases. The two environments tend to converge. Just about the only remaining difference is the volume of data that the two systems are able to process. Last, but not the least, the clearly superior user interface of graphical workstations (as opposed to terminals used in accessing mainframe databases) greatly improves the ease and quality of the users' interaction with a micro-database system.

1.4 RELATIONAL VERSUS NETWORK DATABASE SYSTEM

There are two database standards—relational and network. These two models have evolved since the early seventies. Since then, there has been considerable debate about the superiority of one over another database model. This debate has recently been revived by the formal introduction of the two standards, but it still seems to generate more heat than light. The confusion is overwhelming as the premises of the debate have been unsound—the practical successes of network systems are being confronted with the theoretical promises of the relational model. In reality, the two models tend to converge by assimilating the best features of each other. This tendency has been confirmed in the standards, much to the dislike of the proponents of the pure relational model. The standards, however, are not supposed to express the theoretical foundations and promises of a particular research area (in this case relational theory). The standards must come down to earth. This section and, indeed, the entire book is committed to such a pragmatic approach.

There is one striking difference between the historical evolution of relational and network database systems; the relational systems came out of the research laboratories, whereas the network model evolved from practical implementations. The first network systems (IDS of General Electric in the mid sixties and DMS-1100 of Sperry Univac in the early seventies) were used as blueprints for early network (Codasyl) standards (1969 and 1971). The foundations of the relational databases were laid down in the early seventies by Edgar Codd of the IBM Research Laboratory. However, it has taken ten to fifteen years for the database professionals to accept the relational systems as viable, practical alternatives to the network and other widely used systems.

The *SQL* standard has only been one factor in this recent acceptance. Perhaps the most significant reason for it is linked to the strategic decision of IBM to replace (in the long run) its ageing hierarchical system IMS by the relational DB2. This decision had the immediate effect of attracting computer decision-makers to relational technology. The best of the relational DBMSs, considered superior to DB2 Version 1, have rapidly gained in popularity (ORACLE, INGRES). DB2 has recovered lost ground and, indeed, has gained a leading edge in some respects with the introduction of Version 2 at the end of 1988. In the mid-eighties, vendors of the most recognized network DBMSs (such as IDMS and DMS-1100) encountered selling difficulties and, to regain the lost ground, released relational interfaces to otherwise typically network databases (IDMS/R, IDMS/SQL, RDMS-1100). The trend towards the relational technology in database evolution is now irreversible.

The relational, as opposed to the network model, has sound mathematical foundations. It is based on set theory and the mathematical notions of relation and function. The model is simple, elegant and—within its mathematical framework—very powerful. This mathematical framework is governed by the operations of *relational algebra*. These include four traditional operations (union, intersection, difference and cartesian product) and four special operations (selection or restriction, projection, join and division). To the extent that the relational operations are predictable, the model makes the promise of an extensive use of *declarative programming* (giving rise to the emergence of fourth generation languages (4GLs) and application generators). However, in practice, there are limits to how the relational (*table-at-a-time*) operations can be used. The considerations of maintaining database consistency due to updates and the unpredictability of relational results in view of null values (i.e. unknown and inapplicable values), force programmers to use *procedural (record-at-a-time) programming*. In a practical sense, therefore, the principles of programming relational and network databases are identical.

The relational model, unlike the network model, hides the physical database structures from the user. There is no need for the user, at least theoretically, to know how the database is actually stored in order to process it. This advantage, however, cannot be credited to the relational model per se, but rather to the choice of dynamic storage structures (B-trees) as the implementation strategy for relational databases. After all, even a traditional Cobol programmer needs only to (logically) designate primary and alternate keys to program and to make extensive use of indexed-sequential files (also B-trees). Cobol, not the programmer, is responsible for physical manipulations, that is for the creation, maintenance and reorganization of indexes.

Both Cobol and relational database programmers can program without knowledge of the physical structures in use, but they will write more efficient programs if they have such a knowledge. This may not be an issue for the Cobol programmer, but the sheer complexity of large databases makes this an issue for the relational programmer (or rather designer). As a result, the physical level considerations are quite important for the design and programming of relational databases (indexing, clustering, programming with cursors, etc.). Just about the only difference to the network system is the choice of storage structures.

The network systems use relatively static *multilist structures* and explicitly enforce *navigational programming* (which presupposes programmer knowledge about the way the database is stored). This does not, however, inhibit the building of relational user interfaces (e.g. with SQL as a query language) on top of network data structures (as indeed has been the case with IDMS/R, IDMS/SQL and RDMS-1100). Such interfaces can be built because the underlying physical storage structures in the two models are compatible.

There are a multitude of other issues which can be used as comparison criteria between the relational and network databases (such as repeating attributes in records or tables). There is no need to do this, however, as it can be seen from the examples above that any point in such a debate can be argued either way. We have made our point about the likely convergence of the two models in the not-too-distant future (the DBMS called MDBS III is a move in this direction). From this perspective, it is important to emphasize the similarities and to disregard the differences between the two models.

1.5 PROCESS-DRIVEN VERSUS DATA-DRIVEN APPROACH TO DATABASE DESIGN

One popular approach to database design is to use relational modeling to build a conceptual structure. The conceptual design is done in terms of the well-known relational database design strategies—*synthesis* and *decomposition*—and the relational definitions are derived from the nature of the data, expressed in terms of various dependencies, integrity constraints and inference rules. An immediate consequence of this is a conceptual design methodology which is *data-driven*: the influence of processes (i.e. identified business transactions and events) on data structures is compromised.

The resulting design is quite insensitive to the dominant user requirements for data and tends not to be directly tuned to the current (and desirable) pattern of business functions. Moreover, if relations are used to represent the conceptual design, the demarcation between conceptual and logical structures becomes blurred. An important principle of *semantic modeling*, which is to be independent from any computer-based data model, is lost. Indeed, if the implementation system is relational, then the conceptual and logical designs are almost identical in the sense that a conversion of entity-relationship diagrams to relational structures is an exercise in one-to-one mapping.

Interestingly the data-driven approach, based on relational modeling principles, has not gained wide acceptance in the knowledge areas which are primarily concerned with system development methods (i.e. in systems analysis and software engineering). Methods such as the Jackson System Development (JSD) take the stance that it is just as important to capture the dynamics of the business (what happens? when? how often?) as it is to capture its static properties (what information is stored?). In methods like JSD, which are *process-driven*, the dynamics are described first, and then the information requirements are derived from these dynamics. Such an approach is essential. Ultimately, the process-driven approach invites the use of both the methods which originated in artificial intelligence (such as semantic nets) and the paradigms of object oriented programming (such as abstract data types). In this sense, the process-driven design follows the current trend of integrating database, artificial intelligence and programming techniques.

This book is biased towards the process-driven approach. This can be seen mainly in the requirements analysis and the conceptual design phases (Chapters 3 and 4). The methodology tunes the design to anticipated user transactions. Data semantics are derived completely from the semantics of business functions and any performance-motivated refinements and modifications of data structures are validated against the function specifications. Many of the techniques that employ the data-driven methods, such as normalization and abstractions, are used throughout the book for design refinements. In other words, the design is pretuned to user requirements, before being refined by adherence to access graphs, abstractions and normalization.

In practice, it is rare for a database design methodology to exhibit either a purely data-driven or a purely process-driven approach. Practical methodologies tend to combine best features from both worlds. The methodology presented in this book is no different. The decision of how to classify such methodologies depends on the sequence of actions in the design. If the processes (business functions) are used to derive first-cut data structures, then the design is *process-driven*. If, on the other hand, the first-cut data structures are constructed on the basis of the general semantics of information used in the business, then the design is *data-driven* (no matter how soon such a design is validated against the functions). Both approaches, if thoroughly applied, are likely to lead to similar designs. However, a prevailing opinion is that the process-driven approach is more appealing and natural and it can also ensure savings in system development time. Let us now illustrate this point by means of a short example.

Suppose that the data-driven approach is used in the design of a tiny database system. According to the approach, the designer is first interested in the list of elementary information (attributes) processed in the system. The user provides the following list:

{employee_id#, employee_name, employee_address, employee_phone#, child_name, child_birth_date, child_enroll_grade}

The analysis of the dependencies between attributes leads the designer to determine two clusters of attributes (objects):

```
EMPLOYEE = {employee_id#, employee_name,
                employee_address, employee_phone#}
CHILD = {child_name, child_birth_date, child_enroll_grade}
```

Additionally, there is an obvious need to maintain an association between the above objects. Hence, a third object will be:

```
FAMILY = {employee_id#, child_name}
```

At this initial design stage, consideration is given to the purpose of the system, for instance that the database should maintain personal information about employees and their children (as needed, for example, by a salary department). There is no attempt to analyze specific business functions with a view to deriving the initial objects. However, such analysis is done next in order to refine the original design. For the sake of simplicity and without loss of generality, we will only consider a few possibilities which can emerge as a result of the analysis of business functions.

Suppose that an analysis of user requirements reveals that 95 percent of all functions that use employee attributes also require the child_name. This observation is strengthened by the fact that the remaining 5 percent of functions are classified as having relative design ranks lower than average. As a result, the refined design need only include two objects (child_name becomes a repeating attribute in EMPLOYEE):

```
EMPLOYEE = {employee_id#, employee_name,
                employee_address, employee_phone#, {child_name}}
CHILD = {child_name, child_birth_date, child_enroll_grade}
```

Suppose now that the only (or by far the most important) user of the database in the salary department is the section responsible for deducting children's school fees from employee salaries. Processing convenience can dictate one of two solutions:

```
EMPLOYEE = {employee_id#, employee_name, employee_address,
                employee_phone#, {child_name, child_birth_date,
                child_enroll_grade}}
```

or

```
CHILD = {child_name, child_birth_date, child_enroll_grade, employee_id#,
            employee_name, employee_address, employee_phone#}
```

In the latter case, the assumption is made that if both parents are employees, then only one of them pays the school fees.

Finally, suppose that only 50 percent of employees have children of school age and no information about other children is to be kept in the database. This observation can lead to yet another design:

```
EMPLOYEE = {employee_id#, employee_name, employee_address,
                employee_phone#}
```

CHILD = {child_name, child_birth_date, child_enroll_grade, father_name,
        mother_name}

The tacit assumption made for the CHILD object is that the father_name or mother_name can uniquely refer to employee_id# (if either father or mother, or both, are employees in the company).

The above example, simplified as it is, illustrates indirectly the major difference between data-driven and process-driven designs. An initial design in the data-driven approach is almost destined to miss user requirements in some respects and the later changes due to function analysis are likely to be extensive. So it seems practical to employ function analysis prior to the initial design of database structures, in the hope of getting an accurate design at the beginning. This is precisely the principle behind the process-driven approach. However, there is another consideration: the design achieved by a purely process-driven approach is strictly tailored to the current and anticipated user requirements on data. There is no natural provision in such a system for easy extensions and the dynamic accommodation of changes. Should user requirements significantly change, the redesign of a database derived by the process-driven methodology is likely to be required earlier than in the case of the database derived in a data-driven fashion.

FURTHER READING

In most books on file management and file processing, a database system is presented as an evolutionary extension to the file system concept—a culminating achievement of the file technology (Claybrook 1983, Hanson 1985, Loomis 1983). Although intelligible, such a treatment addresses only those database management features which have evolved directly from file techniques. However, such books prove fundamental to an understanding of principal database concepts, especially those that relate to a lower physical level. An exhaustive, but formal, treatment of physical file structures can be found in Merrett (1984). A one-volume textbook treatment of files and databases is offered by Smith and Barnes (1987).

Several introductory database texts provide a good comparative analysis of the features of database systems (Bradley 1987, Date 1986, Deen 1985). The books by Deen and Bradley also contain large chapters on file structures. In particular, Deen's book is highly recommended for its brief, yet well-targeted and quite exhaustive, treatment of the subject.

For a comparison of IRSs and DBMSs one should search in the general bibliography on information retrieval rather than in the database literature. This is because the discipline of information retrieval is not that distinctly recognized and publications in this area tend to relate more to the fashionable and better-known research in databases. A survey of information retrieval and a comparison with database processing can be found in Bartschi (1985), Kraft (1985) and Rijsbergen (1980). A description of special access methods for text and documents can be found in Faloutsos (1985) and Faloutsos and Christodoulakis (1985). Kerschberg (1986) is an excellent source of information about expert database systems. Discussions concerning extensions to DBMSs to cater for typical IRSs functions can be found in Deasi *et al.* (1987), Haskin and Lorie (1982) and

Stonebraker *et al.* (1983). An introduction to hypertext systems is offered by Conklin (1987).

The best source of information concerning comparison of mainframe and microcomputer databases comes from the analysis of features of typical DBMSs. Unfortunately, this implies a study of difficult-to-obtain technical manuals of the DBMSs under consideration, particularly mainframe DBMSs. Popular microcomputer DBMSs enjoy wider textbook coverage (e.g. Brown (1986) and Townsend (1985) for dBASE III). Distributed databases are discussed in many textbooks and tutorials such as Date (1983), Korth and Silberschatz (1986) and Larson and Rahimi (1984).

The network database model is fully described in some older database texts like Palmer (1975), Olle (1978) and editions 1–3 of Date (1986). Deen's text (Deen 1985) contains a well-balanced discussion of the network and relational systems. The relational model is described in Codd (1970, 1972 and 1979). The practical aspects of relational systems are introduced best in Date (1986) and the theoretical aspects in Maier (1983) and Ullman (1982). The latest standards for the network and relational database languages are available from X3 Secretariat/CBEMA in Washington DC (DRAFT 1985a, DRAFT 1985b). The relational standard is also discussed comprehensively by Date (1987). The compliance of relational DBMSs (and the relational standard) with the relational model is discussed by Codd (1986).

Although much has been written on database design methods, a comparison of data-driven and process-driven approaches is yet to be done from the perspective of an acceptable taxonomy. Most methodologies are not explicit about what constitutes the starting point or what design aspect is emphasized. Some methodologies are quite limited in scope or address only middle design phases. Most tools to support these methodologies are just simple drawing aids without much incorporated semantics and expertise. Indeed, there are only few computer-assisted methodologies that extend (or intend to extend) to an entire design process, from conceptual design to implementation and maintenance (Albano *et al.* 1985, Reiner *et al.* 1986). The relational database design strategies—synthesis and decomposition—are well, though not exhaustively, compared in Hawryszkiewycz (1984). The extended relational model (Codd 1979) and the methodologies that are based on the analysis of natural language sentences or that use binary or functional models represent, almost exclusively, the data-driven approach (e.g. Eick 1984, Housel *et al.* 1979, Orman 1986, Shipman 1981). On the other hand, most of the design tools for production relational databases are process-oriented (ORACLE 1986, SUPRA 1987). Jackson System Development JSD is described in Jackson (1983). The problem of integration of databases, artificial intelligence and programming techniques is exhaustively treated in Brodie *et al.* (1984).

REFERENCES

ALBANO, A., DE ANTONELLIS, V. and DI LEVA, A. (eds) (1985): *Computer-Aided Database Design. The DATAID Project*, North-Holland, 221p.

BARTSCHI, M. (1985): An Overview of Information Retrieval Subjects, *Comp.*, May, pp.67-84.

BRADLEY, J. (1987): *Introduction to Data Base Management in Business*, 2nd ed., Holt, Rinehart and Winston, 669p.

BRODIE, M. L., MYLOPOULOS, J. and SCHMIDT, J. W. (eds) (1984): *On Conceptual Modelling. Perspectives from Artificial Intelligence, Databases, and Programming Languages*, Springer-Verlag, 510p.

BROWN, C. (1986): *Essential dBASE III*, Brooks/Cole, 265p.

CLAYBROOK, B. G. (1983): *File Management Techniques*, John Wiley & Sons, 247p.

CODD, E. F. (1970): A Relational Model of Data for Large Shared Data Banks, *Comm. ACM*, 6, pp.377–87.

CODD, E. F. (1972): Further Normalization of the Data Base Relational Model, in: *Data Base Systems*, ed. R. Rustin, Prentice Hall, pp.33–64.

CODD, E. F. (1979): Extending the Database Relational Model to Capture More Meaning, *ACM Trans. Database Syst.*, 4, pp.397–434.

CODD, E. F. (1986): Is Your Database Management System Really Relational, *Computerworld* (Australia), 7 Feb., pp.18–24.

CONKLIN, J. (1987): Hypertext: an Introduction and Survey, *Comp.*, September, pp.17–41.

DATE, C. J. (1983): *An Introduction to Database Systems*, Vol. II, Addison-Wesley, 383p.

DATE, C. J. (1986): *An Introduction to Database Systems*, Vol. I, 4th ed., Addison-Wesley, 639p.

DEASI, B. C. GOYAL, P. and SADRI, F. (1987): Non-First Normal Form Universal Relations: an Application to Information Retrieval Systems, *Inf. Syst.*, 1, pp.49–55.

DEEN, S. M. (1985): *Principles and Practice of Database Systems*, Macmillan, 393p.

DRAFT (1985a): *Draft Proposed American National Standard Database Language SQL*, Technical Committee X3H2 - Database, X3.135-1985, Project 363-D, 115p.

DRAFT (1985b): *Draft Proposed American National Standard Network Database Language*, Technical Committee X3H2 - Database, X3.133-1985, Project: 355-D, 142p.

EICK, C. F. (1984): From Natural Language Requirements to Good Data Base Definitions—A Data Base Design Methodology, *Proc. Int. Conf. on Data Eng.*, Los Angeles, USA, pp.324–31.

FALOUTSOS, C. (1985): Access Methods for Text, *Comp. Surv.*, 1, pp.49–74.

FALOUTSOS, C. and CHRISTODOULAKIS, S. (1985): Access Methods for Documents, in: *Office Automation. Concepts and Tools*, ed. D.C.Tsichritzis, Springer-Verlag, pp.317–38.

HANSON, O. (1985): *Essentials of Computer Data Files*, Pitman, 176p.

HASKIN, R. L. and LORIE, R. A. (1982): On Extending the Functions of a Relational Database System, in: *Proc. ACM SIGMOD Int. Conf. Mananagement of Data*, ed. M.Schkolnick, pp.207–12.

HAWRYSZKIEWYCZ, I. T. (1984): *Database Analysis and Design*, SRA, 578p.

HOUSEL, B. C., WADDLE, V. and YAO, S. B. (1979): The Functional Dependency Model for Logical Database Design, *Proc. 5th Int. Conf. on Very Large Data Bases*, Rio de Janeiro, Brazil, pp.194–208.

JACKSON, M. A. (1983): *System Development*, Prentice Hall, 418p.

KERSCHBERG, L. (ed) (1986): *Expert Database Systems. Proceedings from the First International Workshop*, The Benjamin/Cummings, 701p.

KORTH, H. F. and SILBERSCHATZ, A. (1986): *Database System Concepts*, McGraw-Hill, 546p.

KRAFT, D. H. (1985): Advances in Information Retrieval: Where is That /#*&@ Record?, *Advances in Computer*, 24, pp.277–317.

LARSON, J. A. and RAHIMI, S. (1984): *Tutorial: Distributed Database Management*, IEEE Computer Society Press, 669p.

LOOMIS, M. E. S. (1983): *Data Management and File Processing*, Prentice Hall, 490p.

MAIER, D. (1983): *The Theory of Relational Databases*, Computer Science Press, 637p.

MERRETT, T. H. (1984): *Relational Information Systems*, Reston Publ., 507p.

OLLE, T. W. (1978): The Codasyl Approach to Data Base Management, John Wiley & Sons, 287p.

ORACLE (1986): *ORACLE SDD User Reference Guide*, Oracle Corporation UK Ltd, Richmond, England.

ORMAN, L. (1986): Functional Data Model Design, *Inform. Systems*, 2, pp.123–35.

PALMER, I. (1975): *Data Base Systems: A Practical Reference*, Q.E.D. Information Sciences, Inc.

REINER, D., BROWN, G., FRIEDELL, M., LEHMAN, J., MCKEE, R., RHEINGAUS, P. and ROSENTHAL, A. (1986): A Database Designer's Workbench, *Proc. 5th Int. Conf. on Entiry-Relationship Approach*, Dijon, France, pp.127–40.

RIJSBERGEN, van C. J. (1980): *Information Retrieval*, 2nd ed., Butterworths, 208p.

SHIPMAN, D. W. (1981): The Functional Data Model and the Data Language DAPLEX, *ACM Trans. Database Syst.*, 1, pp.140–73.

SMITH, P. D. and BARNES, G. M. (1987): *Files and Databases: an Introduction*, Addison-Wesley, 390p.

STONEBRAKER, M., STETTNER, H., LYNN, N., KALASH, J. and GUTTMAN, A. (1983): Document Processing in a Relational Database System, *ACM Trans. Office Inf. Syst.*, 2, pp.143–58.

SUPRA (1987): *SUPRA The Advanced Relational DBMS*, Electronic Brochure, Cincom Systems.

TOWNSEND, C. (1985): *Mastering dBASE III. A Structured Approach*, Sybex, 338p.

ULLMAN, J. D. (1982): *Principles of Database Systems*, Computer Science Press, 2nd ed., 484p.

2

Foundations of Database Design

The purpose of this chapter is to describe various facets of the database design process. Whereas in the previous chapter we explained our standpoint on some important misconceptions relevant to database design, this chapter prepares the reader for a systematic study of the successive design phases. In comparison with Chapter 1, the presentation of the material is more methodical and thorough. Otherwise, the structure of both chapters is similar—a loosely-related conglomeration of topics presented in separate sections.

2.1 DATABASE DESIGN LIFECYCLE

Database design covers the "lifecycle" of a system. It is not only the process of determining the initial database structures, but also the process of programming user applications and the maintenance and evolution of the database. The process is iterative.

The six phases of the database design lifecycle are:

1. **requirements analysis**—strategic planning, business model, implementation plan, data flow modeling;
2. **design of conceptual structure**—entity modeling, functions specifications, access graphs, entity-relationship modeling, view integration;
3. **design of logical schema**—reducing denormalized conceptual objects to relations, converting entity-relationship diagram to relational schema, refining relational schema by normalization;
4. **design of physical schema**—access plans, placement strategies, indexes, external storage estimates, controlling access path selection;
5. **programming user applications**—choosing programmatic interface, programming in embedded SQL, application generation;
6. **testing and maintenance of database system**—structured walkthroughs and inspections, housekeeping, monitoring, auditing, perfective maintenance.

Of the six phases, requirements analysis and conceptual design are independent of the DBMS chosen for the database development. The remaining four phases are dependent upon the database software/hardware platform. The overall design process is iterative and feedback is expected and complied with. Figure 2.1 illustrates the database design lifecycle.

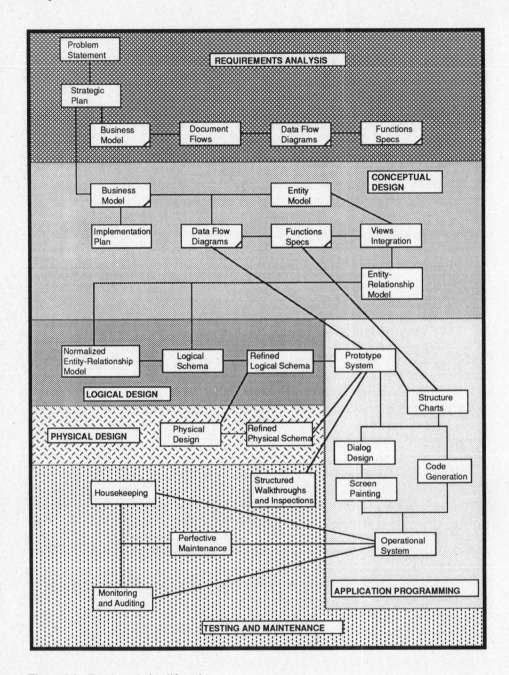

Figure 2.1   Database design lifecycle

2.2 DATA DICTIONARY

A data dictionary (DD) is a single repository for information necessary to the design of an information system. It is the driving force behind the entire design. All information which is used to establish communication links among design stages is required to be stored in the DD. A DD is itself a large database system which stores design information called *metadata*. The concept of metadata encompasses: (1) process object types (e.g. BUSINESS_FUNCTION, PROGRAM, MODULE, TRANSACTION), (2) data object types (e.g. ATTRIBUTE, RECORD, TABLE, RELATIONSHIP), and (3) environment object types (e.g. USER, TERMINAL). At the very least, a DD contains information about the names, aliases and definitions of all metadata objects. It also provides the means to interrelate the objects.

2.2.1 Data dictionary in the process of database design

As a DD is a database system, the methods and techniques used for the development of a typical database system (as described in this book) are also applicable to its construction. We are confronted by a chicken-and-egg problem: do we design the DD database or the application database first? Fortunately, the answer to this question is no longer as difficult as it may seem. DD software packages are available to facilitate the development of the DD's databases. Many businesses have built, and continue to maintain, corporate data dictionaries in the interest of everyday business operations. The CASE/CADE packages that assist in database design feature their own data dictionaries and provide necessary bridge facilities to design tools.

Two standards for DD software, known as Information Resource Dictionary System (IRDS), are available. One was developed by the American National Standards Institute (ANSI), the other by the International Standards Organization (ISO). The former is based on the entity-relationship model, the latter employs a relational SQL data model to describe the proposed schema of the DD database.

The role of the DD in the design is active as it is both the recipient and sender of metadata. A separate DD database must be built for each application database being designed. Naturally, metadata values are entered into the DD database as the design of the application progresses. Some of these values are known as soon as user requirements are spelled out, but other values can only be known later on in the lifecycle of the database system. For example, the values (instances) of a metadata object BUSINESS_ DOCUMENT can be established after initial interviews with the user. However, the values for a metadata object BASE_RELATION can only be known at the completion of the logical design of a relational database. The values for another object VIEW_RELATION will be determined even later during the programming of user applications. Since the definition of a view is derived from base relations, a DD will be interrogated during the design of a view (sender role) and then will be modified to accommodate the view definition (recipient role).

The design and implementation of an information system is an iterative and error-prone activity. It is, therefore, important at all times to ensure the consistency of the DD database used in the design. In some design methodologies, multiple versions of the design are generated and evaluated against each other before choosing the best one. In such methodologies, it is indispensable to have multiple DD database versions. But even if a single design is generated, having a production version and one or more test versions of the DD database is a wise strategy, otherwise, the integrity of the DD database and the successful completion of the design will be at risk.

2.2.2　Data dictionary schema

The DD must be capable of maintaining and generating cross-reference information on the objects defined in the dictionary. In fact, it is this ability which makes the DD a database system. Being a database, the DD has its own database definition or schema. Such a schema can be expressed in terms of a conceptual or logical model, for example,

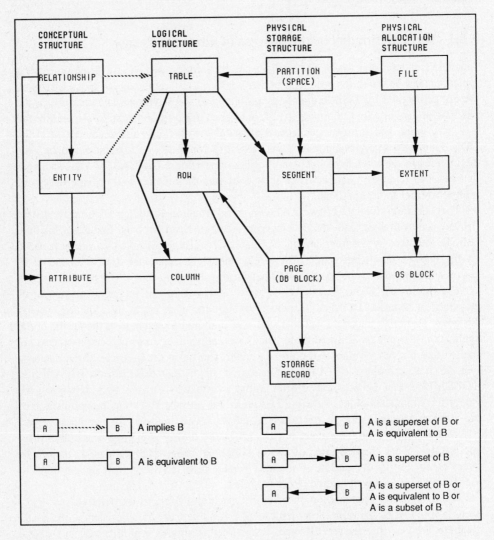

Figure 2.2　Data object types in a data dictionary for relational database design

as an entity-relationship diagram or as a relational database intension (e.g. CREATE TABLE statements). However, as the conceptual and logical models have not been discussed yet, they cannot be used for the presentation of a DD schema here. Also, the DD schema is far too comprehensive for full presentation in this book. Instead, we use a simplified notation to show typical dependencies between the data object types in DDs dedicated to database design. Figure 2.2 shows such dependencies in the DD used in the design of a relational database system. The data object types to assist in the design of a network database system are illustrated in Figure 2.3. Some familiarity with relational and network database structures is required to fully appreciate the information content of the two figures.

2.2.3 Data dictionary as a data inventory

One of the basic functions of the DD is to serve as a data inventory. To this end, the purpose of a DD is storage of information about all data elements known in the system. A *data element* has a recursive definition and can be a *simple* data item or a *group*. A group consists of smaller groups and/or simple data items. In the usual interpretation, the notion of the data element refers to the data object type (rather than process or environment

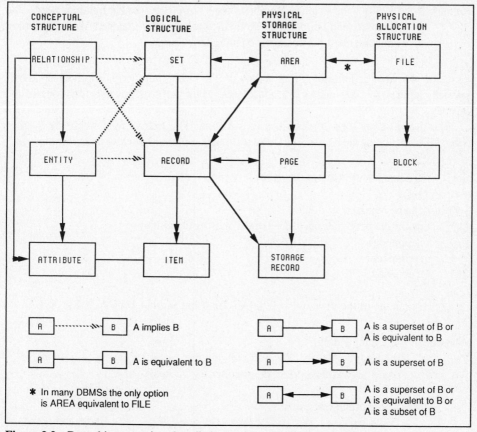

Figure 2.3   Data object types in a data dictionary for network database design

object type). Typically, the information that is kept in a DD for each data element includes name, alias names, type, format, description, value constraints, derivation algorithm and remarks.

The following is an example of a simple data item entry.

Name	order_number
Aliases	business_order_number
Type	string of numeric characters
Format	six digits
Description	This is a unique number assigned by the company and identifies the fact that an order has been received. Since it is the company policy to print a single invoice for each received order, the invoice_number is the same as the order_number.
Constraints	Currently, the first digit of the order_number is zero; it is predicted that this constraint will remain valid for the next three–four years.
Algorithm	For each batch of invoices on a given day, the order_number is initialized to the largest order_number used on a previous day, and incremented by one for each invoice generated.
Remarks	Using the same number for both the order_number and the invoice_number permits the invoice to be easily matched against shipping documents if the customer challenges a charge.

Note, in the above definition, that although the order_number is equivalent to the invoice_number, the two names are not aliases. They perform separate functions in the business.

The definition of a *group* describes its structure. The following symbols are used in some DDs to express such a structure (the right hand column indicates their meanings):

=	is equivalent to (is composed of)
+	and
{ }	can be repeated
[|]	exclusive or (either one data item or another data item)
( )	is optional
* *	a comment
" "	a constant

As an example of their use, we give a DD definition for the group ADDRESS:

```
ADDRESS =[* actual address *
           (house_number + "/") + street_number + street_name + city_name +
           (state_acronym) + postcode_number + ("AUSTRALIA")
           |
           * post office box address *
           "P.O.Box" + post_office_box + city_name + (state_acronym) +
           postcode_number + ("AUSTRALIA")]
```

2.2.4 Commercial data dictionary packages

DDs constitute an integral part of all respectable CASE/CADE tools, such as CASE 2000 DesignAid of Nastec Corporation, Excelerator of Index Technology Corp., FOUNDATION of Arthur Andersen & Co., I-CASE of KnowledgeWare, Information Engineering Facility (IEF) of Texas Instruments and others (see Appendix).

Some large DBMSs have their own full-blown, integrated and active DDs, for example Integrated Data Dictionary (IDD) of IDMS or Extended Data Dictionary (EDD) of System 2000. The other traditional DBMSs, such as ADABAS and DMS-1100, are assisted by comprehensive, but passive, DDs. All relational DBMSs incorporate DDs to support operations, such as query compilation and optimization. Currently, the scope of these DDs is limited.

There are a number of independent DDs that can readily interface to popular DBMSs. The best known are Data Catalogue 2 of Synergetics Corporation, Data Dictionary of Cincom Systems, Data Dictionary of Applied Data Research, Datamanager of Management Systems and Programming (MSP), DB/DC Dictionary of IBM, Dictionary 204 of Computer Corporation of America (CCA) and UCC TEN of University Computing Company.

2.3 DATA FLOW DIAGRAMS

Data flow diagrams (DFD) are a hallmark of structured analysis and design. They enable a graphical, concise and partitioned representation of any analyzed or designed information system. DFDs describe the system at the logical level. The physical characteristics of the system, including the computerized processing environment, are not visualized in the DFDs. As a result, the DFDs are complemented by other methods and techniques, such as document flowcharts, conventional system and program flowcharts, decision tables, structure charts or Nassi-Shneiderman diagrams.

2.3.1 Symbols in data flow diagrams

A DFD consists of five basic elements:

1. *data flows*;
2. *processes* (data transformations);
3. *data stores* (files);
4. *external entities*:
    (a) *data sources* (originators),
    (b) *sinks* (terminators, receivers);
5. *bridges* (connectors).

Typical graphical representations for DFD elements are shown in Figure 2.4. To enhance the diagram layout, data stores and external entities can appear more than once in the same diagram. Simple graphical extensions to DFDs allow easy recognition of the duplicated objects. One common extension uses extra lines inside the data store or external entity—*n* lines for *n* repetitions (not including the first). Another solution is to include asterisks (*) in the repetitious graphical symbols—*n* asterisks for *n* repetitions (not including the first).

Basic principles governing the construction of data flow diagrams are illustrated in Figure 2.5.

2.3.2   Data flows—guidelines and consistency checks

A data flow is a packet of data which moves from one element of the DFD to another. The packet can be a document, an arbitrary grouping of data or an elementary data (i.e. not further decomposable). A data flow does not represent process or control (thus,

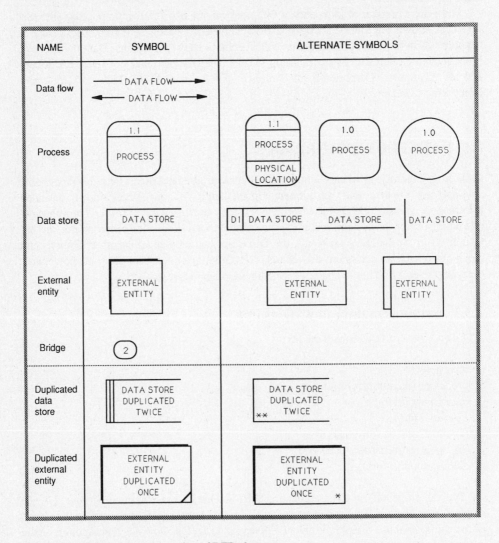

Figure 2.4   Graphical representation of DFD elements

Get_Next_Invoice is not a data flow and neither is Day_of_Fortnight, when it exists only to activate Produce_Payroll process). Diagrammatically, the data flow is a single or double-directional line with a label as shown in Figure 2.6.

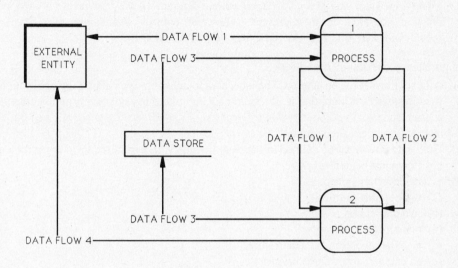

Figure 2.5   Principles for construction of DFD

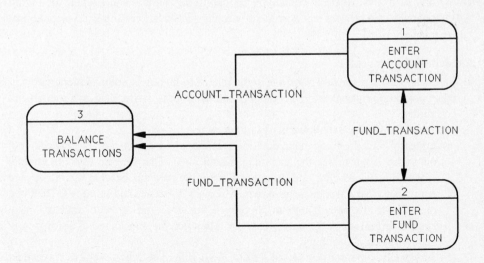

Figure 2.6   Single and double-directional data flows

Guidelines for data flows

1. Double-directional lines should be used infrequently and only at the higher DFD levels.
2. The labels should be nouns joined, if necessary, by adjectives (they must not contain verbs). Generic terms, such as information, data, input and output should be avoided.
3. A signal or flag which triggers a condition or activates (or terminates) a process is not a data flow and it should not be visualized in a diagram. (It may, however, be used in a function specification to represent a flow of control. Remember that function specifications are often considered to be a part of the DFD.)

Consistency checks for data flows

1. All data flows must be labeled. The label should adhere to typical naming conventions used in systems design, that is, it should contain up to thirty characters and begin with a letter, spaces should be replaced by hyphens or underlines, digits are allowed but no special characters are permitted.
2. Each data flow must be defined in the data dictionary. In particular, the composition of any flow must be defined there.
3. A data flow may not span:
   (a) two external entities,
   (b) two data stores,
   (c) two bridges,
   (d) an external entity and a data store,
   (e) an external entity and a bridge.

2.3.3 Processes—guidelines and consistency checks

A process transforms incoming data flow(s) into outgoing data flow(s). It is represented graphically as an oval or circle containing an identifying number and a label (see Figure 2.4). Optionally, the process can also identify a physical location (or person or program) where it is performed.

Guidelines for processes

1. Labels should be strong or transitive verbs related to an object noun. Generic verbs or those implying physical implementation, such as process, write, read or store, should be avoided.
2. A process transforms data flows in one of two ways:
   (a) **logically**—an outgoing data flow(s) is re-classified or its aim is changed, but otherwise it resembles the incoming data flow(s). This implies that the internal structures of incoming and outgoing flow(s), defined in the data dictionary, are equivalent. Logical transforms of data flows are illustrated in Figure 2.7. The three data flows (requested_amount, approved_amount, and granted_amount) have similar definitions in the data dictionary. They may be considered as belonging to a common class—amount.
   (b) **physically**—the transformation results in outgoing data flow(s) which is a distinct data category in comparison with the incoming data flow(s). This implies that without knowing the transformation algorithm it is impossible to establish, on the

basis of the data dictionary entries, the relationship between incoming and outgoing flow(s). An example of the physical transform is shown in Figure 2.8. The outgoing flow total_orders is calculated by adding the numbers of current_order, pending_order and held_order (the held_order is received, but held by the credit department to verify the customer's credit).

Processes which enhance the contents of incoming flows, by automatically generating some data, are the most common examples of physical transforms. One typical example is the processes that use current date and time to identify the outgoing flows.

Consistency checks for processes

1. All processes must be numbered and labeled. The label may contain spaces when written in the diagram's oval or circle, however, the spaces should be converted to hyphens or underlines in the data dictionary. The naming conventions used for data flows apply also to processes.
2. Each process should be defined in the data dictionary.
3. A process is uniquely identified by its number or its label. The processes in the level 0 (overview) diagram are numbered 1, 2, and so on (or 1.0, 2.0, etc.). The processes in level 1 diagrams are identified by concatenating a level 0 number (e.g. 2) with the successive numbers applied in level 1 (e.g. 2.1, 2.2, 2.3, etc.). This convention is continued for lower levels (e.g. 2.2.1, 2.2.2, 2.2.3, etc.).

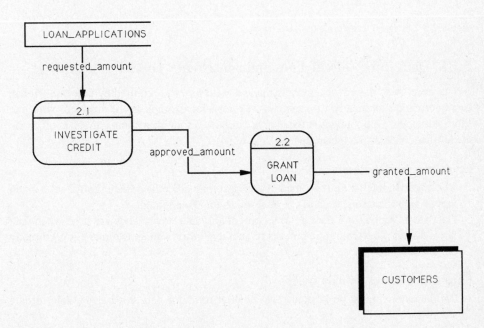

Figure 2.7 Logical transforms of data flows

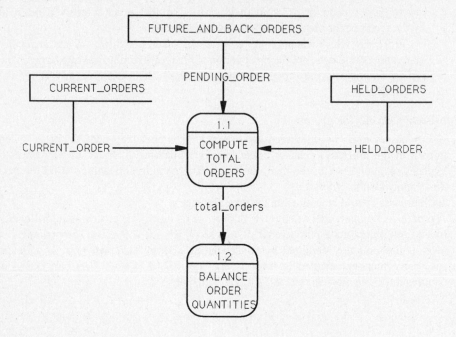

Figure 2.8   Physical transforms of data flows

2.3.4   Data stores—guidelines and consistency checks

A data store holds data. It accepts and releases data flows as required by processes. It can be represented graphically in a number of ways, for example by a rectangle with one short side open. Optionally, the data store can have an identification symbol in a box on the left-hand side of the rectangle (see Figure 2.4).

Guidelines for data stores
1. The labels should be nouns joined, if necessary, by adjectives (they should not contain verbs). Generic terms, such as file or store, should be avoided.
2. Data stores represent a time delay in processing data flows. They are used when data flows do not move from one process to another (or to/from an external entity) directly but are delayed.

Consistency checks for data stores
1. All data stores must be labeled. The labeling rules for data flows apply also to data stores.
2. All data elements in a data store which are not used in any data flows of the DFD must be accounted for. Such data elements may be justified and maintained in order to

support the unpredictable masked functions (see Section 3.2.4), however, in most cases they would uncover an error in the diagram or in the data dictionary. Three possibilities for errors exist:

(a) data elements which are not used in any data flow,
(b) data elements which enter a data store (via an incoming flow) but never leave it (via an outgoing flow),
(c) data elements which leave a data store but are not used in any incoming flow.

3. A data store must have at least one incoming data flow and one outgoing data flow.
4. A data store related to a process at a higher level must also appear and be related to a descendant of that process at the lower level.
5. A data store may appear at any level in the DFD; however, at the first level where a data store appears, all incoming and outgoing flows to it must be shown. In other words, all processes which access the data store must be identified and thereafter, only those processes and their descendants can be allowed to use that data store. Since the direction of data flows is relevant, some of those processes can only use the data store for input, and others only for output.

Figure 2.9 illustrates the consistency enforced on the data store CUSTOMERS by applying the rule that all references to the data store are shown at the first level where the store is used. The store CUSTOMERS is first used in the overview diagram (level 0). It has an outgoing data flow to the process LEND_MONEY and a double-directional flow to/from the process ENTER_ACCOUNT_TRANSACTION. This means that CUSTOMERS is not used by any processes in the DFD except for LEND_MONEY, ENTER_ACCOUNT_TRANSACTION, and their descendants. A descendant of ENTER_ACCOUNT_TRANSACTION is OPEN_ACCOUNT and descendant of LEND_MONEY is VERIFY_CUSTOMER_CREDIT. Note that the directions of data flows to/from CUSTOMERS shown in the overview diagram agree in the lower level diagrams. VERIFY_CUSTOMER_CREDIT is only allowed to read from the store CUSTOMERS because at the overview level the store refers to the parent process (LEND_MONEY) by the outgoing flow. (The black triangles in the processes of the overview diagram indicate that the child diagrams for those processes exist.)

2.3.5   External entities—guidelines and consistency checks

An external entity can be a data source or a data sink (or both). A source is an external system which supplies some data flows to be processed in the system (as determined by the scope of the DFD). A sink is an external system which receives some data flows from the DFD. An external entity is represented graphically by a labeled square or rectangle, possibly stylized (see Figure 2.4).

Guidelines for external entities

1. The labels should be nouns or pronouns.
2. External entities lie outside the boundaries of the designed system. We should not be concerned with the use of data flows by the external entities; in particular, the communication between external entities is of no concern in the DFD.
3. There is no special need to define the external entities in the data dictionary.

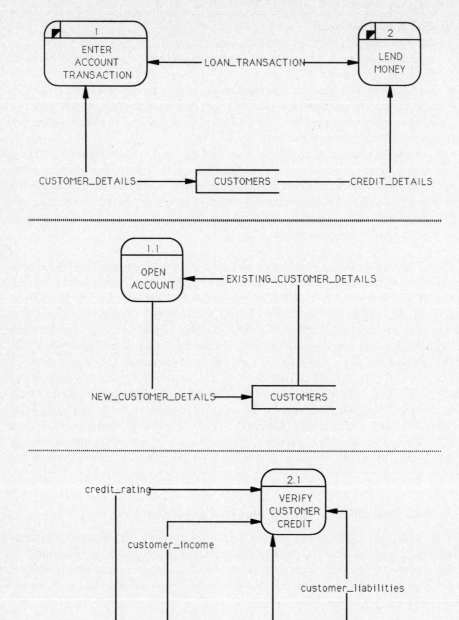

Figure 2.9   Consistency enforcement by showing all references to a data store at the first DFD level where the store is used

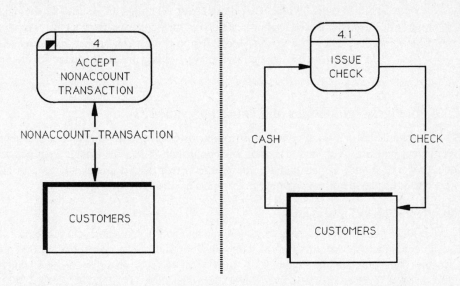

Figure 2.10 Consistency enforcement by showing an external entity in lower DFD levels

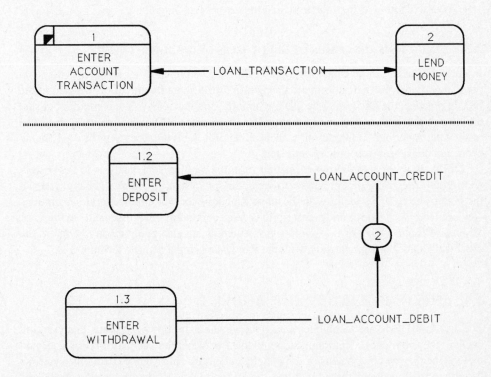

Figure 2.11 Using bridges

Consistency checks for external entities

1. All external entities must be labeled. Unless external entities are defined in the data dictionary, the designer is free to choose a labeling method.
2. An external entity related to a process at a higher level must also appear and be related to a descendant of that process at the lower level. This point is illustrated in Figure 2.10.

2.3.6   Bridges—guidelines and consistency checks

A bridge establishes a special connection from a lower level child diagram to a higher level parent diagram. A special aspect of this connection is that the bridge identifies an uncle process (or aunt, if you prefer). The bridge is represented graphically as a small circle containing an identifying number of the uncle as illustrated by Figure 2.11.

Consistency checks for bridges

1. All bridges must be numbered according to the numbering convention for processes.
2. All uncle processes identified in the parent diagram must have corresponding bridges in the child diagram. In Figure 2.11, LEND_MONEY is an uncle process which becomes a bridge in the lower level decomposition of ENTER_ACCOUNT_ TRANSACTION. As in the case of data stores, the direction of data flows is relevant. Because the flow LOAN_TRANSACTION is bi-directional, there is both an incoming and outgoing flow to/from the bridge in the lower level diagram.

2.3.7   Data flow diagrams in the process of database design

In order to assist in database design, DFDs must cooperate closely with the data dictionary. Every piece of information shown in DFDs should be precisely defined in the DD. In practice, the DFDs and the DD are built up simultaneously. In a computer-assisted design environment, any new information introduced in a DFD is automatically recorded in the DD. Any "old" information is checked against the definitions kept in the DD and necessary consistency checks are activated.

DFDs allow for smooth transformation from the requirements analysis to the design, and from the description of processes to the definition of data structures. The processes of the bottom-level DFDs identify the business functions for which procedural descriptions are needed. Such procedural descriptions are commonly expressed in *natural* or *Structured English* (SE) or as *pseudocodes*. Attempts are also being made to express the processing algorithms graphically, with the *Petri nets* being a favorite technique.

2.4   ENTITY-RELATIONSHIP MODEL

The DD and DFDs are techniques that underlie the activities of systems analysis and design. They introduce a communication channel between the user and the designer and they define the key components of the system and ensure consistency during the system's development. To achieve these functions, the DD and DFDs deal with both processes and data. At no stage is there an attempt to design the data structures to respond to the processing requirements or to derive the programs from the data structures. In this sense, the DD and DFDs belong more to the analysis than to the design phase.

One technique which does allow the design of data structures on the basis of processes (business functions) is known as *entity-relationship* (E-R) modeling. In this approach, information being modeled is grouped into entities or relationships among entities. The resulting design is purely conceptual, that is, it is independent of the implementation issues. Though derived to satisfy the user requirements (processes), the E-R design does not show processes in any explicit way; instead, it offers a diagrammatic conceptual database structure. The structure integrates *user views* on data and needs to be further converted to logical and physical schema corresponding to the chosen DBMS.

2.4.1 Entity

An entity is an object which can be distinctly identified and is important to the information system of the organization. The entity represents a business fact or rule and is usually expressed as the subject or object of a sentence that defines that fact or rule. It is common for the entity name to be a noun. Examples of entities are COURSE, RESEARCH_REPORT, COMMISSION, EMPLOYEE, INVOICE and ITEM.

It is important to distinguish, at all times, between an *entity set (type)* and *entity instance (occurrence)*. For example, COURSE is an entity set and CSCI-335 (Databases) is an instance from the entity set COURSE. Clearly, entity instances must be uniquely identifiable. When the meaning is obvious from the context, we simply use the word entity for both instances and sets. In the diagrammatic representation of a conceptual design, entity sets are visualized by means of rectangular boxes. Entity instances, though not represented graphically, give semantics and interpretation to the diagram.

How to organize information into sets and instances is a difficult design decision. An abstraction process called *classification/instantiation* is involved here. Classification groups entities sharing common characteristics and holding uniform conditions into a class (which we call an entity set or type). The reverse of classification is called instantiation when entity instances (occurrences) are obtained.

2.4.2 Relationship

A relationship is an association between entities from different or identical entity sets. Entities are associated for business reasons. Relationships can usually be denoted by a verb. For example, the entity COURSE may be associated with the entity TEACHER via the relationship TEACHES. An entity EMPLOYEE can be involved in a relationship IS_MANAGER_OF to indicate a multiple-level managerial structure of employees.

As in the case of entities, a distinction is made between a *relationship set (type)* and a *relationship instance (occurrence)*. For instance, TEACHES is a relationship set and 'Leszek teaches CSCI-335' is an instance of the relationship set TEACHES. Relationship instances must be uniquely distinguishable. There are several different methods of graphically representing relationship sets. In the most restricted representation, relationships are indicated by means of lines connecting entities (with or without relationship names written along the lines). However, a frequent method of representation is to use diamonds or oval boxes to connect entities. Different graphical representations for a relationship TEACHES are shown in Figure 2.12. The three representations are called: *simplified, restricted*, and *enhanced* (the semantics of the latter are discussed next).

2.4.3 Attribute

Entities and relationships have *properties* which can be described as *attribute-value* pairs. For example, area_of_expertise might be an attribute of a TEACHER and knowledge bases could be the value of this attribute. Another attribute of the TEACHER may be years_of_teaching_experience, for which the value may be 15. For each entity or relationship instance, each attribute will be assigned a value. If all values of a certain attribute (or set of attributes) are different, then they can serve to uniquely identify entity or relationship instances. Such an attribute is known as an entity (or relationship) *identifier (key)*. An entity or relationship can have many unique identifiers (e.g. course_ number and course_name can be two equivalent identifiers of the entity COURSE).

Attributes can be *simple* or *group* (see Section 2.2.3). A simple attribute can have only atomic values and does not have an internal structure. Sometimes, the internal structure is a matter of semantic interpretation and processing requirements, for example, ADDRESS can be a group attribute in one design and a simple attribute in another. If only the full address is required in processing, then ADDRESS can be designated a simple attribute. However, if a part of the address is explicitly required for processing (in queries like, List all students from a given city), then ADDRESS should be made a group attribute (with city_name being a simple attribute within that group).

2.4.4 Classes of relationships

Relationships can be classified according to four criteria: degree, connectivity, membership and regularity. Since certain classes of relationship are not expressible in

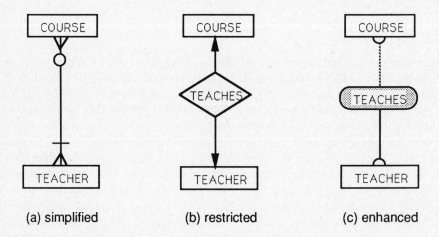

(a) simplified   (b) restricted   (c) enhanced

Figure 2.12   Three graphical representations for a relationship set

simplified and restricted diagrams, enhanced graphical notation is used in the following presentation (however, a comparison with the simplified and restricted representations is made).

2.4.4.1 Degree of relationship

The criterion of degree refers to the total number of entity sets linked by a relationship set. From this point of view we distinguish *sole (unary)* relationship sets (involving one entity set only and expressing recursive dependencies among the values of attributes in that single entity set) from *ample* relationship sets (associating two or more entity sets). Ample relationship sets are usually subject to further classification by degree, which results in *binary* (degree two) and *n-ary* (three or more) relationship sets. Figure 2.13 gives examples of sole, binary and ternary relationships.

To represent a sole relationship, a single line is used that connects a relationship to an entity. Two lines are needed to express a binary relationship, three to express a ternary relationship and so on. In the simplified E-R notation (Figure 2.12), a sole relationship can be shown by a looping line that connects an entity to itself. Relationships of higher than binary degree cannot be represented in simplified notation. In the restricted E-R notation, some difficulties can be experienced when drawing relationships of degree greater than four (though admittedly, such relationships have dubious meaning, are not practical and can easily be converted to lower degree counterparts).

The relationship IS_MANAGER_OF in Figure 2.13 expresses a hierarchical managerial structure of employees in a typical enterprise. Each employee can have only one manager. A manager is also an employee, defined within the entity EMPLOYEE; for example, John Smith can be a chief manager. He is a superior to a number of employees—Nola Tailor and Ian Carpenter among others. Some of these employees can also be managers for other groups of employees; for instance, Ian Carpenter can be a manager of Peter Locksmith, Paul Turner and a few others. Since such a hierarchical structure of employment expresses dependencies internal to one and only one entity set EMPLOYEE, the corresponding relationship IS_MANAGER_OF is sole (sometimes called *recursive*).

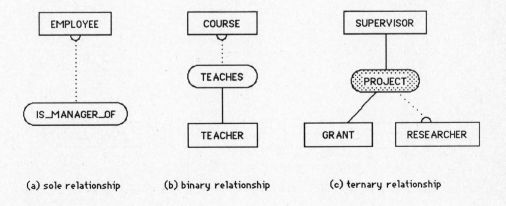

(a) sole relationship   (b) binary relationship   (c) ternary relationship

Figure 2.13 Degree of relationship

The binary relationship TEACHES expresses the fact that a TEACHER teaches COURSEs. Most of the relationship sets in a typical entity-relationship design belong to the binary class.

The ternary relationship PROJECT expresses the fact that a research project requires a SUPERVISOR, a GRANT and RESEARCHERs. Occasionally, a relationship can have a degree larger than three; for example, one could extend PROJECT to a quarternary relationship by adding to it the entity EQUIPMENT. However, increasing the degree of a relationship beyond ternary (some would even say beyond binary) is not recommended practice as the semantics quickly become unclear (that is, without additional narrative explanations to the diagram).

2.4.4.2   Connectivity of relationship

According to the criterion of connectivity we separate out *singular* and *multiple* relationship sets. The multiple relationship sets can be divided further into *univocal* and *nonunivocal* relationship sets. A relationship set is singular when, among its entity instances, the only possible linkings are 1:1. Multiple relationship sets may be of 1:N or N:1, in which case the "subordination" between entities is univocal or they may be of M:N, so that the "subordination" is not univocal. An illustration of binary relationships with different connectivities is given in Figure 2.14.

With reference to the three E-R notations (Figure 2.12), there are no semantic differences in the way the connectivity is represented. Plain lines are used to express 1 (singular) connectivity; to represent M (multiple) connectivity, three similar notations are used: a claw in the simplified, an arrow in the restricted and a semicircle in the enhanced diagram.

The relationship HAS in Figure 2.14 is 1:1 (singular) since the business fact is that each SUPERVISOR must have one, and no more than one, OFFICE and conversely if an OFFICE accommodates a SUPERVISOR then there is no more than one such person in it.

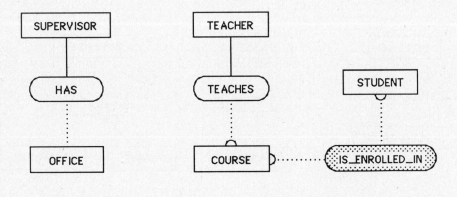

(a) 1 :1 binary relationship   (b) 1 :N binary relationship   (c) M :N binary relationship

Figure 2.14   Connectivity of relationship

The relationship TEACHES is 1:N (univocal) since a TEACHER can be assigned to teach more than one COURSE but a COURSE can have only one TEACHER assigned to it at any moment of time. That is, if teacher x swaps the course a with teacher y within the relationship instance i, then teacher y momentarily replaces teacher x in the relationship i.

The relationship IS_ENROLLED_IN is M:N (nonunivocal) since a STUDENT can be enrolled in many COURSEs and a COURSE is attended by many STUDENTs. In Figure 2.14, there is only one entity set COURSE used in two relationship sets, since it is not possible to have, in one E-R diagram, two entity sets with the same name (the same is true for relationship sets).

2.4.4.3 Membership of relationship

With regard to the membership criterion, the participation of the entities in a relationship can be *total* or *partial*. A total entity of the relationship set means that every instance e of an entity set E involved in the relationship set X occurs in a certain instance x of that relationship set. The entities of a relationship set which do not satisfy this condition are called partial. Figure 2.15 illustrates the concept of membership.

In the enhanced E-R diagram, the total membership of an entity in a relationship is shown by a solid line that connects the two. The partial membership is represented by a dotted line. In the simplified notation (Figure 2.12), a circle on a line expresses partial membership and a bar, total membership. In the restricted notation, the notion of membership is not visualized at all.

The relationship PREREQUISITE in Figure 2.15 shows which courses are prerequisites for the other courses. For example, CSCI-201 and CSCI-223 are the prerequisites for CSCI-335; CSCI-201 is also a prerequisite for CSCI-223; and the prerequisite for CSCI-201 is CSCI-121. The membership of COURSE in the relationship PREREQUISITE is partial since it is possible for the university to provide courses which do not belong to any particular studies, for example, independent courses organized on a "one-off" basis which neither have prerequisites nor are required by other courses.

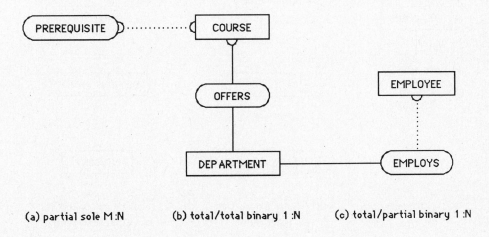

(a) partial sole M:N   (b) total/total binary 1:N   (c) total/partial binary 1:N

Figure 2.15   Membership of relationship

The membership of COURSE in the binary relationship OFFERS is total, as is the membership of DEPARTMENT in OFFERS. This means that every course must be offered by one of the departments and every department must offer at least one course.

The membership of DEPARTMENT in the relationship EMPLOYS is total since a department should only exist if it has employees. However, the membership of EMPLOYEE in EMPLOYS is only partial, as some employees are allowed to not be associated with any department (e.g. independent advisers).

2.4.4.4 Regularity of relationship

A division by the criterion of regularity results in *regular* and *weak* relationship sets. We say that a relationship set is regular when it contains attributes; if it does not, it is weak. This is different from another common interpretation of regularity, which states that a regular relationship is uniquely identifiable by its own attributes. In such an interpretation, the weak relationship may or may not contain attributes. Regularity of relationships is exemplified in Figure 2.16.

In an enhanced E-R diagram, variations in shading of the relationship ovals are used to denote weak or regular relationship sets. The unshaded ovals in Figure 2.16 represent weak relationships, while the shaded ovals denote regular relationships. Neither the simplified nor restricted diagrams (shown in Figure 2.12) have any means of representing regularity.

The relationship TEACHES in Figure 2.16 is weak since it does not contain any attributes. The sole function of this relationship is to relate the entities TEACHER and COURSE.

The relationship ATTENDS_CLASS is regular because information about how many STUDENTs have attended the classes of a particular COURSE is actually kept in this relationship. In fact, regularity in this case is especially strong since ATTENDS_CLASS is likely to contain not only descriptive attributes (e.g. number_of_students), but also identifying attributes (e.g. class_number, with the course identification encoded in it).

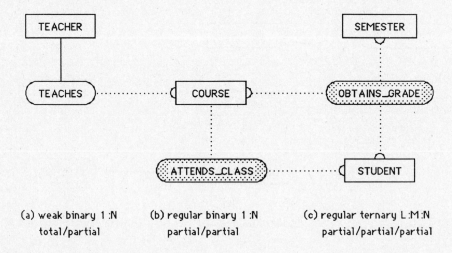

(a) weak binary 1 :N   (b) regular binary 1 :N   (c) regular ternary L:M:N
    total/partial   partial/partial   partial/partial/partial

Figure 2.16   Regularity of relationship

The relationship OBTAINS_GRADE is regular since it contains information about the grade obtained by a STUDENT in a COURSE given in a certain SEMESTER. In general, it is possible for a student to take the same course in more than one semester (e.g. after failing the course).

2.5   RELATIONAL NORMALIZATION

The introduction of the relational model heralded a new approach to database modeling. The mathematical foundations of the relational model produced the basis for such modeling, that is *normalization*. An underlying assumption of normalization is that it supports associations between relations by means of attribute values. This is *logical* representation; thus, normalization is a logical level concept. Under the assumption that entities and relationships of the conceptual model correspond to relations of the relational model, normalization can be used for conceptual design. This implies, however, a semantically limited design in which such concepts as group attributes, repeating attributes, aggregation and generalization cannot be taken advantage of.

There are six normal forms with the acronyms: 1NF, 2NF, 3NF, BCNF, 4NF and 5NF. If a relation is in a higher normal form, then it is also in all lower forms (e.g. a relation in 3NF is also in 2NF and 1NF). Three kinds of dependencies between attributes of relations are considered in the normalization process: *functional* (2NF, 3NF, BCNF), *multivalued* (4NF) and *join* (5NF). Normalization theory is based on *projection* as the relational decomposition operator and on the *natural equi-join* as the reconstruction operator. To illustrate the theory, we will use SQL's SELECT statement to display the contents of tables in particular normal forms.

2.5.1   First normal form

First normal form (1NF) is satisfied by any "flat" relation, that is a relation with no group and/or repeating attributes. All tuples of such a relation must have the same number of attributes. 1NF is a fundamental definitional requirement of the relational model; classical relational theory does not deal with relations which are not in 1NF.

Figure 2.17 represents the relation FIRSTNF which is in 1NF, but is not in 2NF. The example refers to a supplier-parts database, widely used in the literature. The database keeps information about the shipments of parts by suppliers. Each supplier has a unique supplier number (S#), a rating or status value (STATUS), and a location (CITY). Each part has a unique part number (P#), and can be supplied by different suppliers. The quantity (QUANTITY) shipped is also given in each tuple.

A relation which is in 1NF succumbs to so-called *update anomalies*. The anomalies are due to the operations of modification, insertion and deletion. In FIRSTNF, it is possible to modify CITY of a particular S# in one tuple and not in the others (e.g. changing SAN JOSE in the second tuple to SAN DIEGO and leaving the third tuple unchanged, will place the relation in an inconsistent state). A new supplier, who does not yet supply any parts, cannot be inserted into FIRSTNF. This is because P#, which is a part of the relation key {S#, P#}, should not take null values (the null values are indicated by the question mark in Figure 2.17). Similarly, should we delete all the shipments by a supplier, we lose all information about that supplier (such as its CITY and STATUS).

```
SQL> SELECT * FROM FIRSTNF;

S#          STATUS CITY            P#      QUANTITY
----    ---------- ---------------  ----   ----------
S6              20 DARMSTADT         P5           100
S2              30 SAN JOSE          P6          2500
S2              30 SAN JOSE          P11          100
S8              40 WATERLOO          P4           200
S7              10 WOLLONGONG        P3           100
S4              10 FUKUOKA           P2           500
S21              ? ?                 P2           250
```

Figure 2.17　Relation in first normal form

```
SQL> SELECT * FROM SECONDNF;

EMPLOYEE_FAMILY_NAME DEPARTMENT_NAME          LOCATION
-------------------- --------------------     ----------

MACIASZEK            COMPUTING SCIENCE        KEANE BLD
GRAY                 COMPUTING SCIENCE        KEANE BLD
STAFFORD             COMPUTING SCIENCE        KEANE BLD
BLAKE                MATHEMATICS              KEANE BLD
```

Figure 2.18　Relation in second normal form

To avoid update anomalies, a 1NF relation should be decomposed vertically (i.e. by means of the relational operation of projection) into two or more smaller relations. The resulting relations will be in higher normal forms. FIRSTNF could be decomposed into two relations: ONE (S#, STATUS, CITY), TWO (S#, P#, QUANTITY).

2.5.2　Functional dependency

A functional dependency (FD) is one of the most useful concepts of relational analysis. It provides a means for decomposition of relations which are in low normal forms and which exhibit update anomalies.

A set of attributes {B} of an object Y is *functionally dependent* on a set of attributes {C} of Y (denoted {C} $\rightarrow$ {B}) iff (if and only if) each {C} value {v_C} corresponds at any time to exactly one {B} value {v_B}. Such a dependency is *partial* iff {C} is a proper subset of a candidate key {K} of Y, that is {K} $\supset$ {C} and {B} is not a subset of any candidate key. {B} in {C} $\rightarrow$ {B} is *transitive* on {D} iff {D} $\rightarrow$ {C} and {C} $\nrightarrow$ {D}.

In FIRSTNF, there are two functional dependencies: S# $\rightarrow$ STATUS and S# $\rightarrow$ CITY. Each S# has exactly one STATUS and is located in exactly one CITY. Both functional dependencies in FIRSTNF are partial because S# is a proper subset of the key {S#, P#}. STATUS and CITY are not subsets of the key. There are no transitive dependencies in FIRSTNF.

2.5.3   Second normal form

Second normal form (2NF) requires that a relation is in 1NF and has no partial functional dependencies. This means that every non-key attribute (i.e. attribute that is not part of any key) is fully dependent on a key. FIRSTNF was not in 2NF because it contained partial dependencies.

Figure 2.18 shows the relation SECONDNF which is in 2NF, but which is not in 3NF. The example describes the departments and locations of employees. EMPLOYEE_FAMILY_NAME is the key (it is assumed that there are no two employees with the same family name). The functional dependencies of SECONDNF are:
EMPLOYEE_FAMILY_NAME → DEPARTMENT_NAME, EMPLOYEE_FAMILY_NAME → LOCATION and
DEPARTMENT_NAME → LOCATION.
The relation SECONDNF cannot have partial dependencies since it has a single attribute key.

A relation which is in 2NF can also exhibit update anomalies, although for different reasons than anomalies in a 1NF relation. Modification of the location of a department must be done for all employees in that department or SECONDNF will become inconsistent. There is no possibility of inserting into SECONDNF the location of a newly created department that does not have employees. If at some point in time there are no employees in a department, there is no possibility of recording the location of the department.

The update anomalies can be eliminated by decomposing SECONDNF into two relations:
ONE (EMPLOYEE_FAMILY_NAME, DEPARTMENT_NAME), and
TWO (DEPARTMENT_NAME, LOCATION).

2.5.4   Third normal form

A relation is in third normal form (3NF) if it is in 2NF and has no transitive dependencies. SECONDNF is not in 3NF because the functional dependency DEPARTMENT_NAME → LOCATION is transitive. More precisely, LOCATION is transitive on EMPLOYEE_FAMILY_NAME, because:

1. EMPLOYEE_FAMILY_NAME → DEPARTMENT_NAME,
2. DEPARTMENT_NAME → LOCATION,
3. DEPARTMENT_NAME ↛ EMPLOYEE_FAMILY_NAME.

The relation THIRDNF (Figure 2.19) is in 3NF, but is not in the next higher form, BCNF. The relation stores information about grades achieved by students in courses; the students' phone numbers are also kept in the relation. The keys of the relation are: {STUDENT_ID, COURSE#} and {PHONE#, COURSE#}. These are the functional dependencies in THIRDNF:
{STUDENT_ID, COURSE#} → GRADE,
{PHONE#, COURSE#} → GRADE,
STUDENT_ID → PHONE#, and
PHONE# → STUDENT_ID.
There are no transitive or partial dependencies in THIRDNF.

```
SQL> SELECT * FROM THIRDNF;

STUDENT_ID PHONE# COURSE#   GRADE
---------- ------ --------- -----
870001     280001 CSCI223   HD
870001     280001 CSCI335   HD
870002     280002 CSCI335   PT
870002     280002 CSCI957   F
870002     280002 CSCI336   F
```

Figure 2.19   Relation in third normal form

THIRDNF also has some undesirable properties that can lead to update anomalies. The modification of a student's phone number, for example, must be done on multiple tuples. There is no possibility of storing the student's phone number until that student takes at least one course. If a student withdraws from all courses, then the student's phone number is also deleted.

The decomposition of THIRDNF into: ONE (STUDENT_ID, PHONE#) and TWO (STUDENT_ID, COURSE#, GRADE) eliminates the update anomalies. Another decomposition, which eliminates the update anomalies and preserves the dependency {PHONE#, COURSE#} → GRADE, is:
ONE (STUDENT_ID, COURSE#, GRADE) and
TWO (PHONE#, COURSE#, GRADE).

2.5.5   Boyce-Codd normal form

Boyce-Codd normal form (BCNF) is strictly stronger than the three normal forms just discussed, although it does not make any explicit reference to them. The definition of 3NF is concerned with *non-key* attributes, while BCNF considers also those attributes that take part in a composite key. An object Y is in BCNF iff every determinant of functional dependencies in Y is, in fact, a candidate key of Y. THIRDNF is not in BCNF because STUDENT_ID and PHONE# are not keys (they are parts of keys), yet they are determinants.

The relation BOYCECODDNF (Figure 2.20) is in BCNF. The relation keeps basic information about course offerings. Depending on which week it is in the semester and on particular educational needs, the classes can take place in different rooms on the same day of different weeks. The key of the relation combines all its attributes {COURSE#, WEEK_DAY, ROOM}. There are no functional dependencies in this relation.

The update anomalies that arise in BOYCECODDNF are that the rows can only be updated in sets. The modification of a day of teaching of CSCI335 from MONDAY to TUESDAY must be done in two tuples. Addition of a third room for CSCI235 must also be done by inserting two tuples (for Tuesday and Thursday classes). Deletion of the Tuesday's class of CSCI235 will involve removing two tuples.

The update problems of BCNF can be avoided by a further stage of decomposition. Such a decomposition should eliminate the multivalued dependencies from the relation. The multivalued dependencies are discussed next.

```
SQL> SELECT * FROM BOYCECODDNF;

COURSE# WEEK_DAY   ROOM
------- ---------- ----
CSCI235 TUESDAY    R333
CSCI235 THURSDAY   R444
CSCI235 TUESDAY    R444
CSCI235 THURSDAY   R333
CSCI335 MONDAY     R200
CSCI335 MONDAY     R201

6 records selected.
```

Figure 2.20   Relation in Boyce-Codd normal form

2.5.6 Multivalued dependency

Multivalued dependency (MVD) is a generalization of functional dependency, that is, functional dependency is a special case of multivalued dependency. Functional dependencies exclude certain tuples from a relation (if $A \rightarrow B$, then there cannot be two tuples with the same A value but different B values). Multivalued dependencies enforce the existence of certain tuples.

A set of attributes {B} of a relation Y is *multivalued dependent* on a set of attributes {C} of relation Y in a way that does not depend on a set of attributes {D} of Y (denoted {C} $\rightarrow \rightarrow$ {B} | {D}) iff whenever tuples $<v_C, v_B, v_D>$ and$<v_C, v'_B, v'_D>$ exist in Y, then tuples $<v_C, v_B, v'_D>$ and $<v_C, v'_B, v_D>$ are also in Y. Whenever {C} $\rightarrow \rightarrow$ {B} | {D} holds, then {C} $\rightarrow \rightarrow$ {D} | {B} must also hold. We say that {C} multivalue determines {D} in a way which is independent of {B}. A multivalued dependency can exist only if the relation has at least three attributes. The multivalued dependency is *not* the same as an m:n association between attributes (as is often mistakenly stated in the literature).

There is one multivalued dependency in BOYCECODDNF: COURSE# $\rightarrow \rightarrow$ WEEK_DAY | ROOM. This is a "tuple-generating" dependency. For example, if a certain course uses two rooms, then these rooms must be made available for every day of the week on which this course is taught. In other words, if a new room is assigned to a course for a particular day of the week, this room will be used on all days that the course is taught. In this sense, the assignment of a room to a course is independent of the day of the week on which the course is given. ROOM is multivalue determined by COURSE#, but it is independent of WEEK_DAY and vice versa.

BOYCECODDNF relation should be decomposed, because once we know a particular COURSE# value, WEEK_DAY gives us no single-valued information about ROOM and vice versa. The multivalued dependencies are relation-content sensitive. For example, if we did not have the first row in the BOYCECODDNF relation, the multivalued dependency would not hold; the course CSCI235 could use Room R333 on Thursday but not on Tuesday, which contradicts the meaning of the multivalued dependency.

```
SQL> SELECT * FROM FOURTHNF;

S#      P#      E#

-----   -----   -----

S10     P10     E20
S20     P10     E10
S10     P20     E10
S10     P10     E10
```

Figure 2.21   Relation in fourth normal form

2.5.7 Fourth normal form

A relation Y is in fourth normal form (4NF) iff whenever there exists a multivalued dependency in Y, say {C} → → {B} | {D}, then all attributes of Y are also functionally dependent on {C}. In other words, Y is in 4NF iff it is in BCNF and all multivalued dependencies in Y are, in fact, functional dependencies. BOYCECODDNF is not in 4NF because it contains a multivalued dependency which is not a functional dependency.

The existence of multivalued dependencies is object-content sensitive and does not neccesarily lend itself to a realistic explanation in terms of a business rule (hence, multivalued dependencies are difficult to capture). Adding an attribute to Y can invalidate any previous multivalued dependencies in Y. This implies that a non-4NF relation can be converted into a 4NF relation just by adding an attribute to it, although normally a decomposition would be expected to achieve the same result. The current theory does not deal satisfactorily with such issues.

Figure 2.21 represents the relation FOURTHNF that is in 4NF. This relation does not have functional and multivalued dependencies. It is an example of the *all-key relation*. The relation refers to a student-project-equipment database and expresses the business rule ("the real life constraint") that if student S10 works on project P10 (tuple1), and P10 uses equipment E10 (tuple 2), and E10 is used by S10 (tuple 3), then it must be true that S10 uses E10 in P10 (tuple 4).

FOURTHNF exhibits update anomalies that relate to its business rule. For example, if the tuple (S10, P10, E10) is deleted, at least one of the other tuples must also be deleted otherwise the business rule is violated. Similar conditions appear in cases of modification and addition because the business rule must be true at all times.

An implication of such update anomalies is that FOURTHNF should be further decomposed. However, such a decomposition seems to be contrary to the semantic spirit of this relation (i.e. to be a three-way association informing which students use what equipment in what projects). If the designer chooses to decompose FOURTHNF, then such a decomposition will be determined from the notion of join dependency.

2.5.8 Join dependency

Join dependency (JD) is the ultimate form of dependency, when the notion of normalization is applied to decomposition through projection, and reconstruction through join. A relation in 4NF has join dependency because it is possible to decompose such a

```
SQL> SELECT * FROM FIFTHNF;

S#      P#      E#

-----   -----   -----

S10     P10     E20
S20     P10     E10
S10     P20     E10
```

Figure 2.22   Relation in fifth normal form

relation into several relations and to reconstruct the original relation from these decomposed relations. Such a reconstruction does not involve a loss of information (where a loss is understood to constitute extra tuples or the elimination of legitimate tuples from the original relation). Join dependency is a generalization of the multivalued dependency. Both join and multivalued dependencies rely on the *extension*, rather than intension, of the relation.

A set of attributes $\{\{B\}, \{C\}, \{D\}\}$ is *join dependent* in relation Y (denoted $*(\{B\}, \{C\}, \{D\})$) iff whenever tuples $<v_C, v_B, v'_D>$, $<v_C, v'_B, v_D>$ and $<v'_C, v_B, v_D>$ exist in Y, then the tuple $<v_C, v_B, v_D>$ is also in Y. In other words, Y satisfies the join dependency $*(\{B\}, \{C\}, \{D\})$ iff it is equal to the join of its projections over $\{B\}$, $\{C\}$ and $\{D\}$.

2.5.9   Fifth normal form

A relation Y is in fifth normal form (5NF) iff every join dependency in Y is implied by the candidate keys of Y. This means that, though it may be possible to "losslessly" decompose Y according to the join dependency in Y, there is no advantage to doing so if the projected relations will still include the candidate keys of Y.

As in the case of the 4NF, a non-5NF relation can sometimes be converted into a 5NF relation just by adding an attribute to it, although normally a decomposition would be expected to achieve the same result. Clearly, join dependencies are even more difficult to uncover than multivalued dependencies.

The relation FIFTHNF in Figure 2.22 is in 5NF. Any further decomposition of this relation would result in a so-called *connection trap* (i.e. lossy reconstruction). The decomposition of FIFTHNF would bring about the same three relations ((S#,P#), (S#, E#), (P#,E#)) as the decomposition of FOURTHNF (Figure 2.21). If the join of these three relations produces FOURTHNF, then it cannot produce at the same time FIFTHNF. Hence, FIFTHNF is not further decomposable. The business rule which existed for FOURTHNF is not valid for FIFTHNF.

2.5.10   Nonclassical normalization

The 5NF is the ultimate normal form of the classical normalization theory. However, there is an emerging trend to develop a new kind of normalization theory whereby a *restriction/projection* will be used in decomposition and an *outer join* in reconstruction. Such developments are of interest in distributed databases and in semantic modeling that takes advantage of abstractions (aggregation and generalization).

2.5.11   Denormalization

There has been considerable debate about what we call the semantics of normalization. Practically all aspects of normalization can be, and have been, challenged, although such criticisms were only recently given wider publicity and only recently met with wider acceptance. The following is a summary of these challenges:

- All definitions of normal forms other than the first (and, to some extent, BCNF) are not 100 percent sound, and are subject to controversy.
- The reduction in update anomalies with higher normal forms backfires with obvious update problems, due to excessive decomposition of relations. After all, an update is always preceded by a retrieval and key attributes are modified at times (people change names, to use a somewhat trivial example).
- Denormalized structures have been proved to have a similar mathematical appeal to normalized ones and appropriate extensions to relational algebra have been proposed.
- The spirit of normalization contradicts some important principles of semantic modeling and object-oriented database programming.

Denormalized relations can contain *group (relation-valued) attributes*; moreover, attributes and group attributes can be repeating. Using denormalized objects in database design can have a very strong semantic basis. A common argument against the viability of denormalization has been its lack of mathematical soundness and tractability. However, as recent research work has indicated, denormalized structures (sometimes called *NF2—non-first normal form*) have a similar mathematical appeal to normalized ones. This has been proven by recent definitions of the denormalized relational algebra and by the extensions to SQL to handle denormalized relations.

2.6   SEMANTIC ENHANCEMENTS

With the growing convergence of database technology towards artificial intelligence (*semantic nets*) and programming languages (*abstract data types*), there comes the realization that enhancements in conceptual modeling are needed. We discuss here such enhancements from the viewpoint of entity-relationship modeling. One such enhancement is known as database abstraction, another as nested relationships. Such relationships, and the models in which they are used, are sometimes called *hypersemantic*.

An *abstraction* is a model of a real-life situation such that certain details are deliberately omitted. In a sense, the entire database design process is based on the notion of abstraction. The database design uses only essential information, relevant to the users; some facts of potential interest will never be considered in the design. The design introduces a model of the reality but it is not, itself, a reality.

One design abstraction, called *classification/instantiation*, was introduced in Section 2.4.1. and is fundamental to the basic entity-relationship modeling. In this section, we are interested in two special kinds of abstractions which extend the basic entity-relationship model. The abstractions are known as *aggregation/decomposition* and *generalization/*

specialization. An aggregation transforms a relationship between objects (usually entities) into an aggregate object. A generalization turns a class of objects (usually entities) into a generic object (usually an entity). The use of abstractions in a design involves issues of property (attribute) inheritance.

The concept of *nested relationships* is relevant to abstractions. Nested relationships can be used in cooperation with database abstractions and extend the definition of a relationship by allowing the relationship to be directly associated with other relationships.

2.6.1 Aggregation/decomposition

An aggregation transforms a relationship between objects (usually entities) into a higher level aggregate (*superset*) object. The reverse of aggregation is called decomposition. For instance, a relationship among entities LANDLORD, TENANT, and RESIDENTIAL_ PROPERTY can be abstracted into a superset entity LEASE. We make such an aggregation to ignore details about the relationship; for example, we want to think about a lease without bringing to mind such details as an address of the landlord or a credit rating of the tenant.

One implication of aggregation is that the original entities (LANDLORD, TENANT and RESIDENTIAL_PROPERTY) can disappear from the conceptual schema though, clearly, this is only possible if those entities do not participate in some other relationships. In general it would be a harmful modeling practice to eliminate from the conceptual design entities that are abstracted into a superset object. After all, those entities may find existence in their own rights in successive extensions to the conceptual design. A preferred alternative is to indicate, diagrammatically, the existence of an aggregation in the conceptual design, and to introduce separate mechanisms for the conversion of aggregation to logical and physical design structures. In Figure 2.23 we introduce such a graphical notation (black circles) to represent a superset relationship (LEASE_X) and, indirectly (via an aggregate relationship), a superset entity (LEASE_Y). Semantically, the two representations are equivalent. It is up to the personal preferences of the designer to select one of the two.

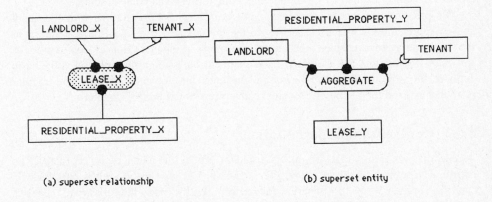

(a) superset relationship   (b) superset entity

Figure 2.23 Aggregation/decomposition

A lease describes a contract under which a landlord grants, to a tenant on behalf of an owner, possession and use of a residential property. The landlord may be the actual owner of the property, or may be a lessee granting a sublease. In Figure 2.23, a lease can be granted to one tenant, or jointly to a group of tenants.

A superset object (such as LEASE) is sometimes known as a HAS-A object (LEASE HAS-A LANDLORD, etc.). We call the component (subset) entities the PART-OF entities (LANDLORD is PART-OF LEASE). In general, PART-OF objects can be relationships.

Implicit in the entity-relationship representation of the aggregation is the concept of *attribute inheritance*. This is an *upward* (bottom-up) inheritance for aggregation and a *downward* (top-down) inheritance for decomposition. However, the downward inheritance has rather theoretical meaning and is not used in modeling practice. Thus, the HAS-A object inherits the attributes of the PART-OF objects, not vice versa. This is graphically illustrated by placing the black circles at a HAS-A object.

In our example, LEASE may inherit from the PART-OF entities such attributes as landlord_name, owner_name, tenant_name, and property_address. These attributes may be inherited in order to constitute a key for LEASE. Alternatively, the key could be a separate attribute of LEASE, that is not inherited (e.g. lease_contract_number). LEASE can also include descriptive attributes (e.g. lease_date or rent_payment).

The attribute inheritance, as shown in an entity-relationship diagram, can be actual or virtual. *Actual inheritance* means that the inherited attributes are stored in a HAS-A object (i.e. they are duplicates of the same attributes in PART-OF entities). *Virtual inheritance* means that the inherited attributes are stored only in PART-OF entities and are transported to a HAS-A object whenever this object is analyzed. All information about the attribute inheritance for aggregations is kept in the DD and is used in the conversion from conceptual to logical and physical designs. If the objects participating in an aggregation are retained in the conversion then, depending on the logical model, virtual inheritance may or may not be sustained. For example, virtual inheritance is not possible in the relational model because of the referential integrity rule.

An aggregation can be built on multiple levels—usually, but not necessarily, creating a tree (hierarchy). Moreover, it is not required for subset objects at any particular level to be mutually exclusive. Both of these topics are open research problems. In practice they are better avoided, usually by a simple remodeling of the conceptual structure.

The first concept, known as *cover aggregation*, has been described in some detail above. Aggregation is also used to refer to the internal structure of an object, that is, to the aggregation of attributes needed to construct an object. This is referred to as *Cartesian aggregation* and manifests itself as an attribute structuring method in the basic entity-relationship model. Attributes are clustered into objects (entities and regular relationships) and the definitions for such clusters are stored in a DD database.

2.6.2 Generalization/specialization

A generalization turns a class of objects (usually entities) into a generic object (usually an entity). The reverse of this is called specialization. For instance, an entity PROPERTY can be regarded as a generic (*supertype*) entity for the class of entities RESIDENTIAL_PROPERTY and INDUSTRIAL_PROPERTY. We use such a generalization to ignore individual differences between *subtype* entities. For example, property_address can belong to PROPERTY, whereas number_of_employees is clearly an attribute of INDUSTRIAL_PROPERTY, not applicable to RESIDENTIAL_PROPERTY.

A supertype entity is sometimes called a CAN-BE entity (PROPERTY CAN-BE a RESIDENTIAL_PROPERTY). A subtype entity is known as an IS-A entity (RESIDENTIAL_PROPERTY IS-A PROPERTY). A relationship that relates a supertype entity to subtype entities is called a *generic relationship*.

In Figure 2.24 we present four generic relationships that are built on top of the superset relationship from Figure 2.23. Black rectangles attached to subtype entities are used to denote a generic relationship.

The first generic relationship in Figure 2.24, called GENERIC_ONE, describes the fact that PERSON CAN-BE a LANDLORD or a TENANT. An explanation for the partial membership of PERSON in GENERIC_ONE could be that there are some PERSON entity instances in the overall conceptual structure that are neither landlords nor tenants (e.g. dependants).

The relationship GENERIC_TWO defines a rule that a LANDLORD CAN_BE a LESSEE or an OWNER. If the landlord is a lessee, then (s)he grants a sublease of the property to a tenant (expressed by the aggregation LEASE). A separate regular relationship RENTS is used to determine owners who rent properties to lessees. The lessees subsequently assume the role of landlords and sublease the properties. The membership of OWNER and LESSEE in GENERIC_TWO is partial, as there is no obligation for an owner or a lessee to become a landlord.

The relationships GENERIC_THREE and GENERIC_FOUR create a generalization hierarchy. In this hierarchy, PROPERTY CAN-BE either a RESIDENTIAL_PROPERTY

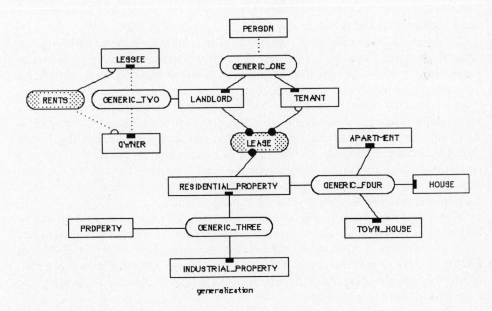

Figure 2.24 Generalization/specialization

or an INDUSTRIAL_PROPERTY. A RESIDENTIAL_PROPERTY CAN-BE an APARTMENT or TOWN_HOUSE or HOUSE.

There is an important difference between the inheritance mechanisms of aggregation and generalization. Unlike aggregation, the inheritance of attributes in generalization is *downward* (top-down). Hence, the black rectangles are placed in IS-A (subtype) entities. LANDLORD and TENANT inherit the generic attributes present in PERSON, such as date_of_birth and, for that matter, person_name. Attributes inherited from PERSON complement the specific attributes of LANDLORD (e.g. interest_on_mortgage) and TENANT (number_of_dependants). In an orthogonal fashion, specialization uses an upward (bottom-up) inheritance. However, the upward inheritance of specialization does not bear a practical importance.

As in the case of aggregation, generalization can be multilevel, but is not necessarily hierarchical. The IS-A entities do not have to be mutually exclusive; for example, it is possible that a landlord could be a tenant in the property which (s)he leases to other tenants. Such information can be stored in the DD, but the handling of it in the database design is not at all obvious. Usually, ad hoc measures are applied, sometimes at the procedural, rather than declarative, level.

2.6.3 Nested relationships

Definitions of object, entity, relationship and attribute are not formal, precise or absolute (and luckily so). For example, COLOR is usually perceived as an attribute (e.g. car_color). However, under certain circumstances, COLOR can be modeled as a higher level object. Such may be the case for a paint factory or a photographic company. COLOR can then be considered to be an entity with such attributes as wavelength, saturation, hue and absorption. Similarly, MARRIAGE can be modeled as an entity in one design and a relationship in another.

In general, it is possible (and indeed likely) that different designers will produce different conceptual structures for the same organization, and yet all such designs may be semantically correct. The objectives of semantic modeling can only be fulfilled if the designer uses the tools which support flexibilty of interpretation: there are no stiff rules.

An immediate consequence of this flexibility of interpretation is the concept of a nested relationship. A relationship is an association between objects (as discussed in Section 2.4.2). The object(s) can be a relationship and such a relationship, that is, one owned by another relationship, is called a nested relationship. We graphically indicate a nested relationship by placing a triangle on the connection line. The triangle is placed near the nested relationship and points towards the owning relationship. In Figure 2.25, the relationship MAJOR is nested in the relationship TAKES.

Figure 2.25 describes a simple conceptual structure, such that the courses offered by various faculties constitute major studies. A student can be enrolled in, at most, one major. In the design, MAJOR is modelled as an M:N relationship between COURSE and FACULTY. Hence, the relationship TAKES, which assigns STUDENTs to a MAJOR, involves a nested relationship (MAJOR). Had MAJOR been modeled as an entity, the nesting would have been avoided.

Although our graphical notation provides enough expressive power to represent deeply nested relationships, an accepted design principle is to try to be evasive in this

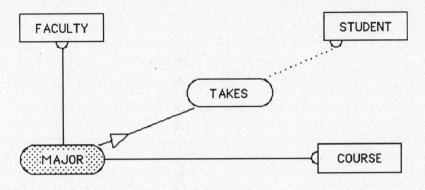

Figure 2.25   Nested relationship

respect. Nesting can easily get out of hand, in particular when the nested relationships are used together with aggregation and generalization structures. The semantics of such designs is obscure; however, the resulting structure has the advantage of being concise. Ultimately, the decision to use nested relationships belongs to the designer.

FURTHER READING

The process of database design has been addressed in many books; however, to the best of our knowledge, the lifecycle of database design, as described in Section 2.1, has not yet been treated as comprehensively and systematically as we have attempted in this book.

The monograph by Furtado and Neuhold (1986) presents in a formal way basic techniques for conceptual and logical design. On the logical design level it refers only to relational databases. A comprehensive text by Hawryszkiewycz (1984) covers the design of data structures for relational, network and hierarchical databases. Its major strength is in conceptual and relational design methods. An interesting, but in our view not very well-structured or consistent, reading is offered by Howe (1983). The book satisfactorily addresses conceptualization, logical design in terms of the relational model and physical design in terms of the network model. A collection of articles edited skillfully by Yao (1985) includes contributions by many recognized experts in database design. However, design of physical schema and presumably issues of application programming are left to the next volume of the book. The book by Vesely (1986) promises more in the title, than it delivers. The presentation is neither complete nor systematic. An important contribution to textbook treatment of database design was made by Teorey and Fry (1982). The book's coverage of physical design is quite superb. Finally, Vetter (1987) contributed an excellent introductory text which does not presuppose any sophisticated background in databases. However, for a database specialist, the book does not provide anything new, except in the way of presentation (quite attractive!).

Tutorial discussions about data dictionaries are offered by Allen *et al.* (1982) and Uhrowczik (1973). From the small selection of textbooks on data dictionaries, the best value is Leong-Hong and Plagman (1982). A systems analysis perspective on data dictionaries is offered by DeMarco (1979) and Gane and Sarson (1979). The ANSI standard for the information resource dictionary system is defined in IRDS (1988a and 1988b), and is also briefly described by Dolk and Kirsch (1987) and Goldfine (1985).

Data flow diagrams were popularized by the books of DeMarco (1979) and Gane and Sarson (1979). Data flow diagrams are routinely described in textbooks on systems analysis (e.g. Aktas 1987, FitzGerald and FitzGerald 1987, Hawryszkiewycz 1988, Jeffrey and Lawrence 1984, Kendall 1987, Page-Jones 1980, Steward 1987, Weinberg 1980). In most of these books, the use of structured English for bottom-level processes in DFDs is also presented. The theory of Petri nets and its use in systems modeling is discussed in Peterson (1981). Application of Petri nets to systems analysis is discussed by Maiocchi (1985).

The entity-relationship model was introduced by Chen (1976). A tutorial description of the entity-relationship model can be found in Chen (1985), Howe (1983), Olle (1981) and elsewhere. The semantics for the model is given by Lien (1980). Czejdo and Embley (1985) and Parent and Spaccapietra (1985) have independently introduced an algebra for the entity-relationship model.

Normalization was introduced by Codd (1970). The same author introduced first, second, third and Boyce-Codd normal forms (Codd 1972). Multivalued dependencies and fourth normal form are due to Fagin (1977). Join dependencies were discovered by Rissanen (1977). Normalization is discussed formally in Maier (1983) and Ullman (1982). An informal discussion of normalization is given in Date (1986). A simple guide to normal forms is presented by Kent (1983). Denormalized relational algebra appears in Schek (1985). An extension to SQL to handle denormalized relations is proposed by Roth *et al.* (1987). Some of our illustrations of normal form relations are based on the well-known examples presented in Date (1986) and Hawryszkiewycz (1984).

The aggregation and generalization abstractions have been defined by Smith and Smith (1977). These abstractions often serve as a basis for semantic data models and are described, under sometimes camouflaged shapes and forms, in the relevant literature. A comparison of semantic data models can be found in Brodie (1984) and King and McLeod (1985). An in-depth tutorial on aggregation and generalization is yet to be written. The same is true for the nested relationships. An introductory treatment of the two abstractions in an entity-relationship setting is available from Hawryszkiewycz (1984).

REFERENCES

AKTAS, A. Z. (1987): *Structured Analysis and Design of Information Systems,* Prentice Hall, 190p.

ALLEN, F. W., LOOMIS, M. E. S. and MANNINO, M. V. (1982): The Integrated Dictionary/Directory, *Comp. Surv.*, 2, pp.245–86.

BRODIE, M. L. (1984): On the Development of Data Models, in: *On Conceptual Modelling. Perspectives from Artificial Intelligence, Databases, and Programming Languages*, ed. M. L. Brodie, J. Mylopoulos and J. W. Schmidt, Springer-Verlag, pp.19–47.

CHEN, P. P. S. (1976): The Entity-Relationship Model—Toward a Unified View of Data, *ACM Trans. Database Syst.*, 1, pp.9–36.

CHEN, P. P. S. (1985): Database Design Based on Entity and Relationship, in: *Principles of Database Design, Volume I, Logical Organizations*, ed. S. B.Yao, Prentice Hall, pp.174–210.

CODD, E. F. (1970): A Relational Model of Data for Large Shared Data Banks, *Comm. ACM*, 6, pp.377–87.

CODD, E. F. (1972): Further Normalization of the Data Base Relational Model, in: *Data Base Systems*, ed. R. Rustin, Prentice Hall, pp.33–64.

CZEJDO, B. and EMBLEY, D. W. (1985): An Algebra for an Entity-Relationship Model and its Application to Graphical Query Processing, in: *Proc. Int. Conf. on Foundations of Data Organization*, Kyoto, Japan, pp.274–79.

DATE, C. J. (1986): *An Introduction to Database Systems*, Vol. I, 4th ed., Addison-Wesley, 639p.

DEMARCO, T. (1979): *Structured Analysis and System Specification*, Prentice Hall, 352p.

DOLK, D. R. and KIRSCH II, R. A. (1987): A Relational Information Resource Dictionary System, *Comm. ACM*, 1, pp.48–61.

FAGIN, R. (1977): Multivalued Dependencies and a New Normal Form for Relational Databases, *ACM Trans. Database Syst.*, 3, pp.262–78.

FITZGERALD, J. and FITZGERALD, A. F. (1987): *Fundamentals of Systems Analysis. Using Structured Analysis and Design Techniques*, John Wiley & Sons, 769p. (+).

FURTADO, A. L. and NEUHOLD, E. J. (1986): *Formal Techniques for Data Base Design*, Springer-Verlag, 114p.

GANE, C. and SARSON, T. (1979): *Structured Systems Analysis: Tools and Techniques*, Prentice Hall, 241p.

GOLDFINE, A. (1985): The Information Resource Dictionary System, in: *Proc. 4th Int. Conf. on E-R Approach*, Chicago, pp.114–22.

HAWRYSZKIEWYCZ, I. T. (1984): *Database Analysis and Design*, SRA, 578p.

HAWRYSZKIEWYCZ, I. T. (1988): *Introduction to Systems Analysis and Design*, Prentice Hall, 373p.

HOWE, D. R. (1983): *Data Analysis for Data Base Design*, Edward Arnold, 307p.

IRDS (1988a): *Information Resource Dictionary System*, American National Standard for Information Systems, X3.138-1988, ANSI.

IRDS (1988b): *Information Resource Dictionary System—Services Interface*, Draft Proposed American National Standard for Information Systems, X3.nnn-1988, ANSI, 325p.

JEFFREY, D. R. and LAWRENCE, M. J. (1984): *Systems Analysis and Design*, Prentice Hall, 225p.

KENDALL, P. A. (1987): *Introduction to Systems Analysis and Design*, Allyn and Bacon, 513p.

KENT, W. (1983): A Simple Guide to Five Normal Forms in Relational Database Theory, *Comm. ACM*, 2, pp.120–25.

KING, R. and MCLEOD, D. (1985): Semantic Data Models, in: *Principles of Database Design, Volume I, Logical Organizations*, ed. S. B. Yao, Prentice Hall, pp.115–50.

LEONG-HONG, B. W. and PLAGMAN, B. K. (1982): *Data Dictionary/Directory Systems. Administration, Implementation and Usage*, John Wiley & Sons, 328p.

LIEN, Y. E. (1980): On the Semantics of the Entity-Relationship Data Model, in: *Entity-Relationship Approach to Systems Analysis and Design*, North-Holland, pp.155–67.

MAIER, D. (1983): *The Theory of Relational Databases*, Computer Science Press, 637p.

MAIOCCHI, M. (1985): The Use of Petri Nets in Requirements and Functional Specification, *System Description Methodologies*, eds D.Teichroew, G. David, Elsevier Science, pp.253–74.

OLLE, T. W. (1981): A Tutorial on Data Modelling using Entity Types, Attributes and Relationships, in: *Data Base Management: Theory and Applications*, eds C. W. Holsapple, A. B. Whinston, D. Reidel Publishing, pp.35–58.

PAGE-JONES, M. (1980): *The Practical Guide to Structured Systems Design,* Prentice Hall, 354p.

PARENT, C. and SPACCAPIETRA, S. (1985): An Algebra for a General Entity-Relationship Model, *IEEE Trans. Soft. Eng.*, 7, pp.634–43.

PETERSON, J. L. (1981): *Petri Net Theory and the Modeling of Systems*, Prentice Hall, 290p.

RISSANEN, J. (1977): Independent Components of Relations, *ACM Trans. Database Syst.*, 4, pp.317–25.

ROTH, M. A., KORTH, H. F. and BATORY, D. S. (1987): SQL/NF: a Query Language for ¬1NF Relational Databases, *Inf. Syst.*, 1, pp.99–114.

SCHEK, H. J. (1985): Towards a Basic Relational NF^2 Algebra Processor, in: *Proc. Int. Conf. on Foundations of Data Organization*, Kyoto, Japan, pp.173–82.

SMITH, J. M. and SMITH, D. C. P. (1977): Database Abstractions: Aggregation and Generalization, *ACM Trans. Database Syst.*, 2, pp.105–33.

STEWARD, D. V. (1987): *Software Engineering with Systems Analysis and Design*, Brooks/Cole, 414p.

TEOREY, T. J. and FRY, J. P. (1982): *Design of Database Structures,* Prentice Hall, pp.57–132.

UHROWCZIK, P. P. (1973): Data Dictionary/Directories, *IBM Syst. J.*, 4, pp.332–50.

ULLMAN, J. D. (1982): *Principles of Database Systems*, 2nd ed., Computer Science Press, 484p.

VESELY, E. G. (1986): *The Practitioner's Blueprint for Logical and Physical Database Design*, Prentice Hall, 405p.

VETTER, M. (1987): *Strategy for Data Modelling (application- and enterprise-wide),* John Wiley and Sons, 344p.

WEINBERG, V. (1980): *Structured Analysis*, Prentice Hall, 328p.

YAO, S. B. (ed) (1985): *Principles of Database Design, Volume I, Logical Organizations*, Prentice Hall, 405p.

3

Requirements Analysis

This chapter deals with analysis and specifications of user requirements. This is the initial phase of system development, often referred to as the system analysis phase. The goal of system analysis is to define what the system is expected to do. This involves examining the current system and building a problem model. Typical structured system analysis techniques, centered around data flow diagram modeling, are used. This chapter includes the problem statement for the case study used in this book.

3.1 STRATEGIC PLANNING

A database design process must be conducted within the framework of the enterprise's strategic plan. In a properly run organization, the strategic plan is the document most essential to determining managerial and operational plans. A strategic plan:

- observes (or establishes) the company mission statement;
- sets strategic objectives of the company;
- identifies specific goals in support of objectives;
- determines strategies and policies whereby the objectives can be achieved;
- controls the allocation of resources;
- ascertains a corporate-wide business model;
- establishes an outward image of the organization;
- assigns priorities to development projects; and
- aligns information system design and implementation with business needs.

3.1.1 Mission statement

The corporate mission is an enduring statement of purpose which describes the long-term vision of the organization. The organization's objectives, goals, strategies and policies are based on the mission and should be evaluated and modified in accordance with it. The corporate mission is a statement of philosophy and business principles. It is usually advantageous to have a customer-oriented, rather than a product-oriented, mission statement. For example, the mission statement for the University of Wollongong reads, in part:

The prime objective of The University of Wollongong is to be strong in both the traditional and new disciplines at both undergraduate and postgraduate levels so as to produce graduates and research outcomes of international distinction and in areas of national importance.

The first step in information system development is to identify an organization's mission. The development of a database system is usually triggered by problems in the execution of managerial or operational functions (e.g. overdue accounts cause significant cash flow problems, as a result of a limited credit verification of customers). Such problems are unraveled as a result of external and internal audits. An *external audit* identifies and evaluates principal political, economic, social and technological factors that affect an organization's performance. It identifies external threats to be avoided and external opportunities to be taken advantage of. An *internal audit* identifies and evaluates key company weaknesses and strengths in the areas of management, marketing, accounting, production and research and development.

The problems identified by these audits are then analyzed within the framework of the existing strategic plan. Two outcomes of such an analysis are possible: either objectives of the strategic plan are not being carried out at managerial and operational levels, or the strategic plan overlooks the issues that caused the problem. In the first case, issues of propagating the objectives of the strategic plan to lower levels must be looked at. In the second case, changes to the strategic plan must be contemplated.

3.1.2   Strategic objectives and goals

The hallmark of strategic planning is effectiveness (doing the right things) rather than efficiency (doing things right). Corporate strategic objectives are the basis for system development. The objectives, although broad, differ for different companies and vary for the same company depending on the current "business climate". The objectives can also overlap, thus giving rise to conflicts in the strategic plan. Such conflicts must be resolved by attaching priorities to the objectives. Normally organizations pursue only one or a few objectives at any given time. Long-term objectives are supported by specific corporate goals (usually expressed as annual targets).

Some examples of strategic objectives and goals are:

- to increase profitability (specific goals might be to increase revenues in the next fiscal year by 3–4 percent and to decrease billing costs in the next fiscal year by 1 percent);
- to improve customer service (a specific goal might be to shorten average overall order processing time to 14 days);
- to seek ownership or increase control over suppliers or competitors;
- to introduce present products into new geographic areas;
- to improve work practices and quality of life within the organization;
- to change the production profile;
- to modernize manufacturing equipment;
- to decrease atmospheric pollution; and
- to decrease incidents of industrial conflicts.

3.1.3 Strategies and policies

Strategies and policies are the means whereby the organization attempts to achieve its strategic objectives and goals. Two typical strategies are acquisition and merger. Policies are instruments for the implementation of strategies. They include administrative procedures and practices, rules, forms, methods and guidelines. Sometimes the policies set constraints and limits on pursuits to achieve strategic goals and objectives.

Some examples of strategies and policies are:

* acquisition of a chain of retailers to meet a profitability objective (a supporting policy might be to open some retail points on Saturday afternoons and Sundays);
* market penetration (a supporting policy might be to make the retailers contribute some percentage of their revenues towards advertising);
* reduction of tax liabilities (a supporting policy might be to lease rather than purchase new equipment).

3.1.4 Strategic planning for conceptual design

Strategic planning belongs to the systems analysis phase, but its influence on the conceptual design cannot be overstated. A business model (a hierarchy of subsystems and processes) is a direct consequence of the strategic plan. The strategic plan also determines the order in which database systems are built. The data flow diagrams for a designed database system relate directly to the managerial and operational plans and to the business model. The data dictionary is put into existence by recording strategic objectives and then by decomposing them into subsystems, functions, events, entities and so on. A top-down decomposition of DFD processes ("bubbles") establishes a hierarchy of business processes. A schematic diagram of dependencies between strategic modeling and typical activities of the conceptual design is given in Figure 3.1.

A broad meaning of strategic planning includes managerial and operational plans. In Figure 3.1, the strategic plan corresponds roughly to a mission statement, the managerial plans are developed in response to strategic objectives and goals, and the operational plans enforce strategies and policies. A business model is the functional structure of an organization (Section 3.2) and is first derived from a strategic plan. As the conceptual design progresses, the model is systematically enriched and improved. The conceptual design proceeds according to the implementation plan. The implementation plan states which subsystems are to be first implemented and schedules design stages (Section 3.3).

Once the implementation plan is known, top-level data flow diagrams (DFDs), for the first subsystem to be implemented, are drawn (Sections 2.3 and 3.4). Drawing top-level (i.e. context and overview) DFDs has two advantages: it is a means of verification of the business model (Section 3.2), and it allows the establishment of a simplified entity-relationship diagram called an entity model (Sections 2.4, in particular Figure 2.6, and 4.1). The entity model is derived by converting composite data flows and data stores into data entities. The relationships between entities are created by analyzing the connectivities between data flows and stores and by studying the corresponding processes of DFDs.

The development of low-level DFDs leads to iterative refinements of the business model and to the functions specifications for (at least) lowest-level processes (Section

4.2). If the entity diagram exists, the function specifications are generalized into access graphs (Section 4.3). In a sound design methodology, supported by computer-assisted software engineering (CASE) tools, function specifications and access graphs can be

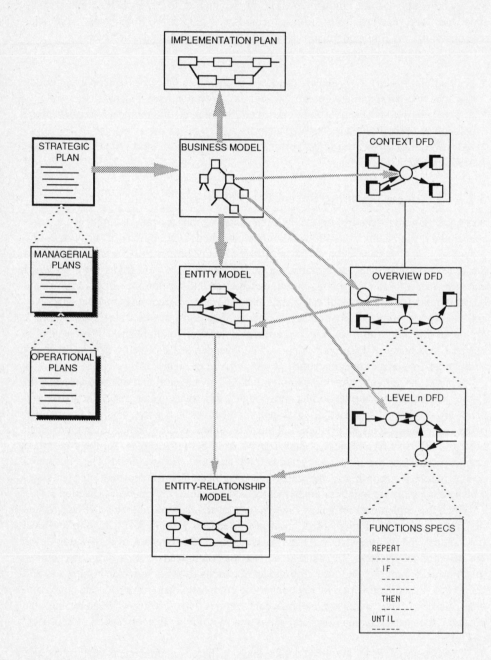

Figure 3.1   Strategic planning for conceptual design

rigorously analyzed and used to derive a provably correct entity-relationship model (Sections 2.4, 2.6 and 4.4). Another approach, that can lead to a feasible solution when pursued by an experienced designer, is to develop the entity-relationship model by the informal studies of the DFDs and by the successive transforms of parts of the entity model. The former approach is advised when designing with the assistance of CASE tools. The latter is akin to manual design (it assumes, however, the use of skillful and experienced designers).

3.2 BUSINESS MODEL

One of the aims of systems analysis (and strategic planning in particular) is to determine the strategy for the development of a new information system. Once it is decided what business application area should be implemented first, the conceptual design phase can be initiated. The conceptual design begins with the identification of business processes. A hierarchy of business processes is constructed to create a high-level business model. Originally, such a model identifies only subsystems and high-level functions. The functions decompose vertically to create a multilevel hierarchical structure.

3.2.1 Correspondence between business model and data flow diagrams

It is neither desirable nor purposeful to attempt to build a multilevel business model at once. An incremental and iterative construction of the business model, that gets feedback from the development of the data flow diagrams for a new system, is a better approach (Figure 3.1). The DFD (Section 2.3) is itself a hierarchically structured technique which can be viewed as a more detailed representation of the business model. Functions of the business model correspond to processes (bubbles) of the DFD. Moreover, they correspond on the basis of levels; that is if a function on level i in the business model matches a process on level j in the DFD, then a function on level $i-1$ must correspond to a certain process on level $j-1$ (Figure 3.2).

3.2.2 Subsystems and functions

A business model is a functional structure of the organization. It consists of subsystems and multilevel functions. A subsystem differs from a function in that it is a jurisdiction rather than a process. A subsystem can be considered as a department name or a jurisdictional area with a physical location in the organization. A function corresponds to a DFD's process.

There are four categories of functions: *query* (Q-function), *update* (U-function), *input* (I-function) and *report* (R-function). An overlap between these functions is possible. This overlap happens when a function, which is otherwise inseparable, is in fact a multiple function. To recognize such a possibility we allow for the concatenation of function identifiers (so we can have a UR-function, QI-function and so on). Some examples of the different functions are:

Q-function	Check if items are in stock.
U-function	Update customer references.
I-function	Enter customer order.
R-function	Produce monthly sales report.
UR-function	Adjust inventory and produce adjustment report.
QI-function	Verify customer existence and enter new customer.

Categorization of functions is important to many crucial design decisions. The overall percentages of query and update functions influence such things as access strategies, physical placements and normalization levels. Input and update functions affect the design of forms (documents) while output functions determine the design of reports and query and update functions govern the design of screens. The relevance of functions to design decisions is discussed in pertinent places in this book.

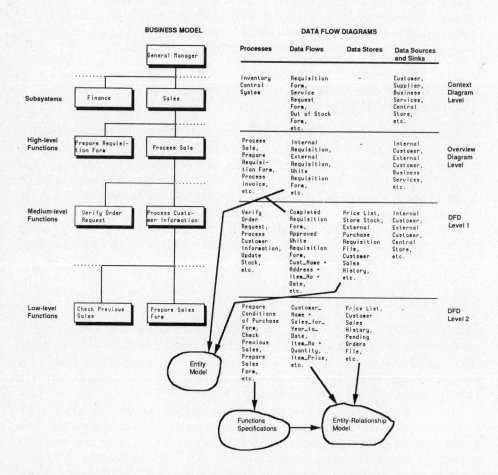

Figure 3.2   Correlations between a business model and data flow diagrams

3.2.3 Housekeeping functions

Some functions are not related to the database application being designed, but to the activities of administering the database application. Such activities are sometimes known as housekeeping. Any housekeeping function (H-function) belongs also to one of the four categories (it is a multiple function). The housekeeping functions are treated separately in the database design process and are not normally considered at the early phases of the design process. In particular, they are not addressed in the systems analysis and the conceptual design phases. Thus, they are not part of the business model. Some examples of housekeeping functions are:

HQ-function   Display information about users currently logged in to the DBMS.
HU-function   Change (upgrade or degrade) user's access privileges.
HI-function   Give access authorization to a new user.
HQR-function   Display current activities on the database and print summary statistics
                         of the system during a set time interval.

3.2.4 Manifest and masked functions

There is one more class of functions that is not identified in the business model. These are the ad hoc functions that are only used occasionally (e.g. Produce an exception report for any sales order which was amended more than twice last week or Determine current sales orders on the ten most profitable products during the last three months). We call such functions masked, as opposed to manifest functions identified in the business model. The masked functions are informational rather than operational. They are important to the decision-making processes of the business, are of interest to executives and often require immediate access (e.g. What is the balance owing of the customer I have on phone?).

Functions which were originally identified as masked, but are of considerable recurrent nature, can be promoted to manifest functions. This way, they will get direct consideration in the business model and in the DFD modeling. However, many functions cannot be predicted when building the conceptual model of the business. They may, for example, become of interest at some future time as a result of a change in business conditions or with the arrival of a new executive. Naturally, the *unpredictable* masked functions cannot be considered in the design. We can only hope that the system will be able to accommodate most of such functions when they eventuate. Current fourth or fifth-generation languages of state-of-the-art DBMSs provide necessary potential toward this aim. The *predictable* masked functions, on the other hand, are considered in the conceptual design. They should be supported by the underlying database structures and, therefore, will be incorporated in the design of the entity model (Section 4.1) and later reaffirmed in the entity-relationship-attribute (ERA) schema (Section 4.4).

3.3 IMPLEMENTATION PLAN

The implementation plan is a "by-product" of the strategic planning and the activities involved in building the business model. The strategic plan and business model determine, even if implicitly and not in detail, a plan of the systems development. There are two aspects of the implementation plan: the application aspect and the methodological aspect. The *application* aspect of the implementation plan concerns the order in which the subsystems will be developed. The strategic plan and the business model provide all necessary information for the application aspect of the implementation plan. The *methodological* aspect determines the order (and overlap) in which major development phases will be conducted. This aspect is only indirectly related to the strategic plan and the business model (e.g. via cost factor or effectiveness considerations). We shall only discuss the methodological aspect of the implementation plan.

A crucial factor in developing the implementation plan is the accuracy of the estimates. The estimation should not be covered in the mist of intuition, past experiences with similar tasks and guesswork. The estimates should apply to all individual stages of a consistent and predefined methodology for systems development. All external and internal assumptions should be spelt out and documented (e.g. a predicted inflation rate in the time horizon of the system's development or the availability of a guru with particular skills). This implies that the building of the implementation plan cannot begin too early. A certain amount of analysis must be done before our estimates can be justified. It is reasonable to expect that the initial version of the implementation plan can be done once an outline of the business model is available. As the development progresses, some estimates of the implementation plan become facts and the remaining estimates can be stated more accurately. The development of the implementation plan is therefore an ongoing activity.

There are two interrelated elements of the implementation plan: *time* and *cost-benefit*. The estimates for these two elements are developed concurrently. The implementation plan is mostly concerned with monitoring time. This is an activity internal to the system's development cycle and, as such, it is performed by project managers. The cost-benefit analysis, on the other hand, is often conducted by senior executives of the company with the cooperation of project managers.

It is worthwhile to employ a project management software package (such as Microsoft Project or MacProject). Such a package would easily accommodate refinements to the plan due to project monitoring activities and would generate a refined plan. It is also likely that the package would contain (or interface with) a spreadsheet software to allow sophisticated cost-benefit analysis. A project management software package can also constitute a part of an integrated CASE tool.

3.3.1　Lifecycle models

The time dimension of an implementation plan is derived from the lifecycle model adapted in the design methodology. Four basic lifecycle approaches can be distinguished:

- the slam dunk approach;
- the baroque approach;
- the waterfall approach; and
- the prototyping approach.

3.3.1.1 The slam dunk approach

The slam dunk approach is centered around the application programming phase. It is based on the principle that programming should begin as soon as the project idea is conceived. It effectively precludes all other project development phases from being used in any systematic way. If documentation of the other phases is required by the management, it is created to justify programming decisions taken, rather than to be a blueprint for programming. The slam dunk approach goes against typical project management practices and, therefore, implementation plans for it are not constructed. Nevertheless, this approach may well be the most commonly used in practice. This is regrettably so, as successes with this approach are rare and even then can be attributed, not to the method, but to the quality of development teams and to managerial skills. Figure 3.3 is an example of the slam dunk approach applied to the database development lifecycle discussed in this book (note that the maintenance and evolution phases are not considered because they do not apply to the development process).

3.3.1.2 The baroque approach

The baroque approach is an overdone attempt to rectify problems of the slam dunk approach. It is an attempt to run a software development process like a manufacturing production line. The next design phase can commence only after the previous phase is completed. There is no overlap. This approach is ill-conceived because software development is an iterative process that requires multiple feedbacks between design phases and stages. Refinements of the seemingly completed design stages must be an accepted practice because the design requirements are never fully specified or understood. The system is built to satisfy the user (requirements); but what is the user satisfaction? Building software is a social phenomenon; the baroque approach, however, tries to work against the social processes. As a result, the design enters the systems analysis and never seems to progress to the next phase. After an unacceptably long attempt to complete the analysis, the developers usually give up and frantically try to complete the remaining design phases. By then, it is usually too late. Figure 3.4 illustrates the baroque approach.

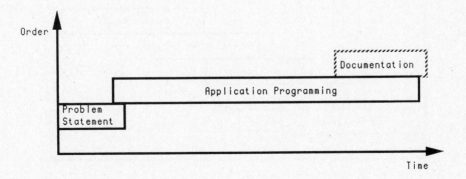

Figure 3.3   The slam dunk approach

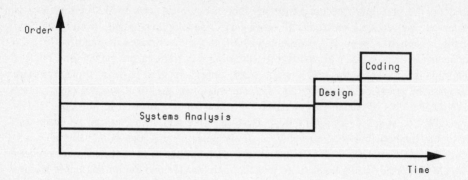

Figure 3.4   The baroque approach

3.3.1.3 The waterfall approach

The waterfall approach is a direct response to the shortcomings of the baroque approach. It allows for overlaps and iterations between design phases and stages. In other respects, however, it is as rigorous and systematic as the baroque approach is. The order in which design phases are entered is strictly defined. The waterfall approach encourages a structured design methodology and stands up for good design practices. However, it introduces a time lag between design commencement and software delivery. This time lag may be long enough to cause users and management dissatisfaction as to the design's progress. Support for the project can drop significantly and, at the same time, expectations about the final product are likely to outgrow what can be delivered. Nevertheless, a patient and well-informed user can be rewarded by quality software once the development is finished. The waterfall approach is exemplified in Figure 3.5.

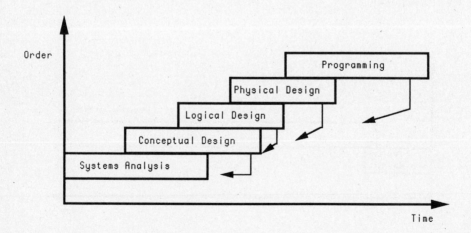

Figure 3.5   The waterfall approach

3.3.1.4 The prototyping approach

The prototyping approach is a relatively new idea which gained momentum with the introduction of nonprocedural programming as a basis for systems development. Nonprocedural (declarative) programming assists dynamic software environments of DBMSs (mainly relational) and knowledge-based development packages. In such environments, changes to data structures can be (at least theoretically) easily accommodated by the existing programs. More importantly, nonprocedural programming provides the power of generating software (rather than writing it). In such a situation, prototyping has become an attractive alternative. A prototype of the system can be built early in the design process and given to users for tests and feedback. There is a danger, however, that the initial development discipline can vanish and deteriorate to the slam dunk approach. Ideally, the prototype should be used to refine the system's design and then discarded. Dynamic software environments encourage, however, the conversion of the prototype to a final product and, in project teams which lack the discipline, the slam dunk style of work can take over. The prototyping approach is illustrated in Figure 3.6.

3.3.2 Time estimation

In the preparation of the time aspect of the implementation plan we turn to graphic techniques. Traditional techniques of project control and job scheduling can be used and probably the most popular tools of this sort are:

- Gantt (milestone) charts; and
- PERT (CPM) charts.

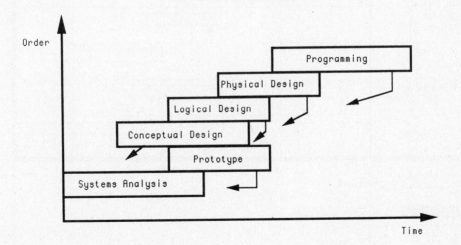

Figure 3.6 The prototyping approach

3.3.2.1 Gantt charts

A Gantt chart is a kind of bar chart. It displays activities on the vertical axis and the time required across the horizontal axis. In a typical Gantt chart, the time durations for activities are shown. A *milestone chart* is a variation of the Gantt chart, such that the starting (and/or finishing) dates for activities are displayed, instead of the time durations. Since popular extensions to Gantt charts permit different time representations and time scales, it is practical not to differentiate between the Gantt and milestone charts. *Activities* (tasks) are significant, measurable and verifiable points in the development of a project. Gantt charts can be applied to projects and to individuals (resources). Commonly, one master Gantt chart is used for the project and separate charts are developed for subactivities assigned to individuals. A blueprint of the Gantt chart for a database development project is shown in Figure 3.7. Only design phases are distinguished as activities. In a practical situation, the design stages would also be considered in the chart (as subactivities).

3.3.2.2 PERT charts

PERT and CPM are synonymous terms for a popular network scheduling technique. PERT is an acronym for Program Evaluation and Review Technique, while CPM stands for Critical Path Method. A Gantt chart does not show dependencies between activities but a PERT (CPM) chart rectifies this shortcoming by explicitly determining which

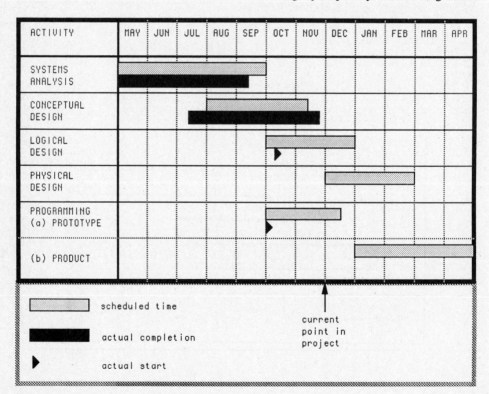

Figure 3.7   Blueprint of master Gantt chart

activities must be completed before another activity can start. *Activities* are represented by arrows (arcs). An *event* marks the beginning or end of an activity, and is represented by a circle (node).

A chart is constructed as a network of activities, of which some must be completed before others can commence. Time durations are assigned to all activities, so it is possible to determine the longest path for the project to complete. This is called the *critical path*. Activities that constitute the critical path do not have a *slack time,* which means that any slippage in the critical path activities will cause slippage in the entire project. Other activities have a slack time and can be delayed without delaying the completion of the project. Each event can be assigned an *event time* (placed in a small rectangle) which is identified by a partial critical path calculated just for that event. A blueprint of the PERT chart for a database development project, that corresponds to the Gantt chart of Figure 3.7, is demonstrated in Figure 3.8. Note that in this simplified example, three equivalent critical paths can be distinguished (our choice of one of them is arbitrary). Moreover, there are only two slack times (in the paths 5–7 and 10–11).

There are many variations and extensions to PERT and CPM charts. One extension, that is a direct consequence of the slack time, is that the activities which are not on a critical path can be assigned the earliest and latest start and finish times. Another extension involves the use of probabilistic time estimates. Instead of a single time estimate for each activity, three estimates are given: optimistic, pessimistic and most likely. On the basis of these three estimates, the mean time is determined and used in the computation of the critical path.

3.3.3 Cost-benefit analysis

Cost-benefit analysis is the second aspect of the implementation plan and is clearly related to time evaluation. Fundamental to successful cost-benefit analysis is the identification of costs and benefits. Some costs and benefits are easily identifiable while others are very hard to capture. Special managerial skills are needed for cost-benefit determination. Systems developers almost invariably underestimate both costs and benefits, mainly because they find it difficult to identify and to assign a monetary value to the cost or to the benefit. Often the task of cost-benefit analysis is passed on to senior executives.

Costs can be categorized into groups:

* personnel (salaries, benefits, consulting fees, etc.);
* hardware (purchase, installation, maintenance, lease, etc.);
* software (CASE tools, DBMS, etc.);
* site preparation (electrical systems, air conditioning, security measures, etc.);
* supply (paper, magnetic media, etc.);
* user preparation (training, documentation, etc.).

Benefits can be derived from an analysis of the strategic plan (Section 3.1) as the objectives, goals and strategies of the strategic plan often directly translate to the benefits identified in the implementation plan for systems development. Most benefits can be identified as:

- increase in revenues;
- decrease in expenditures;
- improvement of services;
- strengthening of position.

Both costs and benefits can be further classified as:

- tangible or intangible (i.e. those which can be assigned a monetary value and those which cannot be easily quantified);

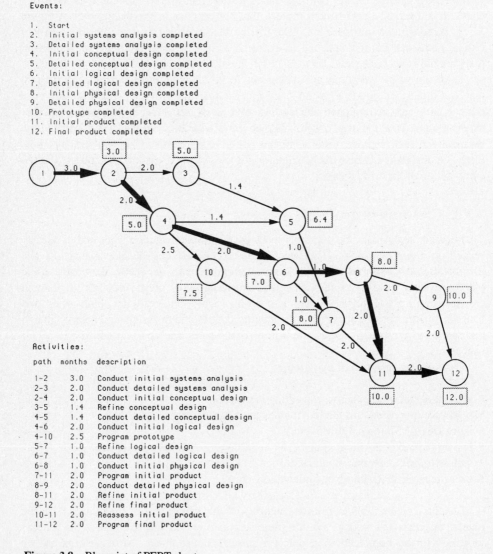

Events:

1. Start
2. Initial systems analysis completed
3. Detailed systems analysis completed
4. Initial conceptual design completed
5. Detailed conceptual design completed
6. Initial logical design completed
7. Detailed logical design completed
8. Initial physical design completed
9. Detailed physical design completed
10. Prototype completed
11. Initial product completed
12. Final product completed

Activities:

path	months	description
1-2	3.0	Conduct initial systems analysis
2-3	2.0	Conduct detailed systems analysis
2-4	2.0	Conduct initial conceptual design
3-5	1.4	Refine conceptual design
4-5	1.4	Conduct detailed conceptual design
4-6	2.0	Conduct initial logical design
4-10	2.5	Program prototype
5-7	1.0	Refine logical design
6-7	1.0	Conduct detailed logical design
6-8	1.0	Conduct initial physical design
7-11	2.0	Program initial product
8-9	2.0	Conduct detailed physical design
8-11	2.0	Refine initial product
9-12	2.0	Refine final product
10-11	2.0	Reassess initial product
11-12	2.0	Program final product

Figure 3.8   Blueprint of PERT chart

- direct or indirect (i.e. those which can be specifically attributed to the system's development and those which are by-products or overheads);
- fixed or variable (i.e. those which are proportional to work volume but are otherwise constant and those which change on a regular scale depending on the work volume).

Once costs and benefits are identified, some method of cost-benefit analysis must be chosen. As mentioned earlier, project management software packages or properly equipped CASE tools can be of assistance. Some common methods of cost-benefit analysis are:

1. Payback (or payout) analysis
   A simple method concerned with the determination of the time needed for the accumulated benefits to equal the accumulated costs. The method does not consider the project life (i.e. costs and benefits after the payback period) and the time value of money (i.e. all calculations are done in terms of present value of money).
2. Return on investment analysis
   This method determines a percentage value which indicates the lifetime profitability of a project. The formula subtracts the lifetime costs from the lifetime benefits, divides this difference by the lifetime costs and multiplies the result by 100 percent.
3. Present value analysis
   This method takes into account both the lifetime profitability and the time value of money. The costs and benefits are derived in terms of present value of money, thus allowing for interest rates, inflation, etc.

3.4 DATA FLOW MODELING

We introduced data flow diagrams (DFD) in Section 2.3, and in Section 3.2 we discussed the correspondence between the business model and DFDs. We are now in a position to introduce the guidelines and methods of applying DFDs in conceptual database design.

Within the framework of conceptual design, the DFDs are used as a means of achieving an entity-relationship-attribute (ERA) model for the system. Ideally, computer-assisted software engineering (CASE) tools should be used to facilitate this goal. With the help of CASE tools, the designer is able to iteratively design DFD and ERA diagrams and ensure at all times design consistency and integrity. If a common data dictionary is used by the CASE tool to support DFD and ERA designs, two additional objectives can be achieved. First, it will be possible to automatically derive an initial ERA diagram from the DFD model. Second, an additional level of consistency and integrity can be enforced, such that changes to DFDs will cause corresponding modifications in the ERA model and vice versa.

Designing with data flow diagrams does not succumb to an algorithmic prescription. The designer must be prepared to modify the diagrams many times before the final version is achieved. Experience with other DFDs is advantageous, but it cannot replace the need for a detailed knowledge about the system being designed. Most of the time, when the designer gets stuck, the reason lies in the lack of information about the ways the system operates.

Data flow diagrams organize the results of the design in a top-down fashion. This does not necessarily imply that the design process is conducted in a top-down fashion also. There is plenty of evidence to suggest that the best method of building data flow diagrams is to start and proceed from both ends, working top-down and bottom-up. The designer is always given information at a microscopic level of detail which is penciled down. Then, using a bottom-up scheme, the designer looks for patterns and regularities in the bag of microscopic information. This activity organizes the results of the investigation with the detailed information being abstracted into a general view of the basic dependencies in the system. The context, overview and lower level diagrams are then sketched in a top-down fashion. The design process proceeds iteratively, emphasizing the top-down scheme at some times and the bottom-up scheme at the other times.

Guidelines for drawing data flow diagrams can be summarized into the four design activities of:

- defining system boundaries;
- forming data dictionary entries;
- concentrating on data flows, rather than processes;
- leveling and balancing the DFD.

3.4.1 Defining system boundaries with the context diagram

In this step, the external entities are identified (Section 2.3.5). A graphical method for this step involves the construction of a context diagram which is a top-level DFD diagram and is the most general diagram possible. It consists of one process with multiple outgoing and incoming data flows. Some of those flows relate to external entities, all of which should be identified in the diagram. The external entities constitute the outer layer of the designed system: they delineate the domain of the design process.

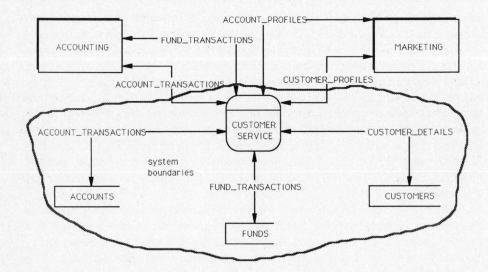

Figure 3.9   Defining system boundaries with the context diagram

An example of a context diagram is given in Figure 3.9. The example refers to a banking environment. The system being designed is dedicated to automate customer services, hence the name of the context "bubble". Two entities external to CUSTOMER_SERVICE are called MARKETING and ACCOUNTING. They are in fact the subsystems of an integrated data processing system for the bank (of which CUSTOMER_SERVICE is a part). Note that we resisted the temptation to include CUSTOMERS as an external entity. In not including it, we avoided a common mistake made in constructing a context diagram. CUSTOMERS is not an external entity in the context diagram because this would imply that the customers are beyond the context of the system. This would even contradict the very name of the system: CUSTOMER_SERVICE. Since the sole purpose of the context diagram is the definition of system boundaries, CUSTOMERS must not be an external entity on that diagram level. However, CUSTOMERS can be an external entity on the lower DFD levels.

Apart from defining system boundaries, the context diagram is redundant; an overview diagram can fulfill the same role. More importantly, the context diagram violates some important principles of constructing DFDs. When used with other DFD levels, it enforces the introduction of exceptional rules for building the diagrams which is a major reason why most CASE tools do not support the maintenance of context diagrams. While we do not reject the use of context diagrams, we rather consider them an undocumented help in defining the system boundaries. By "undocumented" we mean that in the final design specifications we prefer to use the overview diagram to explain the boundaries.

There are at least two general inconsistencies that context diagrams introduce:

1. The process of a context diagram does not have an identifying number and it usually cannot be labeled with a verb-object combination.
2. Since there is only one process, all data flows belonging to the system boundaries must reference data stores. This has one of two implications: either some important data flows are not shown or some data stores are established too early. In the former case, the diagram is incomplete; in the latter the rule that at the first level where a data store appears all flows to it must be shown, is likely to be broken (Section 2.3.4). A related rule—that a store connected to a process at a higher level must also appear, and be related to, a descendant of that process at the lower level (Section 2.3.4)—is also in jeopardy. Because of these problems, at least one popular DFD interpretation (DeMarco) allows the flows in the context diagram to go "nowhere" or to come from "nowhere".

3.4.2   Forming data dictionary entries

Data flow diagrams are pretty meaningless unless the supporting data dictionary (Section 2.2) is complete and precise. Separate data dictionary entries are formed for:

- data flows
    - simple data flow
    - group data flow
    - composite data flow

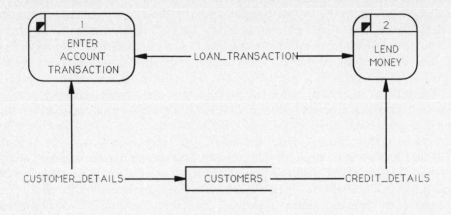

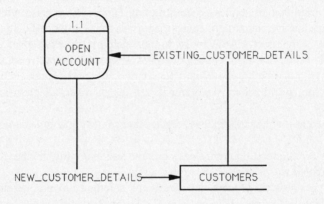

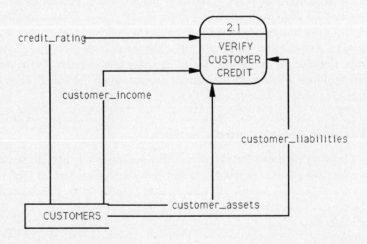

Figure 3.10   Excerpt from a leveled DFD

- data stores
- processes.

The concept of a *simple data flow* is equivalent to the notion of a simple data item as defined in Section 2.2.3. Similarly, a *group data flow* is the same as a group in Section 2.2.3. A *composite data flow* is a composition of simple and/or group and/or composite data flows such that it is not also a group data flow. Hence, a group flow is merely a special case of a composite flow. The difference is that the group flow has the semantics which relate to the entire system rather than a particular flow in the DFD. For example, the group flow ADDRESS is a composition of simple and/or group flows that defines a full address of an object in the entire system scope (Section 2.2.3). Functionally, it is almost like a simple flow except for an internal structure. On the other hand, the composite flow CUSTOMER_DETAILS is a composition of simple and/or group and/or composite flows that provides some information about customers with relation to selected data flows in the DFD. The composite flow is merely a convenient (often arbitrary) grouping of data which represents a flow. The simple and group flows have more universal meaning. They invariably exist outside the DFD. For instance, a group data flow becomes a group attribute (and a simple data flow becomes a simple attribute) in the entity model (Section 4.1) and in the entity-relationship model (Section 4.4).

The definitional entry for a *data store* in the data dictionary is similar to that of a composite data flow. Typically, the definition will contain name, description and the internal structure (all simple and group flows that are held in the data store). As mentioned in Section 2.3.4, the data dictionary should also be able to provide information about those data items in the store which have not been used in any in/out DFD flows.

The level of detail used in the definition of a *process* in the data dictionary depends on whether or not the process belongs to a bottom-level diagram. The bottom-level processes require corresponding function specifications (Section 4.2) while the processes at the upper levels are defined by their names, descriptions and algorithms—the algorithms are normally required for processes which physically transform the data flows (Section 2.3.3).

To illustrate the data dictionary entries corresponding to a DFD, we refer to Figure 2.9 (Section 2.3.4), repeated here for convenience as Figure 3.10.

3.4.2.1 Defining processes

As an example of the data dictionary entry for a process let us consider VERIFY_CUSTOMER_CREDIT from Figure 3.10. This is a process in the level 1 DFD; its parent process is LEND_MONEY. VERIFY_CUSTOMER_CREDIT can be defined in the data dictionary as follows:

Reference	2.1
Name	VERIFY_CUSTOMER_CREDIT
Description	Investigate and determine the financial position of the customer who has applied for a loan. Decide whether an interview should be conducted with the customer and whether references are required. Take the initial decision whether the loan should be approved or declined and forward your recommendation to a senior officer.

Algorithm   For loans not exceeding $100 000:
- If credit_rating is A and total_assets are greater than total_liabilities, then approve the loan (no interview is necessary).
- If credit_rating is B and total_assets are greater than total_liabilities, then (1) conduct the interview, (2) ask for references, (3) approve or decline.
- If credit_rating is C and total_assets are greater than total_liabilities, then forward the matter to a senior officer.
- If credit_rating is A and total_assets are not greater than total_liabilities, then (1) conduct the interview, (2) ask for references, (3) approve or decline.
- If credit_rating is B or C and total_assets are not greater than total_liabilities, then decline the loan.
- For loans exceeding $100 000, refer the matter to a senior officer.

The definition of an algorithm is not normally given for processes which conduct only logical transforms (Section 2.3.3). Nor is it given for processes at the bottom-level diagrams, because such processes will have corresponding function specifications (Section 4.2). For other processes, the algorithm entry is still optional. Sometimes it can be replaced by a reference to a policy statement document or other instructional materials and at other times it can be understood that the functions specifications of the descendant processes provide necessary information.

3.4.2.2 Defining data stores

There is only one data store referred to in Figure 2.10—CUSTOMERS. The definition of a data store contains only three elements:

Name   CUSTOMERS
Description   All current customers of the bank. Only customers of the category "private person" are included. There is a separate data store for customers of the category "corporate organization".
Contents   = [CUSTOMER_DETAILS I NEW_CUSTOMER_DETAILS I
                   EXISTING_CUSTOMER_DETAILS]
                + (EMPLOYMENT_DETAILS)
                + (SPOUSE_DETAILS)
                + (FINANCIAL_POSITION)
                + {(REFERENCE)}

The symbols used in the contents entry are explained in Section 2.2.3. It is not immediately obvious what categories of data flows constitute the data store contents or whether they are simple, group or composite. The data dictionary entries for data flows must be consulted to get the answers. Alternatively, a CASE-based data dictionary can generate a detailed structure for the data store such that the content is defined only in terms of simple and group data flows (with a structure of each group flow also being shown).

3.4.2.3 Defining composite data flows

In Figure 3.10, the composite data flows are labeled in upper-case letters. We will consider NEW_CUSTOMER_DETAILS to illustrate the data dictionary entry:

Name	NEW_CUSTOMER_DETAILS
Description	Personal details concerning a customer (of the category "private person"). These details are needed to open a deposit or loan account.
Equivalent flows	CUSTOMER_DETAILS EXISTING_CUSTOMER_DETAILS
Contents	= person_name + sex + home_address + years_lived_there + (home_phone_number) + (postal_address) + birth_date + marital_status + dependants_number + signature

A peculiar aspect of the DD definition for a composite flow is the entry "equivalent flows". An *equivalent flow* is not an alias, that is, it is not a name by which a composite flow is called on other occasions. It is rather a different name with the same flow contents but with different implications and associations.

The content of a composite data flow is defined in terms of simple and/or group and/or composite flows. Each of the data flows listed in the contents entry is separately defined in the data dictionary. The composite data flow NEW_CUSTOMER_DETAILS consists of only simple (e.g. sex) and group (e.g. home_address) data flows.

3.4.2.4 Defining group data flows

In Figure 3.10, the flows which are likely to be designated as group (rather than composite) data flows are customer_income, customer_assets and customer_liabilities. Let us consider the data dictionary definition for customer_assets:

Name	customer_assets
Description	The entire property (of all sorts) of a customer having money value and that may be sold to pay debts.
Aliases	what_you_own
Contents	= {(home)} + {cash} + (life_policy) + {(vehicle)} + {(other_assets)}

As in the case of data stores and composite data flows, further investigation into the data dictionary is needed to determine the category (simple or group) of the data flows listed in the contents entry. For example, life_policy is probably a group flow consisting of two simple flows: policy_face_value and policy_surrender_value.

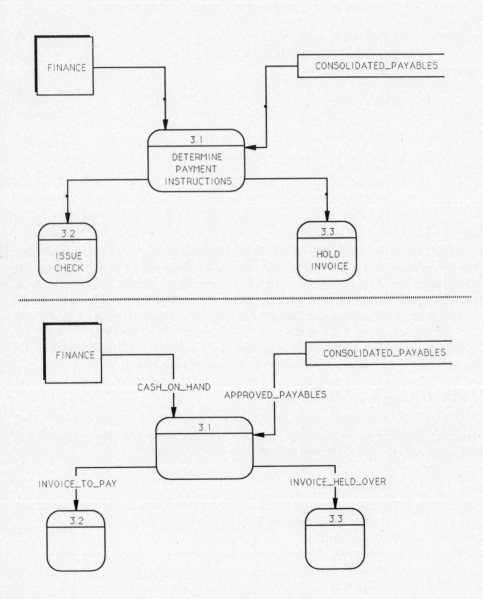

Figure 3.11   Concentrating on data flows rather than processes

3.4.2.5 Defining simple data flows

There is only one simple data flow in Figure 3.10. This is credit_rating. The data dictionary contains the following definition of credit_rating:

Name	credit_rating
Type	choices
Format	A (one alphabetic character)
Description	An indicator of the financial strength of a customer.
Remarks	The rating is made by an independent organization which specializes in rating payment histories and financial integrity of customers.
Constraints	Choices are:
	A (high rating)
	B
	C (low rating)
Aliases	what_you_own

3.4.3 Concentrating on data flows rather than processes

The emphasis in drawing data flow diagrams is on data flows, not processes; data flow diagrams should not be seen as a kind of flowchart. A fundamental issue in drawing DFDs is to determine data flows first, that is, to determine what data inputs are needed to form each data output. Processes introduce only some stages (stops) to these input-output transformations. Originally, the processes can be considered as "black boxes" and can even be named later, after all data flows in the diagram are drawn.

Figure 3.11 illustrates the problem. In the upper part of the diagram, the names of data flows are removed. In the lower part, the names of processes are missing. On reflection, the missing names in the upper diagram are difficult (or even impossible) to fill in, whereas the missing names in the lower diagram can be easily derived. The names of data flows convey enough information to guess process names. To make it possible, however, the names of data flows must be meaningful and specific. For example, Figure 3.11 would not serve its purpose if the data flows INVOICE_TO_PAY and INVOICE_HELD_OVER were replaced by a generic flow INVOICE.

Another important guideline for forming data flow diagrams is to proceed from output data flows to input data flows, not vice versa. A good procedure is to:

1. identify a desired output data flow;
2. create a process responsible for that output (name the process, if you can);
3. define the data dictionary entry for the output data flow (this will identify major subcomponents of that flow);
4. identify input data flow(s).

Figure 3.12 applies the above procedure to the calculation of a current gross pay for employees paid hourly wages.

3.4.4 Leveling and balancing

Structured aspects of data flow diagrams are expressed mainly in leveling (partitioning) and balancing concepts. Leveling is a top-down decomposition of the DFD processes which results in a hierarchical set of diagrams. Processes are decomposed to form next level diagrams until it is decided that a process is a *functional primitive* which cannot be decomposed any further. Such a functional primitive is described by means of a function specification (Section 4.2). There is no requirement that all processes should decompose to the same number of levels.

Balancing forms the complement of leveling. A leveled set of data flow diagrams is balanced if all data which flow into and out of the parent process flow also into and out of the processes in the child diagram. There is one exception to this rule. In order to avoid

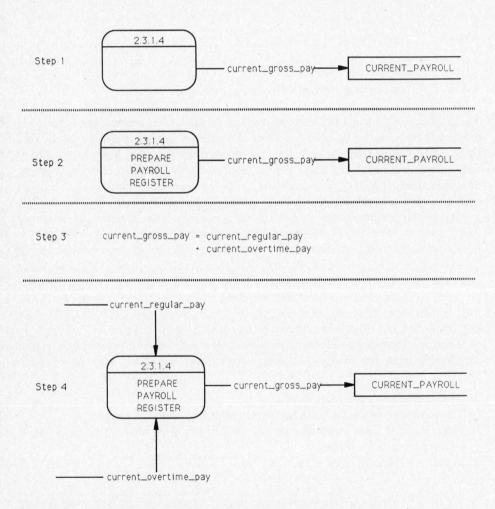

Figure 3.12   Identifying input data flows responsible for an output data flow

cluttering of higher-level diagrams, the data flows which correspond to error and exception conditions are usually considered only on the lower-level diagrams. Such data flows need not be balanced between the parent process and the child diagram.

Consider the example in Figure 3.13. The example concerns the accounts receivable system. As can be concluded from the identifiers of processes, the diagram is on level 2 in the DFD set. All composite data flows are written in capital letters. Lower-case letters are reserved for group and simple data flows.

Figure 3.14 illustrates a child diagram achieved after decomposing the process 2.1.2 APPLY_PAYMENT_TO_INVOICE. Do the diagrams in Figures 3.13 and 3.14 balance? Process 2.1.2 in Figure 3.13 has two incoming flows (UNPAID_INVOICE and PAYMENT_SUMMARY) and two outgoing flows (PAID_INVOICE and OUTSTANDING_INVOICE). There are four incoming flows in the level 3 diagram in

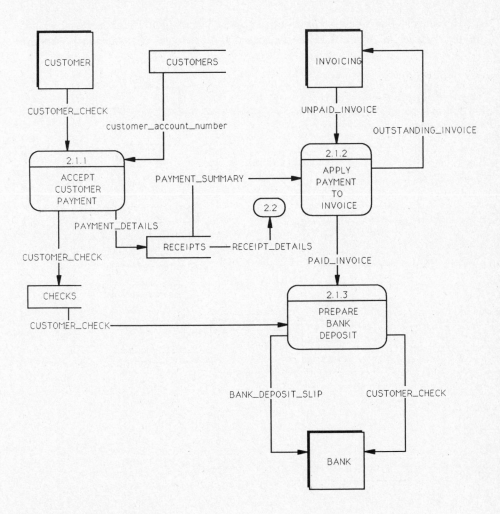

Figure 3.13 Level 2 diagram

Figure 3.14 (customer_account_number, invoice_number, check_info, and invoice_info) and there are three outgoing flows (PAID_INVOICE, OUTSTANDING_INVOICE and NO_MATCH_PAYMENT).

The incoming flows in the two diagrams are balanced despite the fact that they have different names. Balancing does not deal with the names of data flows but is concerned with their contents. The data dictionary must be used to verify whether the diagrams are balanced. In our example, the contents of the incoming data flows to process 2.1.2 are:

UNPAID_INVOICE	= customer_account_number + invoice_info
PAYMENT_SUMMARY	= customer_account_number + invoice_number + check_info

The data dictionary definitions assure us that the incoming flows for process 2.1.2 and for the diagram in Figure 3.14 are balanced. The described phenomenon is called a

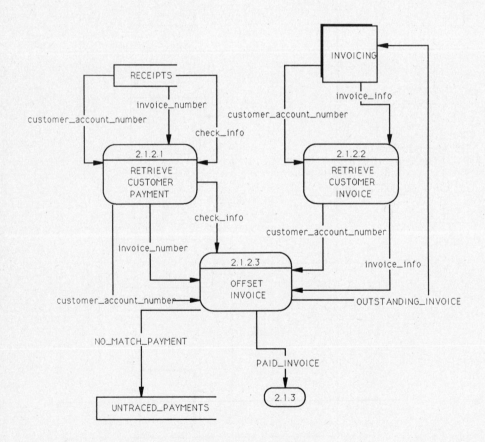

Figure 3.14   Level 3 diagram that may be considered unbalanced

parallel decomposition of data and of function. Processes on higher DFD levels tend to use composite data flows. Decomposition of a process to a lower level diagram is likely to also "decompose" the related flows (from composite flows to group and to simple data flows).

For completeness sake, two of the incoming flows in Figure 3.14 are group flows. The data dictionary entries for them are:

invoice_info = invoice_number
+ date_of_invoice
+ invoice_total

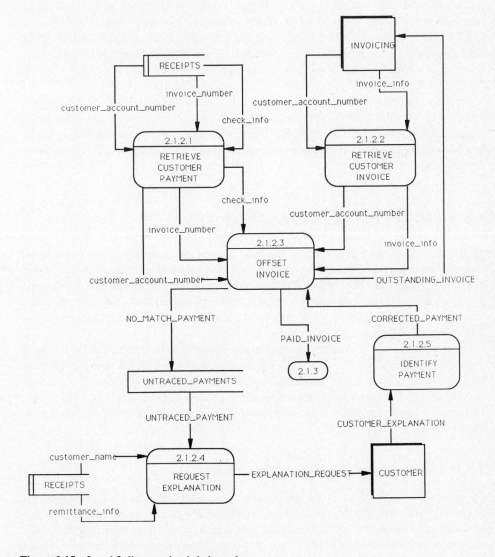

Figure 3.15   Level 3 diagram that is balanced

check_info   = check_number
               + date_of_check
               + check_amount

Are the outgoing flows balanced? This is a matter of interpretation. If the NO_MATCH_PAYMENT is considered an error or exception condition then, according to the definition of balancing, the outgoing flows are balanced. If, however, NO_MATCH_PAYMENT is an important function which was merely overlooked when constructing the parent diagram, then the diagrams are not balanced (even if NO_MATCH_PAYMENT is indeed an error or exception condition).

Suppose that we considered the two diagrams unbalanced. How can the problem be rectified? An obvious solution is to make necessary changes (add NO_MATCH_PAYMENT) to the parent process. Such a modification has a cascading effect and should not be attempted in manual design environments. Some more sophisticated CASE tools, however, can make this task safer. The cascading effect (known also as a *ripple effect*) is due to the fact that "uncle" processes (Section 2.3.6) are affected.

A better solution is illustrated in Figure 3.15. where the NO_MATCH_PAYMENT problem is resolved within the child diagram. Instead of leaving an unbalanced (dangling) flow, NO_MATCH_PAYMENT is further processed in a self-adjusting cycle. NO_MATCH_PAYMENT is changed from a flow out of the diagram to a flow internal to the diagram.

3.5   CASE STUDY: PROBLEM STATEMENT

As the case study used in this book, we have chosen the inventory system of a small company selling and servicing a limited range of hardware and software. The choice was motivated by the fact that the student is likely to be familiar with the operational principles of such an organization. Also, the inventory system has the important advantage of being intuitively clear, even for readers not acquainted with typical business applications. The case study is limited, but realistic.

Even a very limited case study, such as in this book, tends to blow out of proportion if discussed on a step-by-step basis, with strict adherence to the topics raised in the text. This is not surprising if one considers that any design project generates voluminous documentation. Because of this, we are forced to present our case study in terms of the outcomes of the design rather than in terms of the procedures and activities that lead to those outcomes.

3.5.1   Organization and its function model

The company is a small-size organization which specializes in selling computer products to students, staff and departments at the university. It also services the equipment that it sells through a number of service personnel (not directly employed by the company). The company was established three years ago and is located on the university campus. It has a reputation for being a reliable vendor. The company has experienced moderate growth through the years, and rapid expansion has not been considered to be a desirable goal. Nevertheless, the company's growth has led to some customer-related problems caused by the upsurge in new customers.

The company operations are based on the following functions:

- **Sell**   The sell function includes everything that has to do with the actual handling of customers' orders from the time they arrive at the company until merchandise is picked up or shipped to the customer. Sales personnel interact with Business Services and Central Store in the university. Shipment of equipment and software is handled by the company.
- **Service**   The service function is concerned with the repairs and maintenance of equipment sold by the company. Such services are performed by the company or are commissioned to university personnel (i.e. outside the company). This function can involve ordering unavailable parts from the suppliers. Sometimes the equipment must be sent for repair to a supplier. The financial aspect of this function depends on whether or not a warranty is in effect.
- **Purchase**   Merchandise is purchased from different suppliers and kept in the Central Store of the university. Invoices and payments are handled by Business Services of the university (not the company). Central Store confirms received shipments to the company. A close and frequent cooperation between the company and the university administration is required in performing this function.

3.5.2   Additional information about outside environment

The *financial* aspect of the company operation is mostly delegated to Business Services of the university administration. Obviously, financial transactions are initiated by the company personnel, but otherwise transactions are carried out by the Business Services department. At present private customers are expected to pay, in cash, directly to the university cashier. There is a need to introduce more flexibility in this respect, including credit and check payments and possibly mail orders and payments. The Business Services department handles accountancy matters, it keeps track of the company's financial transactions in receivable and payable accounts. The accounts receivable controls the moneys owed to the company. It keeps track of the invoices for sales and records the payments made against invoices. An account is used to send out reminders when payments are overdue. The accounts payable monitors the money owed by the company. It records invoices received from the suppliers and generates payment checks. The Business Services department is also responsible for producing pay checks for the technicians involved in equipment services.

The *personnel* aspect of the company operation is also handled in close cooperation with the university administration. The Personal Services department is involved in this function. It maintains information concerning those who work in and for the company. Both personal and employment history information is recorded. In particular, records of skills, qualifications and special courses attended by employees are kept by the Personal Services department. Information is also kept about people for payroll purposes, including overtime records, current salary levels, leave pays and so on.

3.5.3 Processing overview

An overview of the company processing activities is shown in Figure 3.16 by means of a data flow diagram. Three basic processes are distinguished: sell, service and purchase.

3.5.4 Sell function

Sell function controls customer information (customer name, address, etc.) and information regarding sales made. It should be possible to derive a complete sales history for each customer and product. Consequently, it is necessary to know, for each sale made, what was purchased, when and how much money was paid. If serialized items are purchased, their serial numbers must be known. In addition, if items are ordered from a supplier for a customer, this information should be recorded to ensure that unfilled orders (backorders) are not overlooked.

The central sales document contains such information as: customer's name (e.g. Department of Accountancy), account number to be charged (e.g. cash, department a/c), store item#, units requested, item description, units issued, unit cost, total cost, receipt#, signatures and so on. There are four different prices recognized in the document and identified cryptically as A, B, C, D. They are, respectively, a fixed markup on the item (normally 12.5%), a base (purchase) price, sales tax and a consultancy fee. The last fee is a catchall for special services rendered under some conditions. The university departments buying from the company do not pay sales tax.

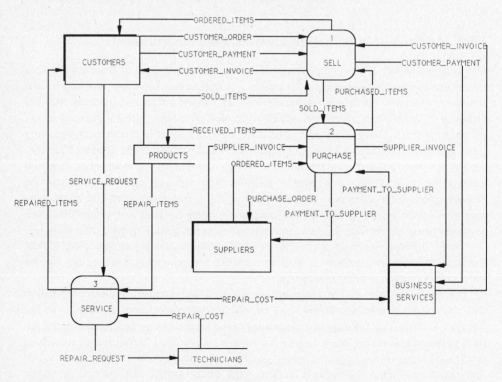

Figure 3.16 Processing overview of the company

The company maintains a complete record of computer systems sold since its operation began. A curious observation about this record is that the equipment name (e.g. "Mac512") is not necessarily the name of the item actually sold, as equipment could have been upgraded at some time. After an upgrade, the system acquires a new name, depending on the upgrade type but it should be possible to derive an item's present description from its service history.

3.5.5   Service function

The service function is either performed by the company or is commissioned to personnel outside the company. Information recorded for a given service includes: the customer who owns the equipment being serviced, the item description (including its serial number, if any), warranty information and, if possible, data regarding when the item was sold to the customer. Other information includes: when it received servicing, when it was returned to the customer, expenses incurred by the service technician, the identity of the service technician and a customer contact. It should be possible to derive a complete service history for any company customer or product.

A special need of the company is the recording of what components are used in services. Many components are modular and modules are replaced on an exchange basis with the suppliers. The company needs to know what modules are currently in stock, which have been ordered, which are to be sent back and so on.

Serviced equipment can be under warranty. Warranties can take three forms: the standard warranty, an extended warranty that the customer can buy and a service contract with the supplier. The warranties are attached to individual items sold.

3.5.6   Purchase function

The purchase function is performed in close cooperation with the university administration. The stock is ordered through the Business Services department and invoices from suppliers are sent to them. The information about the stock which arrived is sent from Central Store to the company on an irregular basis. In fact, the inventory information needs to be accessed in an ad hoc fashion (for example, in the course of dealing with sales enquiries).

Some items are serialized, that is they have unique serial numbers. Other items are unserialized and these items are recorded only as the quantity on hand. The company buys, from time to time, packages that consist of a group of other items. Such packages generally have a lower price than the sum of the prices of their components. However, the company may wish to sell individual components from packages separately (usually at the regular price for those items). If at the later date those items are replaced by identical components, then the overall price of the package must not be affected. A similar inconsistency arises with normal items; their prices change from time to time, but there may be old stock on hand that should still be sold at the old price.

FURTHER READING

Strategic planning is routinely discussed in the books on corporate management techniques and concepts (e.g. David 1986, Wheelen and Hunger 1987). Leslie (1986) describes strategic planning specifically from the viewpoint of the development of information systems.

We do not know of any tutorial-style reference that would broaden our description of the use of the business model in the conceptual design.

The lifecycle approaches used in defining implementation plans are discussed in Peters (1988). An interesting new approach, called the spiral model, is defined in Boehm (1988). The time element of the implementation plan is considered by Awad (1985), Capron (1986) and Kendall (1987). The PERT/CPM technique is examined in most texts on management science and operations research, such as the one by Buffa and Dyer (1978). The cost/benefit element of the implementation plan is addressed in Awad (1985), Kendall (1987) and Leslie (1986).

Surprisingly, a good description of modeling with data flow diagrams is not as easily available as the popularity of the technique might imply. Many books contain errors of interpretation which degrade the technique to a quite useless drawing aid. The original books, which introduced and popularized data flow diagrams in the late seventies, are still the most comprehensive references (DeMarco 1979 and Gane and Sarson 1979). These original texts also include accounts of data dictionaries for data flow diagrams. Some other books which offer interesting observations about data flow diagrams are Awad (1985), Page-Jones (1980) and Peters (1988). The second edition of a popular text by Eliason (1987), which explores common types of business computer applications, uses high-level data flow diagrams.

Our case study example can be better appreciated by readers familiar with typical business computer applications. An outstanding reference on such applications is the textbook by Eliason (1987).

REFERENCES

AWAD, E. M. (1985): *Systems Analysis and Design*, 2nd ed., Richard D. Irwin, 524p.

BOEHM, B. W. (1988): A Spiral Model of Software Development and Enhancement, *Comp.*, May, pp.61–72.

BUFFA, E. S. and DYER, J. S. (1978): *Essentials of Management Science/Operations Research*, John Wiley & Sons, 527p.

CAPRON, H. L. (1986): *Systems Analysis and Design*, The Benjamin/Cummings, 525p.

DAVID, F. R. (1986): *Fundamentals of Strategic Management*, Merrill Publ., 894p.

DEMARCO, T. (1979): *Structured Analysis and System Specification*, Prentice Hall, 352p.

ELIASON, A. L. (1987): *Online Business Computer Applications*, 2nd ed., SRA, 506p.

GANE, C. and SARSON, T. (1979): *Structured Systems Analysis: Tools and Techniques*, Prentice Hall, 241p.

KENDALL, P. A. (1987): *Introduction to Systems Analysis and Design*, Allyn and Bacon, 513p.

LESLIE, R. E. (1986): *Systems Analysis and Design. Method and Invention*, Prentice Hall, 490p.

PAGE-JONES, M. (1980): *The Practical Guide to Structured Systems Design*, Prentice Hall, 354p.

PETERS, L. (1988): *Advanced Structured Analysis and Design*, Prentice Hall, 272p.

WHEELEN, T. L. and HUNGER, J. D. (1987): *Strategic Management*, 2nd ed., Addison-Wesley, 329p.

4

Design of Conceptual Structure

In this chapter we discuss consecutive stages of the second database design phase—conceptualization. This phase is independent of the technical implementation issues as the conceptual design bears no relevance to the DBMS which is to be used as an implementation software. Being independent of the DBMS, the specifications of the conceptualization can be used for the implementation of relational, network, microcomputer-based or any other database system.

In current database design practice, the diagrammatic technique most widely used for conceptualization is Chen's Entity-Relationship Model. The conceptual design presented here is based on Chen's model; however, we have enhanced the model to provide for the required level of semantic support (Chapter 2). Moreover, our objective is not just to describe the diagrammatic technique, but rather to show a methodology whereby the diagrams yield a purposeful design. In doing so, we advocate a method which is conducive to productive reasoning and effective communication between designers and users. The conceptual model is the means, not the end.

4.1 ENTITY MODELING

Up to this point, our approach to system development was process rather than data-driven. Our design was based on a functional business model and was tuned to anticipated user transactions (manifest functions) on a database system being developed. Although we advocate concentrating on data flows rather than processes when constructing the DFDs, the data semantics of the flows are derived completely from the semantics of business functions. Our method assumes that the systems analysis is done prior to conceptualization, and that the strategic plan and business model dictate the design of database structures.

After all the work done in the previous design stages, we are now in a position to attempt, for the first time, to do what the database design is mostly about, to structure data for integrated and shared processing. To this aim, an *entity model* of the database system should be constructed. Technically, the entity model corresponds to the simplified representation of the entity-relationship model (Section 2.4, in particular Figure 2.12). To simplify somewhat, the entity model is a special case of the entity-relationship model such that the relationship sets are not labeled or graphically visualized; further, only sole and binary relationship sets can be expressed.

No practical database design methodology can be totally process-driven or data-driven. A mixed design environment is necessary. If the design starts with processes and derives initial database structures from the processes, then the method is *process-driven*. Alternatively, if the design starts with the determination of data structures that satisfy some desirable properties (Section 2.5) and refines such structures once the processes are specified, then the method is *data-driven*.

In our approach, the building of an entity model at an early design stage (before function specifications (Section 4.2) are determined) results in a mixed design environment which remains, nevertheless, process-driven. The task is difficult: the modeling guidelines are intuitive and less stringent, and arbitrary decisions by designers are unavoidable. A reward for achieving this, however, is that for the first time an integrated database schema, abstracted as an entity model, is produced. Such a schema may not be the best, but it provides an important reference point in the next design stages and is the first attempt to reconcile different, often contradictory, user requirements and views.

Data flow diagrams (DFD) serve as a starting point and they define both data and processes. Two kinds of data defined in DFDs, namely data stores and composite flows, are clusters of attributes similar to those used in entity-relationship-attribute (ERA) diagrams: entity sets. Hence, the initial collection of entity sets in an ERA diagram is equivalent to the list of data stores and composite flows such that:

- duplicate data stores and duplicate composite flows are removed;
- composite flows with contents equivalent to a data store are ignored;
- equivalent composite flows (Section 3.4.2.3) are ignored.

Structurally, composite flows are likely to be nested in, or to overlap with, data stores and other composite flows. As a consequence, the initial collection of entity sets will be redundant. A designer must make conscientious, though quite arbitrary, decisions to minimize the level of redundancy by eliminating some entities and retaining others.

By way of illustration, consider the data flow diagram in Figure 4.1. The diagram is a decomposition of a higher level process ENTER ACCOUNT TRANSACTION. It describes typical bank processes of opening, managing and closing customer accounts. For clarity, composite flows are written in capital letters, while group and simple flows are in lower case.

The data flow diagram contains three data stores (CUSTOMERS, ACCOUNTS and ACCOUNT_TRANSACTIONS) and five composite data flows (CUSTOMER_DETAILS, CUSTOMER_RECORD, APPROVED_LOAN, ACCOUNT_RECORD and TRANSACTION). The data flows CUSTOMER_RECORD, ACCOUNT_RECORD and TRANSACTION are equivalent to the data stores CUSTOMERS, ACCOUNTS and ACCOUNT_TRANSACTIONS respectively. There are no equivalent composite flows.

The contents of the data stores and non-equivalent composite flows are:

CUSTOMERS = [CUSTOMER_DETAILS | APPROVED_LOAN]
             + {account_number}
             + {(loan_number)}
             + customer_type

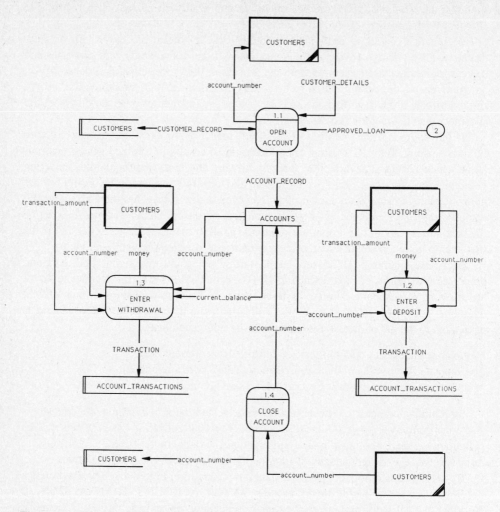

Figure 4.1   Data flow diagram to be used to derive initial collection of entity sets

CUSTOMER_DETAILS = PERSONAL_DETAILS
                   + (EMPLOYMENT_DETAILS)
APPROVED_LOAN = PERSONAL_DETAILS
               + EMPLOYMENT_DETAILS
               + loan_number
ACCOUNTS = account_number
          + (loan_number)
          + {customer_number}
          + current_balance
          + date_last_transaction
          + date_opened
          + date_closed

ACCOUNT_TRANSACTIONS = account_number
                                    + transaction_code
                                    + transaction_amount
                                    + date_transaction
                                    + time_transaction

The initial collection of entity sets, as defined above, is redundant. The data store CUSTOMERS and the composite flows CUSTOMER_DETAILS and APPROVED_ LOAN overlap. To minimize the redundancy, some entities should be eliminated or a more sophisticated analysis (such as normalization) should be undertaken. For our restricted example, based on one data flow diagram from a multi-level set of diagrams, we can only offer intuitive solutions. The simplest solution is to decide on the composition CUSTOMERS, ACCOUNTS and ACCOUNT_TRANSACTIONS.

Another solution might be to consider that APPROVED_LOAN flows from a bridge and implies other related flows in the "uncle" process; then to assume that the bridge identifies the process LEND MONEY, which maintains additional information about CUSTOMERS (such as FINANCIAL_POSITION, SPOUSE_DETAILS and REFERENCES). In these circumstances we could decide to introduce the entity set BORROWERS, apart from CUSTOMERS, to store specific information about customers who have loans from the bank. Alternatively, we could expand the entity set CUSTOMERS to include FINANCIAL_POSITION, SPOUSE_DETAILS and REFERENCES.

Figure 4.2 contains an entity diagram which uses the three entity sets CUSTOMERS, ACCOUNTS and ACCOUNT_TRANSACTIONS. A brief investigation into the data flow diagram of Figure 4.1 enables us to determine the relationship sets. The relationship sets are a "data-structural" support of DFD processes. These supporting relationship sets should be created whenever a process directly uses the data stores (or composite flows) elected as entity sets. In our case, OPEN ACCOUNT and CLOSE ACCOUNT require a direct communication link between CUSTOMERS and ACCOUNTS. Similarly, ENTER DEPOSIT and ENTER WITHDRAWAL need a relationship set between ACCOUNTS and ACCOUNT_TRANSACTIONS.

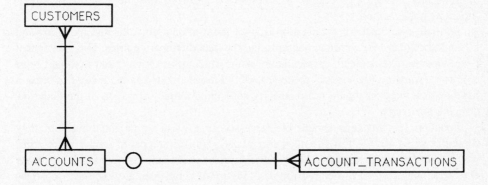

Figure 4.2   Entity diagram derived from a data flow diagram

There is a nonunivocal connectivity (Section 2.4.4.2) between CUSTOMERS and ACCOUNTS because of the existence of joint accounts in which several customers can hold one account (clearly, also, a customer can have many accounts). The membership of this relationship set is total (Section 2.4.4.3): all ACCOUNTS relate to some CUSTOMERS and only information about CUSTOMERS who hold ACCOUNTS is stored in the database.

The relationship set between ACCOUNTS and ACCOUNT_TRANSACTIONS is univocal because any transaction corresponds uniquely to one account_number. This also enforces a total membership of ACCOUNT_TRANSACTIONS in this relationship set. However, the membership of ACCOUNTS in the relationship set is partial because an account can exist with no deposit or withdrawal transactions done against it (e.g. immediately after opening the account).

The presented approach to the derivation of an entity diagram from a data flow diagram is intuitively obvious but it is difficult to apply in a large design situation. A better approach would involve the use of aggregation/decomposition abstractions (Section 2.6.1). This would require a graphical extension to the entity model to illustrate the HAS-A/PART-OF relationships. The aggregation is attractive in this context because it can capture, both graphically and on the data dictionary level, the nesting and overlaps between data stores and data flows on one hand and between entity sets on the other hand. In a CASE environment it should be possible to automatically generate the HAS-A/PART-OF relationships between entities from the data flow diagrams.

4.2   FUNCTIONS SPECIFICATIONS

At the minimum, the bottom-level processes (sometimes called functional primitives) of a data flow diagram need to be specified. The function specification (also called mini-spec) is a concise description of the rules governing the transformation of in-coming data flows into out-going flows. There must be one function specification for each bottom-level process. Optionally, function specs for higher level processes can also be written.

The function specification is a description of *what* the policy governing the transformation within a process is. It is not a description of *how* the policy is or how it should be implemented.

Formally, the function specification is an element of data flow diagram modeling and it should be consistent with the diagrams and the data dictionary entries. This means that it must not be just another representation of the diagram or its part, and it should refer only to information (data items, processes, etc.) defined in the data dictionary. In brief, a function specification should not re-specify something already specified in the diagrams or in the dictionary.

Function specifications should be expressed in a highly orthogonal fashion; they should be structured. To this aim, they should use a limited number of modular structures which are top-down readable. The most popular techique that conforms to these objectives is known as Structured English (SE). Two supplemental tools, decision trees and decision tables, are more specialized and are used either to accompany Structured English or are combined with Structured English to express a part of its description.

4.2.1   Structured English

Structured English is a specification language for the definition of DFD processes. The syntax and other vocabulary of Structured English consists of:

- reserved words for formulation of specification logic;
- terms described in the data dictionary;
- condition statements or imperative commands in English.

Although there is no recognized standard for a Structured English dialect, the principles are basically the same. The specification logic makes use of three constructs: sequence, repetition and decision. These constructs are reminiscent of the constructs used in structured programming.

The *sequence* construct is used to specify a group of actions (policies) which are to be applied together, one after the other. The sequence consists of successive imperative commands in the English language, such as:

write **price** on **PURCHASE_REQUISITION**
write **total** on **PURCHASE_REQUISITION**
send **PURCHASE_REQUISITION** to **PURCHASING_SERVICES**

The *repetition* construct begins with a reserved word <u>REPEAT</u> and finishes with a reserved word <u>UNTIL</u>, a condition statement in English, and the character •, as in:

<u>REPEAT</u>
. . .
<u>UNTIL</u>
   all **ITEMS** in the **INVOICE** are processed
•

The *decision (selection)* construct has one of two forms:

1. <u>IF</u>
   condition statement
<u>THEN</u>
   imperative command
Δ
2. <u>IF</u>
   condition statement
<u>THEN</u>
   imperative command
<u>ELSE</u>
   imperative command
◊

The data dictionary entries are bold-faced in our dialect of Structured English. Moreover, the names of processes called from within a function spec are enclosed by double-quotation marks (" ").

Although rigorous, the Structured English specification is *not executable*. In other words, it is not implementation oriented. Its objective is to specify business functions' requirements and operational logic, not to support the programming language realization; nor is SE a substitute or replacement for a pseudocode or code. In fact, the Structured English specification uses conceptual data definitions while pseudocode and code are based on logical and physical data definitions.

As an illustration, we give a functional specification for the process "OPEN ACCOUNT" (Figure 4.1).

<u>REPEAT</u>
    <u>IF</u>
        CUSTOMER is a borrower (**LOAN** processing)
    <u>THEN</u>
        <u>IF</u>
            existing **CUSTOMER** and **CUSTOMER_RECORD** has changed
        <u>THEN</u>
            write changed **CUSTOMER_RECORD**
            write **ACCOUNT_RECORD (LOAN_ACCOUNT)**
        <u>ELSE</u>
            <u>IF</u>
                new **CUSTOMER**
            <u>THEN</u>
                write new **CUSTOMER_RECORD**
            Δ
        write **ACCOUNT_RECORD (LOAN_ACCOUNT)**
        ◊
    <u>ELSE</u> (i.e. **CUSTOMER** is not a borrower)
        <u>IF</u>
            existing **CUSTOMER**
        <u>THEN</u>
            <u>IF</u>
                CUSTOMER_RECORD has changed
            <u>THEN</u>
                write changed **CUSTOMER_RECORD**
            Δ
            write **ACCOUNT_RECORD (DEPOSIT_ACCOUNT)**
            <u>IF</u>
                CHARGES applicable
            <u>THEN</u>
                "POST CHARGES"
            Δ
        <u>ELSE</u> (i.e. new **CUSTOMER**)
            <u>IF</u>
                customer's bona fide status satisfactory (**REFERENCES** may be required)

<u>THEN</u>
    take specimen signature
    write **CUSTOMER_RECORD**
    write **ACCOUNT_RECORD (DEPOSIT_ACCOUNT)**
<u>IF</u>
    CHARGES applicable
<u>THEN</u>
    "POST CHARGES"
Δ
<u>ELSE</u>
    reject customer request to open an account
        ◊

    ◊

◊
<u>UNTIL</u>
    no more input
•

4.2.2 Decision trees

Decision trees and decision tables (discussed next) are convenient replacements for complicated decision (IF) constructs of a Structured English specification. Whenever there is a large number of condition combinations leading to different actions, the readability of the Structured English description is not good. A graphic representation, by means of a decision tree, is likely to improve the readability.

In fact, the example of a Structured English specification given in the previous section is a good candidate for a graphic representation. The IF construct that dominates this specification is quite complicated. It examines five conditions and delivers up to four different actions for various combinations of those conditions. This is clearly visible in the decision tree representation (Figure 4.3).

4.2.3 Decision tables

A decision table is a tabular representation of a decision tree. It provides a concise visualization of a decision situation. The table consists of four sections: (1) stated conditions (upper left-hand corner), (2) values of conditions (upper right-hand portion), (3) courses of actions (lower left-hand corner) and (4) actions taken or values of actions (lower right-hand portion). The right-hand portion of the table is divided vertically into so-called rules.

There are several kinds of decision table. A "traditional" decision table permits only limited entries for rules namely Yes, No or – (i.e. not applicable) as values of conditions and X or empty space (i.e. no action) as values of actions. The most compressed kind of table allows for textual rule entries. A decision table corresponding to the decision tree of Figure 4.3 is shown in Figure 4.4.

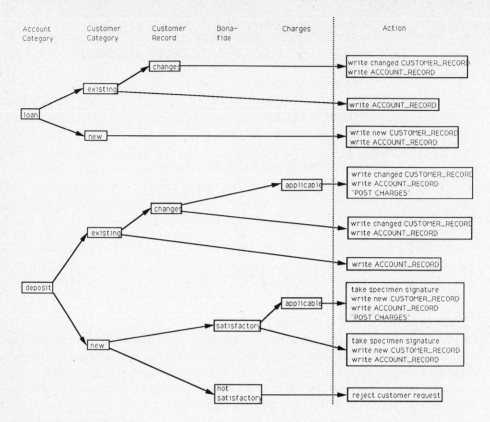

Figure 4.3   Decision tree

	1	2	3	4	5	6	7	8	9
Account Category	loan	loan	loan	deposit	deposit	deposit	deposit	deposit	deposit
Customer Category	existing	existing	new	existing	existing	existing	new	new	new
Customer Record	changes	no changes	–	changes	changes	no changes	–	–	–
Bona-fide	–	–	–	–	–	–	satisfactory	satisfactory	not satisfactory
Charges	not applicable	not applicable	not applicable	applicable	not applicable	not applicable	applicable	not applicable	–
write changed CUSTOMER_RECORD	X			X	X		X	X	
write ACCOUNT_RECORD	X	X	X	X	X	X	X	X	
write new CUSTOMER_RECORD			X						
"POST CHARGES"				X			X		
take specimen signature							X	X	
reject customer request									X

Figure 4.4   Decision table

4.3   ACCESS GRAPHS

Once the functions specifications are in place, the viability of the entity diagram can be verified. To achieve this, the functions specifications are generalized into access graphs (called also access maps or data navigation diagrams). The access graphs show, for each business function, the sequence of accesses through the entity diagram needed to "execute" the function.

A popular way of drawing access graphs is by means of modified (and simplified) *Petri nets*. Graphically, Petri nets are represented by circles (which can contain black dots or tokens), bars (or square boxes) and arcs (to relate circles and bars, and to indicate the flow of tokens). Depending on the application domain, a Petri net system uses a circle to define a place, a predicate or a condition and a bar to represent a transition, event or state. The differences are not just terminological, for example, a place may, in contrast to a condition, carry more than one token. A common interpretation is that circles represent passive and bars active system components.

In a Petri net variation to express access graphs, circles represent entity sets while bars represent relationship sets. The function name, written in an oval, "triggers" the access graph execution. Because the access graphs are based on the entity diagram, the entity sets are named, whereas the relationship sets are not (but they can be numbered to indicate the access sequence). The relationship sets contain "token firing" information, that is, the flow relations from input to output entity sets. As can be expected, four flow relations are possible: one-to-one, one-to-many, many-to-one, and many-to-many. Small black dots are used to represent the "many" relations (Figure 4.5).

Figure 4.6 illustrates two access graphs. The first represents the function OPEN ACCOUNT discussed in the previous section while the second expresses typical activities involved in customer invoicing.

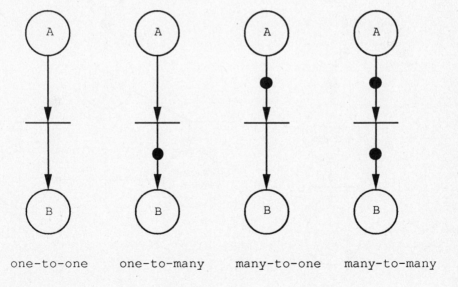

one-to-one   one-to-many   many-to-one   many-to-many

Figure 4.5   Four types of flow relations in access graphs

Equivalent graphs for the same function are possible and this notion of equivalence gives a much desired degree of freedom in the process of constructing access graphs. It is a semantic notion that relates to the concept of semantic maximization. An access graph has *maximal semantic content* if the control which it exerts over the behavior of data objects (represented by entities and relationships) brings about expected results without calling on other access graphs to enforce data integrity and without using redundant data objects. Some candidate equivalent access graphs are shown in Figure 4.7.

It is important to emphasize that access graphs are considered in isolation from each other. It is the task of the next design stages to integrate them into global conceptual database structures. In particular, flow relations are determined solely within the framework of the access graph at hand. They do not express the universal data dependencies between entity sets but only state the maximum possible connectivity of a relationship between entities in a particular access graph. Hence, if the access graph lists all servicing done on a customer's product, then the flow relation between CUSTOMER and PRODUCT is one-to-one (though the connectivity of that relationship set in the universe of discourse is many-to-many).

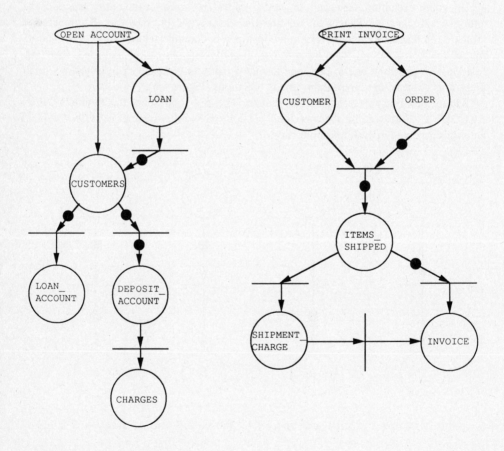

Figure 4.6   Examples of access graphs

The purpose of access graphs is twofold. First, they are used to verify the completeness of the entity diagram. New relationship sets may have to be created in the entity diagram if they are used in the access graphs. Second, they allow for the smooth transformation of the entity diagram into a first-cut entity-relationship diagram (in which more sophisticated relationship sets can be expressed, such as *n*-ary, regular, nested, subset and subtype relationships).

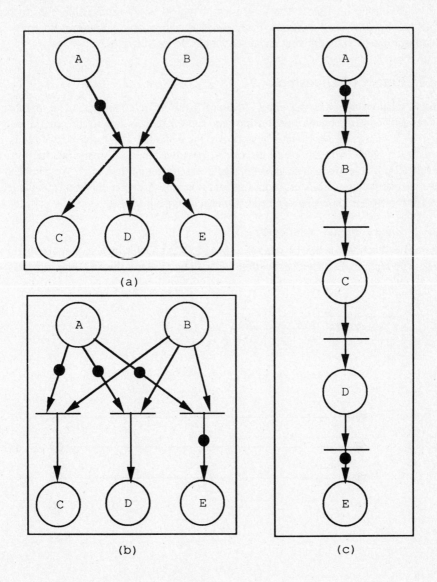

Figure 4.7 Candidate equivalent access graphs

4.4   ENTITY-RELATIONSHIP MODELING

Entity-relationship modeling is central to conceptual design. The goal of conceptual design is to deliver an abstract, nonredundant and unified representation of the data of the application. The entity-relationship model is the most widely used means of such a representation of the data.

In Sections 2.4 and 2.6, an enhanced version of the entity-relationship model was introduced. In this section and in the following, we are interested in the semantics of the entity-relationship diagrams. The semantics of typical entity-relationship constructs are explained by providing excerpts from the data dictionary definitions of entity and relationship sets and by drawing and discussing instance diagrams.

4.4.1   Binary relationships

Binary relationships are the most frequent kind of relationships. The number of theoretically possible binary relationship sets, classified according to the criteria given in Sections 2.4 and 2.6 (excluding nesting), is three hundred and ninety two. It is not, therefore, feasible in this book to discuss all possible kinds of binary relationships (or, indeed, all possible kinds of relationships of degree different than one). We have chosen, rather, to exemplify and discuss more frequent relationship sets in the hope that the reader can extrapolate the knowledge gained to other relationship sets.

4.4.1.1   Binary singular relationships

Figure 4.8 illustrates a binary relationship ALLOCATION which is singular (1:1) and weak. The sections in different face following Figure 4.8 are the DD definitions for this

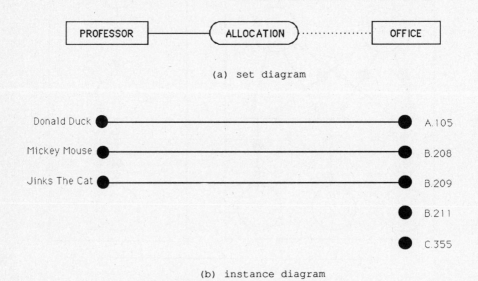

(a) set diagram

(b) instance diagram

Figure 4.8   Binary singular relationship

example. The membership of one entity (PROFESSOR) in this relationship is total and
the second (OFFICE) is partial. The semantics of the relationship ALLOCATE are:

- every professor has one and only one office;
- there is at most one person (professor) in a professorial office;
- there are offices which are not occupied by a professor.

```
================= ENTITIES ==================

Name: OFFICE

Contains the Attributes:
        office_number
        office_size

Primary Key Consists of:
        office_number

Connections:
        via: (1:1 Partial) ALLOCATION (Weak)
                        to: PROFESSOR (1:1 Total)

-------------------------------------------------------------
Name: PROFESSOR

Contains the Attributes:
        professor_name
        professor_expertise_area (repeating)

Primary Key Consists of:
        professor_name

        Connections:
        via: (1:1 Total) ALLOCATION (Weak)
                        to: OFFICE (1:1 Partial)

-------------------------------------------------------------

============== WEAK RELATIONSHIPS ==============

Name: ALLOCATION (binary)

Connections to :
        ENTITY OFFICE (1:1 Partial)
        ENTITY PROFESSOR (1:1 Total)

-------------------------------------------------------------
```

The entities PROFESSOR and OFFICE contain only two attributes each. One of the two attributes in each entity is a key—professor_name for PROFESSOR and office_number for OFFICE. Every instance of an entity set is uniquely identified by its key value. Two entity instances (identified as B.211 and C.355 in Figure 4.8) do not accommodate professors, hence, the partial membership of OFFICE in ALLOCATION.

The attribute professor_expertise_area is repeating. This allows the naming of more than one expertise area of a professor.

4.4.1.2 Binary univocal relationships

An example of the binary univocal (1:N) relationship is shown in Figure 4.9. The relationship EMPLOYMENT is weak. The memberships of the two entities (DEPARTMENT and EMPLOYEE) are total. The semantics of the relationship EMPLOYMENT are:

* department cannot exist without employees;
* all employees work for some, at most one, departments.

```
================== ENTITIES ==================

Name: DEPARTMENT

Contains the Attributes:
        department_name
        department_location

Primary Key Consists of:
        department_name

Connections:
        via: (1:1 Total) EMPLOYMENT (Weak)
                    to: EMPLOYEE (1:N Total)


-------------------------------------------------------------
Name: EMPLOYEE

Contains the Attributes:
        employee_number
        employee_name.first_name
                    .middle_initial
                    .family_name

Primary Key Consists of:
        employee_number

Connections:
        via: (1:N Total) EMPLOYMENT (Weak)
                    to: DEPARTMENT (1:1 Total)
```

```
============== WEAK RELATIONSHIPS  ==============

Name: EMPLOYMENT (binary)

Connections to :
      ENTITY EMPLOYEE (1:N Total)
      ENTITY DEPARTMENT (1:1 Total)

-----------------------------------------------------------------
```

In the instance diagram in Figure 4.9, the Department of Mathematics has three employees and the Department of Astrology has only one employee. Should employee 5500001 retire or quit, the Department of Astrology will be automatically dissolved and will vanish from the database. This is because the integrity constraint (membership class) states that a department must employ at least one person.

Note that one of the attributes (employee_name) is a group attribute. It contains three simple attributes.

4.4.1.3 Binary nonunivocal relationships

A typical example of the binary nonunivocal relationship is shown in Figure 4.10. The relationship ENROLMENT is regular. The memberships of the two entities (STUDENT and COURSE) are partial. The semantics of the relationship ENROLMENT are:

- students may be enrolled in many courses, but some students (e.g. those on leave) may be temporarily not enrolled in any course;
- typically, many students are enrolled in any one course but there can be courses which are currently not taught and such courses do not have any students enrolled.

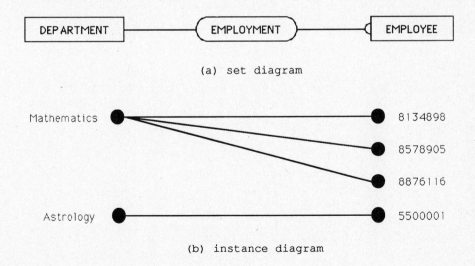

(a) set diagram

(b) instance diagram

Figure 4.9   Binary univocal relationship

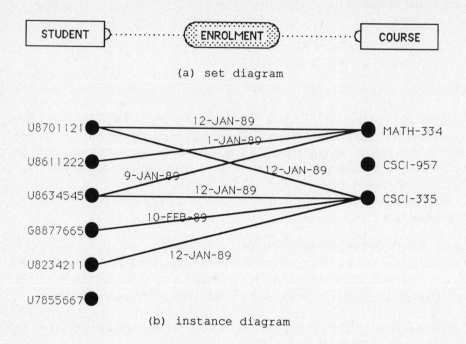

(a) set diagram

(b) instance diagram

Figure 4.10   Binary nonunivocal relationship

```
================== ENTITIES ==================

Name: COURSE

Contains the Attributes:
      course_number
      course_name

Primary Key Consists of:
      course_number

Candidate Key Consists of:
      course_name

      Connections:
      via: (1:N Partial) ENROLMENT (Regular)
                    to: STUDENT (1:N Partial)

------------------------------------------------------------
```

```
Name: STUDENT

Contains the Attributes:
        student_number
        student_name

Primary Key Consists of:
        student_number

Connections:
        via: (1:N Partial) ENROLMENT (Regular)
                        to: COURSE (1:N Partial)

= = = = = = = = = = = = = REGULAR RELATIONSHIPS  = = = = = = = = = = = = =

Name: ENROLMENT (binary)

Contains the Attributes:
        date_of_enrolment

Connections to :
        ENTITY COURSE (1:N Partial)
        ENTITY STUDENT (1:N Partial)


- - - - - - - - - - - - - - - - - - - - - - - - - - - - - - - - - - - - - - - - - - - -
```

There are three students enrolled in MATH-334 and four in CSCI-335 in the instance diagram in Figure 4.10. The course CSCI-957 is not currently on offer. The student U7855667 is not enrolled in any course (presumably, (s)he is on leave).

Courses are uniquely identified by two distinct keys—course_number has been chosen as a primary key and course_name is a candidate key.

The relationship ENROLMENT is regular because it contains the attribute number_of_enrolled_students. Because of its regularity, this relationship exhibits a similar semantic behavior to any entity. In fact, it could be modeled as an entity, but then the entire diagram would have to undergo significant changes in order to fulfill the semantics of the problem.

4.4.2 Unary relationships

Unary (sole) relationships express recursive dependencies between entity instances of a single entity set. The semantics of sole relationships are quite difficult to grasp, yet these relationships play a significant role in modeling real-life situations. Unary relationships can also be divided into three categories: singular, univocal and nonunivocal.

4.4.2.1 Unary singular relationships

Unary singular relationships are rare. The semantics of such relationships are often modeled better by other relationships. A good example of the unary singular relationship is offered by a MARRIAGE relationship, seen from a viewpoint of an employer, in a monogamous society (Figure 4.11). The semantics of the relationship MARRIAGE are:

- an employee can be married to one of the other employees;
- employees who are not married, or who are married to a person that is not an employee of the company, are not admitted to this relationship.

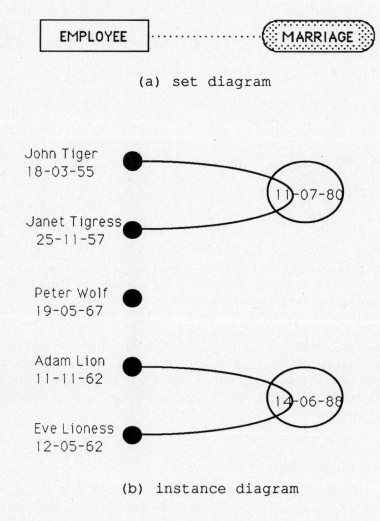

(a) set diagram

(b) instance diagram

Figure 4.11   Unary singular relationship

```
================= ENTITIES =================

Name: EMPLOYEE

Contains the Attributes:
        employee_name
        date_of_birth
        sex

Primary Key Consists of:
        date_of_birth
        employee_name

Connections:
        via: (1:1 Partial) MARRIAGE (Regular)
                        to : apparently only itself

============= REGULAR RELATIONSHIPS =============

Name: MARRIAGE (unary)

Contains the Attributes:
        date_of_marriage

Connections to :
        ENTITY EMPLOYEE (1:1 Partial)

----------------------------------------------------------------
```

There are five employees in the instance diagram in Figure 4.11 and two relationship instances. The employee Peter Wolf does not have one of the other employees as his spouse. The relationship MARRIAGE is regular because it stores information about the date of a marriage between employees.

It is assumed that a unique identification of employees is provided by a composite key consisting of two attributes: date_of_birth and employee_name.

4.4.2.2 Unary univocal relationships

Figure 4.12 illustrates a unary univocal relationship. The example describes a managerial structure of a company in which there are subordinate and superior employees. This will normally give rise to the following semantics:

- a manager can, and usually does, supervise a number of employees;
- an employee can have only one direct supervisor;
- any employee who is supervised can in turn supervise other employees;
- all employees fall into a managerial structure (as supervisor, subordinate or both).

```
================== ENTITIES  = = = = = = = = = = = = =
Name: EMPLOYEE

Contains the Attributes:
     employee_number
     employee_name

Primary Key Consists of:
     employee_number

Connections:
     via: (1:N Total) MANAGERIAL_STRUCTURE (Weak)
                   to : apparently only itself

=============== WEAK RELATIONSHIPS  ===============
Name: MANAGERIAL_STRUCTURE (unary or sole)

Connections to :
     ENTITY EMPLOYEE (1:N Total)
------------------------------------------------------------
```

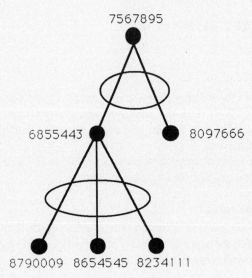

(a) set diagram

(b) instance diagram

Figure 4.12   Unary univocal relationship

There are five employees in the company depicted in the instance diagram in Figure 4.12. Employee 7567895 is a managing director and has two direct subordinates. One of those subordinates, 6855443, supervises the three remaining employees.

4.4.2.3 Unary nonunivocal relationships

The most often used example of a unary nonunivocal relationship refers to the so-called bill-of-material problem. This problem is also known in economics as explosion/ implosion of items (parts). The problem describes a situation in which an item is an assembly of some immediate components but can also be a component of some immediate assemblies (Figure 4.13). The semantics of the relationship BILL_ OF_MATERIAL are:

- an item can be an assembly of any number of items and the same item can be a component in any number of other assemblies;
- an item can be atomic (with no component items) and it may not be needed in any assembly.

(a) set diagram

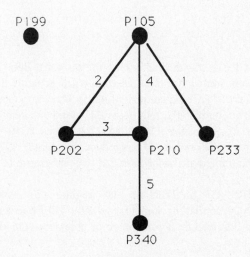

(a) instance diagram

Figure 4.13 Unary nonunivocal relationship

```
================== ENTITIES ==================

Name: ITEM

Contains the Attributes:
      item_number
      item_name

Primary Key Consists of:
      item_number

Candidate Key Consists of:
      item_name

      Connections:
      via: (N:M Partial) BILL_OF_MATERIAL (Regular)
                   to : apparently only itself

 ============= REGULAR RELATIONSHIPS  =============

Name: BILL_OF_MATERIAL (unary or sole)

Contains the Attributes:
      quantity_as_component

Connections to :
      ENTITY ITEM (N:M Partial)


-------------------------------------------------------------
```

There are six items in the instance diagram of Figure 4.13. Item P199 does not participate in the relationship. Item P105 is an assembly that contains three immediate components: P202, P210 and P233. The quantities of immediate components required for one assembly of P105 are: two items P202, four items P210, and one item P233. The item P210 is also an assembly of three items P202 and five items P340. An interesting question is: How many items P202 are needed to produce one item P105? The answer is fourteen (two because of the immediate connection and twelve because of the connection via P210).

The relationship BILL_OF_MATERIAL is regular in order to hold quantity_as_component. This information cannot be stored in ITEM because of the many different ways in which an item can be a component or assembly with relation to other items.

4.4.3 Ternary relationships

Ternary relationships tend to be controversial. Unless they are used within the framework of a stringent semantic interpretation, they can mean different things to different people.

Often, to clarify semantics issues, ternary relationships are given "pair-wise" interpretation. This means that any of the three possible combinations of pairs of entities are interpreted against a remaining entity. In particular, the connectivity of a ternary relationship can depend on whether or not the principle of pair-wise interpretation has been applied.

4.4.3.1 Ternary singular relationships

Figure 4.14 demonstrates an example of a ternary relationship with "unblended" semantics (as opposed to "pair-wise" semantics). This implies that the entities in the relationship FAMILY_UNIT can be interpreted on a one at a time basis. In particular, the connectivity of the relationship is determined by analyzing associations of any one entity with the two remaining entities. Functional dependencies (Section 2.5.2) are helpful in an explanation of the semantics of FAMILY_UNIT. The specification of the semantics is:

- a family unit is considered to consist of a married (possibly "de facto") couple and a residence in which the couple lives;
- some residences may not be occupied by a married couple;

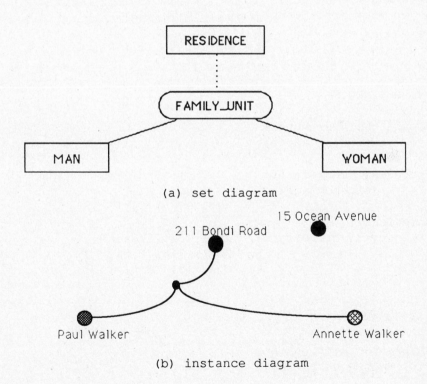

(a) set diagram

(b) instance diagram

Figure 4.14   Ternary singular relationship (unblended semantics)

- only men and women who are married are included in the database;
- the functional dependencies are:
  woman_name → man_name
  woman_name → residence_address
  man_name → woman_name
  man_name → residence_address
  residence_address → woman_name
  residence_address → man_name

```
================== ENTITIES ===================

Name: MAN

Contains the Attributes:
        man_name

Primary Key Consists of:
        man_name

Connections:
        via: (1:1 Total) FAMILY_UNIT (Weak)
                    to: WOMAN (1:1 Total)
                    to: RESIDENCE (1:1 Partial)


    ----------------------------------------------------------------
Name: RESIDENCE

Contains the Attributes:
        residence_address

Primary Key Consists of:
        residence_address

Connections:
        via: (1:1 Partial) FAMILY_UNIT (Weak)
                    to: WOMAN (1:1 Total)
                    to: MAN (1:1 Total)


    ----------------------------------------------------------------
Name: WOMAN

Contains the Attributes:
        woman_name

Primary Key Consists of:
        woman_name
```

```
Connections:
        via: (1:1 Total) FAMILY_UNIT (Weak)
                      to: MAN (1:1 Total)
                      to: RESIDENCE (1:1 Partial)


   =============== WEAK RELATIONSHIPS  ===============

Name: FAMILY_UNIT (ternary)

Connections to :
        ENTITY WOMAN (1:1 Total)
        ENTITY MAN (1:1 Total)
        ENTITY RESIDENCE (1:1 Partial)


------------------------------------------------------------------
```

Ternary relationships with unblended semantics differ from those with pair-wise semantics. However, this difference is seen only in the instance diagram. In general, unless the functional dependencies are stated, the meaning of ternary relationships may not be clear. For example, the unblended semantics of the FAMILY_UNIT relationship in Figure 4.14 do not allow information on previous marriages to be kept in the database. According to the functional dependencies, it is not possible to have the same instance of the entity MAN or WOMAN relating to more than one other instance of the entity WOMAN or MAN. In order to be able to hold such information, the set of functional dependencies would need to be different, thus:

{woman_name, man_name} → residence_address
{residence_address, man_name} → woman_name
{residence_address, woman_name} → man_name

The above set of functional dependencies would transform the FAMILY_UNIT relationship from one with unblended semantics to one with pair-wise semantics. In such a relationship, determinants of the functional dependencies are composite and consist of two attributes. Figure 4.15 illustrates the changes to the instance diagram.

Without knowing the functional dependencies in Figure 4.15, it can be argued that the relationship FAMILY_UNIT is not singular. After all, Paul Walker relates to Annette Walker and Mary Cooper and he is associated with two different residences. This is one reason why the issue of ternary relationships is controversial.

On the other hand, the relationship in Figure 4.14 exhibits other, different problems. Most importantly, the need for a ternary relationship to represent a family unit situation, as shown in Figure 4.14, can be challenged. Under the functional dependencies, any two binary relationships would suffice for the determination of any family unit. For example, binary singular relationships could be used to reconstruct a family unit: (1) between MAN and WOMAN and (2) between RESIDENCE and MAN.

Ternary relationships with unblended semantics are not frequent. This is partly for the reason just stated and partly because they really only happen in relationships of singular connectivity. In the following, the relationships with unblended semantics will not be discussed.

4.4.3.2 Ternary semi-univocal relationships

The connectivity of ternary relationships can be one of four kinds: 1:1:1 or 1:1:M or 1:M:N or K:M:N. It is not necessarily obvious which connectivity is univocal: 1:1:M or 1:M:N or both. Arguably, and without getting into further details, we call the two categories (1:1:M and 1:M:N) semi-univocal.

By way of illustration, a semi-univocal relationship of the 1:1:M kind is shown in Figure 4.16. The relationship JOB records information about current job assignments. A job has a supervisor, is done within a framework of a given project and has employees assigned. The semantics of JOB are:

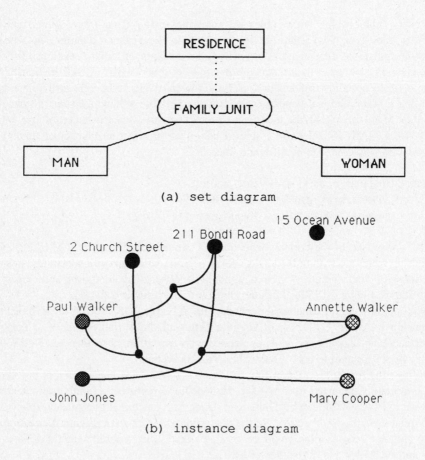

Figure 4.15 Ternary singular relationship (pair-wise semantics)

- only current jobs are held in the relationship;
- not all employees are assigned to jobs;
- all projects and all supervisors have jobs assigned;
- no employee can work on any given project under the supervision of more than one supervisor;
- no supervisor can have any given employee on more than one project;
- the functional dependencies are:

    {employee_number, supervisor_name} → project_number

    {employee_number, project_number} → supervisor_name

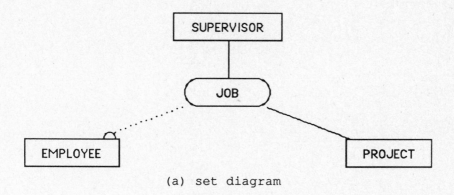

(a) set diagram

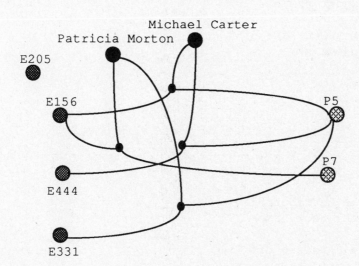

(b) instance diagram

Figure 4.16 Ternary semi-univocal relationship

```
================== ENTITIES ===================
```

Name: EMPLOYEE

Contains the Attributes:
        employee_number
        employee_name

Primary Key Consists of:
        employee_number

Connections:
        via: (1:N Partial) JOB (Weak)
                        to: PROJECT (1:1 Total)
                        to: SUPERVISOR (1:1 Total)

Name: PROJECT

Contains the Attributes:
        project_number
        project_name

Primary Key Consists of:
        project_number

Candidate Key Consists of:
        project_name

Connections:
        via: (1:1 Total) JOB (Weak)
                        to: SUPERVISOR (1:1 Total)
                        to: EMPLOYEE (1:N Partial)

Name: SUPERVISOR

Contains the Attributes:
        supervisor_name

Primary Key Consists of:
        supervisor_name

Connections:
        via: (1:1 Total) JOB (Weak)
                        to: PROJECT (1:1 Total)
                        to: EMPLOYEE (1:N Partial)
```
```

```
============== WEAK RELATIONSHIPS  ==============
```

Name: JOB (ternary)

Connections to :
       ENTITY PROJECT (1:1 Total)
       ENTITY SUPERVISOR (1:1 Total)
       ENTITY EMPLOYEE (1:N Partial)

There are four instances of the relationship JOB shown in Figure 4.16. The functional dependencies hold. The first dependency {employee_number, supervisor_name} $\rightarrow$ project_number is satisfied because:

- {E156, Michael Carter} $\rightarrow$ P5
- {E156, Patricia Morton} $\rightarrow$ P7
- {E444, Michael Carter} $\rightarrow$ P5
- {E331, Patricia Morton} $\rightarrow$ P5

The second dependency {employee_number, project_number} $\rightarrow$ supervisor_name also holds because:

- {E156, P5} $\rightarrow$ Michael Carter
- {E156, P7} $\rightarrow$ Patricia Morton
- {E444, P5} $\rightarrow$ Michael Carter
- {E331, P5} $\rightarrow$ Patricia Morton

However, the pair {supervisor_name, project_number} does not functionally determine employee_number, because:

- {Michael Carter, P5} implies two values of employee_number: E156 and E444.

4.4.3.3 Ternary nonunivocal relationships

The connectivity of a ternary nonunivocal relationship is K:M:N. Figure 4.17 gives an example of such a relationship. The relationship DELIVERY describes a business situation in which trucks are used to deliver goods from warehouses to customers. The semantics of DELIVERY are:

- goods can be delivered by any truck from any warehouse to any customer;
- all trucks and all warehouses are used in deliveries;
- there can be customers who pick up the goods themselves and, therefore, do not participate in the relationship DELIVERY;
- there are no functional dependencies in DELIVERY.

```
================= ENTITIES ===================
Name: CUSTOMER

Contains the Attributes:
      customer_name
      customer_address

Primary Key Consists of:
      customer_name
Connections:
      via: (1:N Partial) DELIVERY (Regular)
                  to: WAREHOUSE (1:N Total)
                  to: TRUCK (1:N Total)
-------------------------------------------------------------
```

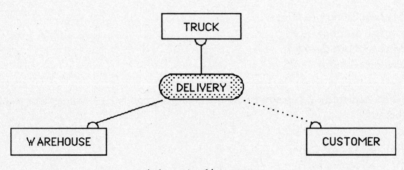

(a) set diagram

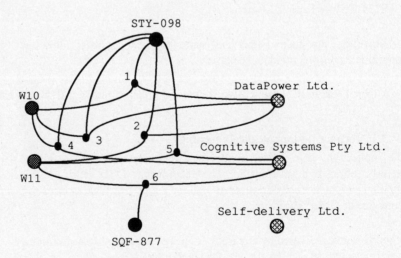

(a) instance diagram

Figure 4.17   Ternary nonunivocal relationship

```
Name: TRUCK

Contains the Attributes:
        truck_registration_number
        truck_make

Primary Key Consists of:
        truck_registration_number

Connections:
        via: (1:N Total) DELIVERY (Regular)
                        to: CUSTOMER (1:N Partial)
                        to: WAREHOUSE (1:N Total)
-------------------------------------------------------------
Name: WAREHOUSE

Contains the Attributes:
        warehouse_number
        warehouse_address

Primary Key Consists of:
        warehouse_number

Candidate Key Consists of:
        warehouse_address

Connections:
        via: (1:N Total) DELIVERY (Regular)
                        to: CUSTOMER (1:N Partial)
                        to: TRUCK (1:N Total)


 ============== REGULAR RELATIONSHIPS  =============
Name: DELIVERY (ternary)

Contains the Attributes:
        delivery_consecutive_number
        delivery_date

Primary Key Consists of:
        delivery_consecutive_number

Connections to :
        ENTITY CUSTOMER (1:N Partial)
        ENTITY WAREHOUSE (1:N Total)
        ENTITY TRUCK (1:N Total)
-------------------------------------------------------------
```

The instance diagram in Figure 4.17 contains six DELIVERY relationships. Because it is possible to have more than one relationship instance among the same three entity instances (one from each entity set), the relationship is identified by its own key (delivery_consecutive_number). In our example, the deliveries numbered 1 and 3 relate to the same entity instances.

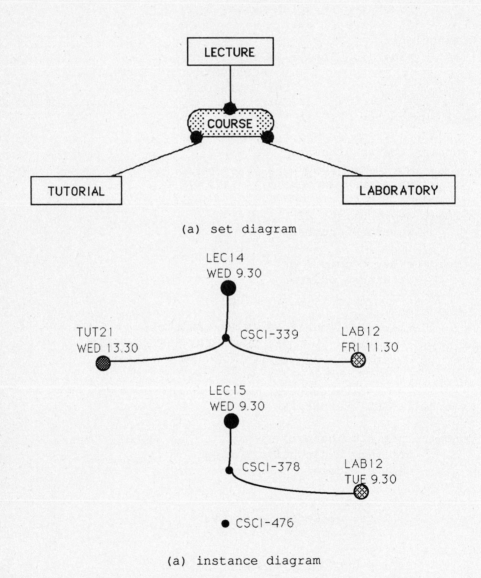

(a) set diagram

(a) instance diagram

Figure 4.18   Aggregate relationship

4.4.4 Hypersemantic relationships

Enhanced conceptual models allow for the representation of hypersemantic relationships. Three categories of hypersemantic relationships (aggregate, generic and nested relationships) were introduced in Section 2.6. The modeling with hypersemantic relationships is very powerful, but at the same time can lead to significant ambiguities. It is crucial that in such a modeling extra caution is exercised.

4.4.4.1 Aggregate relationships

Figure 4.18 shows the hypersemantics involved in the concept of aggregation/ decomposition (Section 2.6.1). The aggregate (superset, HAS-A) relationship COURSE inherits attributes from the three subset (PART-OF) entities. The semantics are:

- a course is understood as a combination of, at most, one lecture per week and/or at most one tutorial per week and/or at most one laboratory per week;
- there is no lecture, tutorial or laboratory which is not a part of a course;
- the courses which are listed, but are not currently run, are also kept in the database;
- since a course can be only a partial combination of any of the three entities, there are no explicitly identifiable inter-entity functional dependencies.

```
================== ENTITIES ==================

Name: LABORATORY

Contains the Attributes:
        laboratory_room
        laboratory_time

Primary Key Consists of:
        laboratory_time
        laboratory_room

Connections:
        via: (1:1 Total Aggregate) COURSE (Regular)
                  to: TUTORIAL (1:1 Total Aggregate)
                  to: LECTURE (1:1 Total Aggregate)
-------------------------------------------------------------
Name: LECTURE

Contains the Attributes:
        lecture_room
        lecture_time

Primary Key Consists of:
        lecture_time
        lecture_room
```

```
Connections:
        via: (1:1 Total Aggregate) COURSE (Regular)
                    to: LABORATORY (1:1 Total Aggregate)
                    to: TUTORIAL (1:1 Total Aggregate)
------------------------------------------------------------------
Name: TUTORIAL

Contains the Attributes:
        tutorial_room
        tutorial_time

Primary Key Consists of:
        tutorial_time
        tutorial_room

Connections:
        via: (1:1 Total Aggregate) COURSE (Regular)
                    to: LABORATORY (1:1 Total Aggregate)
                    to: LECTURE (1:1 Total Aggregate)


  ============= REGULAR RELATIONSHIPS  =============
Name: COURSE (ternary)

Contains the Attributes:
        course_number
        course_name

Primary Key Consists of:
        course_number

Candidate Key Consists of:
        course_name

Connections to :
        ENTITY LABORATORY (1:1 Total Aggregate)
        ENTITY TUTORIAL (1:1 Total Aggregate)
        ENTITY LECTURE (1:1 Total Aggregate)
------------------------------------------------------------------
```

Three instances of the aggregate relationship COURSE are shown in Figure 3.18. The instance identified by CSCI-339 inherits attributes from all three subset entities. The instance identified by CSCI-378 associates two subset entities. The relationship instance CSCI-476 does not relate to any subset entities at all. This is possible because the relationship COURSE has its own key (in fact, it has two keys: course_number and course_name). Note that the existence of relationships such as CSCI-476 may cause the designer to model COURSE as an aggregate (superset) entity, rather than a relationship (Section 2.6.1, Figure 2.23).

4.4.4.2 Generic relationships

Figure 4.19 illustrates the hypersemantics involved in the concept of generalization/specialization (Section 2.6.2). The two subtype (IS-A) entities TELLER and

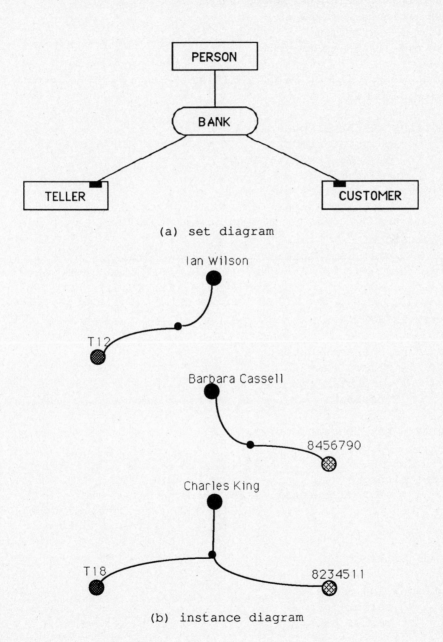

(a) set diagram

(b) instance diagram

Figure 4.19   Generic relationship

CUSTOMER inherit attributes from the supertype (CAN-BE) entity PERSON via the generic relationship BANK. The semantics are:

- a person must be a teller or a customer or both;
- the functional dependencies are:
  teller_id → person_name
  customer_number → person_name

```
================== ENTITIES ==================
Name: CUSTOMER

Contains the Attributes:
        customer_number
        customer_credit_rating

Primary Key Consists of:
        customer_number

Connections:
        via: (1:1 Total Subtype) BANK (Weak)
                       to: TELLER (1:1 Total Subtype)
                       to: PERSON (1:1 Total)
------------------------------------------------------------
Name: PERSON

Contains the Attributes:
        person_name
        date_of_birth
        address

Primary Key Consists of:
        person_name

Connections:
        via: (1:1 Total) BANK (Weak)
                       to: CUSTOMER (1:1 Total Subtype)
                       to: TELLER (1:1 Total Subtype)
------------------------------------------------------------
Name: TELLER

Contains the Attributes:
        teller_id
        teller_salary

Primary Key Consists of:
        teller_id
```

```
Connections:
        via:  (1:1 Total Subtype) BANK (Weak)
                        to: CUSTOMER (1:1 Total Subtype)
                        to: PERSON (1:1 Total)


=============== WEAK RELATIONSHIPS  ===============
Name: BANK (ternary)

Connections to :
        ENTITY CUSTOMER (1:1 Total Subtype)
        ENTITY TELLER (1:1 Total Subtype)
        ENTITY PERSON (1:1 Total)
------------------------------------------------------------
```

Three instances of the relationship BANK are illustrated in Figure 4.19. The attributes which are inherited by subtype entities are person_name, date_of_birth and address. The inheritance mechanism is the same for the disjoint (the first two relationship instances) and overlapping subsets (the last relationship instance).

4.4.4.3 Nested relationships

Figure 4.20 demonstrates the hypersemantics involved in the nested relationships (Section 2.6.3). The relationship ACCOUNT_TRANSACTION is nested in the relationship CUSTOMER-STATEMENT. The semantics are:

- customer statements are issued monthly and separately for each customer's account;

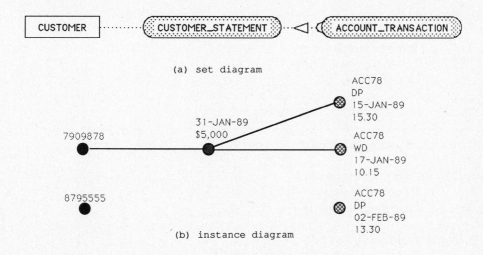

Figure 4.20   Nested relationship

- only the latest customer statement is kept in the database;
- ACCOUNT_TRANSACTION is a relationship among the entities CUSTOMER, TELLER and ACCOUNT (not shown in Figure 4.20).

```
================== ENTITIES ===================
Name: CUSTOMER

Contains the Attributes:
        customer_id
        customer_address

Primary Key Consists of:
        customer_id

Connections:
        via: (1:1 Partial) CUSTOMER_STATEMENT (Regular)
             to: ACCOUNT_TRANSACTION (1:N Partial Nested)

 ============= REGULAR RELATIONSHIPS =============
Name: ACCOUNT_TRANSACTION

Contains the Attributes:
        account_number
        transaction_code
        date_transaction
        time_transaction
        transaction_amount

Primary Key Consists of:
        time_transaction
        date_transaction
        transaction_code
        account_number

Nested in CUSTOMER_STATEMENT
------------------------------------------------------------------
Name: CUSTOMER_STATEMENT (binary)

Contains the Attributes:
        date_of_issue
        closing_balance

Connections to :
    RELATIONSHIP ACCOUNT_TRANSACTION (1:N Partial Nested)
        ENTITY CUSTOMER (1:1 Partial)
------------------------------------------------------------------
```

In the example in Figure 4.20, the relationship ACCOUNT_TRANSACTION is nested in the relationship CUSTOMER_STATEMENT. ACCOUNT_TRANSACTION is identified by a composite key (consisting of four attributes) and it resembles semantically an entity. It is likely that future refinements to the conceptual design will see the relationship ACCOUNT_TRANSACTION converted to an entity.

4.5   VIEW INTEGRATION

In the design of extensive database applications, different designer and user groups adopt their own viewpoints on modeling the same or overlapping processes and data. A view (called also user view or application view) is the model of a database or its portion as perceived by a particular designer or user group. The main goal of the extensive database design is to centralize all local views in a single global database schema (global view). Such an activity is called view integration.

View integration is performed at several phases and stages of the database design process. In a sense, view integration underlies most design activities; for example, the modeling of data flow diagrams, entity diagrams and entity-relationship diagrams are integration tasks. The former concentrates on the integration of processes, the latter integrates data. There are no duplicate processes in the data flow diagram nor are there duplicate entity sets in the entity diagram.

In this section, a methodological approach to the view integration is presented. We propose a method for the view integration whereby final conceptual (entity-relationship-attribute) schemas for extensive database applications can be derived.

4.5.1   Illustration of view integration

Consider a database in an educational organization. Consider further that the following user views have ben identified:

V1   registrar's view,
V2   public relations view,
V3   course evaluation view,
V4   personnel view.

Suppose now that four entity-relationship schemas, corresponding to these views, have been derived (Figure 4.21). The data dictionary definitions for entity and relationship sets have also been given.

The relationship ATTEND is M:N because an apprentice can enroll in many courses and the courses are normally given to many apprentices. The membership of both entities in ATTEND is partial. There may be courses which are not currently offered and there may be apprentices who currently do not take any course. The relationship is regular and contains the attribute date_of_enrolment.

The M:N connectivity of the relationship TEACH informs that a course can be taught by more than one instructor and an instructor can teach many courses. Any course has at least one instructor assigned. There is no instructor who is not delegated to teach a course.

The relationship GRADE connects the same entities (i.e. entity *names* are the same) and is similar to the relationship ATTEND. The connectivity and memberships of the two relationships are identical. The attributes contained in GRADE are course_mark (which is a repeating attribute) and final_grade. It must be noted that the attribute contents of the entities APPRENTICE in ATTEND and GRADE are different.

The generic relationship IS establishes a generalization hierarchy between the supertype entity PERSON and two subtype entities APPRENTICE and INSTRUCTOR. Because of the downward attribute inheritance of generalization (Section 2.6.2), the attribute contents of the two subtype entities are different from the entities with the same names in the other views. The subtype entities can overlap, that is a person can be both an apprentice (and study some courses) and an instructor (and teach other courses).

```
=============== V1 registrar's view ===============
Entity Name: APPRENTICE

Contains the Attributes:
        apprentice_id
        person_name
        date_of_birth
        address
        qualifications_pursued
```

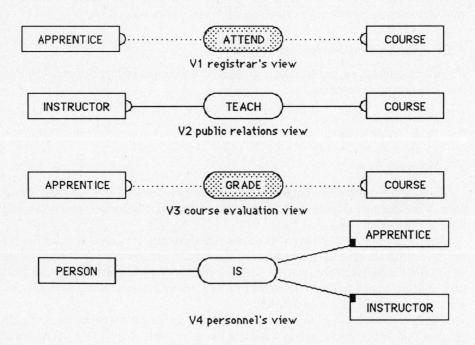

Figure 4.21   Local views

```
Primary Key Consists of:
        apprentice_id

Connections:
        via: (1:N Partial) ATTEND (Regular)
                        to: COURSE (1:N Partial)
-----------------------------------------------------------------
Entity Name: COURSE

Contains the Attributes:
        course_name

Primary Key Consists of:
        course_name

Connections:
        via: (1:N Partial) ATTEND (Regular)
                        to: APPRENTICE (1:N Partial)
-----------------------------------------------------------------
Regular Relationship Name: ATTEND (binary)

Contains the Attributes:
        date_of_enrolment

Connections to :
        ENTITY COURSE (1:N Partial)
        ENTITY APPRENTICE (1:N Partial)
-----------------------------------------------------------------

  ============ V2 pubic relations view  ============
Entity Name: INSTRUCTOR

Contains the Attributes:
        instructor_id
        person_name
        date_of_birth
        address
        salary

Primary Key Consists of:
        instructor_id

Connections:
        via: (1:N Total) TEACH (Weak)
                        to: COURSE (1:N Total)
-----------------------------------------------------------------
```

Entity Name: COURSE

Contains the Attributes:
        course_name

Primary Key Consists of:
        course_name

Connections:
        via: (1:N Total) TEACH (Weak)
                        to: INSTRUCTOR (1:N Total)

Weak Relationship Name: TEACH (binary)

Connections to :
        ENTITY INSTRUCTOR (1:N Total)
        ENTITY COURSE (1:N Total)

=========== V3 course evaluation view ============

Entity Name: APPRENTICE

Contains the Attributes:
        apprentice_id
        person_name

Primary Key Consists of:
        apprentice_id

Connections:
        via: (1:N Partial) GRADE (Regular)
                        to: COURSE (1:N Partial)

Entity Name: COURSE

Contains the Attributes:
        course_name

Primary Key Consists of:
        course_name

Connections:
        via: (1:N Partial) GRADE (Regular)
                        to: APPRENTICE (1:N Partial)

Regular Relationship Name: GRADE (binary)

Contains the Attributes:
      course_mark (repeating)
      final_grade

Connections to :
      ENTITY COURSE (1:N Partial)
      ENTITY APPRENTICE (1:N Partial)

=============== V4 personnel view ================

Entity Name: PERSON

Contains the Attributes:
      person_id
      person_name
      date_of_birth
      address

Primary Key Consists of:
      person_id

Connections:
      via: (1:1 Total) IS (Weak)
                 to: INSTRUCTOR (1:1 Total Subtype)
                 to: APPRENTICE (1:1 Total Subtype)

Entity Name: APPRENTICE

Contains the Attributes:
      qualifications_pursued

Connections:
      via: (1:1 Total Subtype) IS (Weak)
                 to: INSTRUCTOR (1:1 Total Subtype)
                 to: PERSON (1:1 Total)

Entity Name: INSTRUCTOR

Contains the Attributes:
      salary

```
Connections:
        via: (1:1 Total Subtype) IS (Weak)
                        to: APPRENTICE (1:1 Total Subtype)
                        to: PERSON (1:1 Total)

------------------------------------------------------------------
Weak Relationship Name: IS (ternary)

Connections to :
        ENTITY INSTRUCTOR (1:1 Total Subtype)
        ENTITY APPRENTICE (1:1 Total Subtype)
        ENTITY PERSON (1:1 Total)


------------------------------------------------------------------
```

There are many ways of integrating local conceptual schemas into a global one. A necessary requirement is to obtain a global schema which guarantees support for all views or, to be more precise, which guarantees that all business functions will be answerable in an integrated database system. However, some functions will be given preferential treatment and will be directly supported by the underlying database structures, whereas some other functions will be merely answerable. As a consequence, there is a need to *rank* the entire set of business functions in order to establish sound integration criteria (Section 4.5.2).

A global conceptual schema for our example is shown in Figure 4.22. A sample instance diagram and the data dictionary definition for the integrated schema are also given. It should be emphasized that the global schema of Figure 4.22 represents just one possible solution. The superiority of this schema cannot be proven without a detailed analysis of the application domain. Nevertheless, a brief justification is in place.

The schema supports all views and it can be argued that all four views were given equal design considerations, although the relationships ATTEND and GRADE are now integrated in one relationship STUDY. This was the only integration on a *diagram* level. On the *data dictionary* level, the integration affected the attribute contents of some objects. The attributes apprentice_id and instructor_id were dropped altogether, as these attributes would not only be redundant in the global schema, but would also create consistency problems due to the possibility of one person being both an instructor and an apprentice.

The generalization hierarchy plays a central role in the global view. The APPRENTICE and INSTRUCTOR entities inherit attributes from the entity PERSON. The relationship STUDY combines attributes from the relationships ATTEND (view V1) and GRADE (view V3).

```
================== global view ==================


Entity Name: APPRENTICE

Contains the Attributes:
        qualifications_pursued
```

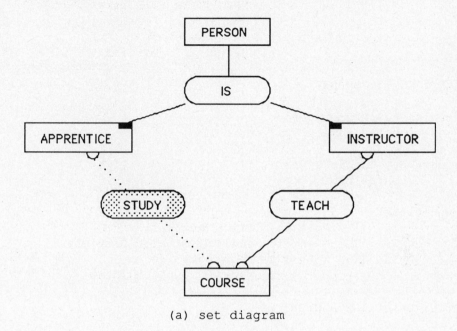

(a) set diagram

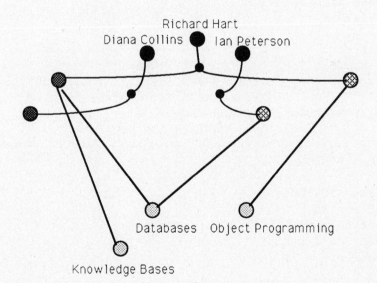

(b) instance diagram

Figure 4.22 Global view

```
Connections:
        via: (1:1 Total Subtype) IS (Weak)
                        to: INSTRUCTOR (1:1 Total Subtype)
                        to: PERSON (1:1 Total)
        via: (1:N Partial) STUDY (Regular)
                        to: COURSE (1:N Partial)
```

```
Entity Name: COURSE

Contains the Attributes:
        course_name

Primary Key Consists of:
        course_name

Connections:
        via: (1:N Partial) STUDY (Regular)
                        to: APPRENTICE (1:N Partial)
        via: (1:N Total) TEACH (Weak)
                        to: INSTRUCTOR (1:N Total)
```

```
Entity Name: INSTRUCTOR

Contains the Attributes:
        salary

Connections:
        via: (1:1 Total Subtype) IS (Weak)
                        to: APPRENTICE (1:1 Total Subtype)
                        to: PERSON (1:1 Total)
        via: (1:N Total) TEACH (Weak)
                        to: COURSE (1:N Total)
```

```
Entity Name: PERSON

Contains the Attributes:
        person_id
        person_name
        date_of_birth
        address

Connections:
        via: (1:1 Total) IS (Weak)
                        to: INSTRUCTOR (1:1 Total Subtype)
                        to: APPRENTICE (1:1 Total Subtype)
```

```
Regular Relationship Name: STUDY (binary)

Contains the Attributes:
        date_of_enrolment
        course_mark (repeating)
        final_grade

Connections to :
        ENTITY COURSE (1:N Partial)
        ENTITY APPRENTICE (1:N Partial)

-------------------------------------------------------------------
Weak Relationship Name: IS (ternary)

Connections to :
        ENTITY INSTRUCTOR (1:1 Total Subtype)
        ENTITY APPRENTICE (1:1 Total Subtype)
        ENTITY PERSON (1:1 Total)

-------------------------------------------------------------------
Weak Relationship Name: TEACH (binary)

Connections to :
        ENTITY COURSE (1:N Total)
        ENTITY INSTRUCTOR (1:N Total)

-------------------------------------------------------------------
```

4.5.2   Calculation of design ranks of business functions

Up till now, business functions have been identified, structured, classified and documented in the data dictionary and function specifications have been defined for all bottom-level data flow diagram processes. Such processes correspond to the *manifest functions* of the business model (Section 3.2). However, as the business model also identifies the *predictable masked functions* (Section 3.2.4), analysis of the functions from both categories should be undertaken. This will establish the prevalent processing patterns in the application, suppress the effects of the interference among user views on the design and alleviate design "noise" (i.e. the strength of "unwanted signals" (functions)).

In brief, we want to add to the quantitative precision of the methodology. To do so, we need to capture and statistically measure dominant characteristics of the set of functions. The problem is difficult and one of the major difficulties stems from the fact that the various functions, tied often to different users, can and will partially overlap. Another difficulty relates to the natural tendency of users to emphasize the relative importance of their own functions.

Three quantitative properties of functions are considered in the calculation of relative function ranks (FR):

f_{ij} *frequency* of realization of function i by user j in a given observation time period (e.g. a month);

p_{ij} the relative *priority* attached by user j to function i according to such criteria as importance, usefulness, required response time, etc. ($\Sigma p_i = 1$ for each user j);

o_i the *overlap* factor that for each function i designates a number of functions K such that at least 50 percent of the attributes of function i occur in function k ($k \in K$).

Consider a simple example that consists of four business functions:

F1   List all servicing between a given pair of dates done on microcomputers purchased by a customer (the customer's name is prompted for).

F2   List all items purchased between a given pair of dates.

F3   List all servicing done between a given pair of dates for items under warranty.

F4   Produce current inventory of serialized items (i.e. items with manufacturer-given serial numbers).

These functions are used by two groups of users (U1 and U2). Suppose that the users declared that the frequencies (f_{ij}) of using the functions over period of one month are as shown in Figure 4.23.

Figure 4.23 is then used to determine the relative frequencies (RF) of functions according to the formula:

$$RF_k = \frac{\displaystyle\sum_{j=1}^{n} f_{kj}}{\displaystyle\sum_{i=1}^{m} \sum_{j=1}^{n} f_{ij}} \qquad (4.1)$$

i \ j	U1	U2
F1	5	1
F2	10	9
F3	7	3
F4	18	17
Σ	40	30

Figure 4.23   Table of frequencies of realization of function i by user j

For our example, the relative frequencies (which sum to 1) are:

$RF_1 = 6/70 = 0.0857$
$RF_2 = 19/70 = 0.2714$
$RF_3 = 10/70 = 0.1429$
$RF_4 = 35/70 = 0.5$

Next, the users declare their individual priorities (p_{ij}) within the scale from zero to one (the sum of priorities of each user is one). The results are shown in Figure 4.24.

Figure 4.24 is used to determine the relative priorities (RP) of functions according to the formula (where n is the number of users):

$$RP_k = \frac{\sum_{j=1}^{n} p_{kj}}{n} \tag{4.2}$$

In our example, the number of users n is equal to 2, and the relative priorities (which sum to 1) are:

$RP_1 = 0.4/2 = 0.2$
$RP_2 = 0.4/2 = 0.2$
$RP_3 = 0.6/2 = 0.3$
$RP_4 = 0.6/2 = 0.3$

Finally, the overlap factors for functions are determined. For this purpose, a cross-reference table of functions and attributes is constructed. Such a table is derivable from function specifications and is a simple matrix which assigns attributes to functions (Figure 4.25).

i \ j	U1	U2
F1	0.1	0.3
F2	0.3	0.1
F3	0.2	0.4
F4	0.4	0.2
Σ	1.0	1.0

Figure 4.24 Table of priorities attached by user j to function i

An *overlap* coefficient for each function (oi) with respect to the others can now be calculated as: $o_i = 1 + (K * 0.5)$. For example, the functions F1 and F2 overlap each other because they have seven common attributes and there are only ten attributes in F1 and nine in F2. Function F1 also overlaps F3. Hence, the overlap factor for F1 is $o_i = 1 + (2 * 0.5) = 2$. Figure 4.26 shows the overlap factors for the example.

The "double-entry calculation" effect of the overlap factors across the involved functions (e.g. if F1 overlaps F2 it is likely that F2 also overlaps F1) is ignored on the basis that the corresponding factors are mutually neutralized. The relative overlaps (RO) of functions are calculated according to the formula:

Function / Attribute	F1	F2	F3	F4
current_date				√
customer_name	√	√	√	√
customer_number	√	√		
from_date	√	√	√	
item_description	√	√	√	√
item_number	√	√	√	√
quantity_sold		√		
requsition_number				√
return_date	√		√	
sale_date		√		
serial_number	√	√		√
serv_request_date	√		√	
serv_request_num	√		√	
to_date	√	√	√	

Figure 4.25 Function-attribute cross-reference matrix

$$RO_k = \frac{O_k}{\sum\limits_{j=1}^{n} O_i}$$ (4.3)

In the example, the relative overlaps are all equal:

$RO_1 = 2/8 = 0.25$
$RO_2 = 2/8 = 0.25$
$RO_3 = 2/8 = 0.25$
$RO_4 = 2/8 = 0.25$

A formula for the calculation of relative function ranks (FR) is:

$$FR(i) = (RF(i) + RP(i) + RO(i)) / 3$$ (4.4)

The function ranks in the example are:

$FR_1 = (0.0857 + 0.2 + 0.25) / 3 = 0.1786$ (4th rank)
$FR_2 = (0.2714 + 0.2 + 0.25) / 3 = 0.2405$ (2nd rank)
$FR_1 = (0.1429 + 0.3 + 0.25) / 3 = 0.2310$ (3rd rank)
$FR_1 = (0.5 + 0.3 + 0.25) / 3 = 0.35$ (1st rank)

The significance of function ranks for the view integration depends on the modeling approach. In the extreme, they can form the basis of an algorithmic procedure to cluster attributes into conceptual objects (entities and relationships). In a less elaborated, but perhaps more practical approach, the function ranks are used to resolve those integration problems in which several alternative database structures are proposed but only one of them should be *directly* supported. This is essentially the answerability problem, as discussed in Section 4.5.1.

i	Overlap functions		Overlap factor
F1	F2	F3	2
F2	F1	F3	2
F3	F1	F2	2
F4	F1	F2	2
Σ			8

Figure 4.26   Overlap table

4.5.3   Resolving integration conflicts

There is no prescriptive, algorithmic way along which the integration of local views can proceed. The design ranks of business functions are helplful, but occasionally they are rendered inapplicable due to some additional semantic information which is not immediately obvious from the diagram. Such hidden semantic information is typically *procedural* (hence, not present in the *descriptive* entity-relationship diagram). The connection trap (Section 4.5.3.5) is a good example.

While potential loss of hidden semantic information is an important consideration in the integration process, there are also other considerations which reflect upon the next database design phases. One of them is the danger of an inferior physical design. This happens when some relationships, which could be crucial to supporting important physical access paths, are eliminated in the view integration process.

4.5.3.1   Data dictionary conflicts

Each local entity-relationship diagram has an associated data dictionary. It is, therefore, likely that the same data dictionary entry will be referred to by different names (*synonyms*) or that different dictionary entries will be described by the same name (*homonyms*). In a process-driven methodology, which derives entity-relationship diagrams from data flow diagrams, data dictionary conflicts are not as severe as in data-driven methodologies. The reason is that data flow diagrams provide the first level of integration during which *naming conflicts* for corresponding dictionary entries are resolved.

The naming conflicts can affect entities, relationships, group attributes and simple attributes. In a computer-assisted design environment, the homonyms are easily dealt with. Any attempt to insert a duplicate name into the data dictionary is disallowed across the board.

The synonyms of entities, regular relationships and group attributes can be discovered by investigating their attribute contents. This presupposes, however, that there are no synonymous attributes. Consider, for example, the entities INSTRUCTOR and LECTURER, identified by instructor_id and lecturer_id, respectively. Suppose also that the remaining attribute contents of the two entities are identical; then the two entities are synonymous if instructor_id and lecturer_id are synonymous (sometimes called the *key conflict*). This is not necessarily the case, however. The two identifiers may identify two different categories (overlapping or disjoint) of teachers; for instance, some courses can only be taught by lecturers, or lecturers are salaried whereas instructors work on an hourly basis.

The discovery of synonymous simple attributes is not easy either. All data dictionary entries for simple attributes must be taken into consideration. The synonymous attributes must have identical (or at least equivalent) types and formats. A synonymous simple attribute is normally entered in the data dictionary as an alias.

The data dictionary conflicts comprise also *inter-object type conflicts*. These are special kinds of synonyms such that, for example, a real-world concept is modeled as an entity in one local view and as a group attribute in another view. The discovery of type conflicts is the responsibility of the database designer. A computer-assisted design tool can only provide supporting documentation in the form of various cross-reference printouts.

4.5.3.2   Abstraction level conflicts

Abstraction level conflicts relate to *aggregation* (Section 2.6.1) and *generalization* (Section 2.6.2) hierarchies. Much of the semantic power of enhanced entity-relationship modeling lies in these two abstractions. In order to maintain this power, it is undesirable to flatten the abstraction hierarchies during the view integration process. Unless justified by other semantic considerations, no aggregate or generic relationships should be eliminated. This introduces, however, extra integration conflicts caused by the fact that entities in aggregation and generalization hierarchies relate to other objects in the entity-relationship diagram.

A related issue is that new abstraction hierarchies can be created as a result of the view integration. Consider two local views with relationships OWNS and HAS (Figure 4.27). The data dictionary definitions of the objects are also shown.

```
================== ENTITIES  ===================
Name: CHECKING_ACCOUNT

Contains the Attributes:
        account_number
        current_balance

Primary Key Consists of:
        account_number

Connections:
        via: (1:N Total) HAS (Weak)
                        to: CUSTOMER (1:1 Partial)
----------------------------------------------------------------
```

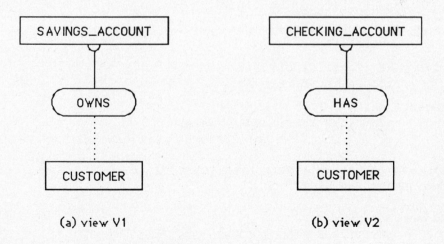

(a) view V1   (b) view V2

Figure 4.27   Local views to be integrated

Name: CUSTOMER (view V1)

Contains the Attributes:
        customer_id
        customer_name
        customer_address

Primary Key Consists of:
        customer_id

Connections:
        via: (1:1 Partial) OWNS (Weak)
                        to: SAVINGS_ACCOUNT (1:N Total)

Name: CUSTOMER (view V2)

Contains the Attributes:
        customer_id
        customer_name
        customer_address

Primary Key Consists of:
        customer_id

Connections:
        via: (1:1 Partial) HAS (Weak)
                        to: CHECKING_ACCOUNT (1:N Total)

Name: SAVINGS_ACCOUNT

Contains the Attributes:
        account_number
        current_balance
        overdraft_limit

Primary Key Consists of:
        account_number

Connections:
        via: (1:N Total) OWNS (Weak)
                        to: CUSTOMER (1:1 Partial)

  ============== WEAK RELATIONSHIPS ==============
Name: HAS (binary)

Connections to :
        ENTITY CHECKING_ACCOUNT (1:N Total)
        ENTITY CUSTOMER (1:1 Partial)

```
Name: OWNS (binary)

Connections to :
        ENTITY CUSTOMER (1:1 Partial)
        ENTITY SAVINGS_ACCOUNT (1:N Total)
```

There are two likely results of the integration of the views V1 and V2; these are shown in Figures 4.28 and 4.29. Treated in isolation from remaining conceptual objects, the two integrated solutions are equivalent. Both employ a newly-discovered generalization hierarchy (ACCOUNT_CATEGORIES); the data dictionary definitions of the entities in the integrated versions are the same; and the subtype entities SAVINGS_ACCOUNT and CHECKING_ACCOUNT do not have a key (in fact, CHECKING_ACCOUNT does not have any attributes at all). The key (account_number) is inherited by the two entities from the supertype entity ACCOUNT. This implies that account_number has a composite format such that the account category (savings or checking account) is built into it. For example, the format may be A99999, where the first alphabetic character would identify the category of the account and the following five digits would be a consecutive number of the account.

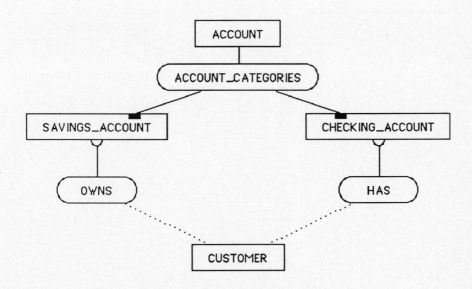

Figure 4.28   View integration in the presence of generalization (version 1)

```
================== ENTITIES ==================
```

Name: ACCOUNT

Contains the Attributes:
        account_number
        current_balance

Primary Key Consists of:
        account_number

```
-------------------------------------------------------------
```

Name: CHECKING_ACCOUNT

Contains no attributes

```
-------------------------------------------------------------
```

Name: CUSTOMER

Contains the Attributes:
        customer_id
        customer_name
        customer_address

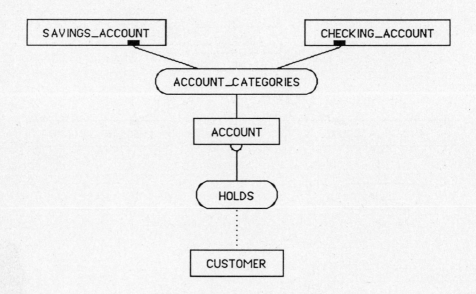

Figure 4.29 View integration in the presence of generalization (version 2)

```
Primary Key Consists of:
        customer_id
- - - - - - - - - - - - - - - - - - - - - - - - - - - - - - - - - - - - - - - - - - - - -
Name: SAVINGS_ACCOUNT

Contains the Attributes:
        overdraft_limit
- - - - - - - - - - - - - - - - - - - - - - - - - - - - - - - - - - - - - - - - - - - - -
```

Note that if connectivity or the memberships of the relationships OWNS and HAS in the local views (Figure 4.27) were not identical, then only the first version of the integrated solution (Figure 4.28) could be used. This would happen, for example, if joint savings accounts (i.e. assigned to two or more persons in joint names) were allowed in the relationship OWNS, but not in the relationship HAS. This would change the connectivity of OWNS from univocal (1:N) to nonunivocal (M:N), thus disallowing the integrated diagram of Figure 4.29.

4.5.3.3 Degree conflicts

Much of the power of semantic modeling lies in the possibility of alternative designs to represent essentially the same information. The integration of alternative solutions does not result in a new integrated diagram; it results in the selection of one of the alternative designs. Degree conflicts are a case in point.

Figure 4.30 shows the degree conflict in two views which relate projects and grants. In the first view, the relationship IS_FINANCED is used to associate projects and grants. In the second view, the same situation is modeled as a repeating group attribute within the entity PROJECT. One of the two solutions must be chosen in the integrated schema. Such a decision should take into account the business functions (according to their ranks) which use the data kept in the objects present in the two views. The first view has a better chance of being accepted, because it caters for those functions which need to access only the data in one of the two entities.

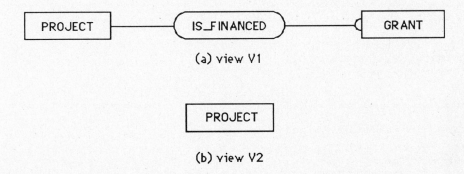

Figure 4.30   Local views with degree conflict (binary relationship versus entity containing the repeating group)

```
================== ENTITIES ==================
```

Name: GRANT

Contains the Attributes:
        grant_number
        granting_body
        grant_amount

Primary Key Consists of:
        grant_number

Connections:
        via: (1:N Total) IS_FINANCED (Weak)
                        to: PROJECT (1:1 Total)

Name: PROJECT (view V1)

Contains the Attributes:
        project_title
        date_started

Primary Key Consists of:
        project_title

Connections:
        via: (1:1 Total) IS_FINANCED (Weak)
                        to: GRANT (1:N Total)

Name: PROJECT (view V2)

Contains the Attributes:
        project_title
        date_started
        grant(repeating).grant_number
                        .granting_body
                        .grant_amount

Primary Key Consists of:
        project_title


```
============== WEAK RELATIONSHIPS ==============
```

Name: IS_FINANCED (binary)

Connections to :
        ENTITY GRANT (1:N Total)
        ENTITY PROJECT (1:1 Total)

Figures 4.31, 4.32 and 4.33 demonstrate three potentially equivalent views which fall into the category of degree conflicts. They describe a typical library situation and the designer must choose one of the views for the integrated schema. This choice should be based on additional semantic information that will reflect the interactions of the three diagrams with the external environment (i.e. with other conceptual objects used by the views and not shown in the three figures).

```
================== ENTITIES ===================

Name: BOOK

Contains the Attributes:
      catalog_number
      bar_code_id

Primary Key Consists of:
      catalog_number

Candidate Key Consists of:
      bar_code_id

Connections:
      via: (1:N Partial) BORROWING_DETAILS (Regular)
                  to: BORROWER (1:N Partial)

-----------------------------------------------------------
Name: BORROWER

Contains the Attributes:
      borrower_id

Primary Key Consists of:
      borrower_id

Connections:
      via: (1:N Partial) BORROWING_DETAILS (Regular)
                  to: BOOK (1:N Partial)

============= REGULAR RELATIONSHIPS =============

Name: BORROWING_DETAILS (binary)

Contains the Attributes:
      date_borrowed
      date_due
```

```
Connections to :
        ENTITY BORROWER (1:N Partial)
        ENTITY BOOK (1:N Partial)
-----------------------------------------------------------------


================== ENTITIES ==================

Name: BOOK

Contains the Attributes:
        catalog_number
        bar_code_id

Primary Key Consists of:
        catalog_number

Candidate Key Consists of:
        bar_code_id

Connections:
        via: (1:N Partial) BORROW (Weak)
                    to: BORROWER (1:1 Partial)
                    to: DATES (1:N Total)
-----------------------------------------------------------------
```

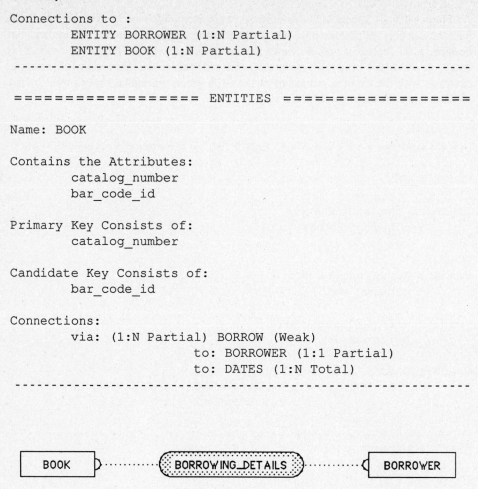

Figure 4.31   Degree conflict—view 1 (binary regular relationship)

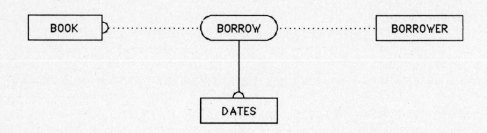

Figure 4.32   Degree conflict—view 2 (ternary semi-univocal relationship with pair-wise semantics)

```
Name: BORROWER

Contains the Attributes:
        borrower_id

Primary Key Consists of:
        borrower_id

Connections:
        via: (1:1 Partial) BORROW (Weak)
                        to: DATES (1:N Total)
                        to: BOOK (1:N Partial)

-----------------------------------------------------------------
Name: DATES

Contains the Attributes:
        date_borrowed
        date_due

Connections:
        via: (1:N Total) BORROW (Weak)
                        to: BORROWER (1:1 Partial)
                        to: BOOK (1:N Partial)

  =============== WEAK RELATIONSHIPS  ===============

Name: BORROW (ternary)

Connections to :
        ENTITY BORROWER (1:1 Partial)
        ENTITY DATES (1:N Total)
        ENTITY BOOK (1:N Partial)

-----------------------------------------------------------------
```

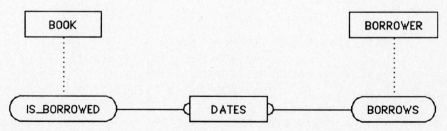

Figure 4.33   Degree conflict—view 3 (two binary univocal relationships)

```
================= ENTITIES ==================
```

Name: BOOK

Contains the Attributes:
        catalog_number
        bar_code_id

Primary Key Consists of:
        catalog_number

Candidate Key Consists of:
        bar_code_id

Connections:
        via: (1:1 Partial) IS_BORROWED (Weak)
                        to: DATES (1:N Total)

Name: BORROWER

Contains the Attributes:
        borrower_id

Primary Key Consists of:
        borrower_id

Connections:
        via: (1:1 Partial) BORROWS (Weak)
                        to: DATES (1:N Total)

Name: DATES

Contains the Attributes:
        date_borrowed
        date_due

Connections:
        via: (1:N Total) BORROWS (Weak)
                        to: BORROWER (1:1 Partial)
        via: (1:N Total) IS_BORROWED (Weak)
                        to: BOOK (1:1 Partial)

```
 ============== WEAK RELATIONSHIPS  ==============
```

Name: BORROWS (binary)

```
Connections to :
        ENTITY BORROWER (1:1 Partial)
        ENTITY DATES (1:N Total)

-----------------------------------------------------------------

Name: IS_BORROWED (binary)

Connections to :
        ENTITY DATES (1:N Total)
        ENTITY BOOK (1:1 Partial)

-----------------------------------------------------------------
```

4.5.3.4 Interpretation conflicts

Interpretation conflicts deal with multiple relationships between the same entities such that these relationships are independent and perform different roles. Such relationships need to be superimposed onto the integrated schema and distinct interpretations attached to these relationships need to be maintained in the global schema. In most cases, the recognition of interpretation conflicts is easy; however, at times, an extra effort is required to understand the problem. One such situation is that illusive similarity between a binary nonunivocal relationship and two circularly placed binary univocal relationships. The instance diagrams in Figures 4.34 and 4.35 illustrate this problem and show clearly that the two views are not equivalent and that the only good integration strategy is to superimpose the views onto the integrated diagram.

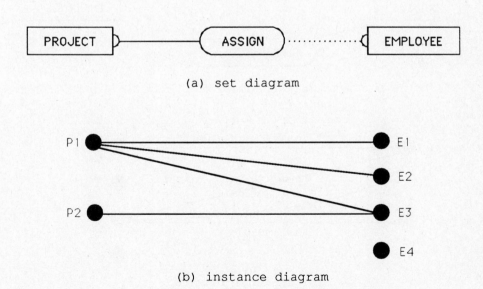

(a) set diagram

(b) instance diagram

Figure 4.34   Interpretation conflict—view 1 (ternary nonunivocal relationship)

View 1 assigns employees to projects. There are many employees on a project and an employee can work on multiple projects. There are also employees (E4) who do not work on any project.

View 2 provides different information. In a sense, it supplements and clarifies the semantic interpretation of the first view. The relationship FULL_TIME_ON_PROJECT lists only employees assigned to a project on a full-time basis; part-time employees (such as E2) working on a project are not connected to that relationship. The relationship SUPERVISED determines those employees who supervise projects. Interestingly, a careful analysis of the two views reveals another piece of semantic information—the only employees who can work on multiple projects are supervisors.

4.5.3.5 Connection traps

One of the objectives of view integration is to eliminate redundant relationships. A relationship is considered redundant if it can be derived from other relationships in the integrated schema. Such a situation arises in a cycle of relationships, as shown in Figure 4.36. In this example, three binary relationships and three entities create a cyclic structure.

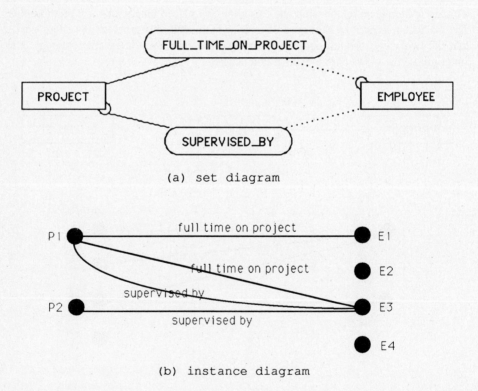

(a) set diagram

(b) instance diagram

Figure 4.35 Interpretation conflict—view 2 (two circularly placed binary univocal relationships)

```
================== ENTITIES ===================

Name: DEPARTMENT

Contains the Attributes:
      department_name

Primary Key Consists of:
      department_name

Connections:
      via: (1:1 Total) PROJECTS (Weak)
                   to: RESEARCH_PROJECT (1:N Total)
      via: (1:1 Total) STAFF (Weak)
                   to: STAFF_MEMBER (1:N Total)

------------------------------------------------------------

Name: RESEARCH_PROJECT

Contains the Attributes:
      project_short_title

Primary Key Consists of:
      project_short_title

Connections:
      via: (1:N Total) PROJECTS (Weak)
                   to: DEPARTMENT (1:1 Total)
      via: (1:1 Total) STAFF_ON_PROJECTS (Weak)
                   to: STAFF_MEMBER (1:N Partial)

------------------------------------------------------------
```

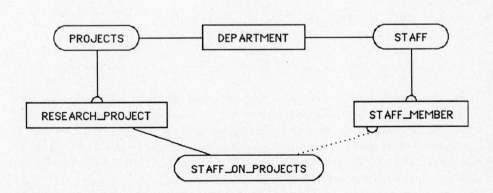

Figure 4.36   Cycle of relationships

```
Name: STAFF_MEMBER

Contains the Attributes:
        staff_member_initials

Primary Key Consists of:
        staff_member_initials

Connections:
        via: (1:N Total) STAFF (Weak)
                    to: DEPARTMENT (1:1 Total)
        via: (1:N Partial) STAFF_ON_PROJECTS (Weak)
                    to: RESEARCH_PROJECT (1:1 Total)


   ============== WEAK RELATIONSHIPS  ==============

Name: PROJECTS (binary)

Connections to :
        ENTITY DEPARTMENT (1:1 Total)
        ENTITY RESEARCH_PROJECT (1:N Total)


------------------------------------------------------------
Name: STAFF (binary)

Connections to :
        ENTITY DEPARTMENT (1:1 Total)
        ENTITY STAFF_MEMBER (1:N Total)


------------------------------------------------------------
Name: STAFF_ON_PROJECTS (binary)

Connections to :
        ENTITY STAFF_MEMBER (1:N Partial)
        ENTITY RESEARCH_PROJECT (1:1 Total)


------------------------------------------------------------
```

Cyclic relationships can give rise to the existence of redundant relationships and such relationships should be eliminated, if they can be reconstructed from the remaining relationships. However, the remaining relationships must not exhibit a *connection trap*. In our example, there are three ways in which one of the relationships in Figure 4.36 can be eliminated. These are illustrated in Figures 4.37, 4.38 and 4.39. The first two possibilities lead to a connection trap while the third possibility does not.

The connection trap in Figure 4.37 occurs because the relationship STAFF_ON_PROJECTS cannot be recovered. As can be seen in the instance diagram, it is not clear which staff members work on which projects and which staff members do not participate in any projects at all. Also, it is not obvious from Figure 4.37 that a staff member can only work on one project at a time (as is indicated by the univocal connectivity of the relationship STAFF_ON_PROJECTS).

A different connection trap exists in the diagram in Figure 4.38. This diagram does not allow for the existence of the relationship STAFF. This is due to the partial membership of the entity STAFF_MEMBER in STAFF_ON_PROJECT. The staff member identified as S.T.N is not involved in any project and, therefore, it is not clear to which department that staff member is assigned.

There is no connection trap in the third diagram illustrated in Figure 4.39. The relationship PROJECT is missing from this diagram, but it can be derived from the remaining two relationships. This diagram represents a nonredundant integrated schema.

In summary, a cycle of relationships may or may not be redundant and each possible simplification of the cycle (such that a potentially redundant relationship is eliminated) should be examined to determine whether a connection trap exists. If it exists in all possible simplifications, then the cycle is nonredundant, otherwise it is redundant (and should be replaced by a simplified "semi-cycle" with no connection trap).

Connection traps in cycles of relationships can usually be explained in terms of the normalization theory. For example, the redundancy within the cycle of relationships in Figure 4.36 can be explained by the existence of a *transitive dependency* (Section 2.5.2):

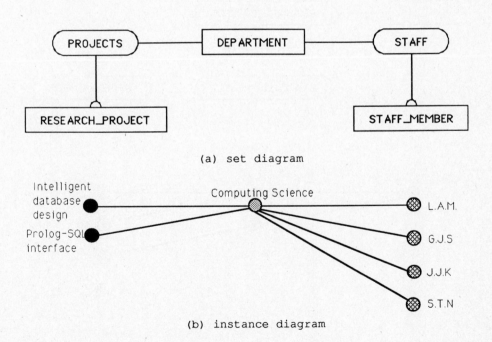

(a) set diagram

(b) instance diagram

Figure 4.37 Redundancy elimination in a university research database—connection trap: Who works on a particular project?

the entity DEPARTMENT (identified by department_name) is transitively dependent on the entity STAFF_MEMBER (identified by staff_member_initials). The set of functional dependencies that produces the transitivity is:

staff_member_initials → project_short_title
project_short_title → department_name
project_short_title ↛ staff_member_initials

Another normalization concept, useful in the context of connection traps, is *multivalued dependency* (Section 2.5.6). Let us refer back to the ternary nonunivocal relationship DELIVERY in Figure 4.17 and let us assume that the relationship DELIVERY is weak. Under this assumption, it is tempting to suggest that the cycle of relationships shown in Figure 4.40 is equivalent to the relationship DELIVERY. (As an aside, the cycle in Figure 4.40 is nonredundant because all relationships are nonunivocal.)

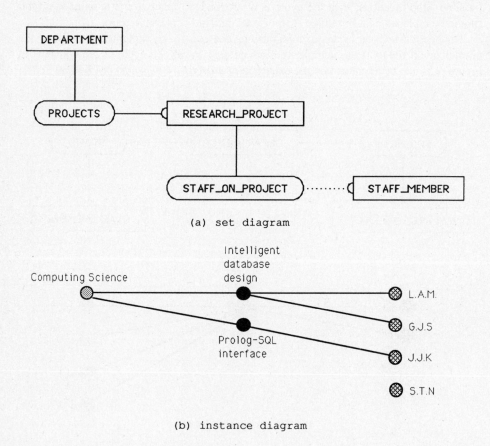

(a) set diagram

(b) instance diagram

Figure 4.38 Redundancy elimination in a university research database—connection trap: List all staff members of a department

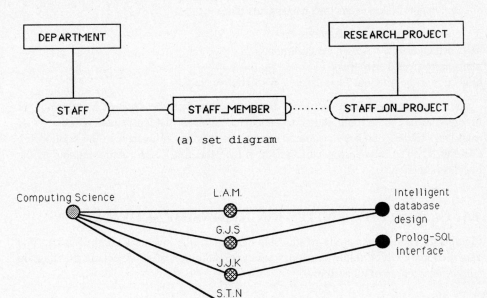

(a) set diagram

(b) instance diagram

Figure 4.39 Redundancy elimination in a university research database—connection trap avoided

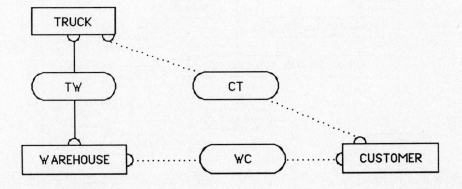

Figure 4.40 Using multivalued dependency to discover a connection trap in a cycle of relationships

The cycle of relationships in Figure 4.40 is equivalent to the relationship DELIVERY if there are no multivalued dependencies in the cycle. In other words, the two diagrams are equivalent if there exists the business rule that:

if   truck T1 is used by warehouse W1
and   warehouse W1 is used for customer C1
and   customer C1 uses truck T1
then   it must be true that T1 is used by W1 to deliver to C1.

If the above "real life constraint" does not occur, then the cycle of relationships in Figure 4.40 has some multivalued dependencies (such as that warehouse_number $\to$ $\to$ truck_registration_number | customer_name) and it is not equivalent to the relationship DELIVERY. The relationship DELIVERY is then the only correct representation of the business situation.

4.6   CASE STUDY: ENTITY-RELATIONSHIP SCHEMA

Figure 4.41 contains the entity-relationship diagram of the inventory control system. The data dictionary which follows includes complete definition of all objects in the diagram and the description of all attributes.

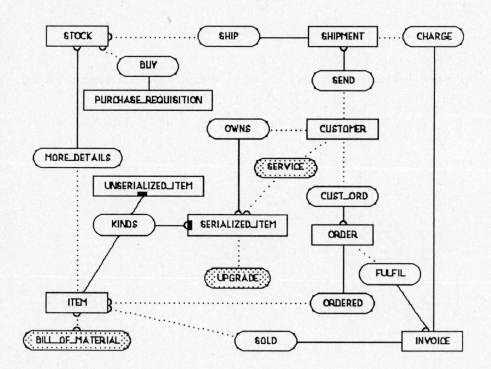

Figure 4.41   Conceptual diagram

Conceptual Schema Definition of: ERA56(DD)

Currently the definition contains:

        9 Entities
        3 Regular Relationships
     11 Weak Relationships
     49 Simple Attributes
and   3 Group Attributes

================== ENTITIES ==================

Name: CUSTOMER

Description: Holds information about person (private or a
           company) who buys.

Contains the Attributes:
       customer_number
       customer_name
       billing_address
       shipping_address

Primary Key Consists of:
       customer_number

Candidate Key Consists of:
       billing_address
       customer_name

Candidate Key Consists of:
       shipping_address
       customer_name

Connections:
       via: (1:1 Partial) CUST_ORD (Weak)
              to: ORDER (1:N Total)
       via: (1:1 Partial) OWNS (Weak)
              to: SERIALIZED_ITEM (1:N Total)
       via: (1:1 Partial) SEND (Weak)
              to: SHIPMENT (1:N Total)
       via: (1:1 Partial) SERVICE (Regular)
              to: SERIALIZED_ITEM (1:N Partial)

Name: INVOICE

Description: Provides the itemized account of the cost of
            sold and shipped items. Sent to the customer
            for payment.

Contains the Attributes:
        invoice_number
        date
        total_item
        total_due

Primary Key Consists of:
        invoice_number

Connections:
        via: (1:1 Total) CHARGE (Weak)
                    to: SHIPMENT (1:1 Partial)
        via: (1:N Total) FULFIL (Weak)
                    to: ORDER (1:1 Partial)
        via: (1:1 Total) SOLD (Weak)
                    to: ITEM (1:N Partial)

Name: ITEM

Description: Provides basic information of business items
            (products).

Contains the Attributes:
        item_number
        item_description
        base_price
        mark_up
        tax
        consultancy_fee

Primary Key Consists of:
        item_number

Connections:
        via: (N:M Partial) BILL_OF_MATERIAL (Regular)
                    to : apparently only itself
        via: (1:1 Total) KINDS (Weak)
                to: SERIALIZED_ITEM (1:N Total Generic)
                to: UNSERIALIZED_ITEM (1:1 Total Subtype)

```
            via: (1:1 Partial) MORE_DETAILS (Weak)
                        to: STOCK (1:N Total)
            via: (1:N Partial) ORDERED (Weak)
                        to: ORDER (1:1 Total)
            via: (1:N Partial) SOLD (Weak)
                        to: INVOICE (1:1 Total)
----------------------------------------------------------------
Name: ORDER

Description: Holds   information   about   open   (unfilled)
            customer orders.

Contains the Attributes:
        customer_order_number
        customer_name
        date
        billing_address
        shipping_address
        payment_method
        shipment_method
        item_on_order (repeating).item_number
                                .quantity_ordered
                                .unit_price
                                .extended_price

        total_amount

Primary Key Consists of:
        customer_order_number

Connections:
        via: (1:N Total) CUST_ORD (Weak)
                    to: CUSTOMER (1:1 Partial)
        via: (1:1 Partial) FULFIL (Weak)
                    to: INVOICE (1:N Total)
        via: (1:1 Total) ORDERED (Weak)
                    to: ITEM (1:N Partial)
----------------------------------------------------------------
Name: PURCHASE_REQUISITION

Description: Defines the purchase order to buy new stock.

Contains the Attributes:
        requisition_number
        supplier_number
        item_to_purchase (repeating).store_item_number
                                    .quantity_required
```

```
        account_number
        date
        requested_by
```

Primary Key Consists of:
```
        requisition_number
```

Connections:
```
        via: (1:1 Total) BUY (Weak)
                      to: STOCK (1:N Partial)
```

Name: SERIALIZED_ITEM

Description: The subtype entity that stores information
             about items with serial numbers. It inherits
             attributes from the supertype entity ITEM.

Contains the Attributes:
```
        serial_number
        date_sold
        warranty_type
        date_warranty_expires
```

Primary Key Consists of:
```
        serial_number
```

Connections:
```
        via: (1:N Total Generic) KINDS (Weak)
              to: UNSERIALIZED_ITEM (1:1 Total Subtype)
              to: ITEM (1:1 Total)
        via: (1:N Total) OWNS (Weak)
                      to: CUSTOMER (1:1 Partial)
        via: (1:N Partial) SERVICE (Regular)
                      to: CUSTOMER (1:1 Partial)
        via: (1:1 Partial) UPGRADE (Regular)
              to : apparently only itself
```

Name: SHIPMENT

Description: Gives information about shipments of ordered
             items to customers.

Contains the Attributes:
```
        our_order_number
        shipping_charge
```

```
      packing_information (repeating).item_number
                                    .quantity_ordered
                                    .quantity_shipped
                                    .quantity_back_ordered
                                    .quantity_canceled
      date
```

Primary Key Consists of:
      our_order_number

Connections:
      via: (1:1 Partial) CHARGE (Weak)
                  to: INVOICE (1:1 Total)
      via: (1:N Total) SEND (Weak)
                  to: CUSTOMER (1:1 Partial)
      via: (1:1 Total) SHIP (Weak)
      to: STOCK (1:N Partial)

Name: STOCK

Description: Defines items in stock.

Contains the Attributes:
      store_item_number
      supplier_number
      supplier_name
      supplier_address
      quantity_on_hand
      reorder_point

Primary Key Consists of:
      store_item_number

Connections:
      via: (1:N Partial) BUY (Weak)
            to: PURCHASE_REQUISITION (1:1 Total)
      via: (1:N Total) MORE_DETAILS (Weak)
                  to: ITEM (1:1 Partial)
      via: (1:N Partial) SHIP (Weak)
                  to: SHIPMENT (1:1 Total)

Name: UNSERIALIZED_ITEM

Description: The subtype entity that stores information
            about items with no serial numbers. It

                  inherits   attributes   (including   its   key:
                  item_number) from the supertype entity ITEM.

Contains the Attributes:
        unit_of_measure

Connections:
        via: (1:1 Total Subtype) KINDS (Weak)
                to: SERIALIZED_ITEM (1:N Total Generic)
                to: ITEM (1:1 Total)

============== REGULAR RELATIONSHIPS ==============

Name: BILL_OF_MATERIAL (unary or sole)

Description: Defines the structural explosion and implosion
             of items.

Contains the Attributes:
        quantity_as_component

Connections to :
        ENTITY ITEM (N:M Partial)

Name: SERVICE (binary)

Description: Identifies and provides details about each
             service requested by a customer on serialized
             items.

Contains the Attributes:
        service_request_number
        date_service_requested
        date_service_completed
        date_service_collected
        technician_name
Primary Key Consists of:
        service_request_number

Connections to :
        ENTITY CUSTOMER (1:1 Partial)
        ENTITY SERIALIZED_ITEM (1:N Partial)

Name: UPGRADE (unary or sole)

Description: Defines upgrades to serialized items that
            result in an item receiving a new item_number
            value.

Contains the Attributes:
        service_request_number
        upgraded_from
        upgraded_to

Primary Key Consists of:
        service_request_number

Connections to :
        ENTITY SERIALIZED_ITEM (1:1 Partial)

   ============== WEAK RELATIONSHIPS = = = = = = = = = =

Name: BUY (binary)

Description: Relates the requisition order to items in
            stock.

Connections to :
        ENTITY PURCHASE_REQUISITION (1:1 Total)
        ENTITY STOCK (1:N Partial)

Name: CHARGE (binary)

Description: Used to include the shipment information (in
            particular, shipment charge) in the invoice to
            the customer.
            The entity SHIPMENT is partial in this
            relationship because of the time delay between
            the shipment and the invoice preparation.

Connections to :
        ENTITY SHIPMENT (1:1 Partial)
        ENTITY INVOICE (1:1 Total)

Name: CUST_ORD (binary)

Description: Relates the unfilled orders to a customer.

Connections to :
        ENTITY CUSTOMER (1:1 Partial)
        ENTITY ORDER (1:N Total)

Name: FULFIL (binary)

Description: Determines invoices sent to the customer in
             partial or full fulfilment of the order.

Connections to :
        ENTITY INVOICE (1:N Total)
        ENTITY ORDER (1:1 Partial)

Name: KINDS (ternary)

Description: Generic relationship that identifies two
             categories of items: serialized and
             unserialized.

Connections to :
        ENTITY SERIALIZED_ITEM (1:N Total Generic)
        ENTITY UNSERIALIZED_ITEM (1:1 Total Subtype)
        ENTITY ITEM (1:1 Total)

Name: MORE_DETAILS (binary)

Description: Cross-references the description of items with
             the stock of those items.

Connections to :
        ENTITY ITEM (1:1 Partial)
        ENTITY STOCK (1:N Total)

Name: ORDERED (binary)

Description: Associates an order with the details of
             ordered items.

Connections to :
        ENTITY ORDER (1:1 Total)
        ENTITY ITEM (1:N Partial)

Name: OWNS (binary)

Description: Defines what serialized items have been
            purchased from the business and owned by the
            customer.

Connections to :
        ENTITY SERIALIZED_ITEM (1:N Total)
        ENTITY CUSTOMER (1:1 Partial)

Name: SEND (binary)

Description: Relates customer information to shipment.

Connections to :
        ENTITY CUSTOMER (1:1 Partial)
        ENTITY SHIPMENT (1:N Total)

Name: SHIP (binary)

Description: Relates shipments of items to items on stock.
            Each shipment causes updates to stock.
            The relationship is univocal. The user is
            interested in items per shipment, but not in
            shipments per item.

Connections to :
        ENTITY STOCK (1:N Partial)
        ENTITY SHIPMENT (1:1 Total)

Name: SOLD (binary)

Description: Relates information about items to the invoice
            that was issued but not paid yet.

Connections to :
        ENTITY ITEM (1:N Partial)
        ENTITY INVOICE (1:1 Total)

=============== SIMPLE ATTRIBUTES ===============

Name: account_number

Definition: Number of the account to which credit or
              debit.

Format: 99/999/999/9999

Type: text

Used in:
        Entity: PURCHASE_REQUISITION

Name: base_price

Aliases: purchase_price

Definition: Base price of the product.

Format: 9(5)V99

Type: number

Used in:
        Entity: ITEM

Name: billing_address

Definition: Customer address to which the invoice should
              be sent.

Format: X(256)

Type: long

Used in:
        Entity: CUSTOMER
        Entity: ORDER

Name: consultancy_fee

Definition: Increases the base_price.

Format: 9(5)V99

Type: number

Remarks: Used as a catchall for services rendered under
             some conditions.

Used in:
        Entity: ITEM

Name: customer_name

Definition: Name of the customer.

Format: X(80)

Type: text

Used in:
        Entity: CUSTOMER
        Entity: ORDER

Name: customer_number

Definition: Identifies the customer.

Format: X(8)

Type: text

Algorithm: Automatically generated by the system.

Used in:
     · Entity: CUSTOMER

Name: customer_order_number

Definition: Identifies the customer's purchase order.

Format: X(8)

Type: text

Used in:
        Entity: ORDER

Name: date

Definition: Date on which something was processed.

Format: DD-MM-YY

Type: date

Used in:
        Entity: INVOICE
        Entity: ORDER
        Entity: PURCHASE_REQUISITION
        Entity: SHIPMENT

Name: date_service_collected

Definition: Date on which the repaired items were returned
             to the customer.

Format: DD-MM-YY

Type: date

Used in:
        Relationship: SERVICE

Name: date_service_completed

Definition: Date on which the serialized item was
             repaired.

Format: DD-MM-YY

Type: date

Used in:
        Relationship: SERVICE

Name: date_service_requested

Definition: Date on which the customer requested the
             service of a serialized item purchased from
             the business.

```
Format:        DD-MM-YY

Type:          date

Used in:
       Relationship: SERVICE
------------------------------------------------------------------
Name: date_sold

Definition:    Date  on  which  the  serialized  item  was  sold  to
               a customer.

Format:        DD-MM-YY

Type:          date

Used in:
       Entity: SERIALIZED_ITEM
------------------------------------------------------------------
Name: date_warranty_expires

Definition:    Date  on  which  the  warranty  of  a  serialized
               item, purchased by the customer, expires.

Format:        DD-MM-YY

Type:          date

Used in:
       Entity: SERIALIZED_ITEM
------------------------------------------------------------------
Name: extended_price

Definition:    Price  of  the  item  line  on  a  customer  order
               form.

Format:        9(6)V99

Type:          money

Algorithm:     unit_price * quantity_required

Used in:
       Group Attribute: item_on_order
------------------------------------------------------------------
```

```
Name: invoice_number

Definition:  Identifies the invoice.

Format:      9(5)

Type:        text
Used in:
      Entity: INVOICE

 ----------------------------------------------------------------
Name: item_description

Aliases:     product_description

Definition:  Description   of   the   item   identified   by
             item_number or by store_item_number.

Format:      X(20)

Type:        text

Used in:
      Entity: ITEM

 ----------------------------------------------------------------
Name: item_number

Aliases:     product_number

Definition:  Internal identifier of the item.

Format:      X(10)

Type:        text

Remarks:     See store_item_number.

Used in:
        Group Attribute: item_on_order
        Group Attribute: packing_information
        Entity: ITEM

 ----------------------------------------------------------------
Name: mark_up

Definition: Fixed mark-up on the base_price.
```

Format: 99V9

Type: number

Used in:
      Entity: ITEM

Name: our_order_number

Definition: The internal number assigned by the business
               to a customer order.

Format: 9(4)

Type: text

Used in:
      Entity: SHIPMENT

Name: payment_method

Definition: Indicates how the customer is willing to pay
               for the order.

Format: X(40)

Type: text

Used in:
      Entity: ORDER

Name: quantity_as_component

Definition: Determines how many items of one kind is
               needed for one item of another kind (bill-of-
               material problem).

Format: 9(3)

Type: integer

Used in:
      Relationship: BILL_OF_MATERIAL

Name: quantity_back_ordered

Definition: Quantity of item ordered by the customer that
              for lack of stock was not filled.
              Another shipment will follow, once sufficient
              stock is available.

Format: 9(3)

Type: integer

Used in:
         Group Attribute: packing_information

Name: quantity_canceled

Definition: Quantity of item ordered by the customer that
              for lack of stock was not filled. A second
              shipment will not follow; if additional
              merchandise is required, the customer is
              expected to reorder.

Format: 9(3)

Type: integer

Used in:
         Group Attribute: packing_information

Name: quantity_on_hand

Definition: Quantity of a particular product in stock.

Format: 9(3)

Type: integer

Used in:
         Entity: STOCK

Name: quantity_ordered

Definition: Quantity of item ordered by the customer.

```
Format:       9(3)


Type:         integer


Used in:
      Group Attribute: item_on_order
      Group Attribute: packing_information
```

```
Name: quantity_required


Definition:   Quantity of item on the purchase requisition
              form or the customer order form.


Format:       9(3)


Type:         integer


Used in:
      Group Attribute: item_to_purchase
```

```
Name: quantity_shipped


Definition:   Quantity of ordered item that was actually
              shipped.


Format:       9(3)


Type:         integer


Used in:
      Group Attribute: packing_information
```

```
Name: reorder_point


Aliases:      reorder_level


Definition:   Quantity of a product below which a new
              purchase order for that product should be
              placed to maintain its stock available at any
              time.


Format:       9(3)


Type:         integer
```

Used in:
        Entity: STOCK

Name: requested_by

Definition: Name of the requisitioning officer.

Format: X(30)

Type: text

Used in:
        Entity: PURCHASE_REQUISITION

Name: requisition_number

Definition: Identifies the external purchase requisition.

Format: 9(5)

Type: integer

Algorithm: Generated automatically as a next consecutive
             number.

Used in:
        Entity: PURCHASE_REQUISITION

Name: serial_number

Aliases: registration_number

Definition: Identifies   an   individual   copy   of   the
             serialized   (hardware)   or   the   registered
             (software) product.

Format: X(20)

Type: text

Used in:
        Entity: SERIALIZED_ITEM

Name: service_request_number

Definition: Identifies the service repair order.

Format: 9(6)

Type: text

Used in:
        Relationship: SERVICE
        Relationship: UPGRADE

Name: shipment_method

Definition: Indicates how the customer wants the ordered
             products to be shipped.

Format: X(40)

Type: text

Used in:
        Entity: ORDER

Name: shipping_address

Definition: Customer address to which the shipment of
             ordered goods should be made.

Format: X(256)

Type: long

Used in:
        Entity: CUSTOMER
        Entity: ORDER

Name: shipping_charge

Definition: Amount of money, charged to a customer, for
             the shipment of ordered products.

Format: 99V99

```
Type:          money

Used in:
        Entity: SHIPMENT
```

```
Name: store_item_number

Aliases:       store_item
               store_product_number

Definition:    Identifies    a    particular    product    in    the
               warehouse.

Format:        X(10)

Type:          text

Remarks:       If  an  item  identified  by  store_item_number  is
               supplied  by  different  suppliers,  then  many
               store_item_number(s)  will  correspond  to  one
               item_number.

Algorithm:     Generated by its supplier.

Used in:
        Group Attribute: item_to_purchase
        Entity: STOCK
```

```
Name: supplier_address

Definition:    Address of the supplier.

Format:        X(512)

Type:          long

Used in:
        Entity: STOCK
```

```
Name: supplier_name

Definition:    Name  of  the  supplier  from  which  products  are
               being purchased.
```

```
Format:        X(512)

Type:          long

Used in:
        Entity: STOCK
```

```
--------------------------------------------------------------
Name: supplier_number

Definition:  Internal code that identifies the supplier.

Format:        X(10)

Type:          text

Used in:
        Entity: PURCHASE_REQUISITION
        Entity: STOCK
```

```
--------------------------------------------------------------
Name: tax

Definition:  Tax on the base_price.

Format:        99V9

Type:          number

Used in:
        Entity: ITEM
```

```
--------------------------------------------------------------
Name: technician_name

Definition:  Full name of the technician who completed a
             service or an upgrade of a serialized item.

Format:        X(30)

Type:          text

Used in:
        Relationship: SERVICE
```

```
--------------------------------------------------------------
```

Name: total_amount

Definition: Total amount of the customer order.

Format: 9(6)V99

Type: money

Used in:
        Entity: ORDER

Name: total_due

Definition: Total invoice charge.

Format: 9(6)V99

Type: money

Used in:
        Entity: INVOICE

Name: total_item

Definition: Amount on an invoice for the item line.

Format: 9(5)V99

Type: money

Used in:
        Entity: INVOICE

Name: unit_of_measure

Definition: Describes a basic unit of manipulation of the
             unserialized item (e.g. dozen, pair, each).

Format: A(4)

Type: text

Remarks: The unit of measure of serialized items is
             always 'each'.

Used in:
        Entity: UNSERIALIZED_ITEM

Name: unit_price

Definition: Item price on the customer order form.

Format: 9(5)V99

Type: money

Used in:
        Group Attribute: item_on_order

Name: upgraded_from

Definition: The item_number before upgrade.

Format: X(10)

Type: text

Used in:
        Relationship: UPGRADE

Name: upgraded_to

Definition: The item_number after upgrade.

Format: X(10)

Type: text

Used in:
        Relationship: UPGRADE

Name: warranty_type

Definition: Determines the warranty given or purchased by
             the customer on purchase of a serialized item.

Format: XX

Type: text

Used in:
        Entity: SERIALIZED_ITEM

=============== GROUP ATTRIBUTES ================

Name: item_on_order

Definition: Details about the item in the customer order
             form.

Composed of the Attributes:
        item_number
        quantity_ordered
        unit_price
        extended_price

Used in:
        Entity: ORDER

Name: item_to_purchase

Definition: Basic details about an item being purchased.

Composed of the Attributes:
        store_item_number
        quantity_required

Used in:
        Entity: PURCHASE_REQUISITION

Name: packing_information

Definition: Identifies quantities of item when filling
             customer order.

Composed of the Attributes:
        item_number
        quantity_ordered
        quantity_shipped
        quantity_back_ordered
        quantity_canceled

Used in:
        Entity: SHIPMENT

FURTHER READING

Principles for drawing entity diagrams are discussed by Martin (1987). However, we do not know about any reference that addresses, to any significant depth, the conversion from data flow diagrams to entity diagrams.

Books on structured analysis are good sources of information about functions specifications. We recommend DeMarco (1979), Gane and Sarson (1979), Page-Jones (1980) and Peters (1988).

Petri nets are subject of many books (e.g. Peterson 1981, Reisig 1985). The use of Petri nets for representing access graphs in conceptual or other design stages is discussed by Atzeni *et al.* (1982), Balbo *et al.* (1984), Borgida *et al.* (1982), De Antonellis and Zonta (1981), Eder *et al.* (1986), Maiocchi (1985) and Sakai and Horiuchi (1984). The relevance of access graphs to the open (and not at all distant) research topic of graphical access to databases is addressed in Elmasri and Larson (1985) and Larson (1986).

Various authors introduce subtle differences in presentation of the semantics of the entity-relationship modeling. Good sources are those by Chen (1976, 1985), De Antonellis and Di Leva (1985), Hawryszkiewycz (1984), Howe (1983), Lien (1980) and Teorey *et al.* (1986).

Tutorial-style discussion on view integration at the conceptual design level is given by Batini *et al.* (1986) and Navathe *et al.* (1986). More formal treatment is available from Biskup and Convent (1986) and Yao *et al.* (1985). The connection traps are well explained by Howe (1983).

REFERENCES

ATZENI, P., BATINI, C., DE ANTONELLIS, V., LENZERINI, M., VILLANELLI, F. and ZONTA, B. (1982): A Computer Aided Tool for Conceptual Database Design, in: *Automated Tools for Information Systems Design*, ed. H. J. Schneider and A. I. Wasserman, North-Holland, pp.85–106.

BALBO, G., DEMO, G. B., DI LEVA, A. and GIOLITO, P. (1984): Dynamics Analysis in Database Design, in: *Proc. Int. Conf. on Data Eng.*, Los Angeles, California, pp.238–43.

BATINI, C., LENZERINI, M. and NAVATHE, S. B. (1986): A Comparative Analysis of Methodologies for Database Schema Integration, *ACM Comp. Surv.*, 4, pp.323–64.

BISKUP, J. and CONVENT, B. (1986): A Formal View Integration Method, in: *SIGMOD'86. SIGMOD Record,* 2, pp.398–407.

BORGIDA, A. T., MYLOPOULOS, J. and WONG, H. K. T. (1982): Methodological and Computer Aids for Interactive Information System Development, in: *Automated Tools for Information Systems Design*, ed. H. J. Schneider and A. I. Wasserman, North-Holland, pp.109–24.

CHEN, P. P. S. (1976): The Entity-Relationship Model—Toward a Unified View of Data, *ACM Trans. Database Syst.*, 1, pp.9–36.

CHEN, P. P. S. (1985): Database Design Based on Entity and Relationship, in: *Principles of Database Design, Volume I, Logical Organizations*, ed. S. B. Yao, Prentice Hall, pp.174–210.

DE ANTONELLIS, V. and DI LEVA, A. (1985): DATAID-1: a Database Design Methodology, Inf. Syst., 2, pp.181–95.

DE ANTONELLIS, V. and ZONTA, B. (1981): Modelling Events in Data Base Applications Design, in: *Proc. 7th Int. Conf. Very Large Data Bases*, ed. C.Zaniolo, C.Delobel, Cannes, France, pp.23–31.

DEMARCO, T. (1979): *Structured Analysis and System Specification*, Prentice Hall, 352p.

EDER, J., KAPPEL, J., TJOA, A. M. and WAGNER, R. R. (1986): BIER—The Behaviour Integrated Entity Relationship Approach, in: *Proc. 5th Int. Conf. on Entiry-Relationship Approach*, Dijon, France, pp.253–72.

ELMASRI, R. A. and LARSON, J. A. (1985): A Graphical Query Facility for ER Databases, in: *Proc. 4th Int. Conf. on E-R Approach*, Chicago, pp.236–45.

GANE, C. and SARSON, T. (1979): *Structured Systems Analysis: Tools and Techniques*, Prentice Hall, 241p.

HAWRYSZKIEWYCZ, I. T. (1984): *Database Analysis and Design*, SRA, 578p.

HOWE, D. R. (1983): *Data Analysis for Data Base Design*, Edward Arnold, 307p.

LARSON, J. A. (1986): A Visual Approach to Browsing in a Database Environment, *Comput.*, June, pp.62–71.

LIEN, Y. E. (1980): On the Semantics of the Entity-Relationship Data Model, in: *Entity-Relationship Approach to Systems Analysis and Design*, North-Holland, pp.155–67.

MAIOCCHI, M. (1985): The Use of Petri Nets in Requirements and Functional Specification, *System Description Methodologies*,ed. D. Teichroew and G. David, Elsevier Science, pp.253–74.

MARTIN, J. (1987): *Recommended Diagramming Standards for Analysts and Programmers. A Basis for Automation*, Prentice Hall, 325p.

NAVATHE, S., ELMASRI, R. and LARSON J. (1986): Integrating User Views in Database Design, *Comput.*, Jan., pp.50–62.

PAGE-JONES, M. (1980): *The Practical Guide to Structured Systems Design,* Prentice Hall, 354p.

PETERS, L. (1988): *Advanced Structured Analysis and Design*, Prentice Hall, 272p.

PETERSON, J. L. (1981): *Petri Net Theory and the Modeling of Systems*, Prentice Hall, 290p.

REISIG, W. (1985): *Petri Nets. An Introduction*, Springer-Verlag, 161p.

SAKAI, H. and HORIUCHI, H. (1984): A Method for Behavior Modelling in Data Oriented Approach to Systems Design, in: *Proc. Int. Conf. on Data Eng.*, Los Angeles, California, pp.492–9.

TEOREY, T. J., YANG D. and FRY, J. P. (1986): A Logical Design Methodology for Relational Databases Using the Extended Entity-Relationship Model, *Comput. Surv.*, 2, pp.197–222.

YAO, S. B., WADDLE, V. and HOUSEL, B. C. (1985): An Interactive System for Database Design and Integration, in: *Principles of Database Design, Volume I, Logical Organizations*, ed. S. B. Yao, Prentice Hall, pp.325–60.

5

Design of Logical Schema

This chapter addresses the logical level design of a relational database. The presentation is practically oriented and is placed within the framework of a lifecycle design methodology. The objective is to provide transformation rules whereby a logical schema is derived from a conceptual (ERA) diagram. Once a first-cut schema is derived, it can be subjected to formal normalization algorithms (synthesis and decomposition). The normalization is discussed in a rigorous fashion but it is based on realistic examples to better relate to typical design situations. A highlight of the chapter is the introduction of a graphical representation of a relational schema. Such a graphical representation is directly convertible to a verbal schema of the database definition (e.g. using SQL's CREATE statements).

5.1 RELATIONAL CONCEPTS REVISITED

Relational approach to database management has at least three different interpretations and contexts: model-theoretic, official standard and implementation-specific.

Three basic components of the relational system are identified below. These components were originally specified in the model-theoretic context and they are:

- object types (two basic data structures: relation and domain);
- operators (as specified in relational algebra or relational calculus);
- integrity rules (mainly entity integrity and referential integrity).

The desired level of cooperation among the above components has been specified by means of Codd's twelve rules (Section 5.1.2).

5.1.1 Relational theory vs. practice

The practice of relational systems often differs from the theory of the relational model. This is evident both in efforts at standardization and in various implementations of the relational model. However, a common denominator for both the standards and the implementations of the model is the use of SQL (often pronounced "sequel"). SQL

(Structured Query Language) is a language for defining, manipulating and controlling data in a relational database. SQL provides both a unifying environment for the definition and access to relational databases. It is so popular that it serves as a trademark for relational databases. One way of identifying the power of a relational DBMS is to compare its SQL capabilities with the properties of the relational model.

The official standard for the database language SQL was ratified by ANSI (American National Standards Institute) in 1986. The ANSI proposal is likely soon to be accepted as an international standard by ISO (International Standards Organization). The ANSI standard concentrates on the *programmatic* (as opposed to interactive) aspects of database language. A major premise of the standard is the portability of programs. The programmatic aspect of the standard enhances portability, but replaces a dynamic, dual-mode (definition and manipulation) interface by a static, schema-based language.

Current relational implementations emphasize the *interactive* aspect of SQL. SQL is highlighted as a stand-alone, dynamic language which can be interactively used, not only to manipulate data, but also to change at any time the data structure definitions. However, the power of interactive SQL is limited and often deceptive. A result of a complex SQL query can be difficult to predict and verify. As a consequence, SQL is not a language for end-users. The user interface to the relational systems is normally form (screen) oriented. The implementation of the forms is partly done by interactive SQL commands (which constitute so-called *triggers*) and partly by SQL commands embedded in a programmatic

Relational Model	Relational Standard (ANSI)	Relational Implementation (ORACLE)
	SCHEMA	
RELATION	BASE TABLE	TABLE
TUPLE	ROW	RECORD
ATTRIBUTE	COLUMN	COLUMN
DOMAIN		
PRIMARY KEY	UNIQUE CONSTRAINT	
FOREIGN KEY		
CATALOG		DICTIONARY
VIEW	VIEWED TABLE	VIEW

Figure 5.1 Equivalence of relational terms

environment of such languages as Cobol or C (called, in form generation environment, *user exits*).

The differences in the three approaches extend also to the terminology. Some principal equivalences of terms are shown in Figure 5.1. The terms shown in the table are discussed in detail below.

The notion of *schema* is explicit only in the standard. A schema defines the database structure and some integrity constraints owned by a specific user. The user is usually identified with an application domain. Typically the database structure comprised by the schema constitutes a part of the complete database definition of an operational system. In this sense, the schema would be better called a *subschema* but such a notion is not defined in the standard SQL. Technically, the schema definition of the database structure consists of the definitions of base tables, viewed tables and privileges (i.e. authorizations to perform some actions on base or viewed tables).

The concept of schema is rejected in the relational model as being a static feature, reminiscent of the network database model. Nevertheless, the model-theoretic research of database design uses the term schema to refer to the definition of a database being designed. More specifically, the relational schema is a set of relation schemes, where a *scheme* is the definition of a relation consisting of its name, a list of candidate keys and a set of attributes.

The relational implementations do not refer explicitly to the concept of schema, but provide most means necessary for its representation.

A *relation*, according to the relational model, is a two-dimensional stored data structure in which:

- all attributes are single-valued and atomic (i.e. no repeating and no group attributes are allowed);
- tuples are unordered;
- attributes are unordered;
- there are no duplicate tuples.

Base table (relational standard) and *table* (most implementations) do not satisfy the last feature and allow for duplicate tuples. This is considered a serious flaw of SQL. Also, the order of tuples is important for some SQL operations and enforced if necessary (ORDER BY clause).

A *tuple* is a set of (attribute name : attribute value) pairs. Each value is drawn from the domain of the respective attribute. Every tuple of the relation has the same cardinality. The tuple is the smallest unit of data that can be inserted into a relation and deleted from a relation. A *row* (relational standard) and *record* (most implementations) are synonymous with the term tuple.

An *attribute* represents the use of the domain within a relation. It is a multi-set (bag) of values that may vary over time. The value of an attribute is the smallest unit of data that can be selected from the relation or that can be updated. *Column* is the SQL counterpart for attribute.

A *domain* is a set of all legal values of an attribute. The actual values, which appear in an attribute, are drawn from that domain. The concept of domain is not used in SQL. Some primitive, syntactic aspects of this concept are only incorporated in data typing.

Each column in SQL is given a *type* (integer, date, etc.), which syntactically restricts the set of legal values in a column.

The relational model specifies that every relation has a primary key. This is a consequence of the requirement that there are no duplicate tuples in a relation. A *candidate* key of a relation is a minimal set of attributes such that the values of these attributes uniquely identify a single tuple in this relation. A relation can have many candidate keys. One of these keys is denoted a *primary key*.

SQL does not have an explicit notion of the primary or candidate key. Nevertheless, the primary or candidate key can be supported by applying some rules. In the relational standard, a *unique constraint*, specified for a set of columns, enforces that no two rows of a table are allowed to have the same values. To simulate the primary key notion, the unique constraint is used together with a *not null constraint*, which forbids null values in a column. In ORACLE, a similar effect is achieved by specifying *unique index* and *not null* for a set of columns.

A *foreign key* is a set of attributes in one relation whose values are either nulls or are required to match the values of a primary key of another relation. This definition is realized in the principle of *referential integrity*, which is used in the relational model to represent conceptual relationships. Currently, most relational DBMSs do not automatically enforce referential integrity at the definitional level. Integrity enforcements are done at the procedural level in application programs. A notable exception is DB2 Version 2, released at the end of 1988, which supports the referential integrity in the database definition (Section 5.1.3).

A *catalog* is a set of relations which contains definitions of all objects (relations, views, indexes, users, etc.) known to the system. It is a database about metadata. Ordinary SQL statements are used to interrogate the catalog as if it was any other database. The relational standard does not specify a catalog structure as it considers that the concept of a catalog is outside the scope of the SQL standard. In ORACLE, the catalog is known as a data *dictionary*.

A *view* is a relation which is derived from other relations and/or views. A view is given a name and is specified as a part of the database definition. A view is never stored in the database. It is a virtual relation which is constructed from its definition whenever needed. In the relational standard, a view is often referred to as a *viewed table*.

5.1.2   Codd's twelve rules for fidelity of a relational system to the relational model

In 1986 the founder of the relational model, Edgar F. Codd, wrote the twelve commandments of relational database theory. These rules can be used to measure the fidelity of relational implementations to the relational model. Since publication of the rules, research has shown that some of the rules are not achievable without significant breakthroughs in the relational theory. In particular, the view updating rule (Rule 6) and the logical data independence rule (Rule 9) will have to be rewritten to become feasible. In the following, Codd's rules are subjected to a critical analysis.

Rule 1: The information rule

> All information in a relational database is represented explicitly at the logical level and in exactly one way—by values in tables.

This rule implies that metadata (data about data) is represented in exactly the same manner as the application data. Accordingly, the same language (SQL) is used to access application data and the metadata in the catalog (cp. Rule 4).

This rule touches upon the concept of *nulls*. In a table-oriented representation of information, it is unavoidable that some values will be nulls. The nulls have at least two different interpretations: (1) value at present unknown (e.g. an address of an employee can be missing); and (2) property inapplicable (e.g. male employee does not have a maiden name). The nulls are addressed explicitly by Rule 3.

Rule 2: Guaranteed access rule

> Each and every datum (atomic value) in a relational database is guaranteed to be logically accessible by resorting to a combination of table name, primary key value and column name.

An essential part of the rule is the *primary key* concept. However, current DBMSs (with the exception of DB2) do not support this concept explicitly, that is, in a data-definitional way. In general, four steps are needed to indirectly enforce the existence of the primary key of a relation by a database designer:

- specify NOT NULL in the attribute(s) definition (i.e. those attributes that constitute a primary key);
- create a UNIQUE INDEX over the NOT NULL attribute(s) (cp. Section 5.6.2);
- never drop that index;
- as a facilitating option, create a table in the catalog to keep track of all indirectly defined primary keys.

The reason for the lack of an explicit primary key concept in current DBMSs can be traced to the related concepts of domain, foreign key, null values and so on. For example, it is possible to have two (or more) relations with different primary keys denoting the same conceptual objects. If the primary keys for such relations were drawn from different domains then it would be unclear how to execute any successful joins. A common situation relates to people who tend to be identified by different key-attributes (e.g. employee_id or tax_register_number or {family_name, birth-date}, etc.).

Rule 3: Systematic treatment of null values

> Null values (distinct from the empty character string or a string of blank characters and distinct from zero or any other number) are supported in fully relational DBMS for representing missing information and inapplicable information in a systematic way, independent of data type.

By definition and common sense, null values must be allowed to exist in relations. This is necessary, for example, if a new tuple is inserted in a relation and the user is not able, even if temporarily, to provide some attribute values. However, it is not at all obvious how to support the null values in relational operations. The suggestions that three-valued, or even four-valued, logic should be used can be challenged. It is well-known that three-valued logic (let alone four) does not have a unique interpretation. For example, in three-valued logic I, p → q is true if p and q are nulls (not known), but in three-valued logic II, p → q is null if p and q are nulls.

Rule 4: Dynamic online catalog based on the relational model

The database description is represented at the logical level in the same way as ordinary data, so that authorized users can apply the same relational language to its interrogation as they apply to the regular data.

This rule is supported by most relational DBMSs. Typically, SQL is used to access relations in the catalog so that the database administrator can access and modify system-level relations and views and a regular user can access information in the catalog about his/her database tables and tables with public authority. New relations can also be created in the catalog for database integrity and tuning reasons. Some generalized applications, built on top of a DBMS, will create and maintain their own tables in the catalog (e.g. ORACLE's form generator SQL*Forms is such an application).

Rule 5: Comprehensive data sub-language rule

A relational system may support several languages and various modes of terminal use (for example, the fill-in-the-blanks mode). However, there must be at least one language whose statements are expressible, per some well-defined syntax, as character strings and that is comprehensive in supporting all of the following items:

- Data definition
- View definition
- Data manipulation (interactive and by program)
- Integrity constraints
- Transaction boundaries (begin, commit and rollback).

Interactive SQL and embedded SQL can be successfully used to support all these items. However, the support for integrity constraints is not straightforward and is subjected to the limitations evident in the discussion of Rule 10.

Rule 6: View updating rule

All views that are theoretically updatable are also updatable by the system.

This rule assumes that it is possible to determine what views are theoretically updatable. However, this assumption cannot be sustained in the current stage of development of relational technology. A popular belief is that a view which is the projection of a base table is updatable and a view which is a join of base tables is not updatable. This belief has been adopted in many commercial DBMSs, including ORACLE. The truth of the matter is that there are projection views which are not updatable and there are join views which are. The updatability of a view depends more on whether the primary key of a base table is included in the view than it does on a relational algebra operation used in the view creation. A DBMS which does not support the primary key concept (cp. Rule 2) is bound to be unreliable in view updating operations.

Rule 7: High-level insert, update and delete

> The capability of handling a base relation or a derived relation as a single operand applies not only to the retrieval of data but also to the insertion, update and deletion of data.

This requirement is clearly in reaction to shortcomings of some SQL implementations in the database modification area. In general, there is no reason why modification operations should be inferior in their relational power to retrieval operations. Yet, this has been the case in some commercial DBMSs, including early versions of DB2. Such DBMSs do not permit, for instance, a "whole-record" update, that is, an update of one or more rows in a relation if a column (or columns) in that row(s) has a certain value. Nor do they permit an update, insert or delete on a relation which is also referenced in the FROM clause of a subquery, for example, "Delete all customers with unpaid balances which are overdue for more than six months".

Rule 8: Physical data independence

> Application programs and terminal activities remain logically unimpaired whenever any changes are made in either storage representations or access methods.

The relational model is defined as purely logical. Hence, by definition, the relational systems attempt to hide physical level characteristics from the user. To the extent to which they are successful in this attempt, the physical data independence is naturally enforced in relational DBMSs.

Rule 9: Logical data independence

> Application programs and terminal activities remain logically unimpaired when information-preserving changes of any kind that theoretically permit unimpairment are made to the base tables.

Difficulties in enforcing logical data independence in relational systems stem precisely from the same reasons as in the view updating rule (Rule 6). Changes to logical definitions of base relations would not affect applications if it was always possible to maintain a pre-change state of the database definition by means of newly created view relations, so that these view relations would "simulate" the old base relations. If such views were updatable then the system would fully support logical data independence. As it stands today, decomposing the relation R by projection to two new relations R1 and R2 would make it impossible to replace R by a join view of R1 and R2 without affecting the applications which refer to R. This is because a join view would not be updatable and it would not be able to assume the role of the old base relation R without hiccups.

Rule 10: Integrity independence

> Integrity constraints specific to a particular relational database must be definable in the relational data sub-language and storable in the catalog, not in the application programs.

As with many of the other rules, the integrity independence rule cannot be supported in a DBMS which does not understand the primary key notion. Two integrity rules are fundamental to every relational database. The *entity integrity* states that the attributes of a primary key cannot accept null values. The *referential integrity* demands that each non-null foreign key value must match some primary key value of a relation to which the foreign key refers. It is expected that the forthcoming releases of relational DBMSs will support these two integrity rules (Section 5.1.3).

Rule 11: Distribution independence

> A relational DBMS has distribution independence.

The meaning of this rule is that the same applications (commands and programs) can be run without changes on distributed and centralized databases. The relational systems are particularly suited for distribution. Relations are easy to fragment and the fragments are easy to recombine by means of optimizable relational operations. However, the implication is that the system needs to be able to support the view updating rule (Rule 6) and the integrity independence rule (Rule 10).

The distribution independence rule should be responsive to three kinds of distribution transparency:

1. Location transparency: A user should be given the impression that (s)he uses a local database (this is really a special aspect of the physical data independence (Rule 8)).
2. Fragmentation transparency: A user does not have to realize that a relation (s)he is using is fragmented (this is an aspect of the logical data independence (Rule 9)).
3. Replication transparency: A user does not have to realize that copies (replicas) of the same relation can exist at many different sites.

Rule 12: Nonsubversion rule

> If a relational system has a low-level (single-record-at-a-time) language, that low level cannot be used to subvert or bypass the integrity rules and constraints expressed in the higher level relational languages (multiple-records-at-a-time).

There are database problems that current DBMSs cannot handle with the exclusive use of a high-level relation-at-a-time language; a typical example of this is a bill of material (part explosion) problem, in which recursive processing is required. As a consequence, all relational DBMSs provide embedded processing facilities in which a modified version of a relational language (typically SQL) is embedded in a host language (a third-generation programming language, such as C, COBOL, or PL/I). Embedded programming relies on the concept of *cursor*—a kind of pointer which at any given time points to one tuple in a relation. This leads to a low-level tuple-at-a-time processing, necessary to solve some practical problems which currently cannot be handled by relational level operations.

5.1.3 Automatic enforcement of referential integrity

At the end of 1988, IBM released Version 2 of DB2 which automatically enforces referential constraints on relations. Other major systems will follow suit; for example,

ORACLE Version 6.0 introduces, as the first step, a syntax support for referential integrity enforcement.

Referential integrity is the design rule in which all references from one relation to another are required to satisfy the mapping between primary and foreign keys of involved relations. Consider the binary univocal relationship EMPLOYMENT in Figure 4.9 in Chapter 4. The membership of both entities (DEPARTMENT and EMPLOYEE) in this relationship is total. In the relational schema (Figure 5.8), later in this chapter, the relationship EMPLOYMENT will be represented by the *foreign key* 'department_name' in the relation EMPLOYEE matching the *primary key* 'department_name' of the relation DEPARTMENT. The relation DEPARTMENT is a *parent relation* while the relation EMPLOYEE is a *dependent relation*.

In DB2 Version 2, this referential integrity can be defined in the CREATE TABLE statements:

```
CREATE TABLE DEPARTMENT
   (DEPARTMENT_NAME  VARCHAR(36)    NOT NULL,
   LOCATION         VARCHAR(20),
   MANAGERID        CHAR(8),
   PRIMARY KEY (DEPARTMENT_NAME));

CREATE TABLE EMPLOYEE
   (EMPLOYEE_NUMBER  CHAR(8)        NOT NULL,
   FAMILY_NAME      VARCHAR(20)    NOT NULL,
   FIRST_NAME       VARCHAR(15),
   DEPARTMENT_NAME  VARCHAR(36),
   PRIMARY KEY (EMPLOYEE_NUMBER),
   FOREIGN KEY (DEPARTMENT_NAME)
        REFERENCES DEPARTMENT
        ON DELETE RESTRICT);
```

The definition of referential integrity in the CREATE TABLE statements decides the way the SQL manipulative operations of INSERT, UPDATE and DELETE work (the SELECT statement is not influenced by the referential integrity). As a general requirement, the manipulative operations must ensure that:

- a primary key value must uniquely identify one tuple in the relation and cannot be null;
- every foreign key value must match a primary key value or be null (subject to the DELETE option in the FOREIGN KEY clause);
- a primary key value may match none, one or many foreign key values.

On an attempt to INSERT a tuple in the dependent relation EMPLOYEE, the system looks for the existence of a corresponding tuple in the relation DEPARTMENT. The INSERT:

```
INSERT INTO EMPLOYEE VALUES
   ('85661200', 'SMITH', 'JOHN', 'MATHEMATICS');
```

will not succeed if a 'department_name', MATHEMATICS, does not exist in the
DEPARTMENT relation. In other words, the total membership of EMPLOYEE in
EMPLOYMENT is enforced during the INSERT operation. If the membership is partial,
the user should put the null value for the 'department_name' column, if appropriate.

The UPDATE operation is organized around the same principle as the INSERT
operation. Whenever a tuple is to be updated in the dependent relation, a new value in the
foreign key is checked to determine if it matches a primary key value of the parent
relation or is null:

```
UPDATE EMPLOYEE
   SET DEPARTMENT_NAME = 'FORTUNE_TELLING'
   WHERE EMPLOYEE_NUMBER = '85661200';
```

As a direct consequence of the UPDATE rule, it is not possible to update a primary
key in a tuple of a parent relation that has a dependent tuple. If this were possible, the
dependent tuple would violate the referential integrity after the update.

As opposed to the previous operations, the DELETE operation applies to a parent
relation, it performs in one of three ways and it can affect tuples in relations other than
subjected to the DELETE action, for example:

```
DELETE FROM DEPARTMENT
   WHERE DEPARTMENT_NAME = 'MATHEMATICS';
```

The three DELETE options are:

RESTRICT   which does not allow the deletion of parent tuples that have dependent
            tuples (this reflects the principle of total membership when considered
            from the viewpoint of the DELETE operation);
CASCADE   which cascades the DELETE operation to all associated dependent tuples,
            after first deleting a tuple in the parent relation;
SET NULL   which deletes a tuple in the parent relation and sets the foreign key values
            in the dependent tuples to null.

The RESTRICT option, to which DB2 defaults, expresses rules such as: "A
department can be dissolved only if it does not have any employees working in it". The
CASCADE option would be applied if the rule were: "If a department is dissolved, all
employees are automatically fired". The SET NULL option should be used if the rule
were: "If a department is dissolved, the employees of this department are not associated
with any department until further action".

The DELETE operation involves:

- the relation for which the DELETE is issued;
- all of the dependent relations;
- all descendants of the dependent relations (such as if EMPLOYEE had a dependent
  relation CHILD), but only if the CASCADE option is defined.

DB2 introduces restrictions and roundabouts to deal with more difficult problems encountered in the enforcement of the referential integrity. One such problem is the foreign key in the same relation as its primary key (*self-reference* problem). Another problem is a *cycle* of references, such as in the following expansion of the definition of the DEPARTMENT and EMPLOYEE relations (to indicate that a manager is one of the employees):

```
CREATE TABLE DEPARTMENT
    (DEPARTMENT_NAME   VARCHAR(36)    NOT NULL,
    LOCATION           VARCHAR(20),
    MANAGERID          CHAR(8),
    PRIMARY KEY (DEPARTMENT_NAME),
    FOREIGN KEY (MANAGERID)
        REFERENCES EMPLOYEE
        ON DELETE SET NULL);


CREATE TABLE EMPLOYEE
    (EMPLOYEE_NUMBER   CHAR(8)        NOT NULL,
    FAMILY_NAME        VARCHAR(20)    NOT NULL,
    FIRST_NAME         VARCHAR(15),
    DEPARTMENT_NAME    VARCHAR(36),
    PRIMARY KEY (EMPLOYEE_NUMBER),
    FOREIGN KEY (DEPARTMENT_NAME)
        REFERENCES DEPARTMENT
        ON DELETE RESTRICT);
```

It is interesting to note that the referential integrity in relational databases is reminiscent of the concept of *membership class* in the network (Codasyl) databases (though the membership class, while quite static, is more powerful). The membership class in a network system is specified as a combination of *insertion class* (AUTOMATIC, STRUCTURAL, MANUAL) and *retention class* (FIXED, MANDATORY, OPTIONAL).

5.2 REDUCING DENORMALIZED CONCEPTUAL OBJECTS TO RELATIONS

Entities and regular relationships of a conceptual database structure may be denormalized, that is, they may contain repeating simple attributes, group attributes and repeating group attributes. Hence, the first step in the derivation of a relational schema from the entity-relationship diagram is to normalize the entities and regular relationships to at least first normal form. To do this, the entity-relationship diagram is converted to a form in which all denormalized objects (mainly entities, and very rarely regular relationships) are reduced to relations. This conversion process is done entirely at a conceptual level and results in a new "normalized" entity-relationship structure.

5.2.1 Eliminating repeating simple attributes

Refer back to the definition of the entity PROFESSOR in Section 4.4.1.1 (Figure 4.8). This entity is denormalized because it contains a repeating simple attribute called professor_expertise_area. The entity PROFESSOR can be reduced to a relation in one of two ways:

1. by deciding on a maximum number of values of professor_expertise_area and replacing the repeating attribute by a set of simple attributes (where the cardinality of the set will be equal to the chosen maximum number);
2. by decomposing the entity to two entities and establishing a new binary univocal relationship between them.

The first solution does not cause changes to the entity-relationship diagram, but the definition of the entity in the data dictionary is affected. Figure 5.2 shows an example of the relation instance, corresponding to the entity PROFESSOR, after this first approach was applied. It is assumed that a professor can have up to three expertise areas. If a professor nominates less than three expertise areas, the null values (indicated by question marks) appear in the column(s). Figure 5.2 illustrates also that the entity-relationship diagram of Figure 4.8 remains unchanged.

The solution in Figure 5.2 is easy to apply. It requires only that the entity be redefined by replacing a repeating attribute with a fixed number of attributes. However, the solution is quite rigid and it may cause the loss of information. In our example, this will happen if some professors would like to nominate more than three expertise areas. Also, the solution introduces null values in attributes.

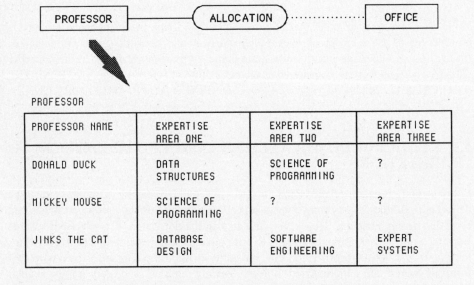

PROFESSOR

PROFESSOR NAME	EXPERTISE AREA ONE	EXPERTISE AREA TWO	EXPERTISE AREA THREE
DONALD DUCK	DATA STRUCTURES	SCIENCE OF PROGRAMMING	?
MICKEY MOUSE	SCIENCE OF PROGRAMMING	?	?
JINKS THE CAT	DATABASE DESIGN	SOFTWARE ENGINEERING	EXPERT SYSTEMS

Figure 5.2   Elimination of a simple repeating attribute in the entity PROFESSOR (Case 1)

The second solution in which the original entity is decomposed into two entities normally preferred. The changes to the diagram may go beyond the definition of a new relationship that joins two decomposed entities. They may, in fact, cascade to the relationships which, directly or indirectly, relate to the original entity. This is a problem of integration (Section 4.5). A normalized version of the diagram from Figure 4.8, obtained by the decomposition technique, is shown in Figure 5.3 and in the data dictionary definition which follows.

```
================= ENTITIES ==================

Name: EXPERTISE_AREA

Contains the Attributes:
        professor_expertise_area

Primary Key Consists of:
        professor_expertise_area

Connections:
        via: (1:N Total) NOMINATES (Weak)
                        to: PROFESSOR (1:1 Total)
```

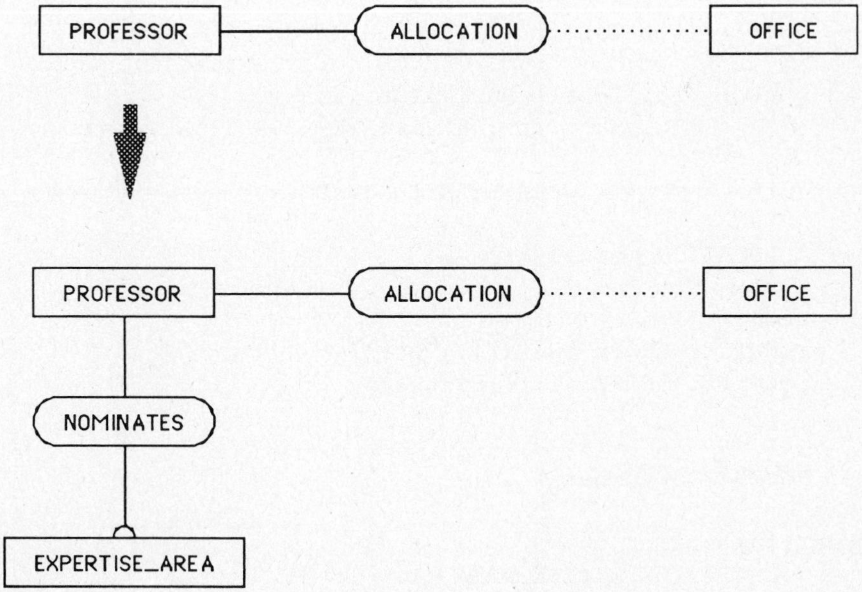

Figure 5.3   Elimination of a simple repeating attribute in the entity PROFESSOR (Case 2)

```
Name: OFFICE

Contains the Attributes:
        office_number
        office_size

Primary Key Consists of:
        office_number

Connections:
        via: (1:1 Partial) ALLOCATION (Weak)
                        to: PROFESSOR (1:1 Total)


----------------------------------------------------------------
Name: PROFESSOR

Contains the Attributes:
        professor_name
        date_of_birth

Primary Key Consists of:
        professor_name

Connections:
        via: (1:1 Total) ALLOCATION (Weak)
                        to: OFFICE (1:1 Partial)
        via: (1:1 Total) NOMINATES (Weak)
                        to: EXPERTISE_AREA (1:N Total)

  = = = = = = = = = = = = = =  WEAK RELATIONSHIPS = = = = = = = = = = =

Name: ALLOCATION (binary)

Connections to :
        ENTITY PROFESSOR (1:1 Total)
        ENTITY OFFICE (1:1 Partial)


----------------------------------------------------------------
Name: NOMINATES (binary)

Connections to :
        ENTITY EXPERTISE_AREA (1:N Total)
        ENTITY PROFESSOR (1:1 Total)


----------------------------------------------------------------
```

5.2.2 Eliminating group attributes

Refer back to the definition of the entity EMPLOYEE in Section 4.4.1.2 (Figure 4.9). This entity is denormalized because it contains a group attribute labeled employee_name. The entity EMPLOYEE can be reduced to a relation in one of two ways:

1. by demoting the group to a loose conglomeration of simple attributes;
2. by decomposing the entity to two entities and establishing a new binary univocal relationship between them.

   The first solution does not cause changes to the entity-relationship diagram, but the definition of the entity in the data dictionary is affected. The entity consists now of simple attributes and the group employee_name is eliminated. A new definition of the entity EMPLOYEE is shown below (cp. Section 4.4.1.2).

```
-----------------------------------------------------------------
Name: EMPLOYEE

Contains the Attributes:
        employee_number
        first_name
        middle_initial
        family_name

Primary Key Consists of:
        employee_number

Connections:
        via: (1:N Total) EMPLOYMENT (Weak)
                        to: DEPARTMENT (1:1 Total)
-----------------------------------------------------------------
```

   The above solution may not be acceptable if the structure of a group is more complicated or if the user wishes to be given full flexibility in referring both to a full name and any part of the name. The second solution responds well to these requirements. Figure 5.4 and the definition of the entity EMPLOYEE_NAME, which follows, illustrates the point. It is assumed, that a full employee name is a key of the entity EMPLOYEE_NAME.

```
-----------------------------------------------------------------
Name: EMPLOYEE_NAME

Contains the Attributes:
        first_name
        middle_initial
        family_name
```

```
Primary Key Consists of:
        family_name
        middle_initial
        first_name

Connections:
        via: (1:1 Total) HAS (Weak)
                        to: EMPLOYEE (1:1 Total)
```

- -

5.2.3   Eliminating repeating group attributes

The problem of the elimination of repeating group attributes has already been discussed in the context of the degree conflicts in view integration (Section 4.5.3.3). The entity PROJECT in view V2 in Figure 4.30 contains the repeating group called grant. The equivalent representation of PROJECT by means of view V1, in this figure, eliminates this repeating group. The elimination of a repeating group attribute is always done by means of decomposition of the entity with a repeating group into two entities and by establishing a binary univocal relationship between these entities. Figure 5.5 illustrates the transformation principle. The data dictionary entries are described in Section 4.5.3.3.

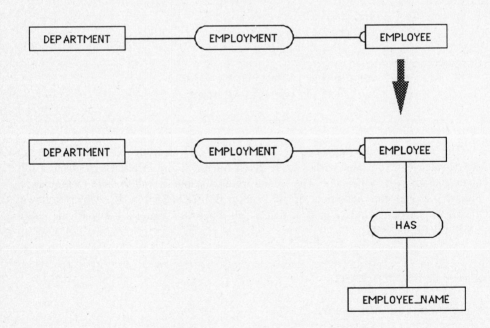

Figure 5.4   Elimination of a group attribute in the entity EMPLOYEE (Case 2).

5.3   CONVERTING PRIMITIVE ENTITY-RELATIONSHIP CONSTRUCTS TO RELATIONAL STRUCTURES

The aim of the reduction of conceptual objects to relations is to facilitate the conversion rules from entity-relationship constructs to relational structures. All conceptual objects are now "normalized", that is, they are at least in first normal form. Under this assumption, we will formulate the conversion rules for all typical entity-relationship constructs. The DD definitions for all constructs discussed are given in Section 4.4.

Because the relationships in the relational model are expressed by means of attribute values (referential integrity), there is a need to show primary and foreign keys of relations in the graphical representation of the relational conversion. A foreign key that matches the primary key in the same or other relation(s) establishes the relationship. Such a relationship can be explicitly shown in the relational diagram by drawing an arrowed line from a foreign key to the primary key.

The line is solid when the foreign key does not admit null values, otherwise it is dotted. An attribute of the primary key is placed in a dark-shaded box while a light-shaded box is used to indicate an attribute of the foreign key. If an attribute of the primary key is also an element of the foreign key, then the primary key visualization (dark shading) is given priority. In such a situation, the connection line is used to indicate that the attribute is also an element of the foreign key.

In most conversion cases, it is possible to have more than one acceptable conversion. Most of the time, however, there is a conversion which is clearly superior to the others. The superiority relates usually to the issue of redundancy minimalization. If it is at all feasible, the conversion which does not introduce null values in a foreign key is superior to a functionally equivalent conversion which allows for null values in a foreign key. Here, only the superior conversions are illustrated diagrammatically and discussed in depth.

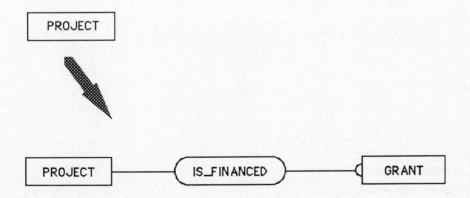

Figure 5.5   Elimination of a repeating group attribute in the entity PROJECT

We note, however, that the superior conversions may sometimes be inapplicable as a result of the existence of relations created by earlier conversions. In general, the history of conversions and the existing relations must be taken into account in converting any next relationship to a relational structure. This issue is addressed by the research into logical view integration.

5.3.1   Converting a binary singular relationship

Figure 5.6 illustrates the conversion of the binary singular relationship ALLOCATION (Figure 4.8) into a relational structure. The primary key of OFFICE relation appears as a foreign key in the PROFESSOR relation. This takes account of the fact that the membership of PROFESSOR entity in ALLOCATION is total. The foreign key 'office_number' does not allow null values. This is indicated by the solid line from it to the primary key of OFFICE.

In general, should the membership of the entity OFFICE in ALLOCATION be total, the primary key of either relation could appear in the other relation as a foreign key. As it stands, placing the foreign key in OFFICE relation would require more storage space than in the solution presented in Figure 5.6.

If the membership of both entities was partial, either relation could contain the foreign key with nulls allowed. A better design, however, would take into consideration the level of partiality, that is, which of the foreign keys would be expected to contain less null values.

If the null values were expected to be frequent in either solution, a preferable design could be to create the relationship relation ALLOCATION (Figure 5.7). Either 'professor_name' or 'office_number' can be chosen as primary key of ALLOCATION. In Figure 5.7, 'office_number' is the primary key and 'professor_name' is a candidate key. Both attributes are foreign keys matching primary keys of the respective entity relations.

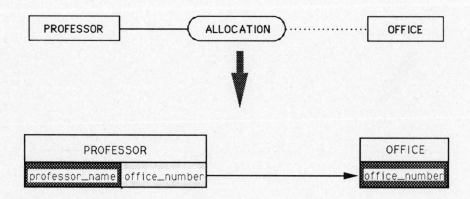

Figure 5.6   Converting a binary singular relationship

5.3.2 Converting a binary univocal relationship

Figure 5.8 illustrates the conversion of the binary univocal relationship EMPLOYMENT (Figure 4.9) into a relational structure. The foreign key appears at the N side of the relationship. Null values are not allowed for the foreign key because the membership of EMPLOYEE entity in EMPLOYMENT is total.

5.3.3 Converting a binary nonunivocal relationship

The conversion of the binary nonunivocal relationship ENROLMENT (Figure 4.10) is shown in Figure 5.9. Such a conversion requires a relationship relation ENROLMENT. This relation obtains the primary key as a concatenation of primary key attributes of both

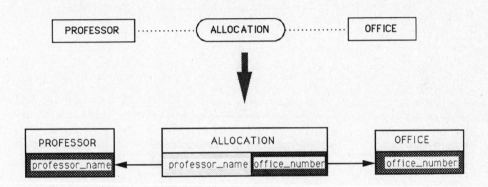

Figure 5.7   Converting a binary singular relationship with partial entities

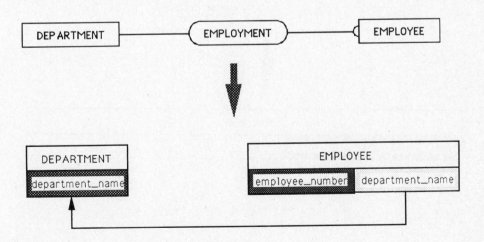

Figure 5.8   Converting a binary univocal relationship

entities. The relationship ENROLMENT is regular and contains the attribute 'date_of_enrolment'. This attribute is incorporated in the relation ENROLMENT.

5.3.4   Converting a unary singular relationship

Figure 5.10 illustrates the conversion of the unary singular relationship MARRIAGE (Figure 4.11) into a relational scheme. The primary key of the relation EMPLOYEE is {employee_name, date_of_birth}. The foreign key {spouse_employee_name, spouse_date_of_birth} consists of attributes drawn from the same domains from which the attributes of the primary key are derived. The foreign key accepts null values, as it is indicated by a dotted relationship line.

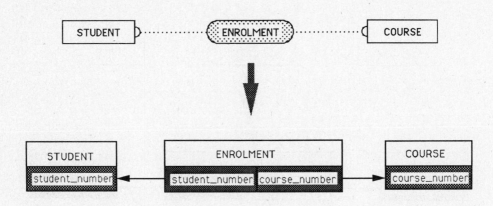

Figure 5.9   Converting a binary nonunivocal relationship

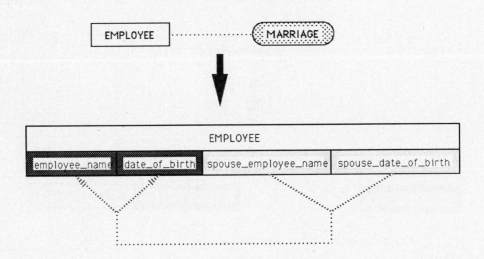

Figure 5.10   Converting a unary singular relationship

If the foreign key is expected to contain many null values, then a preferred solution could be to create a relationship relation MARRIAGE. Such a relationship relation would have identical primary and foreign keys as the relation EMPLOYEE in Figure 5.10. The foreign key in the relation MARRIAGE would not admit null values. In such a solution, the entity relation EMPLOYEE would contain the same attributes as the original entity EMPLOYEE.

5.3.5 Converting a unary univocal relationship

Figure 5.11 illustrates the conversion of the unary univocal relationship MANAGERIAL_STRUCTURE (Figure 4.12) into a relational scheme. The primary key of the relation EMPLOYEE is employee_number. The foreign key manager_ employee_number has been created to support the relationship. Interestingly, the foreign key accepts null values despite the total membership of the entity EMPLOYEE in the relationship. In reality, the foreign key will have only one null value in the tuple describing a top manager (the managing director) of a company. To allow for this one null value the relationship line, which expresses the referential integrity, must be dotted.

5.3.6 Converting a unary nonunivocal relationship

Figure 5.12 illustrates the conversion of the unary nonunivocal relationship BILL_OF_MATERIAL (Figure 4.13) into a relational diagram. The relationship is represented in the relational model by means of a relationship relation. The primary key of the relationship relation BILL_OF_MATERIAL consists of two attributes drawn from the common domain of item_number values. The attributes are named here 'major_item_number' and 'minor_item_number'. They also serve as foreign keys matching the primary key of the entity relation ITEM. Note, that the foreign keys do not accept null values.

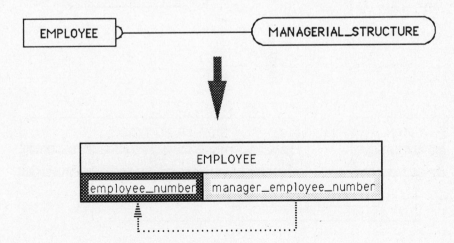

Figure 5.11 Converting a unary univocal relationship

5.3.7 Converting a ternary singular relationship

Figure 5.13 demonstrates the conversion of the ternary singular relationship with unblended semantics FAMILY_UNIT (Figure 4.14) into a relational diagram. The relationship is represented in the relational model by means of a relationship relation. The relationship relation FAMILY_UNIT has three candidate keys. One of these primary keys, namely 'residence_address', is arbitrarily chosen the primary key. The three candidate keys serve as foreign keys matching the primary keys of the three entity relations RESIDENCE, MAN and WOMAN. None of the foreign keys accept null values.

The conversion of the ternary singular relationship with pair-wise semantics FAMILY_UNIT (Figure 4.15) into a relational diagram is shown in Figure 5.14. A major difference with the conversion in Figure 5.13 is that the relationship relation FAMILY_UNIT has different candidate keys. The FAMILY_UNIT relation has three composite candidate keys: {woman_name, man_name}, {residence_address, man_name}, {residence_address, woman_name}. The first of these three possibilities is arbitrarily chosen the primary key.

5.3.8 Converting a ternary semi-univocal relationship

Figure 5.15 illustrates the conversion of the ternary semi-univocal relationship JOB (Figure 4.16) into a relational diagram. The relationship is retained in the relational model as a relationship relation. The relationship relation JOB has two candidate keys: {employee_number, supervisor_name} and {employee_number, project_number}. The first has been chosen the primary key.

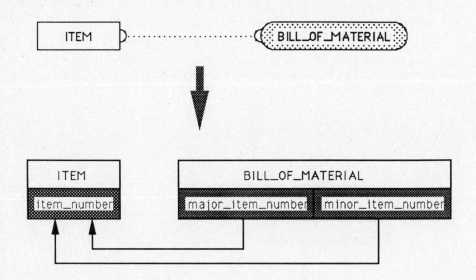

Figure 5.12   Converting a unary nonunivocal relationship

5.3.9   Converting a ternary nonunivocal relationship

Figure 5.16 illustrates the conversion of the ternary nonunivocal relationship DELIVERY (Figure 4.17) into a relational diagram. The relationship DELIVERY is regular and is identified by its own attribute 'delivery_consecutive_number'. This attribute becomes the primary key of the relationship relation DELIVERY. The foreign keys in DELIVERY are 'warehouse_number', 'track_registration_number' and 'customer_name'. They correspond to the primary keys in the entity relations WAREHOUSE, TRUCK and CUSTOMER.

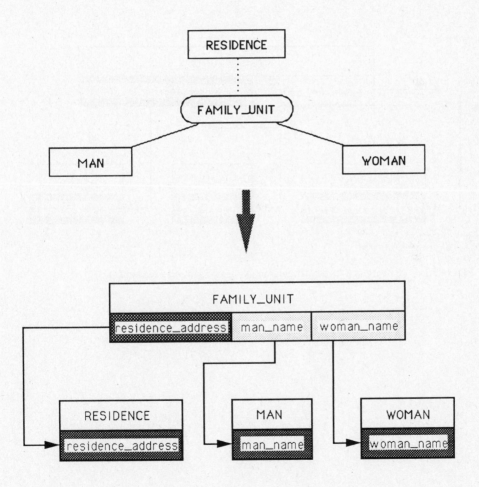

Figure 5.13   Converting a ternary singular relationship (unblended semantics)

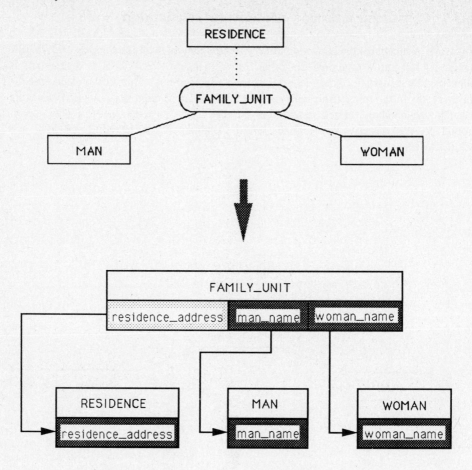

Figure 5.14   Converting a ternary singular relationship (pair-wise semantics)

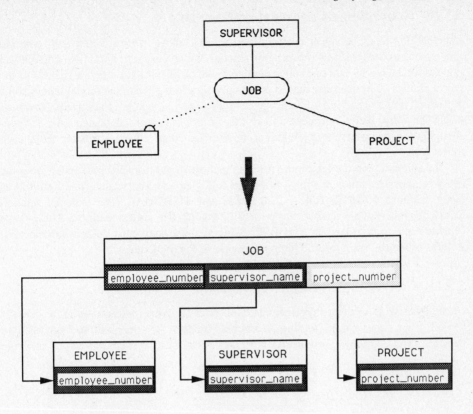

Figure 5.15 Converting a ternary semi-univocal relationship

5.3.10   Converting an aggregate relationship

Aggregation, being a hypersemantic abstraction, allows for a variety of possible conversions to the relational model. One solution which comes to mind is to combine an aggregation hierarchy into one superset relation which physically inherits attributes of the subset entities. (Physical inheritance is the only way in the relational model unless some procedural implementation of inheritance is provided.) Such a relationship, however, would be very badly normalized and this solution is not advocated. As a better alternative, a distinct superset relation can be created to inherit attributes from each subset entity.

The solution presented in Figure 5.17 is the most straightforward conversion from the entity-relationship structure shown in Figure 4.18. The solution retains subset entities as entity relations LABORATORY, LECTURE and TUTORIAL. The superset relation COURSE inherits physically the primary keys of the subset entities. These keys constitute the foreign keys in COURSE. Since a course may exist without laboratories, lectures or tutorial assigned, the foreign keys can accept null values.

5.3.11   Converting a generic relationship

Generalization is another hypersemantic abstraction which allows quite a deal of flexibility in conversion to the relational model. As opposed to aggregation, generalization employs top-down attribute inheritance. This top-down attribute

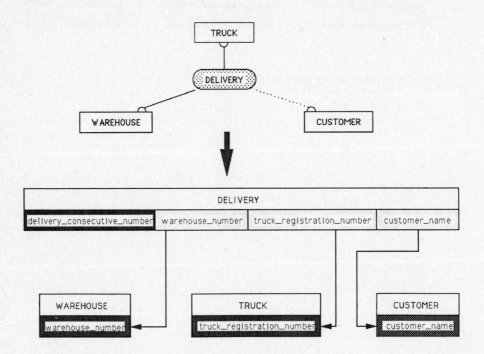

Figure 5.16   Converting a ternary nonunivocal relationship

inheritance is signified by the fact that the foreign keys in the subtype relations match the primary key of the supertype relation (if the supertype relation is retained in the conversion).

Figure 5.18 illustrates the conversion of the generic relationship BANK (Figure 4.19) to a relational structure. Because of the overlapping character of the subtype entities TELLER and CUSTOMER, the supertype entity PERSON must be retained in the conversion. The foreign keys in TELLER and CUSTOMER match the primary key of the supertype relation PERSON. They do not accept null values.

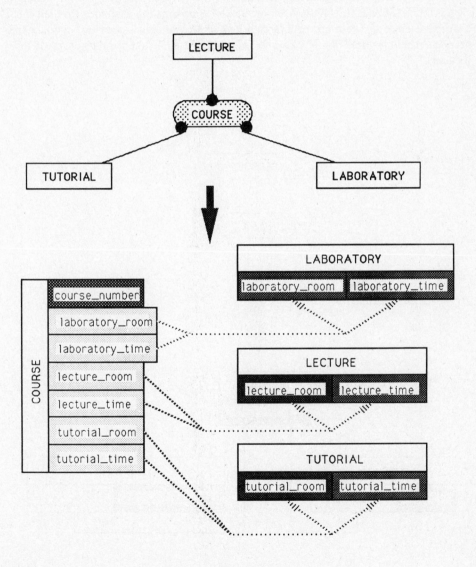

Figure 5.17   Converting an aggregate relationship

5.3.12   Converting a nested relationship

The hypersemantics involved in nested relationships can differ significantly, depending on the database designer's preferences. Hence, it is not possible to specify universal conversion rules. Each nested relationship is specific and should be addressed as such.

Figure 5.19 illustrates the conversion of the nested relationship ACCOUNT_TRANSACTION (Figure 4.20) to a relational structure. In the conversion, all objects from Figure 4.20 have been converted to relations. The primary keys of the entity CUSTOMER and the relationship ACCOUNT_TRANSACTION have been retained in their corresponding relations. The primary key of the relation CUSTOMER_STATEMENT has been created by concatenating attributes from all three conceptual objects. There are two foreign keys which establish necessary associations between relations. Both foreign keys are attributes used in the primary keys of their relations.

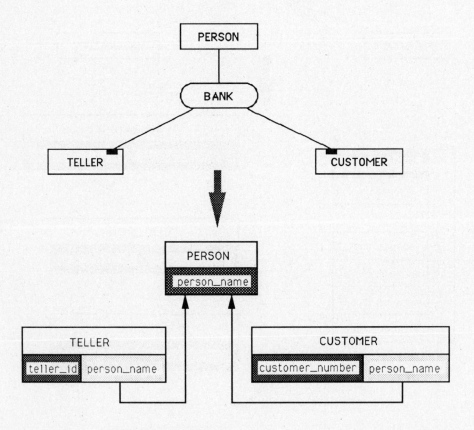

Figure 5.18   Converting a generic relationship

5.4 REFINING RELATIONAL SCHEMA BY NORMALIZATION

At times, the primitive conversions discussed in the previous section may be rendered inapplicable due to restrictions imposed by the relations already existing in the schema. The relations derived in earlier conversions must be considered in the conversions that follow. The conversion process has an incremental character and the order in which the relationships are picked for conversions determines the final relational schema. It is possible, and indeed likely, to obtain different schemas by changing the sequence in which the relationships are converted.

The problem of incremental conversion is a special case of logical view integration in which a new set of relations is superimposed on the current schema. Unless backtracking to previous conversions is allowed, the current schema is not expected to undergo structural changes. A likely result of the incremental building of a relational schema is that relations will have attributes added and the level of normalization will be decreased. There is a need, therefore, to refine the relational schema by normalization.

When establishing a "good" normalization level in a process-driven approach to database design, the designer can rely on information gathered about business functions and anticipated processing patterns. In a data-driven approach, a "good" normalization level (sometimes named, quite groundlessly, "optimal") is usually considered to be BCNF or 3NF (brave souls refer instead to 5NF).

Independently of the design approach, the designer should begin with the observation, which follows, on the two classes of databases and their implications on normalization.

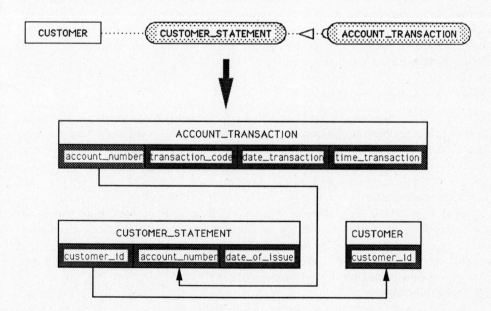

Figure 5.19 Converting a nested relationship

The two classes are: (1) typical data processing systems with frequent updates (e.g. payroll, inventory, wholesale distribution, accounting, banking); and (2) information retrieval systems, oriented towards textual (unformatted) data (e.g. office automation, library information, pharmaceutical and medical databases). The former class is sensitive to update anomalies and data inconsistencies which are known to be preventable by normalization rules. The latter class is mainly interested in minimizing the number of objects that must be retrieved in order to answer a query. That aim can often be achieved by the denormalization of objects.

The above observation can be enriched in a data-driven approach by using the following general heuristic:

General normalization heuristic

Since business functions are classified into queries (Q-functions) and updates (U-functions) (Section 3.2.2), take the relative design ranks of functions FR (Section 4.5.2) and sum them respectively to get FR of the set of Q-functions $\Sigma \, FR_Q$ and FR of the set of U-functions $\Sigma \, FR_U$. Decide on one of the following refinement strategies:

1. If $\Sigma \, FR_Q \geq 0.7$ (hence $\Sigma \, FR_U < \Sigma \, FR_Q$) then you can further denormalize the relations.
2. If $\Sigma \, FR_U \geq 0.7$ (hence $\Sigma \, FR_U > \Sigma \, FR_Q$) then you can further normalize the relations.
3. If $|\Sigma \, FR_U - \Sigma \, FR_Q| < 0.4$ then consider the current design "good" and do not proceed with the refinement by normalization (status quo).

The general normalization heuristic is purposely not very specific on how much to normalize or denormalize. A uniform approach to all relations, such as: "normalize all relations up to BCNF", is not acceptable. The relations should be considered on an individual basis, taking into account access graphs of functions (Section 4.3). The following heuristic addresses this issue.

Specific normalization heuristic

Consider the access graphs of functions and, for each relation R of the relational schema, determine the number of Q-functions $\#Q_R$ and U-functions $\#U_R$ used against them. Apply one of the following refinement principles, depending on the strategy chosen in the general normalization heuristic:

1. Further denormalize:
   (a) if $\#Q_R \geq \#U_R$, then you can denormalize R to 1NF by combining with it, if possible, other relations with the same primary key or other relations which refer to a candidate key of R by means of a foreign key;
   (b) otherwise, if $\#Q_R < \#U_R$, then you can denormalize R by one level down or, if that is not easily possible, leave R unchanged.
2. Further normalize:
   (a) if $\#U_R \geq \#Q_R$, then you can normalize R to 5NF;
   (b) otherwise, if $\#U_R < \#Q_R$, then you can normalize R by one level up or, if that is not easily achievable, leave R unchanged.

5.5   NORMALIZATION ALGORITHMS

There are two classical normalization methods—decomposition and synthesis. The objective of these classical approaches is to achieve the highest possible normalization level of a relational schema. The algorithms aim to achieve 3NF relation schemes for any particular design problem. The problem of determining whether a 3NF relation is in BCNF has been shown to be computationally infeasible (i.e. *NP*-hard). The determination of 4NF and 5NF faces problems of semantic fuzziness, as discussed in Sections 2.5.6–2.5.9.

A common feature of the classical approaches to normalization is that the set of attributes and dependencies is known *a priori*. In addition, the decomposition assumes the existence of some intitial relation schemes. *Decomposition* is a top-down approach which commences with an existing relation, investigates its normal form and decomposes it (using the relational projection operation) until relation schemes in desired normal forms are achieved. *Synthesis* is a bottom-up approach which begins with a nonredundant set of functional dependencies and combines the attributes involved in those dependencies into normal form (in practice, 3NF) relation schemes.

5.5.1   Theory of functional dependencies

Functional, multivalued, join and other data dependencies express integrity constraints that should be preserved by a database. Unfortunately, it is known that higher normal form relations may not be *dependency preserving*. This means that achieving a higher normal form may not always be desirable. The foundation of currently available normalization algorithms lies in the functional dependencies.

When using normalization algorithms, in particular synthesis, it is important to ensure that the initial set of functional dependencies is as complete as possible. In general, given a set of functional dependencies, it can be deduced that certain other functional dependencies also hold in the database. Inference axioms (known as *Armstrong's rules*) are used to derive new dependencies from a given set of dependencies. There are three axioms that are sound and complete. Given that X, Y and W are sets of attributes, these axioms are:

Reflexivity	if $X \supseteq Y$, then $X \rightarrow Y$.
Augmentation	if $X \rightarrow Y$ and $W \supseteq Z$, then $XW \rightarrow YZ$.
Transitivity	if $X \rightarrow Y$ and $Y \rightarrow Z$, then $X \rightarrow Z$.

The axioms are *sound* because they do not infer any incorrect dependencies. They are *complete* because they lead to the derivation of the closure. The *closure* of a set F of dependencies, denoted F^+, is the set of all dependencies that can be derived from F by using a complete set of axioms. In practice, it is convenient to use three additional axioms for the computation of F^+. These are:

Pseudotransitivity	if $X \rightarrow Y$ and $YW \rightarrow Z$, then $XW \rightarrow Z$.
Union	if $X \rightarrow Y$ and $X \rightarrow Z$, then $X \rightarrow YZ$.
Decomposition	if $X \rightarrow YZ$, then $X \rightarrow Y$ and $X \rightarrow Z$.

As an example:

If
$F =$ {{student_id → student_name},
        {student_name → {student_address, student_phone_number}}
then
$F^+ =$ {{student_id → student_name},
        {student_name → {student_address, student_phone_number},
        {student_name} → {student_address},
        {student_name} → {student_phone_number},
        {student_id} → {student_address},
        {student_id} → {student_phone_number},
        {student_id} → {student_address, student_phone_number}}

The presented closure F^+ does not include so-called *trivial* dependencies, such as {student_id} → {student_id}. It can be seen that even for a very small initial set of functional dependencies, the closure is quite large. Therefore, to make the normalization algorithms applicable, we are interested in the minimum size possible which can be representative of the closure. This is done by forming the set F' which has the same closure F^+ as F; such a set is called a *cover* of F. In general, the sets F and F' are said to cover each other if they have the same closure. The minimum size set F' is called a *nonredundant cover* which means that no proper subset of it is a cover of F.

For example, suppose that for a given set of functional dependencies F, the following cover has been derived:

$C' =$ {{invoice_number → order_number},
        {order_number → customer_name},
        {invoice_number → customer_name}}

The cover C' is redundant. A nonredundant cover might be:

$C'' =$ {{invoice_number → order_number},
        {order_number → customer_name}}

Redundant functional dependencies create problems for normalization algorithms. It is important to be able to start normalization with the nonredundant set of functional dependencies. To achieve this, we must be able to determine whether or not any particular functional dependency can be derived from the given set of functional dependencies by applying inference axioms. The method for detecting redundant functional dependencies is known as the *membership algorithm*. From several variations of the membership algorithm, we present the one which has simple interpretation but is computationally expensive.

Membership algorithm

0.   Let $F = \{f_1, f_2, \dots , f_n\}$ be a set of functional dependencies defined over the set of attributes $\{A_1, A_2, \dots , A_m\}$. And let SET be a set of attributes which determines whether or not a functional dependency under consideration is redundant.

1a. Eliminate extraneous attributes from the determinant of each functional dependency of F. An attribute is extraneous if its elimination does not alter the closure F^+ of F. Define new F, if any extraneous attributes have been eliminated.

1b. To obtain a shorter description of F, apply the union axiom to group the functional dependencies with the same determinant into a single functional dependency.

2. Take each f_i from F and determine if it can be derived from $F' = F - f_i$. Initialize SET $= A_i$, where A_i is the determinant of f_i. In doing so, we make use of the reflexivity axiom which can generate a trivial dependency such that $A_i \rightarrow A_i$.

3a. To find new attributes to add to SET, select a functional dependency in F' whose determinant is contained in SET, but whose right side is not. By union and transitivity, the right side of this functional dependency can be added to SET.

3b. Repeat Step 3a every time SET is expanded until no new functional dependencies qualify and no more attributes can be added.

4. If, at the conclusion of Steps 3 and 4, the right side of f_i is in SET then, by decomposition, f_i can be derived from the other functional dependencies and therefore f_i is redundant.

We will now apply the membership algorithm to a simple example:

Step 0   F = {{project_name} $\rightarrow$ {supervisor_name, start_date},
             {project_name, start_date} $\rightarrow$ {grant_name},
             {grant_name, supervisor_name} $\rightarrow$ {start_date},
             {project_name, supervisor_name} $\rightarrow$ {grant_name}}

Step 1a   This is a semantic decision which must remain the designer's responsibility. Any mistakes or omissions are likely to result in a semantically distorted minimal cover. In our case, we assume that the designer discovered an extraneous attribute supervisor_name in the third functional dependency. The new set F is:

           F = {{project_name} $\rightarrow$ {supervisor_name, start_date},
             {project_name, start_date} $\rightarrow$ {grant_name},
             {grant_name} $\rightarrow$ {start_date},
             {project_name, supervisor_name} $\rightarrow$ {grant_name}}

Step 1b   Not applicable

Step 2   Consider {project_name} $\rightarrow$ {supervisor_name, start_date}
            SET = {project_name}

Step 3   No additions can be made to SET

Step 4   {project_name} $\rightarrow$ {supervisor_name, start_date} is not redundant

Step 2   Consider {project_name, start_date} $\rightarrow$ {grant_name}
            SET = {project_name, start _date}

Step 3   SET = {project_name, start_date, supervisor_name} because
{project_name} → {supervisor_name, start_date} and
{project_name, start _date} ⊇ {project_name}

SET = {project_name, start _date, supervisor_name, grant_name} because
{project_name, supervisor_name} → {grant_name} and
{project_name, start_date, supervisor_name} ⊇
{project_name, supervisor_name}

Step 4   Now, {grant_name} is in SET.
Hence, {project_name, start_date} → {grant_name} is redundant and is
removed from F

Step 0   F = {{project_name} → {supervisor_name, start_date},
    {grant_name} → {start_date},
    {project_name, supervisor_name} → {grant_name}}

Step 1   Not applicable (it can never be applicable in other than the first iteration)

Step 2   Consider {grant_name} → {start_date}
SET = {grant_name}

Step 3   No additions can be made to SET

Step 4   {grant_name} → {start_date} is not redundant

Step 2   Consider {project_name, supervisor_name} → {grant_name}
SET = {project_name, supervisor_name}

Step 3   SET = {project_name, supervisor_name, start_date} because
{project_name} → {supervisor_name, start_date} and
{project_name, supervisor_name} ⊇ {project_name}

Step 4   At this step, because {project_name, start_date} → {grant_name} was
redundant and deleted from F, {project_name, supervisor_name} →
{grant_name} must be concluded nonredundant

Therefore, the minimal cover of F is:

F' = {{project_name} → {supervisor_name, start_date},
    {grant_name} → {start_date},
    {project_name, supervisor_name} → {grant_name}}.

5.5.2 Synthesis

A primary application of the membership algorithm is in the preparation for the use of a synthesis algorithm. The best known synthesis algorithm, known as *Bernstein's algorithm*, takes a nonredundant set of functional dependencies and produces a 3NF relational schema.

Bernstein's synthesis algorithm
0. Apply the membership algorithm (Section 5.5.1) to find the nonredundant cover, F', of F.
1. Partition functional dependencies F' into groups such that the determinants in each group are identical.
2. Merge groups with equivalent keys, that is, any two groups with determinants X and Y, such that there is a bijection $X \rightarrow Y$ and $Y \rightarrow X$ in the closure of F'. Repeat this step until no equivalent keys are found.
3. Eliminate transitive dependencies (Section 2.5.2 and 2.5.4).
4. Construct relation schemes from the groups, such that the determinants are candidate keys.

The operations in Bernstein's algorithm are syntactic in nature and the semantic interpretation of them in terms of real world situations must be controlled by the designer. In particular, the designer must ensure that all attributes used in functional dependencies are unique. This means that any two attributes with the same name, used in any of the functional dependencies, must have identical semantic interpretation. For instance, in the two functional dependencies invoice_number $\rightarrow$ date and order_number $\rightarrow$ date, the *uniqueness assumption* is violated. The attribute date means the date of an invoice in the first case, and the date of an order in the second case.

The principle of Bernstein's algorithm is simple. Given a nonredundant cover of a set of functional dependencies, the designer groups all dependencies with the same or equivalent determinants and constructs a relation for each such group. Since, as a result of merging equivalent keys in Step 2, the groups can exhibit transitive dependencies, they are discovered and eliminated in Step 3. In reality, Step 3 is a decomposition process, rather than a synthesizing operation.

As an illustration, let us discuss Bernstein's algorithm in the light of the following set of functional dependencies:

F = {{invoice_number, item_number} $\rightarrow$ {quantity_back_ordered},
    {item_number, requisition_number} $\rightarrow$ {quantity_back_ordered},
    {invoice_number} $\rightarrow$ {requisition_number},
    {item_number} $\rightarrow$ {item_description},
    {item_description} $\rightarrow$ {item_number},
    {item_description} $\rightarrow$ {warehouse_number},
    {item_number} $\rightarrow$ {warehouse_location},
    {item_number} $\rightarrow$ {item_price},
    {item_number} $\rightarrow$ {unit_of_measure}}

Step 0   The dependency {invoice_number, item_number} →
         {quantity_back_ordered} is redundant, as follows:
         SET_1 = {invoice_number, item_number}
         SET_2 = {invoice_number, item_number, requisition_number} because
                 {invoice_number} → {requisition_number} and
                 {invoice_number, item_number} ⊇ {invoice_number}
         SET_3 = {invoice_number, item_number, requisition_number,
                 quantity_back_ordered} because
                 {item_number, requisition_number} → {quantity_back_ordered} and
                 {invoice_number, item_number, requisition_number} ⊇
                 {item_number, requisition_number}
      Now,   {quantity_back_ordered}   is   in   SET.   Hence,   {invoice_number,
      item_number} → {quantity_back_ordered} is redundant.

F' = {{item_number, requisition_number} → {quantity_back_ordered},
     {invoice_number} → {requisition_number},
     {item_number} → {item_description},
     {item_description} → {item_number},
     {item_description} → {warehouse_number},
     {item_number} → {warehouse_location},
     {item_number} → {item_price},
     {item_number} → {unit_of_measure}}

Step 1 $Group_1$ = {item_number, requisition_number, quantity_back_ordered}
         $Group_2$ = {invoice_number, requisition_number}
         $Group_3$ = {item_number, item_description, warehouse_location,
                 item_price, unit_of_measure}
         $Group_4$ = {item_description, item_number, warehouse_number}

Step 2 $Group_1$ = {item_number, requisition_number, quantity_back_ordered}
         $Group_2$ = {invoice_number, requisition_number}
         $Group_3$ = {item_number, item_description, warehouse_location,
                 item_price, unit_of_measure, warehouse_number}

As a result of merging equivalent keys in Step 2, the following transitive dependency is
discovered in the synthesized group $Group_3$:

{item_number} → {warehouse_number},
{warehouse_number} ↛ {item_number},
{warehouse_number} → {warehouse_location}.

$Group_3$ must be decomposed to eliminate the transitive dependency:

Step 3 $Group_1$ = {item_number, requisition_number, quantity_back_ordered}
         $Group_2$ = {invoice_number, requisition_number}

$Group_3$ = {item_number, item_description, item_price,
            unit_of_measure, warehouse_number}
$Group_5$ = {warehouse_number, warehouse_location}

Step 4 $Relation_1$ = {item_number, requisition_number, quantity_back_ordered}
         Key is {item_number, requisition_number}
       $Relation_2$ = {invoice_number, requisition_number}
         Key is {invoice_number}
       $Relation_3$ = {item_number, item_description, item_price,
         unit_of_measure, warehouse_number}
         Candidate keys are: (1) {item_number},
         (2) {item_description}
       $Relation_5$ = {warehouse_number, warehouse_location}
         Key is {warehouse_number}

Apart from its syntactic nature, Bernstein's algorithm has other shortcomings. One such shortcoming is that it cannot be extended to the derivation of BCNF relations, which are often considered preferable to 3NF schemes and which are simpler to understand. Another shortcoming is that Bernstein's algorithm does not ensure *dependency preservation* and the *lossless join property* in the derived 3NF relations.

The first shortcoming, that it cannot be extended to the derivation of BCNF relations, flows from the fact that there are some sets of functional dependencies that cannot be represented by any BCNF relational schema. Consider the following nonredundant cover of functional dependencies:

F' = {{student_name, student_address} → {phone_number},
     {phone_number} → {student_address}

It is clear that, in a relational schema that represents F, one of the relations will contain {student_name, student_address, phone_number} with the key {student_name, student_address}. This relation is not in BCNF. The decomposition of this relation into R1{student_address, phone_number} and R2{student_name, phone_number} is not dependency preserving and, therefore, leads to the second shortcoming, that of not ensuring dependency preservation or the lossless join property.

To explain this second shortcoming, let us refer to a subset of functional dependencies used in our original example:

F =   {{invoice_number, item_number} → {quantity_back_ordered},
     {item_number, requisition_number} → {quantity_back_ordered},
     {invoice_number} → {requisition_number}}

We showed in the above that a nonredundant cover of F can be:

F' =   {{item_number, requisition_number} → {quantity_back_ordered},
     {invoice_number} → {requisition_number}

By Bernstein's algorithm, the following two 3NF relation schemes are obtained:

Relation₁ =   {item_number, requisition_number, quantity_back_ordered}
              Key is {item_number, requisition_number}
Relation₂ =   {invoice_number, requisition_number}
              Key is {invoice_number}

This relational schema does not preserve the dependency {invoice_number, item_number} → {quantity_back_ordered} and it does not satisfy the lossless join property. To illustrate this problem, we show the ORACLE definition (DESCRIBE statement) and content (SELECT * statement) of the original relation LOSSY, then the definition and content of the two 3NF relations LOSSY1 and LOSSY2. These relations are then joined by means of another SELECT command to prove that the decomposition was lossy (there are two spurious tuples in the joined relation).

```
SQL> DESCRIBE LOSSY
 Name                                 Null?      Type
 ----------------------------------   --------   ---------
 INVOICE_NUMBER                       NOT NULL   CHAR(12)
 ITEM_NUMBER                          NOT NULL   CHAR(12)
 REQUISITION_NUMBER                   NOT NULL   CHAR(12)
 QUANTITY_BACK_ORDERED                           NUMBER


SQL> SELECT * FROM LOSSY;

 INVOICE        ITEM           REQUISITION    QUANTITY
 NUMBER         NUMBER         NUMBER         BACK ORDERED
 -----------    -----------    -----------    -----------
 INV157         IT2988         REQ764                   15
 INV158         IT3001         REQ764                   23
 INV160         IT4333         REQ800                   23


SQL> DESCRIBE LOSSY1
 Name                                 Null?      Type
 ----------------------------------   --------   ---------
 ITEM_NUMBER                          NOT NULL   CHAR(12)
 REQUISITION_NUMBER                   NOT NULL   CHAR(12)
 QUANTITY_BACK_ORDERED                           NUMBER


SQL> DESCRIBE LOSSY2
 Name                                 Null?      Type
 ----------------------------------   --------   ---------
 INVOICE_NUMBER                       NOT NULL   CHAR(12)
 REQUISITION_NUMBER                              CHAR(12)
```

```
SQL> SELECT * FROM LOSSY1;

ITEM            REQUISITION  QUANTITY
NUMBER          NUMBER       BACK ORDERED
------------    ------------ ------------
IT2988          REQ764                 15
IT3001          REQ764                 23
IT4333          REQ800                 23


SQL> SELECT * FROM LOSSY2;

INVOICE         REQUISITION
NUMBER          NUMBER
------------    ------------
INV157          REQ764
INV158          REQ764
INV160          REQ800


SQL> SELECT DISTINCT INVOICE_NUMBER, ITEM_NUMBER,
  2               LOSSY1.REQUISITION_NUMBER,
  3               LOSSY1.QUANTITY_BACK_ORDERED
  4             FROM LOSSY1, LOSSY2
  5           WHERE LOSSY1.REQUISITION_NUMBER =
  6                 LOSSY2.REQUISITION_NUMBER;


INVOICE         ITEM         REQUISITION  QUANTITY
NUMBER          NUMBER       NUMBER       BACK ORDERED
------------    ------------ ------------ ------------
INV157          IT2988       REQ764                 15
INV157          IT3001       REQ764                 23
INV158          IT2988       REQ764                 15
INV158          IT3001       REQ764                 23
INV160          IT4333       REQ800                 23
```

To satisfy the lossless join property, an extra relation {invoice_number, item_number, quantity_back_ordered} is needed. This relation is named LOSSLESS in the ORACLE example below. A join of the three decomposed relations is nonloss.

```
SQL> DESCRIBE LOSSLESS
 Name                                     Null?      Type
 ---------------------------------------  ---------  ---------
 INVOICE_NUMBER                           NOT NULL   CHAR(12)
 ITEM_NUMBER                              NOT NULL   CHAR(12)
 QUANTITY_BACK_ORDERED                               NUMBER
```

```
SQL> SELECT * FROM LOSSLESS;

    INVOICE        ITEM           QUANTITY
    NUMBER         NUMBER         BACK ORDERED
    -----------    -----------    ------------
    INV157         IT2988                   15
    INV158         IT3001                   23
    INV160         IT4333                   23

SQL> SELECT DISTINCT LOSSLESS.INVOICE_NUMBER,
  2                         LOSSY1.ITEM_NUMBER,
  3                         LOSSY1.REQUISITION_NUMBER,
  4                         LOSSY1.QUANTITY_BACK_ORDERED
  5              FROM LOSSY1, LOSSY2, LOSSLESS
  6              WHERE LOSSLESS.INVOICE_NUMBER =
  7                     LOSSY2.INVOICE_NUMBER
  8                AND LOSSLESS.ITEM_NUMBER =
  9                     LOSSY1.ITEM_NUMBER
 10                AND LOSSY1.REQUISITION_NUMBER =
 11                     LOSSY2.REQUISITION_NUMBER;

    INVOICE        ITEM           REQUISITION    QUANTITY
    NUMBER         NUMBER         NUMBER         BACK ORDERED
    -----------    -----------    -----------    ------------
    INV157         IT2988         REQ764                   15
    INV158         IT3001         REQ764                   23
    INV160         IT4333         REQ800                   23
```

5.5.3 Decomposition

Decomposition develops the design through the following sequence of refinement steps:

1. Derive an initial set of relations for the database schema.
2. Find the set of functional, multivalued and join dependencies which hold in these relations at all times.
3. Use these dependencies and the normalization heuristics to reorganize the relations to the desired normal forms.

The discipline of decomposition tacitly assumes the existence of the so-called universal relation for a designed database system. The *universal relation* is a term used to denote a single relation which contains all attributes identified in the database system. Under the *universal relation assumption*, all relations in the database schema are projections of the universal relation. Hence, under this assumption, the first step of the decomposition algorithm can be replaced by:

(*) Construct the universal relation.

The usefulness of a universal relation, however, is questionable. First, it leads to a proliferation of attribute names since they must now have a global rather than a local meaning. Second, the inclusion of all attributes in a single relation forces the admission of nulls which can result in very few keys in the universal relation (or even no keys at all). Third, the definition of a multivalued dependency is at stake as it is couched in terms of a particular, usually small, relation and it is sensitive to this relation content.

The decomposition approach to normalization is less stringent than the synthesis, but it has the important advantage of being semantically richer. In fact, we used decomposition in presenting the normalization processes in Section 2.5. In this section, we will use the examples of relations from Section 2.5 to illustrate some fine points of decomposition.

The ORACLE SQL*Plus DESCRIBE command is used to give a full definition of the relations presented in Section 2.5. (The NOT NULL attributes indicate the primary keys of relations.) The contents of the relations are repeated for convenience (with the use of the SELECT * command) and the explanation as to why a discussed relation is in a particular normal form is recalled. Then the DESCRIBE command is used again to define the relations obtained from the decomposition of the original relation and the SELECT * command is then used to display the contents of the new relations. Additional discussion is provided, whenever necessary.

5.5.3.1   Decomposition of 1NF relation

1. Definition of the relation FIRSTNF (which is in 1NF, but not in 2NF):

```
SQL> DESCRIBE FIRSTNF
Name                                    Null?       Type
-------------------------------------   ---------   ---------
S#                                      NOT NULL    CHAR(4)
STATUS                                              NUMBER
CITY                                                CHAR(12)
P#                                      NOT NULL    CHAR(4)
QUANTITY                                            NUMBER
```

2. Current content of FIRSTNF (null values are indicated by the question mark):

```
SQL> SELECT * FROM FIRSTNF;

S#          STATUS CITY            P#        QUANTITY
-----   ----------   ------------   -----   -----------
S6          20 DARMSTADT     P5            100
S2          30 SAN JOSE      P6           2500
S2          30 SAN JOSE      P11           100
S8          40 WATERLOO      P4            200
S7          10 WOLLONGONG    P3            100
S4          10 FUKUOKA       P2            500
S21          ? ?             P2            250
```

In FIRSTNF, there are two functional dependencies: S# → STATUS and S# → CITY. Each S# has exactly one STATUS and is located in exactly one CITY. Both functional dependencies in FIRSTNF are partial because S# is a proper subset of the key {S#, P#} and, hence, FIRSTNF is not in 2NF. If the normalization heuristics (Section 5.4) suggest the need for a higher normal form, the relation FIRSTNF should be replaced by smaller relations.

3. Definition of the relations obtained from the decomposition of FIRSTNF:

```
SQL> DESCRIBE DECOMPOSE1A
Name                                  Null?      Type
------------------------------------- ---------- ---------
S#                                    NOT NULL   CHAR(4)
STATUS                                           NUMBER
CITY                                             CHAR(12)

SQL> DESCRIBE DECOMPOSE1B
Name                                  Null?      Type
------------------------------------- ---------- ---------
P#                                    NOT NULL   CHAR(4)
S#                                    NOT NULL   CHAR(4)
QUANTITY                                         NUMBER
```

4. Contents of the decomposed relations (Natural equi-join of these relations over S# will result in the relation FIRSTNF; such a join can, at the designer's discretion, be implemented as a view table.):

```
SQL> SELECT * FROM DECOMPOSE1A;

S#         STATUS CITY
-----  ----------- ------------
S6          20 DARMSTADT
S2          30 SAN JOSE
S8          40 WATERLOO
S7          10 WOLLONGONG
S4          10 FUKUOKA
S21          ? ?

SQL> SELECT * FROM DECOMPOSE1B;

P#     S#     QUANTITY
-----  -----  ----------
P5     S6          100
P6     S2         2500
P11    S2          100
```

```
P4      S8          200
P3      S7          100
P2      S4          500
P15     S4            ?
P2      S21         250
```

```
8 records selected.
```

5.5.3.2 Decomposition of 2NF relation

1. Definition of the relation SECONDNF (which is in 2NF, but not in 3NF):

```
SQL> DESCRIBE SECONDNF
Name                                    Null?      Type
----------------------------------- ---------- ---------
EMPLOYEE_FAMILY_NAME                    NOT    NULLCHAR(20)
DEPARTMENT_NAME                                CHAR(20)
LOCATION                                      CHAR(9)
```

2. Current content of SECONDNF:

```
SQL> SELECT * FROM SECONDNF;

EMPLOYEE_FAMILY_NAME    DEPARTMENT_NAME            LOCATION
--------------------- ---------------------- ----------
MACIASZEK               COMPUTING SCIENCE          KEANE BLD
GRAY                    COMPUTING SCIENCE          KEANE BLD
STAFFORD                COMPUTING SCIENCE          KEANE BLD
BLAKE                   MATHEMATICS                KEANE BLD
```

A relation which has a single attribute key, such as SECONDNF, must be by definition in at least 2NF. SECONDNF is not in 3NF because the functional dependency DEPARTMENT_NAME → LOCATION is transitive. More precisely, LOCATION is transitive on EMPLOYEE_FAMILY_NAME, because:

  (i) EMPLOYEE_FAMILY_NAME → DEPARTMENT_NAME,
 (ii) DEPARTMENT_NAME → LOCATION,
(iii) DEPARTMENT_NAME ↛ EMPLOYEE_FAMILY_NAME.

If there is a need for a higher normal form, the relation SECONDNF should be replaced by smaller relations.

3a. Definition of the relations obtained from a decomposition of SECONDNF according to the primary key EMPLOYEE_FAMILY_NAME:

```
SQL> DESCRIBE DECOMPOSE2A
Name                                    Null?      Type
-------------------------------- --------- ---------
EMPLOYEE_FAMILY_NAME                    NOT NULL   CHAR(20)
DEPARTMENT_NAME                                    CHAR(20)


SQL> DESCRIBE DECOMPOSE2B
Name                                    Null?      Type
-------------------------------- --------- ---------
EMPLOYEE_FAMILY_NAME                    NOT NULL   CHAR(20)
LOCATION                                           CHAR(9)
```

4a. Contents of the decomposed relations:

```
SQL> SELECT * FROM DECOMPOSE2A;

EMPLOYEE_FAMILY_NAME   DEPARTMENT_NAME
-------------------- --------------------
MACIASZEK              COMPUTING SCIENCE
GRAY                  COMPUTING SCIENCE
STAFFORD              COMPUTING SCIENCE
BLAKE                 MATHEMATICS


SQL> SELECT * FROM DECOMPOSE2B;

EMPLOYEE_FAMILY_NAME   LOCATION
-------------------- -----------
MACIASZEK              KEANE BLD
GRAY                  KEANE BLD
STAFFORD              KEANE BLD
BLAKE                 KEANE BLD
```

5a. Natural equi-join of the relations **DECOMPOSE2A** and **DECOMPOSE2B** over **EMPLOYEE_FAMILY_NAME** results in the relation **SECONDNF**; hence, the decomposition is lossless, but not in a way which is dependency preserving (DEPARTMENT_NAME → LOCATION is not preserved in either relation):

```
SQL> SELECT DECOMPOSE2A.EMPLOYEE_FAMILY_NAME,
  2                     DEPARTMENT_NAME, LOCATION
  3          FROM DECOMPOSE2A, DECOMPOSE2B
  4          WHERE DECOMPOSE2A.EMPLOYEE_FAMILY_NAME =
  5                 DECOMPOSE2B.EMPLOYEE_FAMILY_NAME;
```

```
EMPLOYEE_FAMILY_NAME    DEPARTMENT_NAME           LOCATION
--------------------    ----------------------    ----------
BLAKE                   MATHEMATICS               KEANE BLD
GRAY                    COMPUTING SCIENCE         KEANE BLD
MACIASZEK               COMPUTING SCIENCE         KEANE BLD
STAFFORD                COMPUTING SCIENCE         KEANE BLD
```

3b. Definition of the relations obtained from a decomposition of SECONDNF according to the attribute DEPARTMENT_NAME:

```
SQL> DESCRIBE DECOMPOSE2A
Name                                     Null?       Type
-------------------------------------    ---------   ---------
EMPLOYEE_FAMILY_NAME                     NOT NULL    CHAR(20)
DEPARTMENT_NAME                                      CHAR(20)

SQL> DESCRIBE DECOMPOSE2C
Name                                     Null?       Type
-------------------------------------    ---------   ---------
DEPARTMENT_NAME                                      CHAR(20)
LOCATION                                             CHAR(9)
```

4b. Contents of the decomposed relations (The word DISTINCT in the second SELECT statement is required to eliminate duplicate rows which would otherwise be inserted by ORACLE as a result of the projection operation on SECONDNF; the rows duplication in ORACLE, and other relational DBMS-s, is contrary to the spirit of the relational model [Section 5.1].):

```
SQL> SELECT * FROM DECOMPOSE2A;

EMPLOYEE_FAMILY_NAME    DEPARTMENT_NAME
--------------------    ----------------------
MACIASZEK               COMPUTING SCIENCE
GRAY                    COMPUTING SCIENCE
STAFFORD                COMPUTING SCIENCE
BLAKE                   MATHEMATICS

SQL> SELECT DISTINCT * FROM DECOMPOSE2C;

DEPARTMENT_NAME         LOCATION
--------------------    ----------
COMPUTING SCIENCE       KEANE BLD
MATHEMATICS             KEANE BLD
```

5b. Natural equi-join of the relations DECOMPOSE2A and DECOMPOSE2C over DEPARTMENT_NAME results in the relation SECONDNF; hence, the decomposition is lossless and it is dependency preserving:

```
SQL> SELECT EMPLOYEE_FAMILY_NAME,
  2           DECOMPOSE2C.DEPARTMENT_NAME, LOCATION
  3         FROM DECOMPOSE2A, DECOMPOSE2C
  4        WHERE DECOMPOSE2A.DEPARTMENT_NAME =
  5               DECOMPOSE2C.DEPARTMENT_NAME;

EMPLOYEE_FAMILY_NAME    DEPARTMENT_NAME         LOCATION
--------------------    --------------------    ---------
MACIASZEK               COMPUTING SCIENCE       KEANE BLD
STAFFORD                COMPUTING SCIENCE       KEANE BLD
GRAY                    COMPUTING SCIENCE       KEANE BLD
BLAKE                   MATHEMATICS             KEANE BLD
```

5.5.3.3   Decomposition of 3NF relation

1. Definition of the relation THIRDNF (which is in 3NF, but not in BCNF):

```
SQL> DESCRIBE THIRDNF;

Name                                Null?        Type
---------------------------------   ---------    ---------
STUDENT_ID                          NOT NULL     CHAR(10)
PHONE#                              NOT NULL     CHAR(6)
COURSE#                             NOT NULL     CHAR(7)
GRADE                                            CHAR(5)
```

2. Current content of THIRDNF:

```
SQL> SELECT * FROM THIRDNF;

STUDENT_ID  PHONE#   COURSE# GRADE
----------  ------   ------- -----
870001      280001   CSCI223 HD
870001      280001   CSCI335 HD
870002      280002   CSCI335 PT
870002      280002   CSCI957 F
870002      280002   CSCI336 F
```

The keys of the relation THIRDNF are: {STUDENT_ID, COURSE#} and {PHONE#, COURSE#}. The relation is in 3NF but is not in the next higher form, BCNF. The functional dependencies in THIRDNF are:

- {STUDENT_ID, COURSE#} → GRADE
- {PHONE#, COURSE#} → GRADE
- STUDENT_ID → PHONE#
- PHONE# → STUDENT_ID

There are no transitive or partial dependencies in THIRDNF (the partial dependency occurs when a *nonkey* attribute is dependent on a subset of a key). THIRDNF is not in

BCNF because STUDENT_ID and PHONE# are not keys (they are parts of keys), yet they are determinants.

3. Definition of the relations obtained from a decomposition of SECONDNF according to the two candidate keys {STUDENT_ID, COURSE#} and {PHONE#, COURSE#}:

```
SQL> DESCRIBE DECOMPOSE3A
Name                                 Null?       Type·
----------------------------------   ---------   ---------
STUDENT_ID                           NOT NULL    CHAR(10)
COURSE#                              NOT NULL    CHAR(7)
GRADE                                            CHAR(5)


SQL> DESCRIBE DECOMPOSE3B
Name                                 Null?       Type
----------------------------------   ---------   ---------
PHONE#                               NOT NULL    CHAR(6)
COURSE#                              NOT NULL ·  CHAR(7)
GRADE                                            CHAR(5)
```

4. Contents of the decomposed relations:

```
SQL> SELECT * FROM DECOMPOSE3A;

STUDENT_ID   COURSE#    GRADE
----------   -------    -----
870001       CSCI223    HD
870001       CSCI335    HD
870002       CSCI335    PT
870002       CSCI957    F
870002       CSCI336    F


SQL> SELECT * FROM DECOMPOSE3B;

PHONE#    COURSE#    GRADE
------    -------    -----
280001    CSCI223    HD
280001    CSCI335    HD
280002    CSCI335    PT
280002    CSCI957    F
280002    CSCI336    F
```

5. Natural equi-join of the relations DECOMPOSE3A and DECOMPOSE3B over the common attribute COURSE# results in the relation THIRDNF; note, however, that the use of the word DISTINCT is necessary to eliminate duplicate tuples:

```
SQL> SELECT DISTINCT STUDENT_ID,
  2                      DECOMPOSE3A.COURSE#,
  3                      DECOMPOSE3A.GRADE
  4      FROM DECOMPOSE3A, DECOMPOSE3B
  5      WHERE DECOMPOSE3A.COURSE# =
  6              DECOMPOSE3B.COURSE#;


STUDENT_ID   COURSE#   GRADE
----------   -------   -----
870001       CSCI223   HD
870001       CSCI335   HD
870002       CSCI335   PT
870002       CSCI336   F
870002       CSCI957   F
```

The above decomposition eliminates the update anomalies present in THIRDNF and preserves the dependencies {STUDENT_ID, COURSE#} → GRADE and {PHONE#, COURSE#} → GRADE. Two other dependencies are not preserved. Another possible decomposition of THIRDNF, which also eliminates the update anomalies but which does not preserve {PHONE#, COURSE#} → GRADE, is ONE (STUDENT_ID, PHONE#) and TWO (STUDENT_ID, COURSE#, GRADE).

5.5.3.4 Decomposition of BCNF relation

1. Definition of the relation BOYCECODDNF (which is in BCNF, but not in 4NF):

```
SQL> DESCRIBE BOYCECODDNF
Name                                     Null?       Type
-------------------------------------    ---------   ---------
COURSE#                                  NOT NULL    CHAR(7)
WEEK_DAY                                 NOT NULL    CHAR(9)
ROOM                                     NOT NULL    CHAR(4)
```

2. Current content of BOYCECODDNF:

```
SQL> SELECT * FROM BOYCECODDNF;


COURSE#   WEEK_DAY    ROOM
-------   ---------   ----
CSCI235   TUESDAY     R333
CSCI235   THURSDAY    R444
CSCI235   TUESDAY     R444
CSCI235   THURSDAY    R333
CSCI335   MONDAY      R200
CSCI335   MONDAY      R201


6 records selected.
```

The key of the relation BOYCECODDNF combines all its attributes {COURSE#, WEEK_DAY, ROOM}. There are no functional dependencies in this relation. Hence, by definition, the relation must be in at least BCNF. However, there is a multivalued dependency in BOYCECODDNF, namely, COURSE# $\rightarrow \rightarrow$ WEEK_DAY | ROOM. It may be desirable to decompose BOYCECODDNF in order to overcome the update anomalies caused by the fact that once we know a particular COURSE# value, WEEK_DAY gives us no single-valued information about ROOM, and vice versa.

3. Definition of the relations obtained from a decomposition of BOYCECODDNF according to the attribute COURSE#:

```
SQL> DESCRIBE DECOMPOSEBCNFA
Name                                Null?      Type
--------------------------------    ---------  ---------
COURSE#                             NOT NULL   CHAR(7)
WEEK_DAY                            NOT NULL   CHAR(9)


SQL> DESCRIBE DECOMPOSEBCNFB
Name                                Null?      Type
--------------------------------    ---------  ---------
COURSE#                             NOT NULL   CHAR(7)
ROOM                               NOT NULL   CHAR(4)
```

4. Contents of the decomposed relations:

```
SQL> SELECT DISTINCT * FROM DECOMPOSEBCNFA;

COURSE#     WEEK_DAY
--------    ----------
CSCI235     TUESDAY
CSCI235     THURSDAY
CSCI335     MONDAY


SQL> SELECT DISTINCT * FROM DECOMPOSEBCNFB;

COURSE#     ROOM
--------    -----
CSCI235     R333
CSCI235     R444
CSCI335     R200
CSCI335     R201
```

5. Natural equi-join of the relations DECOMPOSEBCNFA and DECOMPOSEBCNFB over the common attribute COURSE# results in the relation BOYCECODDNF:

```
SQL> SELECT DECOMPOSEBCNFA.COURSE#, WEEK_DAY, ROOM
  2      FROM DECOMPOSEBCNFA, DECOMPOSEBCNFB
  3      WHERE DECOMPOSEBCNFA.COURSE# =
  4              DECOMPOSEBCNFB.COURSE#;


COURSE#    WEEK_DAY   ROOM
--------   ---------  -----
CSCI235    THURSDAY   R333
CSCI235    THURSDAY   R444
CSCI235    TUESDAY    R333
CSCI235    TUESDAY    R444
CSCI335    MONDAY     R200
CSCI335    MONDAY     R201


6 records selected.
```

The above join shows that the projections DECOMPOSEBCNFA and DECOMPOSEBCNFB are lossless (sometimes called *nonloss*). However, the two projections are not *independent* and updates cannot be made to either one without a follow-up update in the other.

5.5.3.5   Decomposition of 4NF relation

1. Definition of the relation FOURTHNF (which is in 4NF, but not in 5NF):

```
SQL> DESCRIBE FOURTHNF
Name                                Null?       Type
----------------------------------- ---------   ---------
S#                                  NOT NULL    CHAR(3)
P#                                  NOT NULL    CHAR(3)
E#                                  NOT NULL    CHAR(3)
```

2. Current content of FOURTHNF (ORDER clause is included to improve the readability):

```
SQL> SELECT * FROM FOURTHNF
  2      ORDER BY S#, P#, E#;


S#    P#    E#
---   ---   ---
S10   P10   E10
S10   P10   E20
S10   P20   E10
S20   P10   E10
```

The relation FOURTHNF is all-key. It is in the 4NF because it does not have functional or multivalued dependencies. The relation expresses the business rule ("the real life constraint") that if student S10 works on project P10 (tuple1), and P10 uses equipment E10 (tuple 2), and E10 is used by S10 (tuple 3), then it must be true that S10 uses E10 in P10 (tuple 4). In other words, FOURTHNF contains a join dependency. As a result, it can be decomposed to the relations in the ultimate normal form, that is, to the 5NF relations. This must be a three-way decomposition.

3. Definition of the three relations obtained from a decomposition of FOURTHNF:

```
SQL> DESCRIBE DECOMPOSE4A
Name                                   Null?       Type
-----------------------------------    ---------   ---------
S#                                     NOT NULL    CHAR(3)
P#                                     NOT NULL    CHAR(3)


SQL> DESCRIBE DECOMPOSE4B
Name                                   Null?       Type
-----------------------------------    ---------   ---------
S#                                     NOT NULL    CHAR(3)
E#                                     NOT NULL    CHAR(3)


SQL> DESCRIBE DECOMPOSE4C
Name                                   Null?       Type
-----------------------------------    ---------   ---------
P#                                     NOT NULL    CHAR(3)
E#                                     NOT NULL    CHAR(3)
```

4. Contents of the decomposed relations:

```
SQL> SELECT DISTINCT * FROM DECOMPOSE4A;
S#    P#
---   ---
S10   P10
S20   P10
S10   P20


SQL> SELECT DISTINCT * FROM DECOMPOSE4B;

S#    E#
---   ---
S10   E20
S20   E10
S10   E10
```

```
SQL> SELECT DISTINCT * FROM DECOMPOSE4C;

P#    E#
---   ---
P10   E20
P20   E10
P10   E10
```

5. A three-way natural equi-join of the relations DECOMPOSE4A, DECOMPOSE4B and DECOMPOSE4C reconstructs the relation FOURTHNF; hence, the decomposition is lossless:

```
SQL> SELECT DISTINCT DECOMPOSE4A.S#,
  2              DECOMPOSE4C.P#, DECOMPOSE4B.E#
  3      FROM DECOMPOSE4A, DECOMPOSE4B, DECOMPOSE4C
  4      WHERE DECOMPOSE4A.S# = DECOMPOSE4B.S#
  5        AND DECOMPOSE4A.P# = DECOMPOSE4C.P#
  6        AND DECOMPOSE4B.E# = DECOMPOSE4C.E#;

S#    P#    E#
---   ---   ---
S10   P10   E10
S10   P10   E20
S10   P20   E10
S20   P10   E10
```

The relations DECOMPOSE4A, DECOMPOSE4B, and DECOMPOSE4C are in the 5NF. They are all-key relations and they do not contain any functional, multivalued or join dependencies.

5.6 CASE STUDY: LOGICAL SCHEMA

The conceptual schema for the inventory control system presented in Section 4.6 should now be normalized and converted to a logical schema. The following discussion is not complete, but the major points are addressed. The reader is invited to complete the design.

5.6.1 Normalizing the conceptual schema

As a result of normalizing the conceptual schema of the inventory control system:

• three denormalized entity sets are reduced to relations (the entity sets are ORDER, PURCHASE_REQUISITION and SHIPMENT);

- three new entity sets are created (ITEM_ON_ORDER, ITEM_TO_PURCHASE and PACKING_INFORMATION);
- three weak relationship sets are created to connect the normalized entities with the newly created entities (TO_ORDER, PURCHASE and PACK).

The normalized conceptual schema is shown in Figure 5.20 and the DD definitions of the six entity sets affected by or created as a result of normalization are presented below. The part of the diagram which is enclosed by a thick, shaded line is converted in Section 5.6.2 to a relational schema.

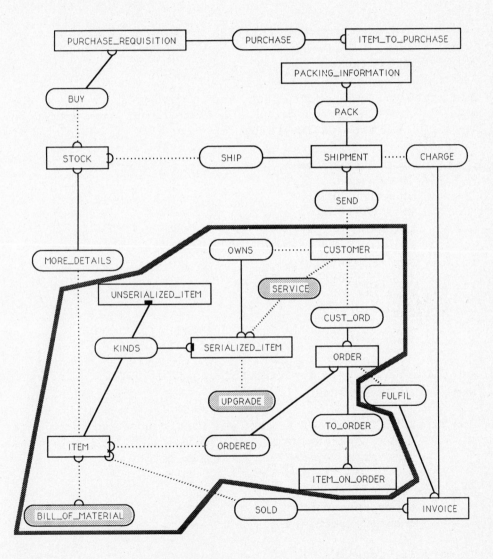

Figure 5.20　Normalized conceptual diagram for the case study example.

Conceptual Schema Definition of: ERA41Norm(DD)

Currently the definition contains:

          12 Entities
           3 Regular Relationships
          14 Weak Relationships
          49 Simple Attributes
    and   3 Group Attributes

================= ENTITIES ==================

Name: ITEM_ON_ORDER

Description: This entity set was introduced to hold the
            repeating group attribute, that was extracted
            from ORDER entity set.

Contains the Attributes:
        item_number
        quantity_ordered
        unit_price
        extended_price

Primary Key Consists of:
        item_number

Connections:
        via: (1:N Total) TO_ORDER (Weak)
                    to: ORDER (1:1 Total)

Name: ITEM_TO_PURCHASE

Description: This entity set was introduced to hold the
            repeating group attribute, that was extracted
            from PURCHASE_REQUISITION entity set.

Contains the Attributes:
        store_item_number
        quantity_required

Primary Key Consists of:
        store_item_number

Connections:
        via: (1:N Total) PURCHASE (Weak)
                    to: PURCHASE_REQUISITION (1:1 Total)

Name: ORDER

Description: Holds   information   about   open   (unfilled)
            customer orders.

Contains the Attributes:
        customer_order_number
        customer_name
        date
        billing_address
        shipping_address
        payment_method
        shipment_method
        total_amount

Primary Key Consists of:
        customer_order_number

Connections:
        via: (1:N Total) CUST_ORD (Weak)
                    to: CUSTOMER (1:1 Partial)
        via: (1:1 Partial) FULFIL (Weak)
                    to: INVOICE (1:N Total)
        via: (1:1 Total) ORDERED (Weak)
                    to: ITEM (1:N Partial)
        via: (1:1 Total) TO_ORDER (Weak)
                    to: ITEM_ON_ORDER (1:N Total)

Name: PACKING_INFORMATION

Description: This entity set was introduced to hold the
            repeating group attribute, that was extracted
            from SHIPMENT entity set.

Contains the Attributes:
        item_number
        quantity_ordered
        quantity_shipped
        quantity_back_ordered
        quantity_canceled

Primary Key Consists of:
        item_number

Connections:
        via: (1:N Total) PACK (Weak)
                        to: SHIPMENT (1:1 Total)

Name: PURCHASE_REQUISITION

Description: Defines the purchase order to buy new stock.

Contains the Attributes:
        requisition_number
        supplier_number
        account_number
        date
        requested_by

Primary Key Consists of:
        requisition_number

Connections:
        via: (1:1 Total) BUY (Weak)
                        to: STOCK (1:N Partial)
        via: (1:1 Total) PURCHASE (Weak)
                        to: ITEM_TO_PURCHASE (1:N Total)

Name: SHIPMENT

Description: Gives information about shipments of ordered
            items to customers.

Contains the Attributes:
        our_order_number
        shipping_charge
        date

Primary Key Consists of:
        our_order_number

Connections:
        via: (1:1 Partial) CHARGE (Weak)
                        to: INVOICE (1:1 Total)

```
via: (1:1 Total) PACK (Weak)
                 to: PACKING_INFORMATION (1:N Total)
via: (1:N Total) SEND (Weak)
                 to: CUSTOMER (1:1 Partial)
via: (1:1 Total) SHIP (Weak)
                 to: STOCK (1:N Partial)
```

5.6.2 Converting to a logical schema

The part of the conceptual diagram in Figure 5.20 which is enclosed by a thick, shaded line is now converted to a relational structure (Figure 5.21). The conversion is relatively straightforward because the conceptual objects have been reduced to relations. Nevertheless, some unexpected design problems can arise and have to be resolved by the designer. In some situations feedback to the conceptualization phase, in order to refine the previous design, may be appropriate.

In the example given, an unexpected design anomaly has arisen, caused by the co-existence in Figure 5.20 of the relationships ORDERED and TO_ORDER. If the two relationships were converted to relations, then the relations ORDERED and ITEM_ON_ORDER would have an identical primary key (item_number) and would represent an identical referential integrity constraint (from the foreign key customer_order_number to the primary key of the relation ORDER). A much better design solution would be to replace the relation ORDERED by an additional referential integrity from the foreign key item_number (which also happens to be the primary key) of ITEM_ON_ORDER to the primary key of ITEM. This retains the same semantics while minimizing redundancy.

The logical schema is created for a particular DBMS (in our case ORACLE) and the restrictions and recommendations of a chosen DBMS must be observed. In the example, the DBMS-motivated changes comprise:

- modifications of data types (in particular, the type 'long', which in the conceptual design meant a 256-characters string, has been converted to CHAR(240)—maximum size in ORACLE (cp. BILLING_ADDRESS and SHIPPING_ADDRESS);
- labeling columns in capital letters, according to a common practice (attributes in our conceptual schema were written in lower case);
- renaming the attribute date as DDATE (because DATE is a reserved word in ORACLE).

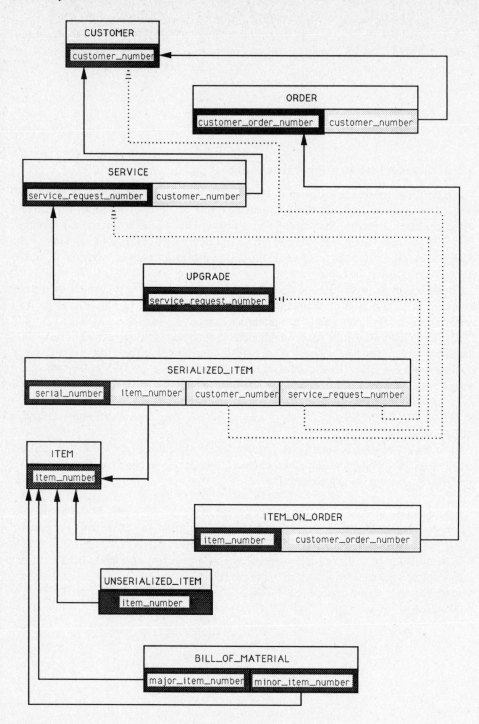

Figure 5.21   Relational structure diagram for the case study example

```
SQL> CREATE TABLE CUSTOMER
  2              (CUSTOMER_NUMBER          CHAR(8)  NOT NULL,
  3               CUSTOMER_NAME            CHAR(80),
  4               BILLING_ADDRESS          CHAR(240),
  5               SHIPPING_ADDRESS         CHAR(240));

Table created.

SQL> CREATE UNIQUE INDEX IND_C
  2              ON CUSTOMER
  3                 (CUSTOMER_NUMBER);

Index created.

SQL> CREATE TABLE ORDER
  2              (CUSTOMER_ORDER_NUMBER    CHAR(8)  NOT NULL,
  3               CUSTOMER_NUMBER          CHAR(8)  NOT NULL,
  4               DDATE                    DATE,
  5               PAYMENT_METHOD           CHAR(40),
  6               SHIPMENT_METHOD          CHAR(40),
  7               TOTAL_AMOUNT             NUMBER(8,2));

Table created.

SQL> CREATE UNIQUE INDEX IND_O
  2              ON ORDER
  3                 (CUSTOMER_ORDER_NUMBER);

Index created.

SQL> CREATE TABLE SERVICE
  2              (SERVICE_REQUEST_NUMBER   CHAR(6)  NOT NULL,
  3               CUSTOMER_NUMBER          CHAR(8)  NOT NULL,
  4               DATE_SERVICE_REQUESTED   DATE,
  5               DATE_SERVICE_COMPLETED   DATE,
  6               DATE_SERVICE_COLLECTED   DATE,
  7               TECHNICIAN_NAME          CHAR(30));

Table created.

SQL> CREATE UNIQUE INDEX IND_S
  2              ON SERVICE
  3                 (SERVICE_REQUEST_NUMBER);

Index created.
```

```
SQL> CREATE TABLE UPGRADE
  2              (SERVICE_REQUEST_NUMBER  CHAR(6)  NOT NULL,
  3              UPGRADED_FROM            CHAR(10),
  4              UPGRADED_TO              CHAR(10));

Table created.

SQL> CREATE UNIQUE INDEX IND_U
  2              ON UPGRADE
  3                (SERVICE_REQUEST_NUMBER);

Index created.

SQL> CREATE TABLE ITEM
  2              (ITEM_NUMBER             CHAR(10)  NOT NULL,
  3              ITEM_DESCRIPTION         CHAR(20),
  4              BASE_PRICE               NUMBER(7,2),
  5              MARK_UP                  NUMBER(3,1),
  6              TAX                      NUMBER(3,1),
  7              CONSULTANCY_FEE          NUMBER(7,2));

Table created.

SQL> CREATE UNIQUE INDEX IND_I
  2              ON ITEM
  3                (ITEM_NUMBER);

Index created.

SQL> CREATE TABLE SERIALIZED_ITEM
  2              (SERIAL_NUMBER           CHAR(20)  NOT NULL,
  3              ITEM_NUMBER              CHAR(10)  NOT NULL,
  4              CUSTOMER_NUMBER          CHAR(8),
  5              SERVICE_REQUEST_NUMBER   CHAR(6),
  6              DATE_SOLD                DATE,
  7              WARRANTY_TYPE            CHAR(2),
  8              DATE_WARRANTY_EXPIRES    DATE);

Table created.

SQL> CREATE UNIQUE INDEX IND_SI
  2              ON SERIALIZED_ITEM
  3                (SERIAL_NUMBER);

Index created.
```

```
SQL> CREATE TABLE ITEM_ON_ORDER
  2               (ITEM_NUMBER              CHAR(10)  NOT NULL,
  3               CUSTOMER_ORDER_NUMBER     CHAR(8)  NOT NULL,
  4               QUANTITY_ORDERED          NUMBER(3),
  5               UNIT_PRICE                NUMBER(7,2),
  6               EXTENDED_PRICE            NUMBER(8,2));

Table created.

SQL> CREATE UNIQUE INDEX IND_IOO
  2              ON ITEM_ON_ORDER
  3                 (ITEM_NUMBER);

Index created.

SQL> CREATE TABLE UNSERIALIZED_ITEM
  2               (ITEM_NUMBER              CHAR(10)  NOT NULL,
  3               UNIT_OF_MEASURE           CHAR(4));

Table created.

SQL> CREATE UNIQUE INDEX IND_UI
  2              ON UNSERIALIZED_ITEM
  3                 (ITEM_NUMBER);

Index created.

SQL> CREATE TABLE BILL_OF_MATERIAL
  2               (MAJOR_ITEM_NUMBER        CHAR(10)  NOT NULL,
  3               MINOR_ITEM_NUMBER         CHAR(10)  NOT NULL,
  4               QUANTITY_AS_COMPONENT     NUMBER(3));

Table created.

SQL> CREATE UNIQUE INDEX IND_BOM
  2              ON BILL_OF_MATERIAL
  3                 (MAJOR_ITEM_NUMBER,
  4                  MINOR_ITEM_NUMBER);

Index created.
```

FURTHER READING

Relational database concepts are comprehensively discussed in numerous books. We recommend Date (1986a), Maier (1983) and Ullman (1982a). The relational model is defined in Codd (1970 and 1979), Date (1986a and b), Maier (1983) and Ullman (1982a). Codd's twelve rules for a relational system are specified in Codd (1986). Codd (1979) and Date (1986b) are invaluable references to understanding the meaning and implications of Codd's rules. The relational standard is introduced in DRAFT (1985a) and Date (1987). The Oracle implementation is discussed in the system's manuals ORACLE (1987a, b and c) and the book by Hursch and Hursch (1987).

Referential integrity is discussed by Date (1986b). A general description of referential integrity enforcement in DB2 Version 2 can be found in IBM (1988). The membership class of network databases is specified in DRAFT (1985b).

The problem of reducing conceptual objects to relations does not require further studies beyond the discussion presented in this book. A good understanding of the definition of relation should suffice for a full understanding of the reduction principles. A methodological approach to the conversion of entity-relationship constructs to relational structures is given in Jackson (1988) and Teorey *et al.* (1986).

Normalization theory is discussed by Maier (1983) and Ullman (1982a). Armstrong's axioms were first published in Armstrong (1974). The membership and Bernstein algorithms are described in Bernstein (1976), Beeri and Bernstein (1979), Hawryszkiewycz (1984) and Lien (1985). The decomposition approach was proposed by Codd (1972) and generalized by Aho *et al.* (1979), Fagin (1977), Rissanen (1977), Zaniolo and Melkanoff (1982) and others. A tutorial-style treatment of decomposition is offered by Hawryszkiewycz (1984), Lien (1985) and Korth and Silberschatz (1986). The universal relation assumption is criticised by Kent (1981), and advocated by Fagin *et al.* (1982), Maier *et al.* (1984), Vardi (1988) and Ullman (1982b). The article by Vardi (1988) sparked a critical response by Codd (1988).

REFERENCES

AHO, A. V., BEERI, C. and ULLMAN, J. D. (1979): The Theory of Joins in Relational Databases, *ACM Trans. Database Syst.*, 3, pp.297–314.

ARMSTRONG, W. W. (1974): Dependency Structures of Data Base Relationships, *Proc. IFIP 74 Congress*, North-Holland, pp.580–83.

BEERI, C. and BERNSTEIN, P. A. (1979): Computational Problems Related to the Design of Normal Form Relational Schemas, *ACM Trans. Database Syst.*, 1, pp.30–59.

BERNSTEIN, P. A. (1976): Synthesizing Third Normal Form Relations from Functional Dependencies, *ACM Trans. Database Syst.*, 4, pp.277–98.

CODD, E. F. (1970): A Relational Model of Data for Large Shared Data Banks, *Comm. ACM*, 6, pp.377–87.

CODD, E. F. (1972): Further Normalization of the Data Base Relational Model, in: *Data Base Systems*, ed. R. Rustin, Prentice Hall, pp.33–64.

CODD, E. F. (1979): Extending the Database Relational Model to Capture More Meaning, *ACM Trans. Database Syst.*, 4, pp.397–434.

CODD, E. F. (1986): Is Your Database Management System Really Relational? *Computerworld (Australia)*, 7 Feb., pp.18–24.

CODD, E. F. (1988): 'Universal' relation fails to replace relational model. Software Letters, *IEEE Soft.*, July, p.4.

DATE, C. J. (1986a): *An Introduction to Database Systems*, Vol. I, Addison-Wesley, 4th ed., p.639.

DATE, C. J. (1986b): *Relational Database: Selected Writings*, Addison-Wesley, p.497.

DATE, C. J. (1987): *A Guide to the SQL Standard*, Addison-Wesley, 205p.

DRAFT (1985a): *Draft Proposed American National Standard Database Language SQL*, Technical Committee X3H2 - Database, X3.135-1985, Project 363-D, 115p.

DRAFT (1985b): *Draft Proposed American National Standard Network Database Language*, Technical Committee X3H2 - Database, X3.133-1985, Project: 355-D, 142p.

FAGIN, R. (1977): Multivalued Dependencies and a New Normal Form for Relational Databases, *ACM Trans. Database Syst.*, 3, pp.262–78.

FAGIN, R., MENDELZON, A. O. and ULLMAN, J. D. (1982): A Simplified Universal Relation Assumption and Its Properties, *ACM Trans. Database Syst.*, 3, pp.343–60.

HAWRYSZKIEWYCZ, I. T. (1984): *Database Analysis and Design*, SRA, 578p.

HURSCH, J. L. and HURSCH, C. J. (1987): *Working with ORACLE*, TAB BOOKS, 228p.

IBM (1988): IBM DATABASE 2 Version 2. General Information, GC26-4373-0, IBM, 45p.

JACKSON, G. A. (1988): *Relational Database Design with Microcomputer Applications*, Prentice Hall, 207p.

KENT, W. (1981): Consequences of Assuming a Universal Relation, *ACM Trans. Database Syst.*, 4, pp.539–56.

KORTH, H. F. and SILBERSCHATZ, A. (1986): *Database System Concepts*, McGraw-Hill, 546p.

LIEN, Y. E. (1985): Relational Database Design, in: *Principles of Database Design, Volume I, Logical Organizations*, ed. S. B. Yao, Prentice Hall, pp.211–54.

MAIER, D. (1983): *The Theory of Relational Databases*, Computer Science Press, 637p.

MAIER, D., ULLMAN, J. D. and VARDI, M. Y. (1984): On the Foundations of the Universal Relation Model, *ACM Trans. Database Syst.*, 2, pp.283-308.

ORACLE (1987a): *SQL*Plus Reference Guide*, Version 2.0, The Relational Database Management System ORACLE, Oracle Corp.

ORACLE (1987b): *SQL*Plus User's Guide*, Version 2.0, The Relational Database Management System ORACLE, Oracle Corp.

ORACLE (1987c): *Database Administrator's Guide*, Version 2.0, The Relational Database Management System ORACLE, Oracle Corp.

RISSANEN, J. (1977): Independent Components of Relations, *ACM Trans. Database Syst.*, 4, pp.317–25.

TEOREY, T. J., YANG D. and FRY, J. P. (1986): A Logical Design Methodology for Relational Databases Using the Extended Entity-Relationship Model, *Comput. Surv.*, 2, pp.197–222.

ULLMAN, J. D. (1982a): *Principles of Database Systems*, 2nd ed., Computer Science Press, 484p.

ULLMAN, J. D. (1982b): The U.R. Strikes Back, in: *Proc. ACM Symp. Principles of Database Systems*, Los Angeles, California, pp.10–22.

VARDI, M. Y. (1988): The Universal-Relation Data Model for Logical Independence, *IEEE Soft.*, March, pp.80–5.

ZANIOLO, C. and MELKANOFF, M. A. (1982): A Formal Approach to the Definition and the Design of Conceptual Schemata for Database Systems, *ACM Trans. Database Syst.*, 1, pp.24–59.

6

Design of Physical Schema

The relational model represents only logical data structures with physical characteristics of data being hidden from the user. Because of the sound theoretical foundations of the model, it is claimed that a relational DBMS should be able to take care of storage and allocation structures in a way which is superior to human expertise. While such a goal has not yet been fully realised, there is little doubt that a human designer will be given less and less opportunity to control physical aspects of a relational database. This is fundamentally different from older database models, such as network, which go as far as providing a Data Storage Definition Language (DSDL), often separate from a logical Data Definition Language (DDL), to describe a physical schema.

The objective of physical database design is performance. A "good" physical design minimizes the number of I/O (input/output) transfers and makes efficient use of external and virtual storage. In achieving these goals, considerations of concurrency and processing efficiency are involved. Physical database design can be based on an external model of the system's behavior or on an internal model of cost estimates obtained statistically by DBMS and based on the analysis of "real" query optimizer decisions. Both models are discussed in this chapter and related to storage structures implemented in two DBMSs—DB2 and ORACLE.

6.1 ACCESS PLANS

In the past, there has been controversy about the performance of relational systems compared to conventional DBMSs that run according to predefined and specifically selected access paths. Relational systems are based on the paradigm of declarative programming and, whenever possible, programmers and users interact with these systems in a declarative, rather than a procedural, fashion. That is, they specify what data are required, but do not determine how these data should be obtained. The determination of access paths is the responsibility of the software module of DBMS called the optimizer. The optimizer performs the analysis of alternative access paths and chooses the one with the lowest cost. The chosen path is called the access plan (execution plan). Recent advances in optimization techniques have shown that optimizers are capable of making very good decisions.

The inputs to the access plan computation are a SQL (or SQL-like) statement, the existing tables and storage structures and cost models of data retrieval and update. The output is an optimal (at least in a heuristic sense) access plan. The general procedure for access plan computation contains the following steps:

1. Translate the SQL statement to an internal relational algebra form. This process resembles parsing in a compiler: the syntax is checked, the existence of referenced relations and attributes is verified and the views, if any, are replaced with relational algebra expressions which compute them.
2. Find equivalent access paths, that is, equivalent relational algebra expressions for evaluating the statement. These include a sequence of operations and intermediate results (temporary relations).
3. Augment the access paths by physical and statistical characteristics (indexes, sort orders, relation sizes, distribution of attribute values).
4. Choose the cheapest access plan, primarily in terms of the number of disk accesses required.

An interesting aspect of access plan calculation is that most commercial DBMSs compile, rather than interpret, SQL statements. This is true not only for a programmatic environment with embedded SQL but also for SQL statements submitted interactively for processing. In a typical sequence of events a SQL statement is compiled, an access plan is generated for it, the plan is executed and the plan is discarded in the interactive case and stored in the catalog in the programmatic case (although some systems, such as current version of INGRES, do not store the plans at all). Research and experiments have shown that compilation is more effective even in interactive processing. Normally, the disadvantage of doing the compilation is outweighed by the advantage of more efficient processing.

In the programmatic environment, access plans generated for SQL statements embedded in a host language program are stored in the catalog as so-called *application plans*. A process of program preparation is shown in Figure 6.1.

An application program is written in a procedural language, such as COBOL, PL/I, C, FORTRAN, ADA or Assembler. In the preprocessing phase, embedded SQL statements are replaced by host language CALL statements. The SQL statements are checked syntactically and stored as a Database Request Module. The host language program constitutes a modified source module.

In the optimizing (also called binding) phase, a relationship between the Database Request Module and the database itself is established. As a result, an application plan is built and normally stored in the catalog.

Compiling and link-editing is the standard programming procedure. The result is a load module ready to execute.

Programmers have the option to validate the application plan at each execution of the program, but usually the program is executed many times without repeating the optimization process. Under some circumstances, the optimization is done automatically and the program is automatically rebound. This happens if some access paths are invalidated due to changes to the database definition.

Current optimizers cannot optimize the sequences of SQL statements, such that a sequence is a single unit of work, because in those sequences there may be some common operations (e.g. the same projection or join) that are needed in many queries. By performing such operations only once for all queries involved, a considerable time saving may be achievable. This problem is known as *multiple-query optimization.* Such optimization is of special importance in databases enhanced with inference capabilities (expert (deductive) database systems) where inferences can be thought of as predefined sequences of SQL statements that express sets of rules activated in search procedures.

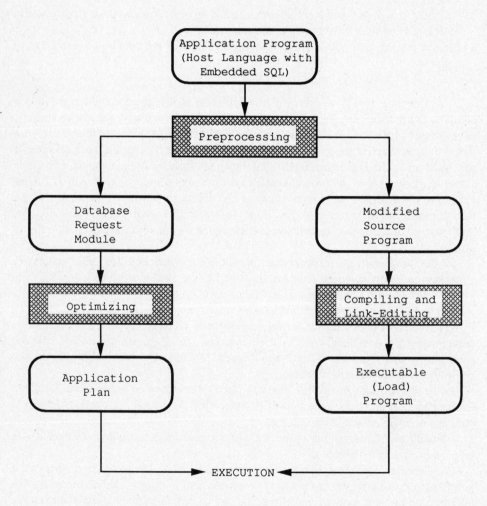

Figure 6.1   Program preparation process

6.2   PLACEMENT STRATEGIES

The aspects of physical database design which are left to the decision of the designer, rather than system, are the database space and placement definitions. These include the definition of databases and mapping relations to files.

6.2.1   Definition of databases

From the viewpoint of a DBMS, a database is a collection of relation spaces and index spaces. It is an operational unit that can be used for starting and stopping access to relations and indexes.

Depending on a DBMS, multiple databases can be created by a special SQL statement or by multiple settings of environment variables on an operating system level. The former approach is superior and is adopted, for example, in DB2. The latter approach is used in ORACLE.

In DB2, a database is created by a SQL statement CREATE DATABASE, for example:

```
CREATE DATABASE DSN8D2PG
  STOGROUP DSN8G200
  BUFFERPOOL BP2;
```

In this definition, the database is called DSN8D2PG. DSN8G200 is the default storage group and BP2 is the default buffer pool to be used for relation and index spaces (the concepts of storage group and buffer pool are explained in Section 6.2.2.1). When the database DSN8D2PG is created, DB2 stores information about it in the catalog relation called SYSIBM.SYSDATABASE. Information about each database occupies a row in this relation.

In ORACLE (running on a Unix machine), a database is identified by a single-letter value of an environment variable $ORACLE_SID written in *.profile* file in ORACLE directory, for example:

```
ORACLE_SID=a; export ORACLE_SID
```

In this definition, the database is identified by the letter 'a'. Each user must repeat the value of this identifier in his/her own *.profile* file to be eligible to access the database:

```
ORACLE_SID=a
. oraenv
```

Because of the restrictions imposed on the use of environment variables, usually only one database is managed by a single ORACLE kernel. In this connotation, the interpretation of the concept *database* is not the same in DB2 and ORACLE. In particular, a DB2 database can also be considered as a unit of *authorization* because a separate database can be created for a user or for an application.

In the relational standard (Section 5.1), the concept of *schema* (rather than database) defines a part of the database that is owned by a specific user or specific application. A user or an application is identified by the AUTHORIZATION clause of the CREATE SCHEMA statement. A schema consists of all relation definitions, view definitions and privilege definitions known to the system for a specified authorization identifier.

6.2.2   Mapping relations to files

Microcomputer-based relational DBMSs usually store each relation and each index in a separate operating system file; however, most large-scale DBMSs do not rely on an underlying operating system for file management and handle the matter for themselves. To this aim, a large operating system file is allocated to the DBMS and the mapping of relations to database "files" is taken care of by the DBMS. If storage expansion is needed to accommodate new relations and indexes, more operating system files can be allocated to the DBMS.

The mapping procedures and the terminology adopted varies between DBMSs. Often the same terms mean entirely different space chunks and remain in a different relationship with the other terms. Instead of attempting to unify the terminology under the assumption of some hypothetical DBMS, we shall describe, separately, the mapping in DB2 (under MVS operating system) and ORACLE (under Unix operating system) environments.

6.2.2.1   Mapping in DB2

DB2 uses *storage groups* to acquire external storage for the database relations and indexes. A SQL statement CREATE STOGROUP is used to create a storage group, for example:

```
CREATE STOGROUP DSN8G200
   VOLUMES (ABC005,DEF008)
   VCAT DSNCAT
   PASSWORD LESZEK;
```

In this example, the storage group DSN8G200 includes two DASD (direct access storage device) volumes: ABC005 and DEF008. DSNCAT is the VSAM (virtual storage access method) catalog name and LESZEK is the VSAM password.

The volumes of a storage group must be of the same device type and must be mounted or permanently resident. However, the same volume may be included in more than one storage group definition. In operating system terms, a storage group is a *VSAM data set (file)*.

When a DB2 database is defined (Section 6.2.1), a default storage group for it can be specified. The default group can be overridden and a different group can be chosen when a relation space or an index space is defined (by means of CREATE TABLESPACE or CREATE INDEX statements).

The use of CREATE STOGROUP is optional. The decision should be based on performance considerations. For example, relations and indexes used most frequently could be assigned to faster devices. At installation time, the storage group SYSDEFLT is created and used automatically when needed. The names of the installation-time group and all other groups defined are kept in the DB2 catalog relation SYSIBM.SYSSTOGROUP.

A database consists of *table spaces* which can contain one or more relations. Each table space is divided into *pages* of either 4K bytes or 32K bytes. A SQL CREATE TABLESPACE statement is used to define a table space, for example:

```
CREATE TABLESPACE DSN8S2DP
   IN DSN8D2AP
       FREEPAGE  7
       PCTFREE  10
   USING STOGROUP DSN8G200
       PRIQTY   52
       SECQTY   20
   LOCKSIZE    ANY
   BUFFERPOOL  BP1
   CLOSE       YES
   DSETPASS    LESZEK;
```

In the example, the table space DSN8S2DP is created within the database DSN8D2AP. The FREEPAGE and PCTFREE options together control the distribution of the free storage space in table spaces. Higher than default settings of these options can be advantageous for table spaces which contain relations with expected high rates of inserts and updates.

The FREEPAGE option specifies that one out of every eight pages in the table space will be left empty during initial database load and during reorganization. The default value for this option is 0 (zero), that is, no empty pages are left during load or reorganization. The PCTFREE option specifies that 10 percent of the space in *each* page will be left empty during initial load and reorganization. The default value is 5 percent.

The STOGROUP keyword identifies the storage group that DB2 should use for the relations belonging to the table space. If this keyword is not specified, a storage group listed in the CREATE DATABASE statement will be used.

The PRIQTY and SECQTY options specify, respectively, the amount of primary and the amount of secondary storage space allocated to the table space. In the example, the primary space allocation is 52K bytes; the secondary, 20K bytes. Since the default values for these parameters are intended for use with relatively small relations, a careful calculation of space requirements is recommended for production database relations. Ideally, an entire relation should be kept within the primary allocation. If secondary allocations must be used, they will probably be located physically adjacent neither to the primary allocation nor to each other. As a result, performance is likely to suffer because DB2 will have to access data from different physical areas.

The LOCKSIZE clause specifies the *locking granularity* for relations in the table space. In general, three levels of locking granularity are possible. They are indicated by the keywords: TABLESPACE, PAGE and ANY. When TABLESPACE is specified, the entire table space is locked on access to any of the relations in this space. This minimizes the overhead processing required for lock maintenance, but it has a negative effect on a level of concurrency. When PAGE is specified, individual pages within the table space are locked as they are required by applications. This allows several applications to concurrently access data within different pages in the table space, but incurs the time and space overhead involved in maintaining additional page locks. When ANY is specified, the decision of whether data should be locked at the page or table space level is left to DB2.

The BUFFERPOOL option is used to override the default buffer pool specification in the CREATE DATABASE statement. DB2 allows the definition of four different buffer pools; the buffer pools BP0, BP1 and BP2 have 4K bytes each and the pool BP32 has the size of 32K bytes.

The choice of a buffer pool name implicitly determines the *page size* in the table space. Whenever a row of the relation is to be processed, the page in an external storage containing the row is brought into a main memory (virtual storage) buffer. The performance can be substantially improved if the page that the application requires can be found in the buffer (as a result of the anticipatory reading of pages and as a result of the correct choice of buffer pools for table spaces).

The CLOSE option indicates whether the VSAM data set (file), corresponding to a storage group, can be closed when the current application run ends. This option can have one of the two values: NO or YES. The NO value should be specified if the table space is frequently needed by many applications. The YES value is recommended for table spaces that are used by relatively few applications, in particular if these applications run in batch mode. The last clause, DSETPASS, determines the password to protect files of the table space.

Multiple relations can be allocated to a single table space. This can be advantageous (because of the reduced I/O cost) for relations which are small and which are related and most of the time used together. Also, fewer table spaces will reduce the file allocation/deallocation cost because the proliferation of files (each table space requires a VSAM data set) is avoided.

However, in most cases, it is better to have one relation per table space. By doing so, we avoid situations in which an application that accesses only one relation can lock the entire table space, thus preventing the other relations from being accessed by other users. Moreover, when there is only one relation in a table space the use of *clustering index* option (see below) is more effective and the *scan* of the relation, when an index cannot be used, is quicker.

By using a more sophisticated variant of the CREATE TABLESPACE statement, a *partitioned table space* can be defined. Partitioning is an advantage if different portions of a large relation have different access patterns and should, therefore, be placed on different device types to improve performance. As an additional advantage, some DB2 utilities can operate on a single partition (e.g. utilities that perform table space reorganization and recovery). This is a consequence of the fact that DB2 creates and manages a separate VSAM data set for each partition.

The use of partitioning has several restrictions. A partitioned table space can only contain one relation and a clustering index must be created on a partitioned relation. A key attribute of a partitioned relation is not directly updatable, therefore, to achieve an update, a row with a pertinent key value must be deleted and then a new row with the updated key value must be inserted.

As with databases and storage groups, the definition of a table space is optional. If a table space is not explicitly defined and a CREATE TABLE statement is issued, DB2 will generate a new table space to accommodate the data of the relation. However, this default space allocation is minimal and it is recommended that an explicit table space is created for all tables that will require more than a few pages for their data rows.

The database and/or the table space to be used for a newly created relation is specified in the IN clause of the CREATE TABLE statement, for example:

```
CREATE TABLE DEPARTMENT
   (DEPTNO      CHAR(4)       NOT NULL,
    DEPTNAME    VARCHAR(36)   NOT NULL,
    MANAGERID   CHAR(8))
   IN DSN8D2AP.DSN8S2DP;
```

In this example, relation DEPARTMENT is created in database DSN8D2AP and table space DSN8S2DP.

In order to keep the same relation in an implicitly created table space of database DSN8D2AP, the following change in the definition statement is needed:

```
CREATE TABLE DEPARTMENT
   (DEPTNO      CHAR(4)       NOT NULL,
    DEPTNAME    VARCHAR(36)   NOT NULL,
    MANAGERID   CHAR(8))
   IN DATABASE DSN8D2AP;
```

One or more indexes can be created for each relation. An index can be created for a single attribute or for any combination of the attributes (the latter is sometimes called a *composite index*). The attribute(s) on which the index is created can have duplicate values, unless a unique index is specified (by means of the UNIQUE clause in CREATE INDEX statement).

A relation can have a *clustering index*, which is specified by means of the CLUSTER clause in CREATE INDEX statement. With the clustering index, DB2 attempts to allocate storage for the relation's rows (records) such that their physical ordering is the same as the corresponding index entries. The clustering index can provide a significant performance advantage for applications which need to retrieve multiple rows in a sequence of the clustering attribute. A clustering index makes no difference for single rows retrievals. There can only be one clustering index defined for any particular relation.

The CREATE INDEX statement is also used to specify how a relation in a partitioned table space should be divided (this is done by means of the PART clause in CREATE INDEX statement). A *partitioned index* must be a clustering index. A comprehensive example of the CREATE INDEX statement is presented below:

```
CREATE INDEX XCPEMPLOYEE
   ON EMPLOYEE
      (WORKDEPT ASC)
   USING STOGROUP DSN8G200
```

```
        PRIQTY   36
        PCTFREE   5  CLUSTER    (PART 1 VALUES('K99'),
                                 PART 2 VALUES('Z99'),
                                 PART 3 VALUES('999'))
BUFFERPOOL BP1
CLOSE YES
DSETPASS LESZEK;
```

In the example a clustering and partitioned index, called **XCPEMPLOYEE**, has been specified for the relation **EMPLOYEE**. The index is built for the ascending order of values in the single attribute WORKDEPT. The considerations for the use of USING, BUFFERPOOL, CLOSE and DSETPASS clauses are the same as in the case of CREATE TABLESPACE statement. The page size of an index, however, is a fixed 4K bytes. This implies that a 32K byte buffer pool (BP32K) is not available for indexes.

Three partitions are defined for the index: partition 1 will contain the range of WORKDEPT values A00 to K99; partition 2 will contain index entries for employees working in the departments L00 to Z99; and partition 3 will contain entries above Z99.

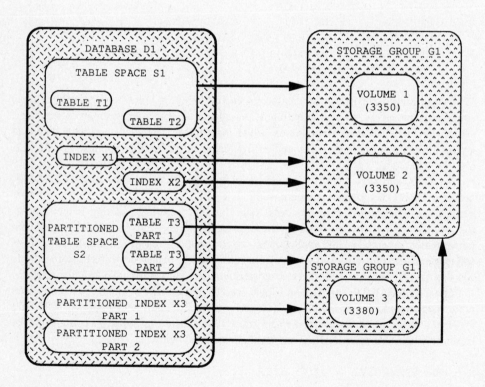

Figure 6.2   Physical data objects in DB2

Each partition uses storage group DSN8G200. In general, a different storage group can be specified for each partition and this could be achieved by defining USING clause immediately after each PART clause.

A summarized account of possibilities in mapping relations to files in DB2 environment is given in Figure 6.2. The figure shows a multitude of possible arrangements in physical database design. The performance of the system can vary considerably depending on the decisions taken.

6.2.2.2 Mapping in ORACLE

ORACLE uses *partitions* to acquire external storage for the database relations and indexes. Conceptually, the ORACLE notion of partition corresponds to the DB2 notion of storage group. A SQL statement CREATE PARTITION is used to create a partition, for example:

```
CREATE PARTITION ORA20MEGA;
```

A partition consists of one or more *operating system files*. A file can be added to the partition by means of a SQL statement ALTER PARTITION, for example:

```
ALTER PARTITION ORA20MEGA
  ADD FILE 'dbs2a.ora';
```

The specification of the file name varies by operating system. Moreover, for certain operating systems (such as Unix) an ORACLE utility called CCF (Create Contiguous File) must be run for every file before adding it to a partition. The CCF utility organizes (allocates and "cleans out") blocks to be used for a file. For example:

```
ccf dbs2a.ora 24000
```

This creates a contiguous file called *dbs2a.ora* which contains 24000 operating system blocks. In a typical Unix environment, the operating system (physical) block is 512 bytes. This converts to an ORACLE (logical) block which, on most operating systems, is either 2048 or 4096 bytes (2048 bytes on Unix). In the example, 6000 ORACLE blocks have been created.

In a newly installed system, a partition called SYSTEM is automatically created. Additional partitions may be added at any time in order to control both placement and accesses across disks to relations. The information about partitions is kept in a data dictionary relation which is made available to users via the view called PARTITIONS.

A partition may contain many relations, but relations may not span partitions; however, a relation may span files in a partition. For every relation that is created (CREATE TABLE), a space definition (CREATE SPACE) controls how and in what partition the table rows will be stored. Indexes (CREATE INDEX) are stored in the same partition as their corresponding tables.

A user has a choice of using the default space definition built into ORACLE or creating a private space definition. A *space* contains pages which are equivalent to ORACLE (logical) blocks. The default space definition, called DEFAULT, is as follows:

```
CREATE SPACE DEFINITION DEFAULT
    DATAPAGES      (INITIAL         5,
                    INCREMENT      25,
                    MAXEXTENTS   9999,
                    PCTFREE        20)
    INDEXPAGES     (INITIAL         5,
                    INCREMENT      25,
                    MAXEXTENTS   9999)
    PARTITION      SYSTEM;
```

The syntax illustrated in the default space definition mirrors the general syntax of creating any space definition. The space is split into two segments: a *data segment* identified by the keyword DATAPAGES and an *index segment* identified by the keyword INDEXPAGES. All indexes created on a relation must use the same space definition as the relation.

The INITIAL parameter determines the number of pages in the first space allocation for relation data or index entries. The minimum value of this parameter is three ORACLE blocks; hence, at least six ORACLE blocks must be available to create a relation. For successful initial allocation, the blocks must be contiguous on a storage medium.

The INCREMENT parameter specifies secondary space allocations after the blocks in the initial *extents* are filled with data. There is no guarantee that the space obtained for incremental extents will be contiguous.

The MAXEXTENTS parameter imposes an upper bound on the number of times ORACLE can allocate an incremental extent. Unless there are special reasons to restrict the sizes of relations and indexes using the space being defined, this parameter should be set very high. The parameter is operating system dependent and, for portability reasons, the default value of 9999 is higher than actually allowed by most operating systems. For example, on VAX/VMS the maximum is about 475 extents, and on MS/DOS the maximum is about 110 extents.

The PCTFREE parameter controls the distribution of the free space during initial load of relation data or during initial creation of index entries. The parameter value can range from 1 percent to 99 percent; the default is 20 percent.

The PARTITION keyword identifies the partition that ORACLE will use for the relations and indexes belonging to the space. If this keyword is not specified, the partition SYSTEM will be used.

The space definition per se does not allocate any storage. Storage is first allocated when a relation (or cluster) is created under the control of this space definition. Multiple relations can be controlled by the same space definition, but, in general, a good practice is to associate the definition with a particular relation.

A *cluster* is an alternative method of storing data in an ORACLE database. It should not be confused with the clustering index concept of DB2. A cluster is created in order to contain two or more relations which have one or more attributes in common (usually keys) and which are frequently accessed together (via join operations).

The purpose of clustering is to improve performance of accessing such relations by storing their rows physically close. For all of the relations in a cluster, rows with the same *cluster attribute* values are stored in the successive logical blocks. Also, each distinct value in each cluster attribute is stored only once, although it is applicable to many relations and rows within relations.

The CREATE CLUSTER statement is used to define a cluster. The *cluster key* is formed by the attribute(s) named in the statement. Relations are added to the cluster by means of the CLUSTER clause of the CREATE TABLE statement. An example of a CREATE CLUSTER statement follows:

```
CREATE CLUSTER PERSONNEL
    (DEPTNUMBER CHAR(4))
    SPACE SP_DEPARTMENT
    SIZE 512
    COMPRESS;
```

The SPACE keyword makes a reference to the space definition. The cluster key values are stored according to the specifications in the INDEXPAGES of CREATE SPACE statement. ORACLE automatically builds an index on the cluster key; however, a CREATE INDEX statement on the attributes which form the cluster key may still be reasonably used, for example, to create a *unique* index for one of the relations in the cluster.

The COMPRESS/NOCOMPRESS switch indicates whether the cluster key index is built compressed or noncompressed. Its functionality is the same as explained for CREATE INDEX statement below.

The SIZE option specifies the size, in bytes, of a cluster (logical) block. Its value should be a divisor of the physical block size and is usually several times smaller than the ORACLE (logical) block. If the specified value is larger than the physical block size, ORACLE will use the physical block size. By choosing a "good" size, space is better utilized and physical scans of rows can be quicker.

To associate a relation with a cluster and/or space definition, the cluster and/or space definition is named in the CREATE TABLE statement, for example:

```
CREATE TABLE DEPARTMENT
    (DEPTNO      CHAR(4)       NOT NULL,
     DEPTNAME    VARCHAR(36)   NOT NULL,
     MANAGERID   CHAR(8))
    SPACE SP_DEPARTMENT
    PCTFREE 8
    CLUSTER PERSONNEL(DEPTNO);
```

When a relation is created, space is immediately allocated for the initial data segment and the initial index segment. The first CREATE INDEX statement begins to fill the initial index extent. For example:

```
CREATE INDEX XEMPLOYEE
    ON EMPLOYEE
        (WORKDEPT ASC)
    PCTFREE 5
    NOCOMPRESS;
```

The PCTFREE parameter specifies the percentage of index entries to leave free during initial index creation. A larger value of PCTFREE permits more data insertions before index block splits occur. The default value is 10 percent.

The COMPRESS/NOCOMPRESS flag indicates whether index data will be compressed or not. Compression saves storage and may speed up some operations that use the index, but it prevents ORACLE from answering the query from the index entries alone without accessing the relation data. The default is COMPRESS.

A relation can have any number of indexes. An index created on a combination of attributes is called a *concatenated index*. The UNIQUE clause in CREATE INDEX statement enforces uniqueness of values of relation attributes which are indexed.

Figure 6.3 illustrates the relationships between physical data objects in an ORACLE database. Although physical characteristics of ORACLE seem a bit simpler than in DB2, they pose equally challenging physical database design problems.

6.3 INDEXES

In most relational DBMSs, indexes are the only access paths to rows in a relation other than a sequential scan of the entire relation, row by row. An exception is INGRES, which

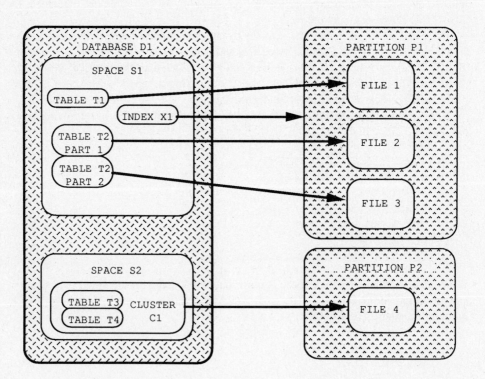

Figure 6.3   Physical data objects in ORACLE

provides hashing and linked lists apart from indexing and scanning, as access mechanisms. The indexes are usually structured as B⁺-trees. The B⁺-tree is an important generalization of the B-tree and B*-tree (where 'B' stands for balanced). In a file management area, the most popular, but much enhanced, implementation of the B⁺-tree is the IBM's virtual storage access method (VSAM).

6.3.1 Internal structure of B⁺-tree indexes

Indexing in database systems is an application of the tree concept to search for records in a file. In a typical B⁺-tree implementation of indexes, each node of the tree contains key-pointer pairs. The key values are kept in sorted order. The pointers of nonleaf nodes point to lower level nodes in the index while the pointers of leaf nodes identify the relation rows which contain a particular key value. Depending on a DBMS, the identifiers of rows (i.e. the pointers in the leaf nodes) are known as row identifiers (ROWID), tuple identifiers (TID) or record identifiers (record-ID). The ROWID structure of ORACLE is described in Section 6.4.2.

Nodes correspond to pages and the distribution of free space within index pages and relation pages is initially controlled by the PCTFREE parameter (Section 6.2). However, the actual space utilization in some index pages may be much less than indicated by the PCTFREE value. This is because the index tree is always *balanced*, that is, all branches of the tree are the same depth. Due to the insertions of new rows into the table, the number of entries in an index page grows and if the page of any index level is full, a *page split* occurs. This causes another page to be added to that level of index and the index entries are re-allocated in such a way that both pages involved are about half-full. Conversely, an opposite effect—*a page concatenation*—can occur due to the deletions of rows in the relation.

Figure 6.4 gives an example of a B⁺-tree index on a single column 'person-name' of some database relation. The index contains three levels of index pages: the root index page, two intermediate index pages and five leaf (or terminal) index pages. The leaf pages

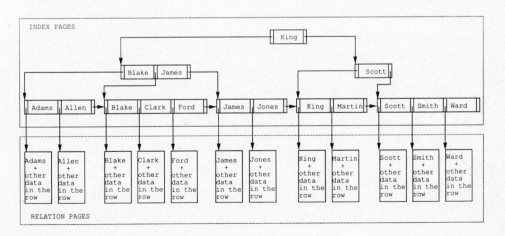

Figure 6.4 Example of a B⁺-tree index on a database relation

are linked together to facilitate sequential processing of the relation records and are termed the *sequence set*. The key values within the sequence set are kept in sorted order. The index implementation shown in Figure 6.4 departs from the theoretical interpretation of the B⁺-tree in that the leaf pages do not contain records (they contain pointers to records).

The B-tree and its variations belong to a category of *multiway trees* which are a generalization of *binary trees* such that a node contains n keys and $n+1$ pointers (instead of one key and two pointers). The specific properties of a B⁺-tree of order M are:

- All nodes, except the root, have at least $\lceil M/2 \rceil$ children and not more than M children (where $\lceil ... \rceil$ is the mathematical notation of the 'ceiling' function on a quotient).
- All leaf nodes appear at the same level, that is, they are the same distance from the root node (this is the balancing feature of the index).
- All nodes always have one less key than pointers.
- Leaf nodes represent the sequence set of the data records.

```
                    Successive index key values:
                        JOHNSON
                        JOHNSTON
                        JOHNSTOWN
                        JOHNTON
```

Forward compression applied:

Find characters at the beginning of each index key value that are the same as in the preceding key value.

Key value:	Count of same characters:	Forward compression result (count and remaining key):
JOHNSON	0 (first key)	0 JOHNSON
JOHNSTON	5	5 TON
JOHNSTOWN	7	7 WN
JOHNTON	4	4 TON

Rear compression applied:

Find characters at the end of each index key value that are the same as in the preceding key value and eliminate them.

Key value:	Forward compression result:	Forward and rear compression result (forward count and remaining key):	Key length:
JOHNSON	0 JOHNSON	0 JOHNSON	7
JOHNSTON	5 TON	5 T	1
JOHNSTOWN	7 WN	7 W	1
JOHNTON	4 TON	4 TO	2

Figure 6.5   Example of forward and rear compression on index key values

The order of the index tree is not always obvious from a brief investigation of its illustration. The index of Figure 6.4 must be at least of order 3 because some nonroot nodes (e.g. Blake, Jones) have three children; however, the order must be less than 5 because some nonroot nodes (e.g. Scott) have only two children. The index is therefore of order 3 or order 4 and further analysis is needed to determine which it is. Such an analysis would show that the index is of order 3 because only two index levels would be needed if the order was 4.

Although indexes in DBMSs are implemented using the general concept of B^+-tree, the implementations vary in details, mainly as a result of different storage allocation schemes. For example, in DB2, indexes are always stored in a space separate from the relation space used to store the data. In ORACLE, on the contrary, all indexes created on a relation must use the same space definition as the relation. Moreover, and partly as a result of the above difference, the concept of the clustering index (Section 6.2.2.1), important in DB2, does not exist in ORACLE.

Indexes can be created for unique (i.e. key) columns or for nonunique columns. The leaf pages contain every indexed data value and its corresponding row identifier that will locate the actual row. For a unique index, there is only one row identifier per data value (Figure 6.4), while for a nonunique index there can be any number of row identifiers per data value. The index entries in leaf pages are sorted on the data value (primary sort) and on the row identifier (secondary sort).

Indexes facilitate database retrieval operations, but they involve some overhead spent keeping them balanced due to update operations. The database designer should strike a balance by taking advantage of knowledge, obtained during the requirements analysis and specifications phase, of the composition of business functions (Section 3.2.2). When deciding on indexes for a particular relation, the access graphs and design ranks of functions, obtained during the conceptual design phase, are invaluable (Sections 4.3 and 4.5.2).

The advantages of indexes are in the query optimization area (Section 6.5). These advantages are derived from the following:

- Retrieval performance remains almost constant when the number of rows in a relation increases.
- Retrieval is fast for both single rows and multiple rows.
- Updates, insertions and deletions are efficient and they maintain index key order for fast retrieval.
- Because all leaf nodes appear at the same level, retrieval of any row from the physical beginning or physical end of the relation takes approximately the same amount of time.
- Indexes are logically and physically independent of the relation data and can be dropped and created any time without invalidating the applications.
- Indexes are maintained automatically by the DBMS.

6.3.2   Index compression

In ORACLE, indexes by default are created compressed. The default can be changed by specifying the NOCOMPRESS option in the CREATE INDEX statement. The aim of compression is to store only the portion of an index key value which distinguishes it from the values immediately before and after it. This is achieved in ORACLE by simultaneously using forward and rear compression. Figure 6.5 illustrates such a compression.

An advantage of compression is that the storage space requirements for index entries is substantially reduced. Because the size of the index page is fixed, this can lead to reduction in the index levels and, as a result, the average time needed to retrieve a relation row can be reduced. It is estimated that compressed indexes require approximately 10 bytes per index entry, whereas noncompressed indexes require about 17 bytes per entry plus the space needed for the entire key value (Section 6.4.2).

A disadvantage of ORACLE compression is that it is never possible to resolve a SQL query directly in the index without accessing rows of the relation, because the characters compressed by the rear compression are not stored. A SQL query can sometimes be resolved with a noncompressed index, if every column referenced in the query is also a part of the index key. There is also an operational overhead involved in compressing and decompressing index values. For example, assuming that a noncompressed index on CITY_NAME exist, the following two queries can be resolved using the index only (Section 6.5):

```
SQL> SELECT CITY_NAME
   2    FROM EMPLOYEE
   3    WHERE CITY_NAME LIKE 'M%K';
SQL> SELECT COUNT (CITY_NAME)
   2    FROM EMPLOYEE
   3    WHERE CITY_NAME LIKE 'WARSAW';
```

6.3.3   Comparison of B$^+$-tree with B-tree and B*-tree

The primary distinction between a B$^+$-tree and a B-tree index is that the latter eliminates the redundant storage of index key values. In the B$^+$-tree, any index key which appears in a nonleaf node is repeated in the leaf. Depending on a variation, the B-tree nodes can hold only index keys or complete data records. Alternatively, because index keys that appear in nonleaf nodes appear nowhere else in the B-tree, an additional pointer to a data record must be included in each nonleaf node.

In general, the B-tree uses fewer tree nodes than a corresponding B$^+$-tree and the searches to data records pointed to by nonleaf nodes are slightly faster; however, the operations on B-tree indexes, including splitting and concatenation, are more complicated. The sequential processing in a B-tree is more complex than traversing the sequence set of a B$^+$-tree and the structural simplicity of B$^+$-trees seems to outweigh the few advantages of B-trees for database implementations.

The B*-tree is an interesting variation of the B-tree, which can be mixed with the B$^+$-tree, if desired. The distinguishing feature of the B*-tree is that its nodes are not split until a node and an adjacent node are both full and one of them is about to overflow. When this happens, the two nodes (rather than one) are split, making three nodes. This ensures that every node is about two-thirds (rather than one-half) full. As a result, the overall number of nodes is smaller than in a corresponding B-tree or B$^+$-tree and, hence, searching a B*-tree is faster on average than searching a B-tree or B$^+$-tree. However, the operations on indexes due to insertions and deletions are more complex and the implementation of a B*-tree is more difficult.

6.4 EXTERNAL STORAGE ESTIMATES

An important consideration in physical database design is the efficient use of direct access storage space. Basic allocation and placement strategies for relations were discussed in Section 6.2 and for indexes in Section 6.3. In this section, we give further details about the implementation of DB2 and ORACLE and provide formulas for the estimation of storage needs in both DBMSs.

6.4.1 Storage estimates in DB2

Inside DB2, a relation is known as a *table* and is treated as a collection of records of the same type. A *record* is the storage representation of a tuple (row) of attributes (columns) values. Records are stored within *pages* (Section 6.2.2.1) and cannot span pages. A page size can be either 4K bytes or 32K bytes. A CREATE TABLE will fail unless the maximum size of table records is less than the page size. If a table space contains many relations, a page will have records of different types.

A record type in a page can be either fixed-length or variable-length. In most cases, *fixed-length records* are preferable as they enable optimization of DB2 processing. Also, a fixed-length record, once stored, is never moved from its original page. There are three situations which result in *variable-length records*:

1. when a relation is created with an edit procedure (EDITPROC clause of the CREATE TABLE statement). The edit routine performs the encoding (encryption or compression) on the data when a row is being stored and decoding when the row is being retrieved;
2. when a relation is created with a varying-length character string column (VARCHAR data type in the CREATE TABLE statement);
3. when a column is added to a previously created relation (ADD clause of the ALTER TABLE statement), for example:

```
ALTER TABLE DEPARTMENT
  ADD DEPTLOCN CHAR(4);
```

Every record has a 6 byte prefix. Additionally, one byte of overhead is needed for each column that may contain null values and two bytes of overhead are required by each VARCHAR column.

The format of DB2 page is shown in Figure 6.6. Every page containing data records (as opposed to index entries) has a 22 byte header. A 2 byte directory entry is kept for each record stored in the page. A directory entry plus a record prefix constitute together a fixed overhead of 8 bytes for each record. The size of a column depends on its data type; for example, assuming that NOT NULL is specified, a SMALLINT column value takes 2 bytes, an INTEGER value is 4 bytes and a FLOAT value is 8 bytes. A DECIMAL value is from 1 to 8 bytes depending on the precision (e.g. a DECIMAL(11) value occupies 6 bytes).

The space available to store records in a 4K byte page is 4074 bytes (4096 with a 22 byte header); however, a DB2 page can contain a maximum of 127 records. This means that space is wasted in a table space if its pages contain only short records, that is, smaller than 32 bytes (4074 : 127 ≅ 32). An excessive normalization can contribute to such a waste. On the other hand, even more space is wasted in a table space that contains records slightly longer than 2037 because only one record can fit in each page. A design aim should be to minimize the number of pages needed to store all records in a table space. If an index cannot be used in a relation processing, DB2 scans every page of the table space.

A page in the index space has the header of 29 bytes. Every nonunique index entry has a 6 byte prefix, every non-leaf index entry has a 3 byte pointer to a lower level index entry and every leaf index entry has a 4 byte pointer, which is a row ID in the relation. Additionally, one byte of overhead is needed for each column that is part of the key and may contain null values. The overall length of an index entry is the sum of the key length and the index overhead.

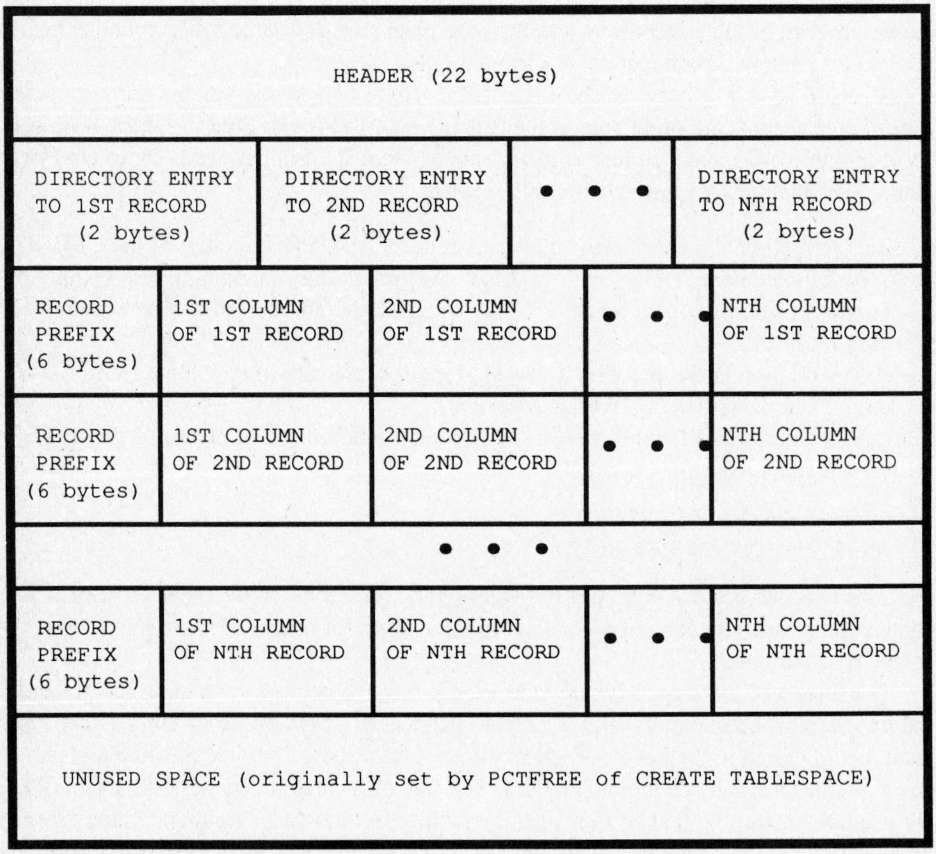

HEADER (22 bytes)				
DIRECTORY ENTRY TO 1ST RECORD (2 bytes)	DIRECTORY ENTRY TO 2ND RECORD (2 bytes)	• • •		DIRECTORY ENTRY TO NTH RECORD (2 bytes)
RECORD PREFIX (6 bytes)	1ST COLUMN OF 1ST RECORD	2ND COLUMN OF 1ST RECORD	• •	NTH COLUMN OF 1ST RECORD
RECORD PREFIX (6 bytes)	1ST COLUMN OF 2ND RECORD	2ND COLUMN OF 2ND RECORD	• •	NTH COLUMN OF 2ND RECORD
		• • •		
RECORD PREFIX (6 bytes)	1ST COLUMN OF NTH RECORD	2ND COLUMN OF NTH RECORD	• •	NTH COLUMN OF NTH RECORD
UNUSED SPACE (originally set by PCTFREE of CREATE TABLESPACE)				

Figure 6.6   DB2 page format

The degree of normalization is crucial not only for space utilization. As the number of relations increases due to normalization, the processing costs can become prohibitive in an exponential fashion as it is not unusual for the join of many large relations to take hours. Moreover, DB2 imposes an upper limit of fourteen relations that can be joined (this limit can be significantly less if an underlying SQL statement is especially complex). In many cases, the introduction of *controlled redundancy* can alleviate these problems. Consider the design in which relations EMPLOYEE and DEPARTMENT (identified by DEPT_NUMBER) both have the attribute DEPT_NAME. This attribute should be eliminated from EMPLOYEE to achieve better normalization; however, the lack of normalization here does not create update problems (department names do not change very often and, after all, the update propagation is easy in this case). Thus, performance should be weighed against normalization in the design.

The storage needs for user data constitute a fraction of overall DB2 storage needs (which include the space required by system libraries, log files, catalog files, temporary database, etc.). Three typical database sites are recognized in storage calculations:

1. the small site of approximately 20 application plans, 50 storage groups and 300 relations;
2. the medium site of approximately 200 application plans, 200 storage groups and 1200 relations;
3. the large site of approximately 400 application plans, 400 storage groups and 2400 relations.

The following formula can be used to make an approximate estimate of overall DASD (direct access storage device) storage needs:

$$NUMVOL = 3 * \frac{2 * TOTDAT}{VOLCAP} \qquad (6.1)$$

where:

NUMVOL is the number of DASD volumes,
TOTDAT is the total amount of data in megabytes,
VOLCAP is the volume capacity in megabytes.

In Formula 6.1, the multiplier 2 is made up of:

- 10 percent for record overhead (this assumes that the average row size is about 80 bytes);
- 5 percent free space within page (i.e. the default value of PCTFREE parameter);
- 15 percent for unusable space on disk track (e.g. only four 4K byte pages can fit on a 19K byte track of a 3350 disk volume);
- 25 percent for unused space within VSAM data set allocated by CREATE STOGROUP statement;
- 20 percent for indexes;
- 25 percent for future growths.

The multiplier 3 in Formula 6.1 is made up of non-user data, such as:

- system libraries (which require a fixed amount of space of about 66M bytes regardless of the site size);
- catalog data sets (about 15M bytes in the small site, 60M bytes in the medium site and 120M bytes in the large site);
- active log data sets to record transactions and data changes; they are periodically off-loaded to the archive log (about 120M bytes in the small site, 240M bytes in the medium site and 2400M bytes in the large site);
- a temporary database to keep intermediate results of certain SQL statements (about 5M bytes in the small site, 20M bytes in the medium site and 40M bytes in the large site).

The value of VOLCAP variable depends on the storage device. It equals, for example, 317M bytes for 3350 disk volumes or 630M bytes for 3380 disk volumes.

The formula for the approximate estimate of storage needs can be made more precise by taking into account the page formats in table and index spaces. This is best explained by means of the following example.

Assume the default settings of PCTFREE and FREEPAGE parameters of the CREATE TABLESPACE statement; these defaults are 5 percent of a page and no free pages, respectively (Section 6.2.2.1). Assume also that the page size is 4K bytes and that the user database contains:

- 1 relation;
- 100 000 rows;
- 20 fixed-length columns, NOT NULL, totalling 200 bytes;
- 5 fixed-length columns with nulls allowed, totalling 30 bytes;
- 1 varying-length column with nulls allowed, averaging 100 bytes;
- 1 unique index over 3 columns, totalling 28 bytes.

The number of pages in the table data space immediately after load can now be calculated in the following steps:

1. Usable page size is 4074 bytes (4096 with 22 bytes of page header).
2. Stored record length is 346 bytes (330 bytes of user data + 8 bytes of record overhead + 6 bytes of null overhead + 2 bytes of variable field overhead).
3. Maximum record per page equals 11 (i.e. the 'floor' function of the quotient 4074 : 346 = 11.775).
4. Records per page after load equals 10 (11 * 95% = 10, where 95 percent is the percentage of the available space after deducting 5 percent enforced by the value of PCTFREE parameter).
5. Number of pages in the table space equals 10 000 (100 000 records : 10 records per page).

The number of pages in the index space immediately after load is determined in the following steps:

1. Usable page size is 4067 bytes (4096 with 29 bytes of page header).
2. Index entry length is 32 bytes (28 bytes of key length + 4 bytes of address pointer).
3. Maximum index entries per page equals 127 (i.e. the 'floor' function of the quotient $4096 : 32 \cong 127.1$).
4. Index entries per page after load equals 114 (127 * 90%, because the PCTFREE default value for index space is 10 percent).
5a. Number of leaf index pages equals 878 (i.e. the 'ceiling' function of the quotient $100000 : 114 \cong 877.2$).
5b. Number of second level index pages equals 8 (i.e. the 'ceiling' function of the quotient $878 : 114 \cong 7.7$).
5c. There is 1 root index page (i.e. the 'ceiling' function of the quotient $8 : 114 \cong 0.07$).
5d. Total number of index pages is 887 (878 + 8 + 1).

6.4.2 Storage estimates in ORACLE

Inside ORACLE, a relation is known as a *table* and is treated as a collection of records of the same type. A *record* is the storage representation of a tuple (row) of attributes (columns) values. Records are stored within *pages* (Section 6.2.2.2) and can (as opposed to DB2) span pages by creating so-called *chained blocks*. A page size is 2K bytes, for most systems, or 4K bytes. Unless the relation is stored within a *cluster* (Section 6.2.2.2), a page contains only records of one relation.

ORACLE attempts to use minimum space when storing data records and index entries. Virtually all records are *variable-length*. This is accomplished by keeping rows and column lengths for all data stored in a page. Also, by default, indexes are created compressed (Section 6.2.2.2).

Every record has four bytes of overhead in an unclustered page or five bytes in a clustered page. Two bytes are needed for row total length and two bytes are used for row sequence number (i.e. the order of insertion). An extra byte in a cluster is required to indicate table number.

Every non-null column data is stored with two bytes of overhead. One byte for column identification and one byte for column length. NULL values are not stored at all. CHAR data values are stored in variable length strings (maximum is 240 characters). NUMBER data values are also stored in variable length format (maximum is as high as 1 followed by 128 zeroes). Columns defined as LONG can store variable length strings containing up to 65 536 characters. Only DATE values are stored in fixed length fields of seven bytes each.

Figures 6.7 and 6.8 show the formats of unclustered and clustered ORACLE pages, respectively. Every unclustered page has 76 bytes of overhead, of which 32 bytes are used for the header of the ORACLE logical block (equivalent to the page itself) and 44 bytes are used for the header of the physical block. For a clustered page, the overhead can increase in steps of 32 bytes if there are two or more cluster logical blocks per physical block (Section 6.2.2.2).

The space available to store records in a 2K-byte page is 1972 bytes (2048 with a 76 byte header). This space is further reduced for initial load by the value of the PCTFREE parameter of CREATE SPACE statement (which, by default, is 20 percent). In reality, space reserved by PCTFREE parameter is exclusively reserved for updates and is not available for insertion of new rows. Only when enough rows have been inserted to fill all pages in the *initial extent* allocated for the relation (by means of CREATE SPACE statement), is the first *incremental extent* allocated.

Chained pages (chained blocks) are used in the following circumstances:

- on an insert of a row which is larger than a page;
- on an update to a row which cannot fit in the current page;
- on an insert to clustered data if it does not fit entirely in the cluster logical block for that cluster key.

A chained block is an additional physical block that makes up a logical block. The next and previous block addresses in the page header are used to establish the chain. Chained blocks do not have to belong to the same extent. From the performance point of view, chained blocks are undesirable.

Associated with every row in a page is the *row sequence number*. This number constitutes a part of the complete address of any row in the database. That address is known as ROWID and can be used in SQL queries. Technically, the ROWID is visualized in hexadecimal representation and it consists of three parts:

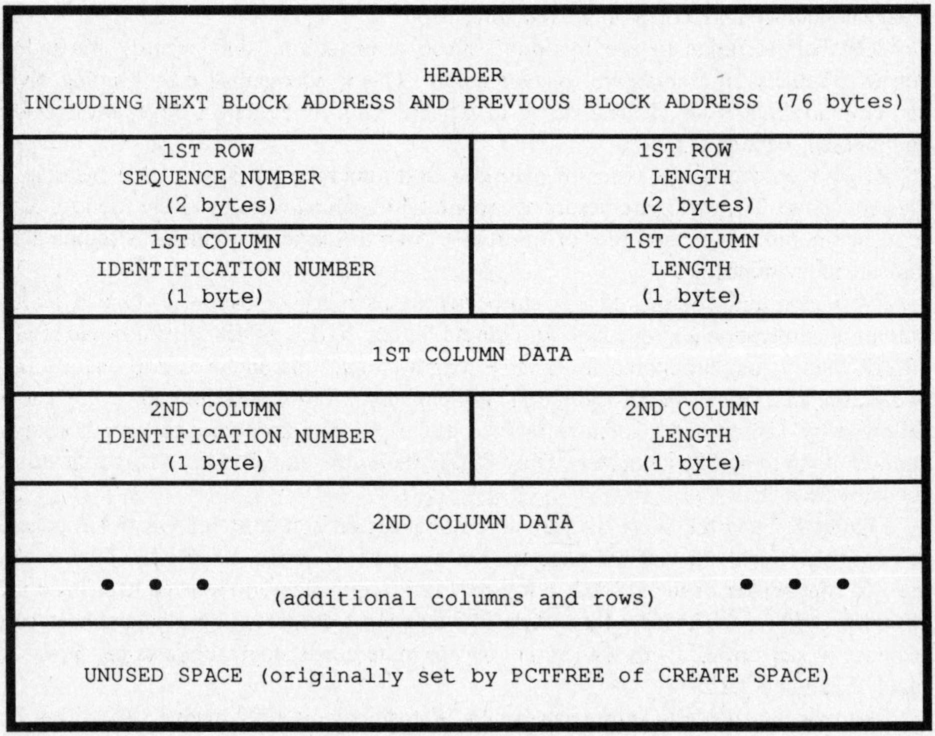

HEADER INCLUDING NEXT BLOCK ADDRESS AND PREVIOUS BLOCK ADDRESS (76 bytes)	
1ST ROW SEQUENCE NUMBER (2 bytes)	1ST ROW LENGTH (2 bytes)
1ST COLUMN IDENTIFICATION NUMBER (1 byte)	1ST COLUMN LENGTH (1 byte)
1ST COLUMN DATA	
2ND COLUMN IDENTIFICATION NUMBER (1 byte)	2ND COLUMN LENGTH (1 byte)
2ND COLUMN DATA	
• • • (additional columns and rows) • • •	
UNUSED SPACE (originally set by PCTFREE of CREATE SPACE)	

Figure 6.7   ORACLE page format (unclustered)

- *logical partition block number*—which identifies a page in the partition that contains the row;
- *row sequence number*—the row number within the table (stored as overhead for each row);
- *partition id*—which identifies the partition.

The following query, run under Unix, selects ROWID numbers for records in the relation ITEM. The function SUBSTR was used to break the information in ROWID into its three components: partition block number, row sequence number and partition id. The example shows that the ITEM rows are stored in partition 1 (SYSTEM), in relative block 34B8 with 7 records in a 2K byte ORACLE block.

```
SQL> SELECT ROWID, SUBSTR(ROWID, 1,8) BLOCK,
  2                 SUBSTR(ROWID,10,4) RSN,
  3                 SUBSTR(ROWID,15,4) PID,
  4          IT_NUMBER, IT_DESCRIPTION
  5              FROM ITEM;


ROWID                 BLOCK     RSN     PID    IT_NUMBER IT_DESCRIPTION
------------------    --------  ------  -----  --------- --------------
000034B8.0001.0001    000034B8  0001    0001   68246789  amplifier
000034B8.0002.0001    000034B8  0002    0001   42687420  tuner
000034B8.0003.0001    000034B8  0003    0001   68714321  compact disc
000034B8.0004.0001    000034B8  0004    0001   77882169  video tapes
000034B8.0005.0001    000034B8  0005    0001   30002468  television
000034B8.0006.0001    000034B8  0006    0001   12345678  video recorder
000034B8.0007.0001    000034B8  0007    0001   56788001  speaker
```

ROWID in a SQL statement is used as if it were a column of a table. This perception is misleading because ROWID is *not* stored in the database at all and, hence, it cannot be referenced in UPDATE, INSERT or DELETE statements. A ROWID value is *not* constant for any row over time (because the physical location of a row may change). The advantages of using ROWIDs are:

- they provide the fastest access to a row of the table;
- they can be used to improve concurrency by obtaining row-level locks;
- they allow determination of storage needs of a table.

Some rules of thumb for managing space in ORACLE databases are:

1. Use fewer larger extents rather than more smaller extents. In an optimal arrangement, all data for a relation should be stored in its initial extent.
2. Increase the value of PCTFREE parameter if, during initial load of the relation, many columns are left NULL and they are expected to be filled in later. Such updates will make individual rows wider because NULLs in ORACLE do not use any space.

```
┌─────────────────────────────────────────────────────────────────────┐
│                             HEADER                                    │
│  INCLUDING NEXT BLOCK ADDRESS AND PREVIOUS BLOCK ADDRESS (76 bytes)   │
├─────────────────────────────────────────────────────────────────────┤
│                          CLUSTER KEY                                  │
├──────────────────────┬──────────────────────┬──────────────────────┤
│      1ST ROW         │      1ST ROW         │       TABLE          │
│  SEQUENCE NUMBER     │      LENGTH          │       NUMBER         │
│     (2 bytes)        │     (2 bytes)        │     (1 byte)         │
├──────────────────────┴───────┬──────────────┴──────────────────────┤
│      1ST COLUMN              │          1ST COLUMN                  │
│  IDENTIFICATION NUMBER       │            LENGTH                    │
│     (1 byte)                 │          (1 byte)                   │
├──────────────────────────────┴─────────────────────────────────────┤
│                      1ST COLUMN DATA                                 │
├──────────────────────────────┬─────────────────────────────────────┤
│      2ND COLUMN              │          2ND COLUMN                  │
│  IDENTIFICATION NUMBER       │            LENGTH                    │
│     (1 byte)                 │          (1 byte)                   │
├──────────────────────────────┴─────────────────────────────────────┤
│                      2ND COLUMN DATA                                 │
├─────────────────────────────────────────────────────────────────────┤
│   ● ● ●      (additional columns and rows)        ● ● ●              │
├─────────────────────────────────────────────────────────────────────┤
│                       UNUSED SPACE                                   │
└─────────────────────────────────────────────────────────────────────┘
```

Figure 6.8   ORACLE page format (clustered)

3. Do not specify the MAXEXTENTS parameter unless the application requires the limiting of space for a relation.
4. Ensure the existence of contiguous blocks for initial data and index extents when the relation is created, otherwise the CREATE will not be successful.

Oracle Corporation provides formulas to estimate the sizes of a single nonclustered relation and a single index. These formulas can be expanded to approximate the storage needs for all user data.

The number of pages required for a relation is calculated as follows:

$$\text{NUMPAG}_R = \frac{\text{NUMROW} * \text{AVEBYT}}{(1 - \text{PCTFRE}) * 1972} \tag{6.2}$$

where:

> NUMROW is the number of rows in the relation;
> AVEBYT is the average number of bytes per row;
> PCTFRE is the decimal value of the PCTFREE parameter;

1972 is the number of bytes available to store rows in a 2048 bytes page (2048 with a 76 byte page header) (Figure 6.7).

The AVEBYT value in Formula 6.2 is determined as:

$$AVEBYT = \sum_{i=1}^{n} ((1 - N_i) * (C_i + 2)) + 4 \qquad (6.3)$$

where:

i = 1, ..., n identifies a column in the relation;

N_i is the fraction of ith column with null value;

C_i is the average length of ith column;

2 is the number of bytes needed for 'column identification number' and 'column length' (Figure 6.7);

4 is the number of bytes needed for 'row sequence number' and 'row length' (Figure 6.7).

To illustrate Formula 6.2, consider (and compare with the example in Section 6.4.1) the database which contains:

- 1 relation;
- 100 000 rows;
- 20 columns, NOT NULL, averaging 200 bytes (i.e. C = 200);
- 5 columns with nulls allowed, averaging 130 bytes, and with Ni = 0.2 for each of the five columns;
- PCTFREE value is set at 20 percent.

For this example:

$$AVEBYT = (200 + (20 * 2)) + ((1 - 0.2) * (130 + (5 * 2)) + 4$$
$$= (222 + (0.8 * 140) + 4$$
$$= 222 + 112 + 4$$
$$= 338$$

$$NUMPAG_R = \frac{100\ 000\ *\ 338}{(1 - 0.2)\ *\ 1972}$$
$$= \frac{33\ 800\ 000}{1578}$$
$$= 21\ 420$$

Hence, 21 420 pages are needed to store this rather large relation in the database.

Index space is more difficult to estimate than relation space. A rule of thumb is that on average about 20–30 percent of the space needed for the relation is required for indexes to that relation. In more detailed calculations the following parameters should be taken into account:

- the number of indexes for the relation;
- distribution of values in the indexed column(s) (in particular, the number of distinct values in comparison with the number of all values);
- the length of the indexed columns;
- the percentage of NULLs in the indexed columns;
- the use of compressed or noncompressed index;
- the time of index creation (i.e. before or after the relation is loaded with data).

The number of pages required for an index can be calculated according to the formula:

$$\text{NUMPAG}_I \;=\; 1.1 \;*\; \frac{\text{NUMROW} \;*\; \text{ESTKEY}}{(1 \;-\; \text{PCTFRE}) \;*\; 1972} \tag{6.4}$$

where:

NUMROW is the number of rows in the relation;
ESTKEY is the estimated key length;
PCTFRE is the decimal value of the PCTFREE parameter;
1972 is the number of bytes available to store rows in a 2048 bytes page
(2048 with a 76 byte page header) (Figure 6.7);
1.1 factor stands for the additional 10 percent to account for the upper nodes of the B-tree index.

The estimated key length is:

ESTKEY= 10 for compressed indexes, or otherwise
ESTKEY= 16 + (number of columns in key) + (sum of lengths of columns in key)

For example, assume that an index is created on a 100 000 row relation and that:

- PCTFREE value is 20 percent;
- the index is compressed;
- the index is over 3 columns, totaling 28 bytes.

In this situation, the number of pages needed for a compressed index is:

$$\text{NUMPAG}_I \;=\; 1.1 * \frac{100\,000 \;*\; 10}{(1 - 0.2) \;*\; 1972}$$

$$=\; \frac{1\,000\,000}{1578}$$

$$=\; 634$$

If the index were noncompressed, the number of pages required would be:

$$NUMPAG_I = 1.1 * \frac{100\,000 * (16 + 3 + 28)}{(1 - 0.2) * 1972}$$

$$= \frac{4\,700\,000}{1578}$$

$$= 2979$$

The number of pages required for a cluster is determined by the space definition used in the CREATE CLUSTER statement (Section 6.2.2.2). That space definition controls the space available for all relations in the cluster. It is desirable to allow one cluster (logical) block for each unique cluster key. The parameter PCTFREE does not apply for clusters.

The formats of ORACLE page do not show overheads for relations. Every relation requires two data pages and one index page of overhead. The first data page is known as the 'extent block'. It contains information about pages in the extent (the start address (TAB$RBA) of each extent used by relation data, the last extent address and the number of pages in the extent). The second data page duplicates some data dictionary information, such as relation definitions. This reduces contention on the data dictionary operations. The overhead required for an index segment is an 'extent block' that contains information about extents used by all indexes for a particular relation.

6.5 CONTROLLING ACCESS PATH SELECTION

In general, the determination of access paths to data is the responsibility of the DBMS's query optimizer module (Section 6.1). A principal advantage of the relational model is based on the assumption that a user can communicate with a database in a nonprocedural language in which no access paths are specified. While this assumption can be enforced in principle, current query optimizers are often unable to stand up to the difficulty of the optimization problems. A user can greatly improve the performance of database systems by judiciously influencing the optimizer's choices of access paths. This can be achieved through creating useful indexes and through formulating SQL statements with the deep understanding of potential optimization strategies. In this sense, there is a close connection between the technical issues of query optimization per se and the problems traditionally addressed by physical database design.

The access path selection by a query optimizer is primarily motivated by the existence of indexes. In a typical relational DBMS, five different access paths are possible:

1. *Relation scan*—a sequential scan of data pages of a relation.
2. *Random relation access through index*—a search which exploits an index tree structure to evaluate predicates defined on the index key attributes and to access data pages containing qualifying relation tuples.
3. *Sequential relation access through index*—a search which exploits the sequence set of an index tree without making use of the tree structure (all the index leaf pages are read, but only data pages containing qualifying tuples are retrieved).

4. *Random index only access*—a search which exploits an index tree structure, as in 2, but without accessing the relation data pages (all the predicates can be evaluated using the index and only index entries are referenced).
5. *Sequential index only access*—a search which exploits the sequence set of an index tree, as in 3, but without accessing the relation data pages (all the predicates can be evaluated using the index sequence set and only index entries in leaf pages are referenced).

Performance-wise, random access is most desirable. If a random access cannot be used, for example, in the case of queries which are not selective enough, a sequential index only access can be an attractive alternative (the *selectivity factor* is the reciprocal of the number of different values of an attribute, e.g. if there are only five different values in a column than the selectivity factor is 0.2—because $5 * 0.2 = 1$).

As a relation scan is the most expensive access path it should only be used if more than 25 percent of the relation rows is to be selected. When more than 25 percent is selected by means of an index the overhead caused by using the index to locate data is too high. However, for large relations and queries with the selectivity factor of less than 25 percent the use of an index is likely to be a critical performance factor.

Indexes are created by a database designer as a result of a careful analysis of the overall processing requirements. Such an analysis involves the overall transaction workloads, the composition of business functions (Section 3.2.2), the access graphs (Section 4.3), the design ranks of functions (Section 4.5.2) and so on. Once an index is created, a database programmer should understand the circumstances under which the query optimizer is able to use or not use this index and formulate SQL statements to take advantage of it.

A typical query optimizer will not use an existing index where:

- there is no WHERE clause in the SQL statement;
- the predicate modifies the indexed column via a function or arithmetic expression;
- the predicate contains either IS NULL or IS NOT NULL options;
- the SELECT statement contains the DISTINCT keyword and/or the ORDER BY clause and/or the GROUP BY clause;
- the indexed column is referenced in an IN list of the subquery;
- the relation is joined to itself;
- a NOT predicate is used and it cannot be converted to its counterpart without a negation;
- there are some categories of the OR clauses (note, however, that the categories which are affected vary from system to system);
- the WHERE clause does not name the first column of a concatenated (multicolumn) index;
- the column specified in the WHERE clause of an UPDATE statement is also specified in the SET clause of this statement.

An index can only be used if it is referenced in a predicate clause. A predicate (condition) appears within the WHERE clause and is used to include or exclude tuples from a result; for example, the following WHERE clause of an UPDATE statement has two predicates:

```
SQL> UPDATE EMPLOYEE
  2    SET COMMISSION = NULL
  3    WHERE CITY = 'DALLAS'
  4    AND JOB = 'TRAINEE';
```

An index cannot be used if the indexed column must be modified to meet the selection criteria, as in the following WHERE clauses:

```
• WHERE COMMISSION * 12 = 6000
• WHERE SUBSTR(EMP_NAME,1,1) = 'M'
• WHERE TO_CHAR(RENT_DATE, 'DD-MON-YY') = '15-NOV-88'
```

However, an index will be used in ORACLE (but not in DB2) on a column that is being compared to an arithmetic expression; for example, the last WHERE clause above can easily be converted so that ORACLE will use the index to do the search:

```
WHERE RENT_DATE = TO_DATE('15-NOV-88', 'DD-MON-YY')
```

In ORACLE, indexes are not used if the predicate contains either of the phrases IS NULL or IS NOT NULL, as in the example:

```
SQL> SELECT * FROM EMPLOYEE
  2    WHERE COMMISSION IS NOT NULL;
```

However, for numeric columns and for the IS NOT NULL case, it is relatively easy to write a SQL statement so it will use an index, if desirable:

```
SQL> SELECT * FROM EMPLOYEE
  2    WHERE COMMISSION >= 0;
```

Indexes are not generally used to process SELECT statements that involve the sort operation. The statements in this category are: the queries that suppress presentation of identical tuples by using the DISTINCT keyword, the queries that use the ORDER BY clause to specify the order in which the results of a query are to be displayed, and the queries that use the GROUP BY clause to display one line for each group of selected tuples with the same values of one or more specified columns or expressions. However, at times, the optimizer may use the index (if available) and avoid the sort.

Normally, an optimizer will not use an index created on the column referred to in a subquery within the IN predicate; therefore, if the use of an index is desirable, an attempt should be made to use a join instead of the subquery. For example, the following subquery will suppress the use of an index on EMPL#:

```
SQL> SELECT NAME, PHONE#
  2    FROM EMPLOYEE
  3    WHERE EMPL# IN
  4        (SELECT MANAGER# FROM DEPARTMENT);
```

Converting the above subquery to a join will allow a DBMS to use the index on MANAGER#. Note, however, that the two queries are not equivalent if EMPL# and MANAGER# contain non-unique (duplicate) values (then the join query might return more tuples than the subquery).

```
SQL> SELECT NAME, PHONE#
  2   FROM EMPLOYEE, DEPARTMENT
  3   WHERE EMPL# = MANAGER#;
```

In ORACLE, certain subqueries are automatically converted to joins, thus allowing the use of indexes. For example:

```
SQL> SELECT * FROM EMPLOYEE
  2   WHERE EMPLOYEE.DEPT# IN
  3          (SELECT DEPT# FROM DEPARTMENT);
```

can be processed as the following "join" query which, incidentally, is not in valid SQL syntax:

```
SQL> SELECT EMPLOYEE.A FROM EMPLOYEE, D:
  2          (SELECT DISTINCT DEPT# FROM DEPARTMENT)
  3   WHERE D.DEPT# = EMPLOYEE.DEPT#;
```

In general, if the join uses columns which are indexed, the index will be used (by executing so-called nested loops algorithm); however, there are situations in which a join cannot take advantage of indexes (leading to a so-called sort/merge algorithm). One such situation is a join of a relation to itself, that is, a join that compares a column with another (or the same) column in the same relation, for example:

```
SQL> SELECT ONE.EMPL_NAME, TWO.EMPL_NAME
  2   FROM EMPLOYEE ONE, EMPLOYEE TWO
  3   WHERE ONE.DEPT_NAME = TWO.DEPT_NAME
  4    AND ONE.EMPL_NAME < TWO.EMPL_NAME;
```

When a *nested loops join* is performed on two relations, the optimizer selects one of the relations as the outer relation and the other as the inner relation. For each qualifying tuple t'_i of the outer relation, the system scans the inner relation for the tuples t''_i that satisfy the join condition. If we let T' (T'') be the number of tuples of the relation in the outer (inner) loop, then, under the unrealistic assumption that one storage access is needed for each tuple read, $T' + (T' * T'')$ secondary storage accesses are needed to evaluate a nested loops join. However, if an index on the join attribute of the inner relation can be used, then only $T' + (T' * T'' * js)$ accesses are required (where js is a join selectivity factor describing the reduction of the Cartesian product of T' and T'' by the join condition).

When a *sort/merge join* is performed on two relations, the system first sorts the relations on the join attribute and then merges the tuples according to the join condition.

Once sorted, the relations being joined are scanned only once; hence, T' + T"+ S' + S" secondary storage accesses are needed (where S' and S" denote the number of storage accesses necessary to sort the relations).

When a NOT predicate is used, a query optimizer will try to change the predicate to the counterpart or opposite query; for example, NOT <= will be changed to >. If such a transformation is possible, a DBMS will consider using an index if available. The cases for which the transformation is not possible, and an index cannot be used, include:

- NOT = (which, in ORACLE, can also be written as: != or ^= or <>)
- NOT BETWEEN x AND y
- NOT LIKE
- NOT IN

SQL statements with OR clauses use indexes under some circumstances. These circumstances can be quite different depending on a DBMS. In DB2, the use of an index is only considered if the OR clauses use the equality operator in comparisons and refer to the same column for multiple OR clauses.

In ORACLE, the indexes can be used even if different columns are referred to by multiple OR clauses, provided that indexes exist on all these columns. ORACLE achieves this by splitting the original SQL statement into multiple queries and performing something like (but not exactly equivalent to) the union of those queries. For example, a query such as:

```
SQL> SELECT * FROM EMPLOYEE
  2   WHERE COMMISSION = 6000
  3    OR POSITION = 'SALESMAN';
```

can be split into the following two queries (to be "unioned"):

```
SQL> SELECT * FROM EMPLOYEE
  2   WHERE COMMISSION = 6000;
```

and

```
SQL> SELECT * FROM EMPLOYEE
  2   WHERE POSITION = 'SALESMAN'
  3   AND COMMISSION NOT = 6000;
```

A query optimizer will attempt to use a concatenated index to resolve any query which, in the WHERE clause, refers to the first column(s) of that index. Hence, if the following concatenated index exists:

```
SQL> CREATE INDEX THREE_COLUMNS
  2   ON EMPLOYEE (DEPTNAME, STATE, CITY);
```

then it will be used in the following two queries:

```
SQL> SELECT * FROM EMPLOYEE
  2   WHERE DEPTNAME = 'ACCOUNTING'
  3     AND CITY = 'NEWCASTLE'
  4     AND STATE = 'NSW';
SQL> SELECT * FROM EMPLOYEE
  2   WHERE DEPTNAME = 'SALES'
  3     AND CITY = 'NEWCASTLE';
```

However, in the next two examples, the index cannot be used because the WHERE clause does not refer to the first column in the concatenated index:

```
SQL> SELECT * FROM EMPLOYEE
  2   WHERE CITY = 'BURWOOD'
  3     AND STATE = 'NSW';
SQL> SELECT * FROM EMPLOYEE
  2   WHERE STATE = 'VIC';
```

An index will not be used in an UPDATE statement when the column specified in the WHERE clause is also specified in the SET clause, for example:

```
SQL> UPDATE MANAGERS
  2   SET SALARY = 1.1 * SALARY
  3   WHERE SALARY > 40000;
```

The reason for this restriction is that an index controlled update could cause an infinite loop during execution.

Occasionally, the use of an index can decrease performance. One reason for that could be the 25 percent selection factor, mentioned earlier in this section. If more than 25 percent of the relation rows is to be selected, then the use of an index may not be advantageous. Also, the use of an index on small relations can only add overhead. Finally, since all indexes that are appropriate in answering a query need to be first combined together and re-sorted, the overall performance of a query can decrease because sort-merge operations are expensive.

A simple way to suppress the use of an index is to use a "dummy" function or an arithmetic expression with the column which is an index key. Normally, a zero would be added to a numeric column or an empty string would be concatenated to a character column, as in (assuming DEPT# is numeric):

```
SQL> SELECT EMPLNAME, DEPT#, PHONE#
  2   FROM EMPLOYEE
  3   WHERE DEPT# + 0 = 40;
```

6.6   USING INTERNAL MODEL IN PHYSICAL DESIGN

Physical database design can be based on an *external model* of the system's behavior or on an *internal model* of cost estimates obtained statistically by DBMS. It is expected that, with the improvements of query optimizers, the internal models will supersede external techniques. The better the optimizers, the more likely that they will ignore externally motivated access paths and choose superior access plans based on their own models. In this relatively new scenario, the physical design will be dynamically generated by a CASE tool integrated with the DBMS's optimizer.

In Section 6.1, a four-step general procedure for access plan computation was given. A closer look at this procedure reveals a number of difficult efficiency problems which should be addressed by a physical database design tool, whether based on an external or an internal model. These problems are listed below.

1. When determining equivalent access paths, the semantic knowledge about a particular application, represented by statistics, access graphs, integrity constraints, intersecting requirements and so on, should be utilized.
2. Data is retrieved from external storage in blocks or records and many such blocks can be kept simultaneously in virtual storage. This should be exploited by the design tool by incorporating in it the knowledge about the strategies used by the buffer manager for block replacements.
3. A model should incorporate the index and tuple maintenance costs due to update operations.
4. When selecting indexes, multiple-relation functions and SQL statements should also be considered. Moreover, the concatenated (composite) indexes on multiple columns should be dealt with.
5. A model should challenge statistical assumptions whenever contradicting events can be easily observed. Typical assumptions that may not be satisfied in practice are:
    (a) uniformity of attribute values (i.e. that all values of an attribute appear equi-frequently in a relation);
    (b) attribute independence (i.e. that values of different attributes in a relation are not interrelated);
    (c) uniformity of business functions (i.e. that the functions refer attribute values equi-frequently);
    (d) constant number of records per page;
    (e) random placement (i.e. that each record of the relation has the same probability to qualify in a SQL statement, independently of its placement among the pages of external storage).

The major premise of using an internal model for physical database design comes from the belief that attempts to outmaneuver the optimizer are misguided. In order to be able to base the design on an internal model, a DBMS must collect information about the optimizer's choices in the catalog and must make this information available to a design tool. ORACLE does not yet provide such information, but DB2 does. The SQL language of DB2 contains the EXPLAIN statement which obtains information about how another SQL statement will be executed. In general (though not with the current DB2 version of EXPLAIN), the physical design could be done even if the database relations are not yet populated with tuples. In such a case, the designer would have to provide statistics describing the database configurations which would then be loaded in the catalog.

The EXPLAIN statement causes optimizer to choose an access plan for the SQL statement being explained. Once chosen, the information about the access plan is stored in an explanation relation owned by the user performing EXPLAIN. In DB2 such a relation is called PLAN_TABLE. The DBMS does not actually execute the statement being explained, nor is an access plan for executing that statement stored anywhere for future use. The EXPLAIN statement computes the optimizer's cost estimates rather than actual costs.

The EXPLAIN statement is conceived to contain four options: REFERENCE, STRUCTURE, COST and PLAN. Only the last option is implemented in DB2 (Version 1 Release 3). The following is an example of EXPLAIN PLAN statement for SQL query number 157:

```
SQL> EXPLAIN PLAN SET QUERYNO = 157 FOR
  2             SELECT EMPLNAME, DEPT#, PHONE#
  3             FROM EMPLOYEE
  4             WHERE EMPL# IN
  5                 (SELECT MANAGER#
  6                  FROM MANAGERS);
```

After execution of this statement, in order to obtain the results, the designer will have to perform the following:

```
SQL> SELECT * FROM PLAN_TABLE
  2   WHERE QUERYNO = 157;
```

The REFERENCE option identifies:

1. the type of SQL statement (SELECT, DELETE, INSERT, or UPDATE);
2. the relations referenced in the statement;
3. the columns referenced in the statement in such ways that they support the use of indexes (called *plausible columns*).

The STRUCTURE option determines:

1. the structure of the subquery tree in the statement;
2. the estimated number of tuples accessed by the statement and its subqueries;
3. the estimated number of times the statement and its subqueries are executed.

The COST option indicates:

1. the estimated cost of execution of the statement and its subqueries in the chosen access plan.

The PLAN option describes:

1. access paths chosen to access each relation, including indexes to be used;
2. order in which relations are accessed and joined;

3. join method selected (nested loops or sort/merge);
4. indication of sorts to be performed;
5. locking strategy.

A physical database design based on the internal model provided by the EXPLAIN statement has five major steps:

1. Determine:
   (a) referenced relations (i.e. those which should be designed for);
   (b) plausible columns (determined by the system according to the optimizer's choices as discussed in Section 6.5).
2. Collect statistics on:
   (a) relations (relation cardinality (i.e. number of tuples) and relation size (i.e. number of pages);
   (b) columns (average length, column selectivity, maximum and minimum values);
   (c) indexes (number of leave entries, number of levels).
3. Evaluate atomic costs (i.e. costs of configurations with, at most, one index per relation (atomic configurations); costs for all other configurations can be computed from atomic costs) including:
   (a) relation access cost;
   (b) relation update cost;
   (c) index maintenance cost.
4. Perform index elimination (based on heuristic criteria for deciding which plausible indexes are likely to be chosen as access paths and which are not. This step is necessary because the choice of plausible columns in Step 1 is based on the ways the columns are used in statements, not on the costs of access paths).
5. Generate solutions according to the parameters supplied by the designer, including:
   (a) the expected workload characterized by set of business functions (Section 3.2.2) and their ranks (Section 4.5.2);
   (b) the maximum number of pages available for indexes.

Physical database design strategies, in particular those based on an internal model, establish special interest in so-called *semantic query optimization*. This is an approach to query optimization that uses knowledge of the semantics of data (expressed as integrity constraints) to produce a semantically equivalent SQL statement that is less expensive to process than the original statement. This new statement is guaranteed to produce the same result because the knowledge used to transform the statement is the same knowledge used to ensure the semantic integrity and consistency of the database.

Suppose that the following integrity rule is in existence: "All Macintosh software must be purchased through an Apple Consortium salesman". Then consider the query: "List salesmen who sell more Macintosh software than average". A semantic query optimizer should now be able to transform this query to the simpler (i.e. cost-reducing): "List Apple Consortium salesmen who sell more Macintosh software than average". The transformed query is cost-reducing because it restricts the processing to one category of salesmen, that is, those who work for Apple Consortia. Similarly, the query: "Who bought dBASE Mac software through an Apple Consortium last month?" could be converted to: "Who bought dBASE Mac last month?" This transformation eliminates a join because it removes a superfluous constraint on a dealer. The transformed queries can now be optimized with the standard optimization techniques.

Semantic query optimization gives rise to intelligent physical database design, that is, a design enhanced with inference capabilities. If applied with a conventional DBMS, semantic query optimization creates new opportunities for performance improvements. The usefulness of semantic optimization is further extended when applied with an expert (deductive) DBMS. Such DBMSs, which integrate the database and knowledge base technologies, should soon be available commercially. One of the advantages of an expert DBMS lies in the possibility of answering *fuzzy (imprecise) queries*. Such queries are not expressed in terms of the user's knowledge of database structures (i.e. what relations and attributes actually exist), but rather in terms of the user's current interests and perception of the "real world". An example of the fuzzy query is: "Is dBASE Mac expensive?"

To answer a fuzzy query, an expert DBMS evaluates relevant integrity rules stored in a database. For the query "Is dBASE Mac expensive?", the rules could be:

Rule 1. A microcomputer DBMS is expensive if it costs more than $2000.
Rule 2. A microcomputer DBMS is expensive if it costs more than $1200 and it is a single-user system.
Rule 3. A microcomputer DBMS is expensive if it costs more than $1000, it is a single user and it does not have a report generation facility.

Assuming that in a question answering session, a user will explain that dBASE Mac is a microcomputer single-user DBMS with report generation facility, an expert DBMS will answer the original query. In doing so, an expert DBMS will analyze the integrity rules and construct SQL queries for them. To provide the answer, the system will evaluate a SQL query built for Rule 3 and expanded (or joined) by a subquery to find the current price of dBASE Mac. In general, expert database systems provide special opportunities for semantic query optimization and give rise to a relatively unexplored problem of *multiple-query optimization* (Section 6.1).

6.7   CASE STUDY: PHYSICAL SCHEMA

The physical design of an ORACLE database cannot be based on the internal model because the system does not yet provide for the explanation (SQL EXPLAIN) of its access plans (Section 6.6). Therefore, the accuracy of index selection and the possibilities of performance tuning are limited. The physical design must be based on an external model that is not necessarily in agreement with the query optimizer's actions. The best one can do is to create indexes and clusters which, according to the external model, have a good chance of being used by the query optimizer.

In this section, the physical design is applied to a part of the logical schema obtained in Section 5.6.2. Only the index and cluster selection problem is addressed. The performance tuning and space calculation (to be realistic) would require a large amount of detail about the contents of relations, the composition of business functions, their access graphs and design ranks.

Business functions are specified on multiple levels (Section 3.2.2). This multiple-level specification corresponds broadly to the leveling of processes in the data flow diagram. A higher level function contains many, more detailed, lower level functions. The following eight high level functions, called modules, are distinguished for the subset of the case study comprised by the logical schema in Section 5.6.2:

M1 Initiate service request.
Record the details of the service being requested. Enter information about the customer, item and fault. Create service request document.

M2 Enter service details.
Enter the repair details when the faulty piece of equipment has been serviced.

M3 List completed repairs and process payments.
List all the customers whose equipment has been serviced and is awaiting collection. Contact the customer and process payment for the service.

M4 Initiate external repair order.
Create an external repair order document for service requests which cannot be performed internally by the company.

M5 Record a returned external repair order.
Record the details of the service performed externally.

M6 Process external repair monthly statements.
Enter the repair summaries received from external repairers. Compare with the company's records.

M7 Process upgrades and installations.
Enter the system upgrades and installations (anchor pads, etc.) details.

M8 Generate reports.
Generate and print servicing reports.

Each module contains lower level functions. These lower level functions are classified as queries (Q-function), updates (U-function), inputs (I-function), reports (R-function) or combinations of these (Section 3.2.2). For example, module M1 contains three functions (attribute definitions for these are given in Section 4.6):

M1F1 Identify the customer (IQ-function).
Enter 'customer_number' or the first several letters of 'customer_name'. If 'customer_number' is entered, then a single 'customer_name' should be found in the database and automatically displayed, together with 'billing_address' and 'shipping_address'. If the first several letters of 'customer_name' are entered, then a list of all customers whose 'customer_name' starts with these letters is searched for and displayed. Use 'billing_address' to differentiate between two customers with the same name. Select a desired 'customer_name' from the list. Move to function M1F2.

M1F2 Identify the faulty equipment (IQ-function).
Display a list of equipment (serialized items) owned by a customer. If the faulty equipment is not listed, then enter information about it ('item_number', 'item_description', 'serial_number', 'date_sold', 'warranty_type' and 'date_warranty_expires'). If the 'item_number' is not known, enter the first several

letters of 'item_description' to search for it. Select a desired 'serial_number' from the list. Move to function M1F3.

M1F3 Enter problem details (IQ-function).

Display information about the customer and the piece of equipment to be serviced. Generate the default 'service_request_number', check it, and overtype it with another number if the default is not good. Enter 'problem_description'. Print service request document and forward it to a technician.

When developing the logical schema, the indexes to enforce the primary keys of relations were created (Section 5.6.2). The purpose of these indexes is logical (integrity enforcement), although they may also be useful for the physical access. Even if they are not, however, they must not be discarded by the physical design. During the physical design new indexes and clusters are added according to business functions needs.

Consider function M1F1. This function will certainly benefit from the unique index on 'customer_number' created in Section 5.6.2; however, a new nonunique index on 'customer_name' seems to be beneficial (it is assumed, that duplicate values of 'customer_name' are not frequent and, therefore, there is no need for a concatenated index on 'customer_name' and 'billing_address'). The nonunique index created would be:

```
SQL> CREATE INDEX IND_CUST_NAME
  2              ON CUSTOMER
  3              (CUSTOMER_NAME);
```

Index created.

For the purposes of function M1F1, the index IND_CUST_NAME will support the access path termed "random relation access through index" in Section 6.5. However, this index is likely to be used by many other functions of the designed application also and some of these other functions will probably use it for the fastest access path, that is for "random index only access". In general, the index IND_CUST_NAME has a good chance of being used often by the query optimizer because many business functions will refer to 'customer_name' in their retrieval predicates.

The analysis of function M1F2 leads to two conclusions. First, a unique index on 'item_description' may be desirable (with a justification similar to that for the index IND_CUST_NAME), that is:

```
SQL> CREATE INDEX IND_ITEM_DESC
  2              ON ITEM
  3              (ITEM_DESCRIPTION);
```

Index created.

Second, and probably more importantly, a cluster of the relations ITEM and SERIALIZED_ITEM on 'item_number' should be considered (Section 6.2.2.2). These two relations are accessed together by M1F2 and there are probably many other functions in the designed application which would benefit from such a cluster, as set out below:

```
SQL> CREATE CLUSTER EQUIPMENT
  2              (ITEM_NUMBER CHAR(10))
  3              SPACE STOCK
  4              SIZE 512
  5              COMPRESS;
```

```
Cluster created.
```

ORACLE will automatically build an index on the cluster key 'item_number'. This index does not contradict or supersede the unique index IND_I on 'item_number' created for relation ITEM during the logical design (Section 5.6.2). The two indexes serve different purposes (Section 6.2.2.2). The last function, that is, M1F3, does not involve the need for creating indexes or clusters.

In general, the creation of indexes and clusters, as well as other physical design decisions, must be justified by the analysis of the entire range of business functions. For this reason, the access graphs (Section 4.3) and the design ranks (Section 4.5.2) of functions should be considered. Indexes and clusters should only be created when implied by the functions with high design ranks and/or when many functions are likely to use them. Superfluous indexes and clusters increase processing overhead and penalize update operations.

FURTHER READING

The concept of access plan is discussed by Date (1986), in both an interactive and programmatic environment. Additional information can be found in technical manuals of DBMSs with relatively open architectures, such as DB2 (IBM 1986, 1987a and 1987b). Multiple-query optimization is addressed by Sellis (1988).

The problem of mapping relations to files is discussed in Korth and Silberschatz (1986) and technical DBMS manuals should be consulted for detailed information. Physical data objects of DB2 are described in IBM (1986), IBM (1987a), and IBM (1987b). Figure 6.2 has been borrowed from IBM (1987b). Physical data objects of ORACLE are explained in ORACLE (1987).

The problem of assigning records to pages, to minimize the total number of pages accessed in response to a set of queries, is addressed by Yu *et al.* (1985). Formulas for storage estimates in DB2 are given in IBM (1987b). The storage requirements of ORACLE relations and indexes are discussed in ORACLE (1987).

The B-tree, as a way of organizing indexes for files, was introduced by Bayer and McCreight (1972). They also suggested a variation of the B-tree which was termed the B*-tree by Knuth (1973). Knuth (1973), on the other hand, proposed a variation of the B-tree that Comer (1979) designated the B$^+$-tree. Comer (1979) gives a tutorial survey of B-trees. A textbook discussion of B-trees and their variations can be found in Korth and Silberschatz (1986), Loomis (1983), Peterson and Lew (1986) and Smith and Barnes (1987). VSAM implementation is nicely presented by Grauer and Crawford (1979). The implementation of indexes in DB2 is described in IBM (1987b) and the implementation of indexes in ORACLE is explained in ORACLE (1987).

Query optimization has an extensive literature (Jarke and Koch 1984, Kim *et al.* 1985). Date (1986) includes an overview of the optimization process. Ceri and Gottlob (1985) provide a good learning aid by translating a set of SQL queries from Date (1986) into relational algebra expressions. An interesting index selection algorithm is due to Whang (1985). Effects of SQL statements on the use of indexes in DB2 are discussed in IBM (1986). Similar information for ORACLE can be found in ORACLE (1987).

Arguments for using an internal, rather than an external, model in physical database design are given in Finkelstein *et al.* (1988). The use of SQL EXPLAIN facility in physical design is discussed in Finkelstein *et al.* (1988) and IBM (1986). Cost model for database updates is given in Schkolnick and Tiberio (1985) and for database retrievals in Finkelstein *et al.* (1988). A database perspective on buffer management is given in Korth and Silberschatz (1986) and in Stonebraker (1981). Some potentially misleading statistical assumptions in physical database design and in query optimization are discussed by Christodoulakis (1984). A monograph on semantic query optimization was written by King (1984). Expert database systems are discussed in the book edition of conference proceedings edited by Kerschberg (1986).

REFERENCES

BAYER, R. and McCREIGHT, E. (1972): Organization and Maintenance of Large Ordered Indexes, *Acta Informatica*, 1, pp.173–89.

CERI, S. and GOTTLOB, G. (1985): Translating SQL into Relational Algebra: Optimization, Semantics, and Equivalence of SQL Queries, *IEEE Trans. Soft. Eng.*, 4, pp.324–45.

CHRISTODOULAKIS, S. (1984): Implications of Certain Assumptions in Database Performance Evaluation, *ACM Trans. Database Syst.*, 2, pp.163–86.

COMER, D. (1979): The Ubiquitous B-tree, *Comp. Surv.*, 2, pp.121–37.

DATE, C. J. (1986): *An Introduction to Database Systems*, Vol. I, Addison-Wesley, 4th ed., 639p.

FINKELSTEIN, S., SCHKOLNICK, M. and TIBERIO, P. (1988): Physical Database Design for Relational Databases, *ACM Trans. Database Syst.*, 1, pp.91–128.

GRAUER, R. T. and CRAWFORD, M. A. (1979): *The COBOL Environment*, Prentice Hall, 464p.

IBM (1986): *IBM DATABASE 2 Application Design and Tuning Guide*, Document Number GG24-3004-00, IBM, International Technical Support Center, Santa Teresa, 125p.

IBM (1987a): *IBM DATABASE 2, Data Base Planning and Administration Guide*, Program Number 5740-XYR, Order Number SC26-4077-3, Release 3, IBM, 226p.

IBM (1987b): *IBM DATABASE 2, System Planning and Administration Guide*, Program Number 5740-XYR, Order Number SC26-4085-3, Release 3, IBM, 319p.

JARKE, M. and KOCH, J. (1984): Query Optimization in Database Systems, *Comp. Surv.*, 2, pp.111–52.

KERSCHBERG, L. (ed) (1986): *Expert Database Systems. Proceedings from the First International Workshop*, The Benjamin/Cummings, 701p.

KIM, W., REINER, D. S. and BATORY, D. S. (eds) (1985): *Query Processing in Database Systems*, Springer-Verlag, 365p.

KING, J. J. (1984): *Query Optimization by Semantic Reasoning*, UMI Research Press, 122p.

KNUTH, D. E. (1973): *The Art of Computer Programming, Vol. 3, Sorting and Searching*, Addison-Wesley, 722p.

KORTH, H. F. and SILBERSCHATZ, A. (1986): *Database System Concepts*, McGraw-Hill, 546p.

LOOMIS, M. E. S. (1983): *Data Management and File Processing*, Prentice Hall, p.490.

ORACLE (1987): *Database Administrator's Guide*, Version 2.0, The Relational Database Management System ORACLE, Oracle Corp.

PETERSON, W. W. and LEW, A. (1986): *File Design and Programming*, John Wiley & Sons, 381p.

SCHKOLNICK, M. and TIBERIO, P. (1985): Estimating the Cost of Updates in a Relational Database, *ACM Trans. Database Syst.*, 2, pp.163–79.

SELLIS, T. K. (1988): Multiple-Query Optimization, *ACM Trans. Database Syst.*, 1, pp.23–52.

SMITH, P. D. and BARNES, G. M. (1987): *Files and Databases: an Introduction*, Addison-Wesley, p.390.

STONEBRAKER, M. (1981): Operating System Support for Database Management, *Comm. ACM*, 7, pp.412–18.

WHANG, K-Y. (1985): Index Selection in Relational Databases, in: *Proc. Int. Conf. on Foundations of Data Organization*, Kyoto, Japan, pp.369–78; also in: *Foundations of Data Organization*, ed. S. P. Ghosh, Y. Kambayashi, K. Tanaka, Plenum Press (1987), pp.487–500.

YU, C. T., SUEN, C-M., LAM, K. and SIN, M. K. (1985): Adaptive Record Clustering, *ACM Trans. Database Syst.*, 2, pp.180–204.

7

Programming User Applications

In any practical, commercial environment, interactive SQL access to the database system is restricted to database professionals (administrators, programmers, designers). The relation-at-a-time access of interactive SQL makes it a powerful and optimizable language, but at the same time unsafe and computationally limited. Interactive SQL is not a language for "naive" users such as managers, clerks and secretaries. Such users need a menu-driven, form oriented, functionally tailored and intuitively obvious interface. The tools provided by a DBMS to facilitate building such interfaces are broadly termed application generators and interactive SQL plays only a limited role in such tools. In application generators a programmatic (embedded) SQL access to the database is emphasized instead. Some reasons for this are that tuple-at-a-time processing of embedded SQL makes recursive queries manageable; it also gives better control to a programmer over data manipulation results and increases concurrency in the multi-user processing.

This chapter is about building user applications. Any self-respecting DBMS has its own, usually proprietary, application generator. In ORACLE, the generator is called SQL*Forms while in DB2, an interactive tool (called DB2I) is provided which uses Interactive System Productivity Facility (ISPF) to help develop and execute application programs. This chapter introduces the official ANSI standard for programmatic SQL and uses ORACLE's Pro*C and SQL*Forms to exemplify application programming and generation.

7.1 PROGRAMMATIC INTERFACES TO DATABASE

The expressive power of SQL is limited, and it cannot perform some kinds of computations. One common class of computation that defeats SQL is recursive processing (such as the one involved in the bill-of-material problem (Section 4.4.2.3)). Some relatively simple arithmetic expressions are also not directly supported, nor can the user define a function in pure SQL to compute them (e.g. variance). As a result, SQL needs to be interfaced with an ordinary programming language to obtain adequate expressive power.

7.1.1   Types and persistence in programmatic interfaces

SQL and most other database sublanguages are not able to perform arbitrary computations. This is the price that these languages pay in order to be optimizable and simple for the user (although this simplicity is deceptive). An attractive, but still not fully developed, solution to this problem is to interface SQL with Prolog; such that SQL is responsible for retrieving information from the database and Prolog performs computations and logical inferences. The current practical solution to the problem involves interfacing SQL with conventional programming languages (COBOL, PL/I, FORTRAN, C, Pascal, Ada, etc.).

When a relational statement is executed, it returns a relation, that is, a *multiset* of tuples (in practice duplicate tuples are allowed; hence multiset rather than set). In a programmatic environment, the returned relation must be handled by programming language expressions. A better way of handling this is to represent relations as *arrays of structures* (records) of an ordinary programming language, such as Pascal; however this solution is not feasible for most conventional programming languages.

The reason why this is not feasible is twofold. First, most such languages do not permit *dynamic arrays* in which sizes can be determined at run-time (such as originally introduced in ALGOL 68). Such arrays would be required for processing relations because the number of tuples in a relation is not known statically (at compile time). Second, even if a language had dynamic arrays, it would probably not have *macroscopic operations*, like the operations of the relational algebra, to process a relation as a unit.

As a result of the above difficulties, the data is conveyed across the interface in a *piped mode*, in which individual tuples, one at a time, are delivered from a database relation to the application program. The piped mode can be implemented in two ways, of which the second is more popular:

1. By using a *workspace*.
   The workspace is a data buffer in virtual storage, accessible only by special operations provided with the programming language. These operations use the workspace as if it were a file or list of records; thus the workspace is not an object of the programming language itself. The ordinary expressions and statements of the language cannot access the workspace data.
2. By using a *cursor*.
   The cursor is a kind of pointer which is defined for a set of tuples returned as the result of a database access. At any particular moment the cursor points to a single tuple on the set, thus providing a tuple-at-a-time addressability. A database operation (e.g. FETCH command) moves a tuple into program variables for further processing; hence, a cursor is even more separated from the programming language than a workspace. It is an object of the database sublanguage (typically SQL).

Most problems in interfacing application programming and databases can be reduced to the notions of data type and persistence. The concept of *type* denotes a set of values (possibly infinite) and, in a programming language context, a *variable* of a particular type can only accept values of that type. The types allowed by ordinary programming languages are quite simple as they are more syntactic than semantic in nature (e.g. INTEGER, STRING). In a database environment, however, more sophisticated types are often available (e.g. DATE, MONEY). In database theory, the concept of type is extended and replaced by the notion of *domain* (Section 5.1.1), which is a highly semantic type (e.g. FIRST_NAME, a set of all names that are legal representations of first names of people).

From the viewpoint of a programmatic database interface, the database definition (or schema) corresponds to an elaborate type declaration, of which the contents of the database is but one value. However, as mentioned before, such sophisticated types are not supported by conventional programming languages. In the case of an entire database, an array of arrays of structures would be needed.

A type in a programming language determines the operations that are valid for variables and constants of that type. Most languages are *strongly typed*, meaning that an operation on a value of an inappropriate type is rejected.

Only a limited flexibility is allowed in constructing new types from the ones which are predefined. In the ALGOL/Pascal family of languages, *type constructors* are limited to **array** and **record**. In general, it is desirable to have *parameterized types*, that is, to have the possibility of expressing new types by parameterizing the existing types. For example, if the language permits a **record** α **end** construct, then α should be allowed to be any type already defined.

The principle of *data type completeness* demands that parameterized types be applicable to procedures and functions, the types of which are determined by the types of their arguments and results. Such types are called *polymorphic* and are available in some new languages (ML, CLU, Miranda, Poly, and Ada in which a "generic package" supports polymorphism). Although one can argue that for a well-defined database model, such as the relational model, only a fixed set of type constructors is needed, the lack of some kind of polymorphic type system is a major restriction encountered in building a programmatic database interface. If there are no parameterized type constructors, a piped mode processing, discussed earlier, is necessary.

Another notion that is important in understanding a programmatic database interface is persistence. The *persistence* of an object created according to its type definition is defined as the duration for which it remains accessible. In databases most objects (relations) must persist beyond the duration of the program whereas in traditional programming languages the only persistent objects are files.

In a typical Pascal scenario, in order to process, say, customer records, a 'customer' record *type* is first created. Next, an *extent* for this type is defined which permits reference to all 'customer' records. The extent is a more complex data structure such as a linked list, binary tree or B-tree. Processing is conducted on the extent in memory. In order to ensure persistence, the customer records in the extent must be stored in the only persistent data type in Pascal, that is a *file*. Since the Pascal file cannot accommodate the extent's structure, additional processing is needed to map between the extent and the file.

Polymorphism is applicable to persistent data types. In Pascal, files may be parameterized by some other types, thus allowing for the persistence of other objects; however, the polymorphism of Pascal is restricted and, for instance, the parameterization of files cannot extend to pointer types. In general, the possibility of persistence in a programming language is of fundamental importance in native syntax interfaces (Section 7.1.4). In explicit and implicit interfaces (Sections 7.1.2 and 7.1.3), database persistence is the responsibility of the database sublanguage (SQL).

7.1.2 Explicit procedure interface

The easiest way to implement a programmatic database interface is to enhance a programming language which has a subroutine facility capable of calling separately compiled procedures written in another language (SQL in our case). In the relational standard, the invoked *procedures* consist of SQL statements and are contained in a *module* associated with the application program which is compiled by a standard programming language compiler. The module is compiled by the DBMS. The method for linking the program to the module is DBMS implementor defined, that is it is not encapsulated by the SQL standard specifications. The application calls each procedure in the module by name. A procedure can have parameters corresponding to variables defined in the application program.

An example of the explicit procedure interface follows. The application selects company employees in any Sydney-based department, displays their names and salaries, and gives them a 5 percent salary raise. The example assumes that the EMPLOYEE relation has been loaded. The calling program, written here in pseudocode, consists of 17 lines. The SQL module has five procedures spanning 26 lines.

```
1    DECLARE E_NAME CHAR(30),
2            E_SALARY DECIMAL,
3            RETCODE INTEGER;
4    CALL EMPOPEN USING RETCODE;
5    WHENEVER (RETCODE < 0) THEN
6        CALL EMPROLLBACK;
7        DISPLAY ('PROGRAM ERROR', RETCODE);
8        STOP RUN;
9    ENDWHENEVER;
10   CALL EMPFETCH USING E_NAME, E_SALARY, RETCODE;
11   WHILE (RETCODE = 0) DO
12       DISPLAY (E_NAME, E_SALARY);
13       CALL EMPMODIFY USING E_NAME RETCODE;
14       CALL EMPFETCH USING E_NAME, E_SALARY, RETCODE;
15   ENDWHILE;
16   CALL EMPCOMMIT;
17   STOP RUN;

1    MODULE
2            LANGUAGE PSEUDOCODE
3            DECLARE RAISEPAY CURSOR FOR
4                  SELECT EMP_NAME, EMP_SALARY
5                    FROM EMPLOYEE
6                    WHERE DEPT_LOCATION = 'SYDNEY'
7    PROCEDURE EMPOPEN
8            SQLCODE
9        OPEN RAISEPAY
10   PROCEDURE EMPFETCH
11           NAME    CHARACTER(30)
```

```
12              SALARY  DECIMAL
13              SQLCODE
14          FETCH RAISEPAY INTO NAME SALARY
15   PROCEDURE EMPMODIFY
16              NAME    CHARACTER(30)
17              SQLCODE
18          UPDATE EMPLOYEE
19              SET EMP_SALARY = 1.05 * EMP_SALARY
20               WHERE EMP_NAME = NAME
21   PROCEDURE EMPCOMMIT
22              SQLCODE
23          COMMIT WORK
24   PROCEDURE EMPROLLBACK
25              SQLCODE
26          ROLLBACK WORK
```

In the calling program, lines 1–3 define program variables. E_NAME and E_SALARY correspond to the attributes EMP_NAME and EMP_SALARY in EMPLOYEE relation. The corresponding parameters in the SQL module are NAME and SALARY. RETCODE accommodates a return code value passed to the program on each execution of a SQL statement contained in a procedure. At any particular moment of program execution, the RETCODE value is equivalent to a current value of the module's SQLCODE parameter. A SQLCODE value of 0 (zero) indicates the successful completion of a SQL statement. A value of +100 means that no tuples were found to satisfy the predicate of the SQL statement and a negative value is returned on occurrence of an error.

The procedures of the module are invoked by CALL statements in the calling program (such as the CALL in line 4). The SQL module has five procedures which consist of a PROCEDURE clause that specifies the procedure's name (e.g. line 7 in the module) followed by a list of parameter definitions and exactly one SQL statement. Normally one of the parameters is SQLCODE. This is an output parameter because its value is going to be passed to the calling program. In general the parameters are either of input or output kind. An input parameter accepts values passed to it from the calling program.

The CALL statement in line 4 of the calling program invokes the procedure EMPOPEN defined in lines 7–9 in the module. This procedure opens the cursor declared in lines 3–6 in the module. The opening of the cursor means that the SQL query specified within the cursor is executed. In the example the opening of the RAISEPAY cursor causes the collection of EMPLOYEE tuples, such that the employees are located in Sydney, to be associated with the cursor. This collection is ordered and OPEN RAISEPAY statement positions the cursor immediately before the first tuple in the collection. Any subsequent FETCH statement (line 14 in the module) will position the cursor on the next tuple or immediately after the last tuple, if there is no next tuple.

The WHENEVER statement (lines 5–9 in the calling program) is a convenient way of handling exceptions during program execution and it improves the clarity of the pseudocode. In a practical language, with a good exception handler (such as the ON

CONDITION in PL/I or EXCEPTION in Ada), the WHENEVER statement is directly usable. In other languages it will have to be replaced by a looping statement with a nested IF enclosed. The meaning of WHENEVER is that if (at any time of program execution) a SQLCODE value passed to RETCODE is negative then the program should: (1) roll the database back to its initial state (line 6), (2) display an error message together with the SQLCODE value (line 7), and (3) terminate the run.

The CALL statement on line 10 is used to position the cursor on the first tuple of a temporary relation obtained by the execution of OPEN RAISEPAY (line 9 in the module). The first execution of the procedure EMPFETCH is expected to be successful and, therefore, to return a zero value in SQLCODE and to enable entry to the WHILE loop (lines 11–15 in the calling program). The actions taken in the loop are: (1) display the employee name and his/her current salary, (2) increase the salary by 5 percent and (3) fetch next employee located in Sydney. The statements in the loop are executed until the value of SQLCODE becomes different to zero, presumably +100 after no more tuples can be fetched.

The CALL statement in line 16 invokes a procedure that commits the changes (i.e. salary increases) to the EMPLOYEE relation. Implicitly, it also closes the cursor, thus making the changes available to other database applications.

An advantage of the explicit procedure interface is that no changes need to be made to the existing specifications of the programming language and so an existing compiler can be used. All that is needed is the ability to call independently compiled subroutines written in a different language and the ability to convert between database and programming language data types.

However, there are several important disadvantages in the explicit procedure interface:

1. The concept of the database module is introduced in the SQL standard, but existing SQL implementations do not yet support it.
2. The programmer must write two programs instead of one, and must duplicate names in order to link calls in the calling program to procedures in the SQL module.
3. Low level programming is encouraged in which many "housekeeping" details must be addressed in the calling program, such as the explicit declaration of I/O buffers and of communication areas.
4. Call parameters can only be dynamically interpreted at run-time, leading to poor error detection. Even trivial syntactic errors may not be discoverable statically, that is at compile-time.
5. The protection of sensitive virtual storage areas containing control information (such as cursor areas or description of the results of SQL operations) can be compromised.

7.1.3 Implicit procedure interface

The implicit procedure interface is the most popular method of interfacing application programming and databases. In this approach SQL statements are embedded directly into the application (host) program and are distinguished from host language statements by a common prefix, typically EXEC SQL. The implicit procedure interface uses a *preprocessor* to translate the embedded SQL statements into the host language CALL statements capable of compilation by a host language compiler. The preprocessor also produces a separate database request module for interface to the DBMS (Section 6.1, Figure 6.1).

An example of the implicit procedure interface, which uses PL/I as a host language, is now presented. The example solves the problem discussed in the previous section.

```
1     EMPSAL: PROC OPTIONS (MAIN);
2       EXEC SQL BEGIN DECLARE SECTION;
3           DCL E_NAME            CHARACTER(30);
4           DCL E_SALARY          FIXED DECIMAL(8,2);
5           DCL SQLCODE           FIXED BINARY(15);
6           DCL  MORE_EMPLOYEESBIT(1);
7       EXEC SQL END DECLARE SECTION;
8       EXEC SQL WHENEVER SQLERROR GOTO EMPROLLBACK;
9       EXEC SQL WHENEVER NOT FOUND GOTO EMPCOMMIT;
10      EXEC SQL DECLARE RAISEPAY CURSOR FOR
11                  SELECT EMP_NAME, EMP_SALARY
12                     FROM EMPLOYEE
13                     WHERE DEPT_LOCATION = 'SYDNEY';
14      EXEC SQL OPEN RAISEPAY;
15      MORE_EMPLOYEES = '1'B;
16      DO WHILE (MORE_EMPLOYEES);
17        EXEC SQL FETCH RAISEPAY
18            INTO :E_NAME, :E_SALARY;
19        IF (SQLCODE = 100) THEN
20            MORE_EMPLOYEES = '0'B;
21        PUT SKIP LIST (E_NAME, E_SALARY);
22        EXEC SQL UPDATE EMPLOYEE
23            SET EMP_SALARY = 1.05 * EMP_SALARY
24            WHERE EMP_NAME = :E_NAME;
25      END;
26    END EMPSAL;
27      EMPCOMMIT:
28        EXEC SQL COMMIT WORK;
29        RETURN;
30      EMPROLLBACK:
31        PUT SKIP LIST ('PROGRAM ERROR' || SQLCODE);
32        EXEC SQL ROLLBACK WORK;
33        RETURN;
```

Line 1 in the above code gives a name to the program (EMPSAL) and identifies it as a main program which may call other procedures (MAIN option). The DECLARE SECTION (lines 2–6) contains definitions of host language variables and provides the DBMS with information about data types.

The WHENEVER statements in lines 8 and 9 specify the actions to be taken when a SQL statement causes an exception condition. There are two possible conditions:

SQLERROR and NOT FOUND. The SQLERROR condition (line 8) is activated whenever the value of SQLCODE is negative, that is whenever any other SQL statement in the program fails and returns error. The action taken by the program in such a situation is indicated by the GOTO label constant (i.e. DBERROR); as a result, the lines 30–33 are executed. An error message is printed, the database is rolled back to its original state and the program terminates.

The NOT FOUND condition (line 9) is equivalent to a value of SQLCODE of +100. In general, this code value can be returned as a result of any of the following events:

- a FETCH for which no next tuple could be found;
- a SELECT or INSERT ... SELECT for which no tuples were found;
- an UPDATE for which there were no tuples to update;
- a DELETE for which there were no tuples to delete.

In the example, on the NOT FOUND condition, control is passed to the EMPCOMMIT label. The changes to the database are committed and the program terminates (lines 27–29).

Lines 10–13 define the cursor to be constructed by the preprocessor. Line 14 opens this cursor (RAISEPAY) to select all employees located in Sydney. The assignment statement in line 15 sets the bit string variable MORE_EMPLOYEES to a value of 1. This represents the "true" condition necessary to initiate the execution of DO WHILE loop (lines 16–25).

The loop provides sequential access to the selected employee tuples. The host program variables referenced in SQL statements (lines 18 and 24) are preceded by a colon (:). The employees' names and salaries are printed (line 21), and the salaries are updated (lines 22–24). The loop and the program terminate when no more tuples can be fetched (lines 19–20).

The implicit procedure interface has some advantages over the explicit interface: a single, self-contained application program is written; the programmer is not concerned with generating names for SQL procedures or with matching parameters; and the preprocessor performs the data type conversions and is able to conduct some static checks.

The disadvantages are:

1. The syntax of the usual programming operations in the embedded SQL statements (arithmetic, logical, etc.) is likely to be different to that of the host language.
2. The checks normally performed by the preprocessor can be bypassed if the programmer attempts to modify the already preprocessed code (e.g. to correct errors or to save a preprocessor run).
3. Although automatic conversion of data types by the preprocessor is advantageous, the resulting type system is likely to be weaker than that supported by the database itself.

7.1.4 Native syntax interface

The native syntax approach requires that database operations be an integral part of a programming language. This approach has led to the development of a new category of languages called *database programming languages.* Types and persistence issues (Section 7.1.1) are central to the development of native syntax interfaces. A database becomes just a new persistent kind of data type, except that it is shared by many applications and often exceeds the lifetime of the applications. One syntax applies to both database and non-database objects.

The SQL standard has been developed quite independently from standards of programming languages, and currently the native syntax approach is not the subject of any standardization effort by any language committee. Nevertheless, research in this area is flourishing and has led to the development of many experimental database programming languages, such as Pascal/R, Adaplex, Taxis, Galileo, Modula/R, and DBPL. In Version 6.0 of ORACLE, a native syntax interface based on Ada is introduced (it is called PL/SQL).

The following example shows how some database operations can be integrated into the COBOL language. The database operations provide the functionality of SQL statements, but syntactically may or may not resemble SQL. The example refers to the problem used for the illustration of procedure interfaces in Sections 7.1.2 and 7.1.3.

```
1      IDENTIFICATION DIVISION.
2          PROGRAM-ID. EMPSAL.
3      ENVIRONMENT DIVISION.
4      DATA DIVISION.
5      SUB-SCHEMA SECTION.
6      DB EMPLOYEEDB.
7          SQLCODE IS DB-STATUS.
8      TD TABLE DESCRIPTION.
9      01 EMPLOYEE.
10         02 EMP-NAME       PIC X(30).
11         02 EMP-SALARY      PIC S9(6)V99.
12         02 DEPT-LOCATION  PIC A(20).
13     WORKING-STORAGE SECTION.
14     01  LAST-RECORD PIC A(3)  VALUE 'NO'.
15     01  DB-STATUS   PIC S9(5) VALUE 0.
16     PROCEDURE DIVISION.
17     DECLARATIVES.
18     NOT-FOUND SECTION.
19         USE FOR DB-EXCEPTION ON +100.
20         MOVE 'YES' TO LAST-RECORD.
21     SQLERROR.
22         USE FOR DB-EXCEPTION ON OTHER.
23         DISPLAY 'PROGRAM ERROR' DB-STATUS.
24         ROLLBACK.
25         STOP RUN.
26     END DECLARATIVES.
27     MAIN SECTION.
28     OPEN-CURSOR.
29         OPEN RAISEPAY CURSOR FOR
```

```
30              SELECT EMP_NAME, EMP_SALARY
31                 FROM EMPLOYEE
32                 WHERE DEPT-LOCATION = 'SYDNEY'.
33       FETCH-FIRST-AND-COMMIT.
34           FETCH RAISEPAY.
35           PERFORM UPDATE-AND-FETCH
36                   UNTIL LAST-RECORD = 'NO'.
37           COMMIT.
38           STOP RUN.
39       UPDATE-AND-FETCH.
40           DISPLAY EMP-NAME EMP-SALARY.
41           COMPUTE EMP_SALARY = 1.05 * EMP_SALARY
42           UPDATE EMPLOYEE USING EMP-NAME.
43           FETCH RAISEPAY.
```

The IDENTIFICATION DIVISION (line 1) is the first statement in any COBOL program. It names the program as EMPSAL. Lines 3 and 4 refer to two further divisions of a COBOL program. These divisions each consist of sections. A section in the PROCEDURE DIVISION can contain paragraphs.

The SUB-SCHEMA SECTION (lines 5–12) is an extension to standard COBOL. It provides tight binding between database objects and COBOL variables. Line 6 identifies the database to be accessed by the application.

Line 7 binds the SQLCODE parameter to the DB-STATUS variable. There is only one relation, EMPLOYEE, in our simple database. This relation is bound, in lines 8–12, to a COBOL record having the same name as the relation. The record items are also given names identical to the names of the relation attributes. As a result, a tight binding is achieved in which the database objects and program variables are not distinguishable.

The DECLARATIVES procedures (lines 17–26) are executed by the program in response to database exception conditions raised by database operations. The procedures fulfill the same role as WHENEVER statements discussed in Section 7.1.3.

The MAIN SECTION contains three paragraphs (lines 27–43). The OPEN-CURSOR paragraph opens a cursor over employees who are located in Sydney. The FETCH-FIRST-AND-COMMIT paragraph retrieves the first selected employee and activates a loop to run the UPDATE-AND-FETCH paragraph. In the loop the salary of each selected employee is increased by 5 percent (line 41) and the raise is recorded in the EMPLOYEE relation (line 42). The loop terminates once a NOT-FOUND condition is raised and the LAST-RECORD variable is assigned the value 'YES' (lines 19–20). The program commits changes and halts (lines 37–38).

The major advantage of the native syntax approach is that it offers to the programmer a single language in which all database manipulations may be performed. Moreover, such a language provides more expressive power because it integrates the relation-valued expressions with algorithmic techniques like iterations, conditionals and assignments.

The most important disadvantages are:

1. A different syntax must be defined in different languages for the same database operations.

2. Existing SQL implementations (with the exception of ORACLE Version 6.0) do not support the native syntax approach.
3. No standards exist.

7.2 PROGRAMMING IN EMBEDDED SQL

Programming in embedded SQL is a practical and widely-used realization of the implicit procedure interface (Section 7.1.3). In this approach, a preprocessor translates SQL statements embedded in the application program into host language code. This code is then compiled and linked with the appropriate run-time libraries to form an executable program.

DBMSs usually support a range of host languages, although under some operating systems some of them may not be available. DB2 supports APL2, BASIC, COBOL, FORTRAN, LISP and PL/I. ORACLE supports C, COBOL, FORTRAN, PL/I, Pascal and Ada. The ORACLE products which allow programming in embedded SQL are termed Pro* products; hence the product which supports Ada is called Pro*Ada, etc. (As an aside, Oracle offers also an explicit procedure interface (Section 7.1.2) called ORACLE Call Interface OCI. This acronym is normally prefixed with a language name, e.g. Ada/OCI. The OCI is not often used for programming but it may be used to better understand low level mechanisms of Pro* calls.)

7.2.1 Composition of a Pro*C program

A Pro*C application consists of two parts:

- a prologue, which contains declarative SQL statements and one executable SQL statement (CONNECT),
- a body, which contains executable SQL statements except for CONNECT.

The declarative SQL statements of the application *prologue* generate no actual calls to the database. These statements are:

- BEGIN DECLARE SECTION
- END DECLARE SECTION
- WHENEVER ...
- DECLARE CURSOR ...
- INCLUDE ...

The executable SQL statements in the application *body* do generate calls to the database and cause return codes to be set after their execution. These return codes are contained within the SQL Communications Area (SQLCA). The first executable SQL statement that is not CONNECT, starts a *transaction*, that is a logical unit of work that can be either completely successful (COMMIT operation) or unsuccessful (ROLLBACK operation). Since an application can activate many transactions, any new transaction begins with the first executable statement encountered after a CONNECT, COMMIT or ROLLBACK.

7.2.1.1 The DECLARE section

The DECLARE section names all the host and indicator variables (next section) used in the application. The data types of *host* variables do not have to match exactly the data types of the corresponding ORACLE attributes defined when the relation was created as ORACLE will make necessary conversions, if that is possible. The following DECLARE section names three host variables, which match three columns of the relation EMP_TEST as shown. The 'int' is the integer data type of C. The VARCHAR is a pseudo-type of Pro*C which extends the data typing of C (Section 7.2.1.3).

```
EXEC SQL BEGIN DECLARE SECTION;
      int empno;
      VARCHAR ename[15];
      VARCHAR job[10];
EXEC SQL END DECLARE SECTION;
```

```
SQL> DESCRIBE EMP_TEST
Name                                 Null?      Type
--------------------------------     ---------  ---------
EMPNO                                           NUMBER
ENAME                                           CHAR(15)
JOB                                             CHAR(10)
```

In SQL statements the host variables are preceded by a colon (:) and must be used in the same upper/lower case format as they are declared, as illustrated:

```
EXEC SQL SELECT EMPNO, JOB
      INTO :empno, :job
      FROM EMP_TEST
            WHERE ENAME = :ename;
```

7.2.1.2 Indicator variables

An indicator variable can optionally be associated with a host variable. ORACLE uses the indicator variable to signify either that the value returned in the host variable is *null* or that *truncation* of the returned value has been performed. The indicator variables must be declared as two-byte integers (i.e. 'short' or 'short int' depending on C implementation; FIXED BIN(15) in PL/I). The return codes of the indicator variable are:

- zero, if the host variable was not null or if the variable was the same length or shorter than the program buffer provided;
- negative value, if the host variable was null;
- positive value, if the host variable was truncated (this positive value is the actual length of the variable *before* truncation).

If the host variable does not have an associated indicator variable and a null value is returned, a negative SQLCODE value will be returned to the program (which will probably be addressed by a WHENEVER statement). The previous example can be extended to associate an indicator variable with the host variable 'job':

```
EXEC SQL BEGIN DECLARE SECTION;
      int empno;
      VARCHAR ename[15];
      VARCHAR job[10];
      short indjob;
EXEC SQL END DECLARE SECTION;
```

Having done this, a programmer can indicate actions to be taken upon the detection of the null value in the JOB attribute, for example:

```
EXEC SQL SELECT EMPNO, JOB
      INTO :empno, :job:indjob
      FROM EMP_TEST
            WHERE ENAME = :ename;
if (indjob == -1)
   job = "na/";
printf(...
```

A programmer can also use an indicator variable (such as 'indjob') to insert a null value into the JOB attribute:

```
empno = 7;
ename = "diana";
indjob = -1;
EXEC SQL INSERT INTO EMP_TEST
         (empno,ename,job)
               VALUES(:empno,:ename,:job:indjob);
```

The above code is considered a better programming practice than a "hard-coding" style, as in:

```
empno = 7;
ename = "diana";
EXEC SQL INSERT INTO EMP_TEST
         (empno,ename,job)
               VALUES(:empno,:ename,NULL);
```

7.2.1.3 The VARCHAR pseudo-type

The VARCHAR pseudo-type is provided to facilitate the declaration of varying length character strings. The above VARCHAR declaration of 'ename' is delivered by the preprocessor to the C compiler as the following structure variable:

```
struct {
   unsigned short len;      /* 2 bytes */
   unsigned char arr[15];
   } ename;
```

The size of the character array is the same as given in the VARCHAR definition. The *len* part of the VARCHAR structure specifies the string length. If the VARCHAR variable is used on output, the *len* is set by ORACLE. On input, the value of *len* must be set by the programmer. An obvious conclusion is that VARCHAR variables are not null-terminated, as normally done in C for character strings.

7.2.1.4 The SQLCA communication area

The execution of any SQL statement causes ORACLE to provide feedback information to the application program. This is done by means of the SQL Communications Area (SQLCA). To this aim, the program must contain the INCLUDE statement:

```
        EXEC SQL INCLUDE SQLCA;
```
or
```
        EXEC SQL INCLUDE SQLCA.H;
```

The SQLCA or SQLCA.H file (the two are identical), as provided by Oracle, must be accessible to the program. This can be achieved by copying it into the directory from which the program is compiled. The SQLCA contains variables, such as error codes, warning flags and event information and diagnostic text, in which the status of various operations is recorded. The full content of the SQLCA file is:

```
$ cat SQLCA

#ifndef SQLCA
#define SQLCA 1

struct sqlca {
    /* ub1 */ char      sqlcaid[8];
    /* b4  */ long      sqlabc;
    /* b4  */ long      sqlcode;
    struct {
        /* ub2 */ unsigned short  sqlerrml;
        /* ub1 */ char            sqlerrmc[70];
        { sqlerrm;
    /* ub1 */ char      sqlerrp[8];
    /* b4  */ long      sqlerrd[6];
    /* ub1 */ char      sqlwarn[8];
    /* ub1 */ char      sqlext[8];
};

struct sqlca sqlca
# ifdef SQLLIB_INIT
        = {
        {'S', 'Q', 'L', 'C', 'A', ' ', ' ', ' '},
        sizeof(struct sqlca),
        0,
        { 0, {0}},
```

```
            {'N', 'O', 'T', ' ', 'S', 'E', 'T', ' '},
            {0, 0, 0, 0, 0, 0},
            {0, 0, 0, 0, 0, 0, 0, 0},
            {0, 0, 0, 0, 0, 0, 0, 0}
        }
# endif
        ;


#endif
```

By using the variables in the SQLCA, a programmer can control event and exception handling. A convenient access to the SQLCA is provided by the WHENEVER declarative statement. The first two elements of the SQLCA (*sqlcaid* and *sqlcabc*) are relevant mainly to FORTRAN, not C. Two other elements (*sqlerrp* and *sqlext*) are currently unused. The meanings of the other elements are:

sqlcode   indicates the result of executing a SQL statement, as explained in Section 7.1.2 (except that ORACLE uses the value of 1403 instead of 100).

sqlerrm   explains error message. This varying length structure contains (in *sqlerrmc*) the error text corresponding to the error number found in *sqlca*; the length of *sqlerrmc* is determined in *sqlerrml*.

sqlerrd   contains six integers, of which only the third *[2]* is currently used. The value of this third element gives the number of tuples processed by manipulative SQL statements (such as INSERT or UPDATE).

sqlwarn   contains eight single-character elements that act as warnings for different conditions which may occur during preprocessing of a program. A warning flag is set if it contains 'W'; the first element *[0]* is set to 'W' if any of the other seven flags is set, thus serving as a global indicator of any problems. The problems addressed by the seven flags are:

    [1] Truncation of character data occurred. This flag should be used together with a positive value returned in an indicator variable (and the length of the host variable should be increased accordingly).

    [2] One or more null values were ignored in the computation of a group function, such as AVG, MIN, MAX, or SUM. This flag may be used in association with the null value function NVL (in order to temporarily assign values for the null data (e.g. zero), thus achieving a correct result from a group function).

    [3] Warns that the number of columns in the SELECT list does not match the number of host variables in the INTO clause.

    [4] Signifies an unconditional UPDATE or DELETE, that is coded without a WHERE clause and therefore leading to the update or deletion of every tuple in the relation.

    [5] Currently unused.

    [6] Indicates the implicit rollback of a transaction, that is a rollback which is not caused by an explicitly coded ROLLBACK WORK statement; for example, an implicit rollback may be due to a deadlock.

[7] Signifies that a column in a SELECT list, which also appears in a relation named in a FOR UPDATE clause, has changed between the time the SELECT started and the time the tuple was FETCHed and locked.

The SQLCA of ORACLE is intended to conform to the relational standard, thus improving the system's compatibility with other DBMSs. For example, of all the elements discussed above, only the last flag *[7]* of *sqlwarn* is not compatible with DB2, which does not have this feature.

However, compatibility aside, ORACLE provides for its users another communication area, called ORACA. The ORACA provides more information from the run-time environment of the preprocessor, such as the line number in the program file that returned error or the first seventy characters of a SQL statement with a parsing error. For reasons of efficiency and compatibility, the use of ORACA is optional.

7.2.1.5 The WHENEVER statement

The WHENEVER statement in ORACLE slightly expands the standard interpretation attached to this statement (Section 7.1.3). The ORACLE format of the WHENEVER statement is:

```
          EXEC SQL WHENEVER <condition> <action>
where <condition> is:
      SQLERROR    if sqlcode is negative,
      SQLWARNING  if sqlwarn[0] is set to "W",
      NOT FOUND   if sqlcode is +1403 (i.e. no tuple
                  found, which corresponds to +100 in the
                  standard and DB2),
and where <action> is:
      STOP        terminate the program and roll the
                  transaction back,
      CONTINUE    ignore the SQLCA condition and execute
                  the next instruction in the program,
      {GOTO | GO TO} <label> pass the control to the
                  statement at the specified label
```

The ORACLE extensions to the standard include the introduction of the SQLWARNING condition and the STOP action. The STOP action, however, is not recommended for normal use because it does not give any feedback to the user upon the program's unexpected termination.

When using the WHENEVER statement, it is crucial to remember that, being a declarative statement, its scope is determined by its physical location in the program rather than by the program's logic. To this extent, the WHENEVER statements should precede the SQL statements to be tested.

In the following example, the control goes to the label *target* if a NOT FOUND condition occurs. Because any SQL statement can end in error, the WHENEVER SQLERROR CONTINUE statement is used to prevent a possible program loop if the next statement (**COMMIT WORK RELEASE**) fails. Similar action should be taken to avoid loops due to warning conditions (by using WHENEVER SQLWARN CONTINUE).

```
    EXEC SQL WHENEVER NOT FOUND GOTO target;
    ...
target:
    printf("\nRelation fetches completed.\n");
    EXEC SQL CLOSE CURSOR1;
    EXEC SQL WHENEVER SQLERROR CONTINUE;
    EXEC SQL COMMIT WORK RELEASE;
    exit(0);
```

The RELEASE option should always be used when terminating the last transaction in a program. This option releases all resources (including ORACLE cursors) and logs the user off the database. If RELEASE is not specified, the locks on relations obtained by the user are held despite program termination (they are held until ORACLE determines that the user process is no longer active). This can have an adverse effect on the system's throughput in a multi-user environment.

7.2.1.6 Connecting to DBMS

An ORACLE user can be given a manual or automatic login by the database administrator. In the *manual login* mode, a user is expected to provide his/her ORACLE username and password whenever signing on to ORACLE. A programmer can code the program to prompt the user for a valid username and password each time the application is started. Alternatively, the programmer can hard-code the username and password to the application, as illustrated:

```
    VARCHAR uid[20];
    VARCHAR pwd[20];
    ...
    strcpy(uid.arr,"MAC");
    uid.len = strlen(uid.arr);
    strcpy(pwd.arr,"LES");
    pwd.len = strlen(pwd.arr);
    EXEC SQL CONNECT :uid IDENTIFIED BY :pwd;
```

The host variables for username (*uid*) and password (*pwd*) are declared as variable character strings. The two variables are initialized to 'MAC' and 'LES', respectively. The *strlen* functions return the number of characters in the varying-length elements of the VARCHAR structures. These numbers are assigned to the *len* elements of the structures. The CONNECT statement must be the first executable statement in an application.

ORACLE users who have an *automatic login* do not need to type their ORACLE username and password to log on to ORACLE. Their identification is tied to their operating system controlled username and password. The automatic login could be achieved by the following code (where "/" is the default character to identify the automatic login specified in the preprocessor's run-time options):

```
VARCHAR uid[20];
...
strcpy(uid.arr,"/");
uid.len = strlen(uid.arr);
EXEC SQL CONNECT :uid;
```

7.2.1.7 Performing SQL statements using host variable arrays

An important extra feature of ORACLE is the possibility of using host language variable arrays in performing SQL statements. This important feature provides for a direct support of multi-tuple SQL operations in the host environment. Pro*C allows host variables declared as arrays to be used in SELECT, FETCH, INSERT and UPDATE statements. When used with SELECT or FETCH, the activity is referred to as an *array fetch*. It is called an *array bind* if used for INSERT or UPDATE operations.

In the following example three host arrays are declared. Two of these arrays (*empno* and *job*) are used to accommodate up to 100 tuples SELECTed from EMP_TEST relation.

```
EXEC SQL BEGIN DECLARE SECTION;
      int empno      [100];
      VARCHAR ename [100] [15];
      VARCHAR job    [100] [10];
EXEC SQL END DECLARE SECTION;

EXEC SQL SELECT EMPNO, JOB
      INTO :empno, :job
      FROM EMP_TEST;
```

This solution is unsatisfactory if more than 100 tuples need to be retrieved. Repetitive execution of the SELECT statement will not help because the statement always retrieves the first 100 tuples. To be able to look past the first 100 tuples, cursor-driven processing must be performed in which a FETCH statement is executed repeatedly in a loop until more than 100 tuples are placed in the arrays as indicated in the next example.

```
EXEC SQL DECLARE CURSOR1 FOR
      SELECT EMPNO, JOB
      FROM EMP_TEST;
...
EXEC SQL OPEN CURSOR1;
...
EXEC SQL FETCH CURSOR1
      INTO :empno, :job;
```

Array fetches are subjected to the important restriction that in a SELECT statement (independent or as part of a cursor) a WHERE clause can never refer to a host array. For example, the following SELECT is invalid if *ename* is an array:

```
EXEC SQL SELECT EMPNO, JOB
     INTO :empno, :job
     FROM EMP_TEST
          WHERE ENAME = :ename;
```

This restriction is waived for carefully used *array binds* in UPDATE statements. The requirement there is that the arrays of the same type and size are used in the SET and WHERE clause of the UPDATE statement. Assuming the previous declaration section, the following UPDATE is valid:

```
EXEC SQL UPDATE EMP_TEST
     SET JOB = :job
     WHERE ENAME = :ename;
```

The use of array binds in INSERT statements is relatively straightforward but requires that arrays are loaded with data prior to insertion:

```
EXEC SQL INSERT
     INTO EMP_TEST (EMPNO, ENAME, JOB)
     VALUES (:empno, :ename, :job);
```

To control the number of tuples subject to array fetches or binds, the FOR keyword is provided by ORACLE. The programmer must ensure that the variable controlling the execution of a FOR loop (*maxrepeat* in this example) does not exceed the actual array sizes.

```
EXEC SQL BEGIN DECLARE SECTION;
     int empno      [100];
     VARCHAR ename  [100] [15];
     VARCHAR job    [100] [10];
     int maxrepeat;
EXEC SQL END DECLARE SECTION;

maxrepeat = 50;
EXEC SQL FOR :maxrepeat
     SELECT EMPNO, ENAME, JOB
        INTO :empno, :ename, :job
        FROM EMP_TEST;
```

7.2.2   Programming without cursors

If SQL statements in an application are known to return exactly one tuple, then the application can be programmed without cursors. Typical examples include SQL statements with equality predicates (in their WHERE clause) based on a value in a unique index. In the following example a simple 'create-search-display-rollback' program without cursors is illustrated in four steps. First a brief description is given, then the source code is provided, followed by a source analysis and an execution example.

7.2.2.1 Description

The program is named *nocursors*. It creates a database relation EMP_TEST under the user MAC. The relation has three attributes: EMPNO, ENAME and JOB. The application prompts for the values of attributes to be entered at the terminal by a user. Upon entry of a set of three values, a new tuple is inserted into the relation and the user is again prompted to enter another set of three values. The insertion process ends once the user enters the value 0 (zero) for the EMPNO attribute. As verification, the user is prompted to enter an ENAME value and the application finds corresponding EMPNO and JOB values. The application ends by undoing all the changes done, that is by rolling the database back to its original state. The program is quite insecure. It does not contain exception handling functions.

7.2.2.2 Source code

```
1    /* Pro*C application with no cursors used */
2    #include <stdio.h>
3
4    EXEC SQL BEGIN DECLARE SECTION;
5          VARCHAR uid[20];
6          VARCHAR pwd[20];
7          int empno;
8          VARCHAR ename[15];
9          VARCHAR job[10];
10   EXEC SQL END DECLARE SECTION;
11   EXEC SQL INCLUDE SQLCA.H;
12   main()
13   {
14     int sret;
15     strcpy(uid.arr,"MAC");
16     uid.len=strlen(uid.arr);
17     strcpy(pwd.arr,"LES");
18     pwd.len=strlen(pwd.arr);
19     EXEC SQL CONNECT :uid IDENTIFIED BY :pwd;
20     printf("\nConnected to ORACLE as user: %s \n",
                 uid.arr);
21     EXEC SQL CREATE TABLE EMP_TEST
22          (EMPNO NUMBER,
23            ENAME CHAR(15),
24            JOB CHAR(10));
25     printf("Relation EMP_TEST created. \n\n");
26     while (1)
27     {
28      printf("Enter employee number (or 0 to end):
                 ");
29       sret = scanf("%d",&empno);
30       if (sret==EOF || sret==0 || empno==0)
31               break;
```

```
32          printf("Enter employee name: ");
33          scanf("%s",ename.arr);
34          ename.len = strlen(ename.arr);
35          printf("Enter employee's job: ");
36          scanf("%s",job.arr);
37          job.len = strlen(job.arr);
38          EXEC SQL INSERT INTO EMP_TEST
39              (EMPNO, ENAME, JOB)
40                  VALUES(:empno,:ename,:job);
41          printf("Employee %s added.\n\n",ename.arr);
42        }
43      printf("\nEnter existing employee name: ");
44      scanf("%s",ename.arr);
45      EXEC SQL SELECT EMPNO, JOB
46          INTO :empno, :job
47          FROM EMP_TEST
48              WHERE ENAME = :ename;
49      printf("Employee details are:   empno: %d
                empjob: %s \n",empno,job.arr);
50      EXEC SQL ROLLBACK WORK RELEASE;
51      exit(0);
52    }
```

7.2.2.3 Source analysis

Line 1 is a comment line. In line 2 the standard input/output library is included into the program. Lines 4–10 contain the DECLARE section, as explained in Section 7.2.1.1 (the VARCHAR pseudo-type is discussed in Section 7.2.1.3 and the use of username (uid) and password (pwd) variables is described in Section 7.2.1.6). In line 11 the SQL Communication Area is included into the program (Section 7.2.1.4).

Execution of a C program begins with a call to a function with the name *main*. This function begins in line 12. The parentheses after the word *main* indicate that the function takes no parameters. Line 14 declares an integer variable, called sret, within the scope of the *main* function. The ORACLE user MAC with the password LES connects to the system as a result of the code on lines 15–19 (Section 7.2.1.6). Line 20 calls a library function *printf* which prints output on the terminal. The output informs that the user MAC is connected to ORACLE. The sequence \n in the string is C notation for the newline character (i.e. move to the next line). The sequence %s is a formatting instruction which says that the value of the variable *uid.arr* will be printed as a string.

Lines 21–24 contain an embedded SQL statement to CREATE the relation EMP_TEST in the database, and line 25 is an output message to this effect. Line 26 initiates a *while* loop, the body of which is enclosed by the braces { } (lines 27–42). The parentheses after the word *while* contain the expression to be evaluated in order to determine the true/false condition for the loop execution. If the expression is non-zero, the loop is executed and the expression is evaluated. In this case, 1 (one) is taken as permanently true, thus leading to an infinite loop, presumably to be broken by other means (such as a *break* function).

Line 28 prompts for an employee number which is read by the function *scanf* in line 29. The input value is interpreted according to *%d* specification, meaning a decimal number. The unary operator *&* returns the address of *empno* (the arguments to scanf must be pointers). The result of *scanf* is assigned to the variable *sret*. An *if* statement in lines 30–31 terminates (*break*) the *while* loop if:

- *sret* is equal to the end of file (EOF) condition; or
- *sret* is equal to zero (0), meaning that the next input character does not match the *%d* specification of *scanf*; or
- *empno* is equal to zero (0).

The assignment statements in lines 34 and 37 are needed to establish the length of character strings entered as ename and job values, respectively. The function *strlen* returns the length of a character string, excluding the null character (\0) which marks the end of strings in C. The tuples are INSERTed into the relation EMP_TEST by a SQL statement in lines 38–40. Each insert is confirmed to the user in line 41.

Line 43 prompts for an employee name, which is read by the function *scanf* in line 44. The employee name entered (ename) is an argument in evaluating the retrieval condition of the SELECT statement (lines 45–48). Line 49 displays *empjob* and *empno* corresponding to the *ename* accepted in line 44. Line 50 rolls the database back to its original state, releases all resources and logs the user off ORACLE (Section 7.2.1.5). The standard library function exit terminates program execution (line 51). A return value of 0 in this function signals a normal termination (various abnormal situations are signaled by non-zero values).

7.2.2.4 Execution example

An example of the execution of the application *nocursors* is shown below. After the relation EMP_TEST is created, one tuple is inserted into it. After entering the value 0 for *empno* in response to the second prompt, the application proceeds by asking the user to enter an employee name. Since the employee name entered (GARY) corresponds to the one previously inserted into the relation, the remaining two attributes are displayed.

```
$ nocursors

Connected to Oracle as user: MAC
Relation EMP_TEST created.

Enter employee number (or 0 to end): 5
Enter employee name: GARY
Enter employee's job: BOSS
Employee GARY added.

Enter employee number (or 0 to end): 0

Enter existing employee name: GARY
Employee details are: empno: 5 empjob: BOSS
```

7.2.3   **Programming with cursors**

In most applications, the SQL executable statements may return more than one tuple. Such applications require the use of cursors (Sections 7.1.1 and 7.1.3), unless *arrays* are used (Section 7.2.1.7). Technically, a cursor is a work area used by the system to store the results of a multiple tuple SQL statement. The cursor operations consist of six SQL statements:

- DECLARE CURSOR
- OPEN CURSOR
- FETCH
- UPDATE ... WHERE CURRENT
- DELETE ... WHERE CURRENT
- CLOSE CURSOR.

A cursor is specified by the declarative DECLARE CURSOR statement which must precede any other SQL statement referencing that cursor. The syntax is:

```
EXEC SQL DECLARE CURSOR FOR <query expression>
```

where <query expression> is a SQL SELECT statement.

A cursor is in either the *open state* or the *closed state*. The initial state of the cursor (i.e. after the DECLARE CURSOR) is closed. A cursor is placed in the open state by an OPEN CURSOR statement and returned to the closed state by a CLOSE CURSOR statement, a COMMIT WORK statement or a ROLLBACK WORK statement.

A cursor in the open state designates all the tuples resulting from its associated query. These tuples form the *active set* of the cursor. The active set remains unchanged until the cursor is closed and re-opened with new values for its input host variables (i.e. host variables in the WHERE clause).

A FETCH statement advances the position of an open cursor to the next tuple in the cursor's sequence and retrieves the values of the columns of that *current* tuple. The cursor may only move forward and the only way to fetch a tuple previously accessed is to close and re-open the cursor, starting again from the beginning of the active set. The *sqlcode* is set in ORACLE to +1403 (+100 in the standard) if the active set is empty or the last tuple has previously been fetched.

A DELETE ... WHERE CURRENT statement deletes the current tuple of the cursor. Similarly, an UPDATE ... WHERE CURRENT statement updates the current tuple of the cursor, as in:

```
EXEC SQL UPDATE EMPLOYEE
        SET EMP_SALARY = :new_salary
        WHERE CURRENT OF RAISEPAY;
```

7.2.3.1   **Description**

In the following example, a complete program which uses cursors is presented. The program refers to the well-known example of the suppliers-parts-projects database. The definition and contents of the relations S (suppliers) and J (projects) are shown below:

```
SQL> DESCRIBE S

 Name                              Null?      Type
 -------------------------------   ---------  ---------
 S#                                NOT NULL   CHAR(4)
 SNAME                                        CHAR(15)
 STATUS                                       NUMBER
 CITY                                         CHAR(12)


SQL> DESCRIBE J

 Name                              Null?      Type
 -------------------------------   ---------  ---------
 J#                                NOT NULL   CHAR(4)
 JNAME                                        CHAR(15)
 CITY                                         CHAR(12)


SQL> SELECT * FROM S;

 S#    SNAME                 STATUS CITY
 ----  ---------------              ------------
 S1    DELOBEL                  20  GRENOBLE
 S8    STAFFORD                 40  WATERLOO
 S7    MACIASZEK                10  WOLLONGONG
 S2    GHOSH                    45  SAN JOSE
 S3    GINSBURG                 20  LOS ANGELES
 S4    KAMBAYASHI               10  FUKUOKA
 S5    SIKLOSSY                 40  AMSTERDAM
 S6    SCHEK                    20  ZURICH

8 records selected.


SQL> SELECT * FROM J;

 J#    JNAME            CITY
 ----  ---------------  ------------
 J1    PROCESSOR        PARIS
 J2    TERMINAL         AMSTERDAM
 J3    DISK DRIVE       LOS ANGELES
 J4    TAPE UNIT        SAN JOSE
 J5    TERMINAL         LONDON
 J6    CONSOLE          WATERLOO
 J7    PRINTER          ROME

7 records selected.
```

The program presented provides a solution to the problem in which a list of all suppliers (in S# order) and all projects for those suppliers (in J# order) is requested. The program is more robust than the application *nocursors* in Section 7.2.2 (and it adopts a different programming style). It provides limited exception handling by direct checking of *sqlcode* values (rather than by using the WHENEVER statement).

7.2.3.2 Source code

```
1    /* Pro*C application with cursors used */
2    #include <stdio.h>
3
4    EXEC SQL BEGIN DECLARE SECTION;
5         VARCHAR uid[20];
6         VARCHAR pwd[20];
7         VARCHAR sno[6];
8         VARCHAR sname[21];
9         VARCHAR scity[16];
10        int     status;
11        VARCHAR jno[5];
12        VARCHAR jname[11];
13        VARCHAR jcity[16];
14   EXEC SQL END DECLARE SECTION;
15
16   EXEC SQL DECLARE C1 CURSOR FOR
17        SELECT S#, SNAME, STATUS, CITY FROM S
18        ORDER BY TO_NUMBER(LTRIM(S#, 'S'));
19
20   EXEC SQL DECLARE C2 CURSOR FOR
21        SELECT J#, JNAME, CITY FROM J
22        WHERE J# IN
23             (SELECT J# FROM SPJ WHERE S# = :sno)
24        ORDER BY TO_NUMBER(LTRIM(J#, 'J'));
25
26   EXEC SQL INCLUDE SQLCA.H;
27
28   main()
29   {
30     strcpy(uid.arr,"MAC");
31     uid.len = strlen(uid.arr);
32     strcpy(pwd.arr,"LES");
33     pwd.len = strlen(pwd.arr);
34     EXEC SQL CONNECT :uid IDENTIFIED BY :pwd;
35     if (sqlca.sqlcode)
36       { printf("Unable to login as %s\n", uid.arr);
            exit(!0); }
37     EXEC SQL OPEN C1;
38     for (;;)
```

```
39        {
40            EXEC SQL FETCH C1 INTO :sno, :sname, :status,
                                      :scity;
41            if (sqlca.sqlcode) break;
42            sno.arr[sno.len] = '\0';
43            sname.arr[sname.len] = '\0';
44            scity.arr[scity.len] = '\0';
45            printf("%-6s %-21s %-5d %-16s\n",
46                     sno.arr,
47                     sname.arr,
48                     status,
49                     scity.arr);
50         EXEC SQL OPEN C2;
51         for (;;)
52         {
53             EXEC SQL FETCH C2 INTO :jno, :jname,
                                       :jcity;
54             if (sqlca.sqlcode) break;
55             jno.arr[jno.len] = '\0';
56             jname.arr[jname.len] = '\0';
57             jcity.arr[jcity.len] = '\0';
58             printf(" %-5s %-11s %-15s\n",
59                     jno.arr,
60                     jname.arr,
61                     jcity.arr);
62         }
63         EXEC SQL CLOSE C2;
64         putchar('\n');
65        }
66      EXEC SQL CLOSE C1;
67    }
```

7.2.3.3 Source analysis

Lines 1–14 and 26–34 are as explained in Section 7.2.2. The cursors named C1 and C2 are declared in lines 16–24. The cursor C1 is associated with a query which retrieves tuples from the relation S, in order of S# values. Because S# is declared as CHAR(4), and to achieve more reliable and portable code, the ORACLE functions LTRIM and TO_NUMBER are used in the ORDER clause. The LTRIM function removes, in an S# string, all initial characters up to the first character which is not 'S'. This means that S# values ('S1', 'S2', etc.) are stripped to numeric characters ('1', '2', etc.). The function TO_NUMBER converts these character values to numbers (1, 2, etc.). The cursor C2 is associated with a query which retrieves tuples from the relation J for each current S# and orders them by J# values (in a way similar to that in cursor C1).

The if statement in lines 35–36 terminates the program with an appropriate message if the value of *sqlcode* is nonzero (i.e. the preceding CONNECT was unsuccessful). In C, if the value in an IF condition is non-zero (positive or negative) it is interpreted as true. A return value of non-zero (!0) of the function *exit* signals an abnormal termination.

Line 37 opens the cursor C1, that is it defines an active set of tuples returned as a result of its query. The for loop in lines 38–65 is permanently true (as indicated by the absence of any loop condition). This is equivalent to an infinite loop programmed as *while (1)* (Section 7.2.2). The loop is broken by a *break* in line 41 once the value of *sqlcode* is non-zero, presumably as a result of an attempt to fetch a tuple (in line 40) from beyond the end of the active set. Those fetched values which are strings are null-terminated according to C rules (lines 42–44). The function *printf* produces formatted output of each tuple's values.

Line 50 opens the cursor C2. The *for* statement begins an inner loop which ends in line 62. In this loop the tuples from the relation J are fetched and printed. Since these loops are nested, the cursor C2 is being closed and re-opened for each execution of the outer loop. The function *putchar* (line 64) generates a newline character, that is it causes a carriage return action on a terminal. The application terminates after closing the cursor C1 (line 66).

7.2.3.4 Execution example

In the following example the presented application, conveniently named *cursors*, is executed against the extensions (i.e. the contents) of the relations shown earlier.

```
$ cursors
S1      DELOBEL                    20      GRENOBLE
   J1      PROCESSOR    PARIS
   J4      TAPE UNIT    SAN JOSE

S2      GHOSH                      45      SAN JOSE
   J1      PROCESSOR    PARIS
   J2      TERMINAL     AMSTERDAM
   J3      DISK DRIVE   LOS ANGELES
   J4      TAPE UNIT    SAN JOSE
   J5      TERMINAL     LONDON
   J7      PRINTER      ROME

S3      GINSBURG                   20      LOS ANGELES
   J1      PROCESSOR    PARIS
S4      KAMBAYASHI                 10      FUKUOKA
   J2      TERMINAL     AMSTERDAM
   J3      DISK DRIVE   LOS ANGELES
S5      SIKLOSSY                   40      AMSTERDAM
   J3      DISK DRIVE   LOS ANGELES
S6      SCHEK                      20      ZURICH
   J3      DISK DRIVE   LOS ANGELES
S7      MACIASZEK                  10      WOLLONGONG
   J1      PROCESSOR    PARIS
S8      STAFFORD                   40      WATERLOO
   J1      PROCESSOR    PARIS
```

7.2.4 Programming with dynamic SQL

At times a database user needs to be given more processing power than that provided by applications whose executions can only vary in response to new input data values (such as in the application *nocursors* in Section 7.2.2). Some users may require the construction of on-line applications in which they may need to be prompted for a SQL statement, not just data. To this aim, DB2, ORACLE and other systems provide extra embedded SQL statements that can interpret and process input of conventional SQL statements from the user. This form of embedded SQL application is called a dynamic SQL application. Dynamically defined SQL statements are statements which are not known at compile time.

In ORACLE, four methods of programming dynamic SQL statements are recognized:

1. the EXECUTE IMMEDIATE statement;
2. the PREPARE and EXECUTE statements;
3. the PREPARE and FETCH statements;
4. the DESCRIBE statement.

7.2.4.1 Using the EXECUTE IMMEDIATE statement

A SQL statement dynamically defined at the run time can be bound and executed by means of another SQL statement called EXECUTE IMMEDIATE. For example, in the EXECUTE IMMEDIATE statement:

```
EXEC SQL EXECUTE IMMEDIATE :sqlstat;
```

sqlstat is a host variable that represents another valid SQL statement entered entirely or partially from the terminal.

In general, the EXECUTE IMMEDIATE method can only be applied if the dynamically defined SQL statement is not a SELECT and the dynamically defined SQL statement does not contain a host variable.

The application below uses the EXECUTE IMMEDIATE method of dynamic SQL. The user at a terminal is prompted for a WHERE clause to be concatenated with a partial UPDATE statement hard-coded in the program. The full statement is used with EXECUTE IMMEDIATE.

```
1    /* Pro*C application with dynamic SQL (EXECUTE
        IMMEDIATE method) */
2    #include <stdio.h>
3    EXEC SQL INCLUDE SQLCA.H;
4
5    EXEC SQL BEGIN DECLARE SECTION;
6            VARCHAR uid[20];
7            VARCHAR pwd[20];
8            char    sqlstat[132];
9    EXEC SQL END DECLARE SECTION;
```

```
10
11
12   main()
13   {
14           char    where[80];
15
16           strcpy(uid.arr,"MAC");
17           uid.len = strlen(uid.arr);
18           strcpy(pwd.arr,"LES");
19           pwd.len = strlen(pwd.arr);
20           EXEC SQL WHENEVER SQLERROR STOP;
21           EXEC SQL CONNECT :uid IDENTIFIED BY :pwd;
22           strcpy(sqlstat, "UPDATE S SET STATUS =
                                  STATUS * 1.2 WHERE ");
23           printf("Enter WHERE clause for the
                          following: \n");
24           printf("%s", sqlstat);
25           gets(where);
26           strcat(sqlstat, where);
27           EXEC SQL EXECUTE IMMEDIATE :sqlstat;
28           printf("Relation updated. \n");
29           EXEC SQL WHENEVER SQLERROR CONTINUE;
30           EXEC SQL COMMIT WORK RELEASE;
31           exit(0);
32   }
```

The function *strcpy* in line 22 copies the first (fixed) part of the UPDATE statement to the string variable *sqlstat*. Lines 23 and 24 prompt the user for the second (dynamic) part of the UPDATE statement. The function *gets* accepts the user's input into the variable *where* (line 25). The function *strcat* in the next line concatenates the string *where* to the end of the string *sqlstat*. This allows the EXECUTE IMMEDIATE statement to bind and execute the dynamically defined UPDATE statement (line 27). The output from two executions of the application *dynamic1* is shown below. In the first execution, the user entered the expression S# = 'S1'. In the second execution, the user typed in SNAME = 'MACIASZEK'.

```
$ dynamic1
Enter WHERE clause for the following:
UPDATE S SET STATUS = STATUS * 1.5 WHERE S# = 'S1'
Relation updated.

$ dynamic1
Enter WHERE clause for the following:
UPDATE S SET STATUS = STATUS * 1.5 WHERE SNAME =
'MACIASZEK'
Relation updated.
```

7.2.4.2 Using the PREPARE and EXECUTE statements

Dynamic programming with the EXECUTE IMMEDIATE statement allows part, or all, of the SQL statement to be entered dynamically during run-time. On each execution of the application, the dynamic statement is parsed and then executed. If the same dynamic statement is entered for many executions of the program, then the method which uses the PREPARE and EXECUTE statements is advantageous. In this method the dynamic SQL statement is parsed (PREPAREd) only once. As an additional advantage, the dynamic SQL statement can contain host variables.

In this example, a user is prompted for a WHERE clause to be used in an UPDATE statement (line 23). The UPDATE statement includes an input host variable (sometimes called a *bind variable*) for STATUS. The user is requested to enter a value for that variable before the update takes place.

```
1    /* Pro*C application with dynamic SQL (PREPARE
     and EXECUTE method) */
2    #include <stdio.h>
3    EXEC SQL INCLUDE SQLCA.H;
4
5    EXEC SQL BEGIN DECLARE SECTION;
6            VARCHAR uid[20];
7            VARCHAR pwd[20];
8            int status;
9            char    sqlstat[132];
10   EXEC SQL END DECLARE SECTION;
11
12
13   main()
14   {
15           char    where[80];
16
17           strcpy(uid.arr,"MAC");
18           uid.len = strlen(uid.arr);
19           strcpy(pwd.arr,"LES");
20           pwd.len = strlen(pwd.arr);
21           EXEC SQL WHENEVER SQLERROR STOP;
22           EXEC SQL CONNECT :uid IDENTIFIED BY :pwd;
23           strcpy(sqlstat, "UPDATE S SET STATUS =
                               :status WHERE ");
24           printf("Enter WHERE clause for the
                      following: \n");
25           printf("%s", sqlstat);
26           gets(where);
27           strcat(sqlstat, where);
28           EXEC SQL PREPARE STAT1 FROM :sqlstat;
29           printf("Enter status, please: ");
30           scanf("%d",&status);
```

```
31                    EXEC SQL EXECUTE STAT1 USING :status;
32                    printf("Relation updated. \n");
33                    EXEC SQL WHENEVER SQLERROR CONTINUE;
34                    EXEC SQL COMMIT WORK RELEASE;
35                    exit(0);
36    }
```

This program (called *dynamic2*) can be executed for different WHERE clauses and for different values of the bind variable (*status*). A general restriction on the PREPARE and EXECUTE method is that a dynamic SQL statement cannot be a query (SELECT statement).

```
$ dynamic2
Enter WHERE clause for the following:
UPDATE S SET STATUS = :status WHERE CITY = 'LOS ANGELES'
Enter status, please: 8
Relation updated.

$ dynamic2
Enter WHERE clause for the following:
UPDATE S SET STATUS = :status WHERE STATUS = 10
Enter status, please: 12
Relation updated.
```

While the program *dynamic2* takes advantage of the possibility of initiating the values of the bind variable, it executes the dynamic statement only once in each run. A better use of the PREPARE and EXECUTE method would be to EXECUTE the PREPAREd statement many times within the same run (or, to be more precise, within the same transaction, that is within the logical unit of work). In *dynamic2*, the desired result would be achieved by replacing the lines 29–32 with, for example:

```
            printf("Enter status, please: ");
            scanf("%d",&status);
            while (status != 0)
            {
                EXEC SQL EXECUTE STAT1 USING :status;
                printf("Relation updated. \n");
                printf("Enter status, please: ");
                scanf("%d",&status);
            }
```

7.2.4.3 Using the PREPARE and FETCH statements

This method relaxes the restrictions on the two methods described above, and permits the use of dynamically defined SELECT statements. The SELECT list must be known in the program but the search criteria (WHERE clause) and ordering (ORDER BY) may vary between runs. The method uses cursors because a SELECT statement may return multiple tuples.

The following program prompts for a WHERE clause to be used in a query. Once the query is PREPAREd, a corresponding cursor is DECLAREd and OPENed, and the tuples are FETCHed in a loop (lines 34–40).

```
1    /* Pro*C application with dynamic SQL (PREPARE
     and FETCH method) */
2    #include <stdio.h>
3    EXEC SQL INCLUDE SQLCA.H;
4
5    EXEC SQL BEGIN DECLARE SECTION;
6            VARCHAR uid[20];
7            VARCHAR pwd[20];
8            VARCHAR sno[6];
9            VARCHAR sname[21];
10           char    sqlstat[132];
11   EXEC SQL END DECLARE SECTION;
12
13
14   main()
15   }
16           char    where[80];
17           int     loop;
18
19           strcpy(uid.arr,"MAC");
20           uid.len = strlen(uid.arr);
21           strcpy(pwd.arr,"LES");
22           pwd.len = strlen(pwd.arr);
23           EXEC SQL WHENEVER SQLERROR STOP;
24           EXEC SQL CONNECT :uid IDENTIFIED BY :pwd;
25           strcpy(sqlstat, "SELECT S#, SNAME FROM S
                            WHERE ");
26           printf("Enter WHERE clause for the
                    following: \n\n");
27           printf("%s", sqlstat);
28           gets(where);
29           strcat(sqlstat, where);
30           EXEC SQL PREPARE STAT1 FROM :sqlstat;
31           EXEC SQL DECLARE CURS1 CURSOR FOR STAT1;
32           EXEC SQL OPEN CURS1;
33           EXEC SQL WHENEVER NOT FOUND GOTO terminate;
34           for (loop=0; ;loop++)
35           {
36                   EXEC SQL FETCH CURS1 INTO :sno,
                                            :sname;
```

```
37                          sno.arr[sno.len] = '\0';
38                          sname.arr[sname.len] = '\0';
39                          printf("%-6s %-21s\n", sno.arr,
                                                     sname.arr);
40              }
41    terminate:
42              printf("\n%d tuples selected.\n", loop);
43              EXEC SQL WHENEVER SQLERROR CONTINUE;
44              EXEC SQL COMMIT WORK RELEASE;
45              exit(0);
46    }
```

In the example of execution below, the program *dynamic3* searches for suppliers with status equal to 12, then displays their numbers and names.

```
$ dynamic3
Enter WHERE clause for the following:

SELECT S#, SNAME FROM S WHERE STATUS = 12
S4 KAMBAYASHI
S5 SIKLOSSY

2 tuples selected.
```

7.2.4.4 Using the DESCRIBE statement

The fourth method of programming dynamic SQL statements allows the most flexibility but requires more sophisticated programming and additional knowledge of ORACLE concepts. In this method the SELECT list may not be known to the program; hence the number and type of host variables cannot be determined until run-time. The SQL statement which enables an examination of the SELECT list of a query, entered dynamically by a user, is called DESCRIBE. The DESCRIBE statement determines the number of columns in the SELECT list and the datatype of each column. In general, the DESCRIBE method can be used for any dynamically entered SQL statements, and not just queries.

A typical application which uses the DESCRIBE method to run a dynamically entered query contains ten steps:

1. Declare the SQL Descriptor Area (SQLDA) structure.
   The SQLDA storage area is used by the application to hold one tuple of the query's result, that is to hold information about columns in the SELECT list (called *define variables*). Optionally, the SQLDA area holds information about input host variables (i.e. *bind variables*). An INCLUDE statement can be used to declare the SQLDA:

   ```
   EXEC SQL INCLUDE SQLDA;
   ```

   If a query uses both define and bind variables, then two SQLDA areas are necessary.

In the example, the define variables are *sno* and *sname*, and the bind variables are *status* and *scity*.

```
EXEC SQL SELECT S#, SNAME
     INTO :sno, :sname
     FROM S
     WHERE STATUS = :status AND CITY = :scity;
```

Multiple SQLDA areas can be declared by means of pointer variables:

```
EXEC SQL INCLUDE SQLDA;
SQLDA *intoda, *whereda;
```

2. Prepare the dynamically entered SQL query, for example:

```
EXEC SQL PREPARE STAT FROM :sqlstat;
```

3. Declare a cursor for the query, for example:

```
EXEC SQL DECLARE CURS CURSOR FOR STAT;
```

4. Allocate a descriptor (i.e. an instance of the SQLDA) using the routine *sqlald*, for example:

```
whereda = sqlald(whereSize, maxChars, 10);
```

5. De-allocate a descriptor using the routine *sqlclu*, for example:

```
sqlclu(whereda);
```

6. Describe the bind descriptor (to store the input variables used in evaluating the query), for example:

```
EXEC SQL DESCRIBE BIND VARIABLES
     FOR STAT
     INTO whereda;
```

7. Open the cursor, for example:

```
EXEC SQL OPEN CURS USING DESCRIPTOR whereda;
```

8. Describe the select descriptor (to associate with it items in the SELECT list), for example:

```
EXEC SQL DESCRIBE SELECT LIST
     FOR STAT
     INTO intoda;
```

9. Fetch tuples from the active set, for example:

```
EXEC SQL FETCH CURS USING DESCRIPTOR intoda;
```

10. Close the cursor, for example:

```
EXEC SQL CLOSE CURS;
```

7.3   APPLICATION GENERATION

Programmatic interfaces to databases contradict the spirit of relational database theory as they are procedural rather than declarative. However, in being procedural, they permit the processing of information by any method and can respond precisely to any user requirements. Furthermore, in the current state-of-the-art of relational theory and practice, some procedural processing is unavoidable. To minimize the need for programmatic interfaces in building database applications, relational DBMSs provide application generators (known also as 4th generation languages).

The application generator provided with ORACLE is called SQL*Forms. It allows the programmer to generate, on a terminal screen, default forms based on the definitions of database relations. These forms can then be customized and improved by means of a utility called the *screen painter*. Once designed, the forms can be used for data entry, retrieval, update and delete operations. With SQL*Forms, initial applications can be built rapidly and modified easily. This gives rise to the *prototyping* approach to systems development (Section 3.3.1.4). Extensive consistency checks, update propagation procedures and recursive algorithms can be implemented in SQL*Forms through *triggers* or by calling programmatic interfaces (called *user exits*).

Version 2.3 of SQL*Forms takes advantage of a terminal's keyboard and defines powerful functions for the keys to achieve easy form manipulation. Pop-up menus are used to guide the user in designing and operating a form. Version 3.0 introduces Macintosh-style menu bars. Many additional utilities are provided by Application Foundation—a tool that runs on top of SQL*Forms. Two other ORACLE products are accessible from within Version 3.0 of SQL*Forms: SQL-Menu (for setting-up application-oriented menus) and PL/SQL (an Ada-based native syntax interface (Section 7.1.4)). The use of a mouse is expected to be added to SQL*Forms (firstly, in a version of ORACLE for Macintosh computers).

7.3.1   Concepts of form generation

Figure 7.1 illustrates a *default form* generated by SQL*Forms from the definitions of the relations A_CUSTOMER and A_ITEM:

```
SQL> DESC A_CUSTOMER;
 Name                                       Null?       Type
 ------------------------------------------ ----------- ----------
 CUSTOMER_NUMBER                            NOT NULL    CHAR(5)
 SOLD_TO_ADDRESS                                        CHAR(40)
 SHIP_TO_ADDRESS                                        CHAR(40)
```

```
SQL> DESC A_ITEM;
Name                               Null?      Type
----------------------------------- ---------- ---------
ITEM_NUMBER                        NOT NULL   CHAR(10)
ITEM_DESCRIPTION                              CHAR(40)
UNIT_OF_MEASURE                              CHAR(5)
PRICE                                        NUMBER
```

A form can have a complex structure and it can contain many pages (screens). A *page* is the part of the form displayed on a terminal's *screen*. A user can move between pages in one keystroke. *Page 0* (zero) of a form is special and can never be displayed by the form operator. For a form designer, it is a convenient place for hiding confidential information and intermediate calculations.

A page can contain one or more blocks. A *block* is the part of the page that corresponds to, at most, one relation in a database. Triggers (Section 7.3.6) can be used to access other relations from the block. There are two blocks in Figure 7.1.

A relation for which a block is constructed is known in SQL*Forms as a *base table*. A single tuple displayed in the block is referred to as a *record*. An attribute (column) of a tuple is called a *field*. A field may also be calculated from other fields on the form. A block can be designed to display one record at a time (*single-record block*) or more than one record at a time (*multi-record block*). The form in Figure 7.1 contains two single-record blocks. In general, the default setting of form generation allows a quick construction of either single-record or multi-record blocks.

A special kind of block, called *control block*, does not represent any relation in the database. The field values in a control block are either entered by the user or calculated

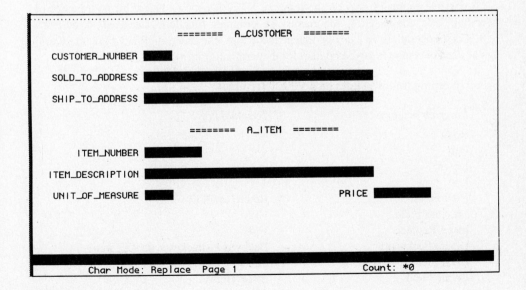

Figure 7.1   Default form

by triggers (from the values of other fields in the form or from the attribute values of any database relations). The purpose of a control block is to serve as a:

- *custom menu* (a list of choices in form operation); or
- *custom help screen*; or
- *temporary holding area* (e.g. to store values of previous record while processing the current record).

A *field* in a block is classified as one of the following:

- *base table field* (called also a *database field*)—corresponding to a column in the base table for the block;
- *table lookup field*—corresponding to a column in other than the base table for the block (retrievable by a trigger, but not modifiable from this block);
- *temporary data field*—not corresponding to any single table column (calculated and displayed by a trigger operating on values in the database, on other fields in the form, on user input or on other forms called by the current form).

7.3.2 Program functions

SQL*Forms can be used with a variety of display terminals. A utility is provided to generate a *keyboard map*, that is to match program functions required by SQL*Forms to the terminal keys and to take advantage of special characteristics of terminals (such as reverse video, bold, highlighting or underlining). A separate set of program functions is used for a screen painting (modify) mode and for running the form. Different terminals use different keyboard maps. A designer can also modify a map, for example to incorporate functions unique to a specific form.

A possible keyboard map for the terminal VT220 is shown below for both modes of operation. For convenience, the names of program functions are used to describe SQL*Forms operations in a device-independent way. The function [Show Function Keys] can be used to display a keyboard map for the terminal from which SQL*Forms is run.

Screen painting (modify) keys on a VT220 terminal

Program function	Terminal key
Right	→
Left	←
Down	↓
Up	↑
Next Field	Return or Tab
Previous Field	F12
Insert/Replace	F14
Delete Backward	Backspace (the key with <X] sign)
Clear Field	F20
Create Field	Insert Here
Select	Select
Select Block	Next Screen

Define	Find
Resize Field	F18
Cut	Remove
Paste	F17
Draw Box/Line	Prev Screen
Undo	F19
Accept	Do
Exit/Cancel	PF4 or ^Z
Print	F9
Redisplay Screen	^R
Run-Options Window	PF2
Show Function Keys	PF1

Form run keys on a VT220 terminal

Program function	*Terminal key*
Right	→
Left	←
Scroll Right	F11 →
Scroll Left	F11 ←
Next Field	Return or Tab
Next Primary Key Field·	^K
Next Record	↓
Next Set of Records	F10
Next Block	Next Screen
Previous Field	F12
Previous Record	↑
Previous Block	Prev Screen
Insert/Replace	F14
Delete Backward	Backspace (the key with <X] sign)
Clear Field	F20
Clear Record	F19
Clear Block	F18
Clear Form/Rollback	F17
Delete Record	Remove
Create Record	Insert Here
Duplicate Field	^F
Duplicate Record	F7
Enter Query	Select
Count Query Hits	F8
Execute Query	Find
Commit Transaction	Do
Exit/Cancel	PF4 or ^Z
Print	F9
Redisplay Page	^R
Help	Help
List Field Values	F13

Display Error	PF3
Block Menu	PF2
Show Function Keys	PF1

7.3.3 Creating a default form

In Version 2.3, SQL*Forms offers a set of pop-up multiple-item windows which serve as menus in painting and running forms and in Version 3.0, Macintosh-style menus are introduced. In a completed and fully customized application, these windows and menus are not normally visible to a user. They are replaced by an application-specific interface (which can, and usually will, include application-specific menus).

Figure 7.2 presents the CHOOSE FORM window which serves as a kind of main menu from which major SQL*Forms operations can be initiated. The window provides a box to fill in the name of the form and a list of items (*actions*) to select. These are:

CREATE	to build a new form;
MODIFY	to change an existing form;
LIST	to display a list of existing forms (e.g. for selection into the Name field);
RUN	to run a form;
DEFINE	to change a form name or define form-level triggers (Section 7.3.6);
LOAD	used for migration of existing forms between different SQL*Forms versions or installations;
FILE	to save or discard changes to a form, to drop the form, to duplicate or rename the form;
GENERATE	to generate an executable version of a form after it has been created or modified.

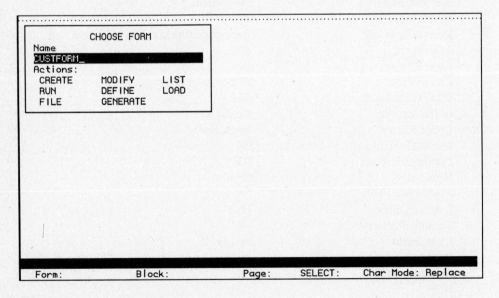

Figure 7.2   The CHOOSE FORM window

The last two lines near the bottom of the screen are the message line and the status line. The *message line* displays prompts, error messages and similar information. The *status line* is the last line on the screen. It informs about the form, block and page currently in use and how many times the [Select] function key has been pressed (used in selecting an object on the screen to be moved, copied, erased, etc.). It also reminds whether the form is being used in the replace or in the insert mode. In the former, the characters being typed replace existing characters under the cursor; in the latter, the typed characters are inserted to the left of the cursor. The Page and SELECT items apply only in the screen painting mode.

After the CREATE action in the CHOOSE FORM window is selected, the CHOOSE BLOCK window pops up (Figure 7.3). The actions in the CHOOSE BLOCK window include:

CREATE   to create a new block with the name and page number specified and to enter the screen painter;

MODIFY   to make changes to an existing block;

DROP   to delete the named block from the form;

LIST   to display a list of existing blocks in the form;

FIELDS   to display a list of existing fields in the block;

DEFAULT   to create a new block with default settings;

PREVIOUS   to display the. name of the block with the previous sequence number (assigned in the screen painter);

NEXT   to display the name of the block with the next sequence number (assigned in the screen painter).

A new block can be created by selecting the CREATE or DEFAULT action. Usually the DEFAULT action is chosen first to automatically obtain the default form. The default form can later be re-designed, enriched and customized by performing the MODIFY

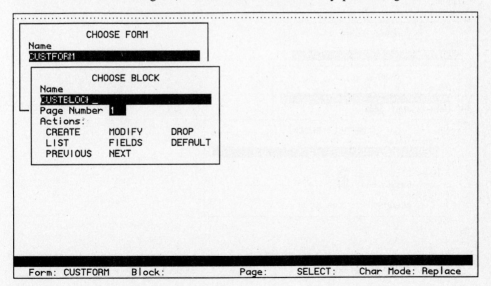

Figure 7.3   The CHOOSE BLOCK window

action. After selecting the DEFAULT action, the DEFAULT BLOCK window pops up (Figure 7.4). It contains the following items:

Table Name	to name the base table or the view table for the block (it can be different from the block name);
Rows Displayed	to specify the number of rows to display (it determines whether the block will be single-record or multi-record; the value 1 indicates a single-record block);
Base Line	to specify the screen line number on which the block will begin;
COLUMNS	to display a list of available column names;
TABLES	to display a list of available tables (from which the base table or the view table for the block can be chosen).

A default form with two single-record blocks is shown in Figure 7.1. Figures 7.5 and 7.6 illustrate a default form with two pages (screens). Either page contains one single-record and one multi-record block. The form is generated from the base tables A_SHIPMENT, A_SHIPMENT_LINE, A_INVOICE and A_INVOICE_LINE.

```
SQL> DESC A_SHIPMENT;
 Name                                   Null?       Type
 ----------------------------------     ---------   ---------
 OUR_ORDER_NUMBER                       NOT NULL    CHAR(5)
 SHIPMENT_DATE                                      DATE
 SHIPMENT_MEDIUM                                    CHAR(20)
 CUSTOMER_NUMBER                                    CHAR(5)
 CUSTOMER_PURCHASE_ORDER_NUMBER                     CHAR(8)
 SHIPMENT_WEIGHT                                    NUMBER
 SHIPMENT_CHARGES                                   NUMBER
```

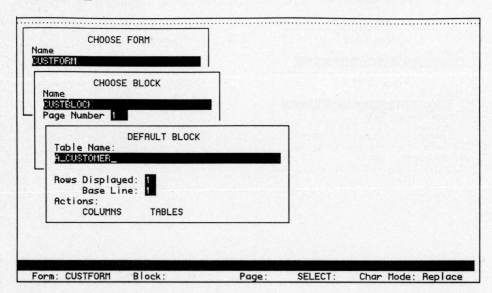

Figure 7.4   The DEFAULT BLOCK window

```
SQL> DESC A_SHIPMENT_LINE;
Name                              Null?       Type
-------------------------------- ---------   ---------
OUR_ORDER_NUMBER                 NOT NULL    CHAR(5)
ITEM_NUMBER                      NOT NULL    CHAR(10)
QUANTITY_ORDERED                             NUMBER
QUANTITY_SHIPPED                             NUMBER


SQL> DESC A_INVOICE;
Name                              Null?       Type
-------------------------------- ---------   ---------
INVOICE_NUMBER                   NOT NULL    CHAR(5)
INVOICE_DATE                                 DATE
OUR_ORDER_NUMBER                             CHAR(5)
CUSTOMER_NUMBER                              CHAR(5)
CUSTOMER_PURCHASE_ORDER_NUMBER               CHAR(8)
SALESPERSON_NAME                             CHAR(30)


SQL> DESC A_INVOICE_LINE;
Name                              Null?       Type
-------------------------------- ---------   ---------
INVOICE_NUMBER                   NOT NULL    CHAR(5)
ITEM_NUMBER                      NOT NULL    CHAR(10)
QUANTITY_BACK_ORDERED                        NUMBER
QUANTITY_CANCELED                            NUMBER
AMOUNT                                       NUMBER
```

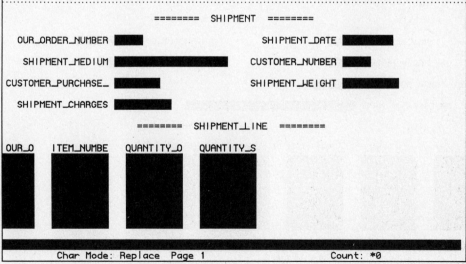

Figure 7.5   First page of a default form

7.3.4 Running a form

A created form gives complete data entry, query, update and delete facilities. Prior to running a form, it should be saved and generated in the CHOOSE FORM window (using the FILE and GENERATE actions). The RUN action in the CHOOSE FORM window executes the form.

Using a form for data entry can be a convenient substitution for the INSERT statement in SQL. Figure 7.7 uses a default form obtained for the base table A_ITEM in order to enter several tuples at a time into the table. Basic checks are performed by SQL*Forms (such that an alphabetic character cannot be entered in the value of a numeric field).

Querying from within a form can be done by typing the selection criteria directly into the appropriate fields after first pressing the [Enter Query] function key. The query is executed by hitting the [Execute Query] function key. The query in Figure 7.8 is interpreted: "Find items which contain the string PENCIL in their description *and* which price is less than 9 dollars". Two special characters facilitate pattern matching of search operations: the percent character (%) represents any combination of a number of characters (including no characters) and the underline character (_) represents any character.

An answer to the query in Figure 7.8 is given in Figure 7.9. All pencil items cheaper than $9.00 are retrieved.

In general, SQL*Forms allows search criteria of almost any complexity. In particular, the WHERE clause of SQL can be specified in the message line at the bottom of the screen. The WHERE clause can be defined for any field in the form or any combination of fields. Such fields are required to be indicated by *placeholders*, that is the ampersand (&) or colon (:) character, followed by a letter or a short word. After pressing the

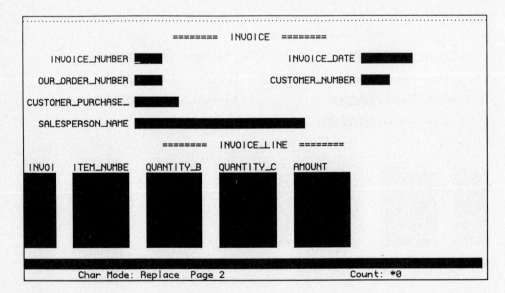

Figure 7.6   Second page of a default form

[Execute Query] key, SQL*Forms prompts for a WHERE clause in which the placeholders can be referred to.

Retrieved records can be easily modified in the form. To *modify* any particular field (i.e. column) in the base table, the cursor must be moved to that field and the new value typed over the old one. To *delete* a record (i.e. a tuple) from the base table, the cursor can be located anywhere in the record and then the [DELETE] function key pressed.

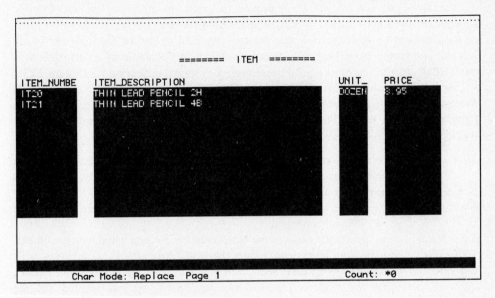

Figure 7.7   Using a default form for data entry

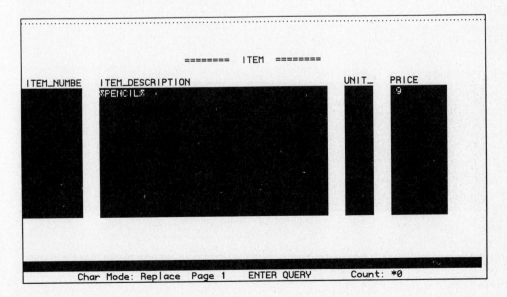

Figure 7.8   Entering a simple query in a field

7.3.5 Modifying a form

A default form provides basic layout and functionality of a form-driven application. It is a quick and easy way of building an application prototype. For a production database system, the forms need to be modified to improve both their layouts and functions. This can be done by selecting the MODIFY action in the CHOOSE FORM window (Figure 7.2).

The layout of a form can be improved to create an effective and user-friendly appearance. The screen painter of SQL*Forms allows for any changes to a form. Any text on the form can be edited or new text entered; any field or part of the form can be re-located; and boxes around the blocks can be drawn. An example of a form that was modified in order to represent a good user interface is shown in Section 7.4 (Figure 7.23).

To modify a block of the form, the MODIFY action in the CHOOSE BLOCK window needs to be selected (Figure 7.3). Two additional keystrokes, [Select Block] and [Define], are then needed to open the DEFINE BLOCK window (Figure 7.10). The window contains fill-in items and a set of actions:

Seq#	to specify the order in which the cursor moves to the block when the [Next Block] or [Previous Block] function key is pressed;
Name	to name or modify the name of the block;
Description	to provide a description of the block to be displayed when the function key [Menu] is pressed;
Table Name	to specify the name of the base table or view associated with the block;
TRIGGER	to define a block-level trigger (Section 7.3.6);
ORDERING	to specify WHERE and ORDER BY clauses that apply to all queries for the block and control the way queries retrieve records into the block;

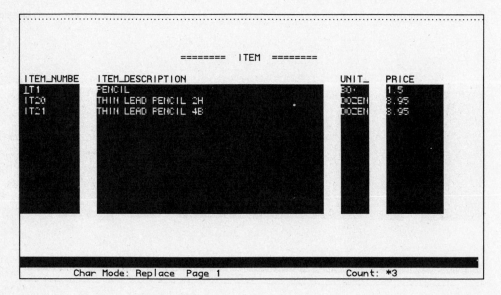

Figure 7.9   Result of a simple query

OPTIONS	to determine various block characteristics (such as the number of records buffered in the memory at one time);
COMMENT	to comment about the block;
TABLES	to list tables from which the base table for the block can be selected.

The functionality of a form can be enhanced by using many additional utilities of SQL*Forms. A number of these utilities is available from the DEFINE FIELD window

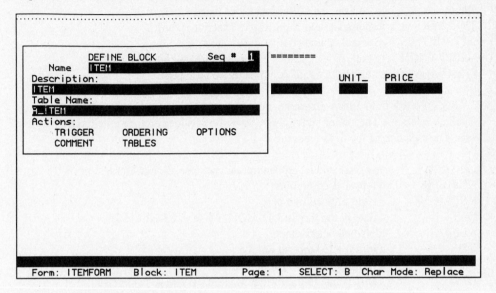

Figure 7.10 The DEFINE BLOCK window

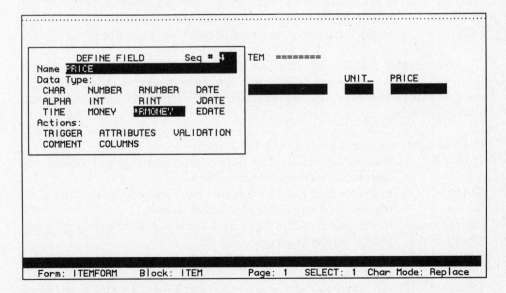

Figure 7.11 The DEFINE FIELD window

(Figure 7.11). This window can be invoked by moving the cursor to the field in the screen painter and pressing the [Select] and [Define] function keys. The meanings of the items in the DEFINE FIELD window are:

Seq#	to specify the order in which the cursor moves to the field when the [Next Field] or [Previous Field] function key is pressed;
Name	to name the associated column in the base table;
Data types	to choose one of the data types listed for the field;
TRIGGER	to define a field-level trigger (Section 7.3.6);
ATTRIBUTES	to select characteristics for the field;
VALIDATION	to control how values in the field are validated;
COLUMNS	to display a list of columns in the base table.

SQL*Forms field types are more numerous and elaborated than column types of database relations. They offer better control over how values are presented to the terminal user. The meaning of the field types are:

CHAR	any displayable, alphanumeric and special characters;
NUMBER	a left-aligned number;
RNUMBER	a right-aligned number;
DATE	a date in the format DD-MON-YY (e.g. 23-DEC-88);
ALPHA	alphabetic characters;
INT	a left-aligned integer number;
RINT	a right-aligned integer number;
JDATE	a Julian date in the format MM/DD/YY (e.g. 12/23/88);
TIME	a time of day in the format HH24:MM:SS (e.g. 23:09:57);
MONEY	a left-aligned number representing a sum of money (e.g. 5.99);
RMONEY	a right-aligned number representing a sum of money;
EDATE	an European date in the format DD/MM/YY (e.g. 23/12/88).

Attributes of a field are defined in the SPECIFY ATTRIBUTES window (Figure 7.12). The window contains a menu of choices that can be toggled on and off. A selected choice is indicated by an asterisk and can be shown in inverse video on some terminals. The attributes are:

Database Field	represents a column in the base table;
Primary Key	enforces uniqueness of the field values (alone or in combination with other fields) across the records of the form;
Displayed	makes the field (i.e. the name and value) visible when the form is run (the field is always visible in the screen painter);
Input allowed	informs that a value of the field can be entered or changed by the user;
Query allowed	permits the user to query on the field;
Update allowed	permits the user to change a value in the field in a record retrieved by a query;
Update if NULL	permits the user to change a value in the field in a record retrieved by a query, but only if this value is null;

Fixed Length	enforces a fixed number of characters in a value of the field;
Mandatory	requires a value in the field;
Uppercase	converts lowercase letters in a value of the field to capitals;
Autoskip	causes an automatic movement to the next field upon entering the last character in the field;
Automatic help	displays the help message (defined in the SPECIFY VALIDATION window) whenever the field is entered;
No echo	suppresses the display of characters typed into the field.

Each field is assigned validation characteristics in the SPECIFY VALIDATION window (Figure 7.13). The window contains the following fill-in items:

Field Length	defines the maximum number of characters that can be entered in the field;
Query Length	defines the maximum number of characters that can be entered in the field as a query condition;
Copy Field ...	specifies the block name and the field name from which the value of the field is copied (e.g. in Figure 7.5, the field OUR_ORDER_NUMBER from SHIPMENT block can be copied to the field OUR_ORDER_NUMBER in SHIPMENT_LINE block);
Default	determines a default value of the field;
Range ...	determines the minimum and maximum valid values for the field;
List of Values ...	specifies the table and column that contain a list of valid (suggested) values for the field; works in conjunction with the [List Field Values] function key;
Help	contains an explanatory message displayed upon pressing the [Help] function key.

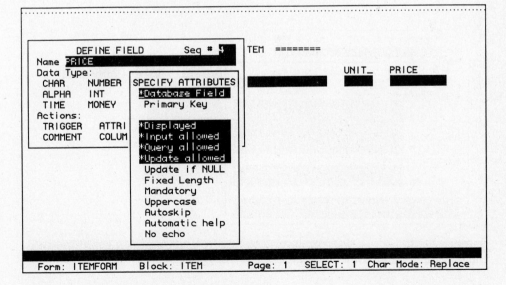

Figure 7.12 The SPECIFY ATTRIBUTES window

7.3.6   Using triggers in a form

A trigger is a set of SQL commands (including special SQL*Forms commands) that are triggered by a certain event when a form is run (e.g. to verify that an employee identification number exists in the database).

Triggers are usually set up after a basic prototype of the form has been created and tested. They serve as powerful means of data validation, integrity and security enforcement, update propagation, field calculation, and function keys expansion.

7.3.6.1   Trigger levels and scope

Triggers can be defined at three levels of a form and a trigger scope is determined by the level at which it is defined. The higher the level, the broader the scope; for example, a trigger defined at the block level applies to every field in the block, that is it is triggered by operations on any field in the block. However, if a trigger of the same type is defined at more than one level, the lower level trigger overrides the higher ones. The levels, from the highest to the lowest, are:

1. *form level* (from the DEFINE FORM window)—to determine general actions and those taken on entering or leaving the form (Figure 7.14);
2. *block level* (from the DEFINE BLOCK window)—to determine actions taken:
   (a) on entering or leaving the block or a record in it,
   (b) on inserting, updating, or deleting a record in the block (Figure 7.15);
3. *field level* (from the DEFINE FIELD window)—to determine actions taken on entering, changing, or leaving the field (7.16).

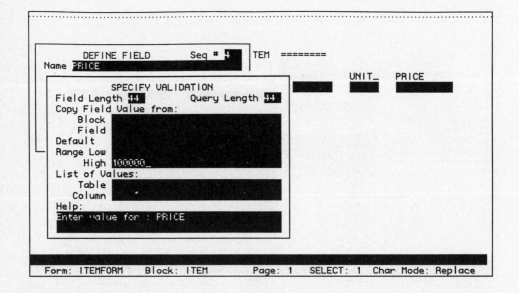

Figure 7.13   The SPECIFY VALIDATION window

The CHOOSE TRIGGER window contains a fill-in item and nine actions. The fill-in item *Name* gives a name to the trigger. Except for so-called user-named triggers, a trigger name is also its type. The actions are:

CREATE   to create a new trigger;
MODIFY   to modify the specified trigger (beginning with the first step of that trigger);

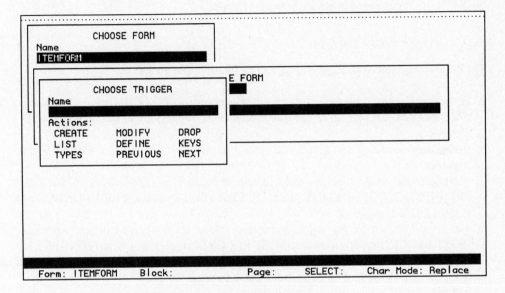

Figure 7.14   The CHOOSE TRIGGER window (form level)

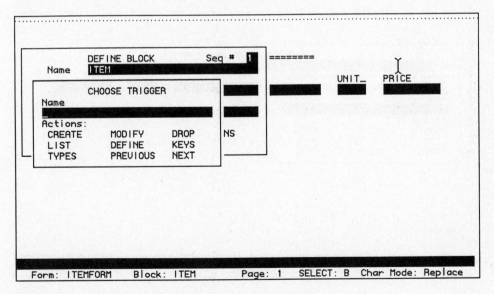

Figure 7.15   The CHOOSE TRIGGER window (block level)

DROP   to delete the specified trigger;
LIST   to display a list of existing triggers;
DEFINE   to change the name of the specified trigger (or menu description of a key
                trigger);
KEYS   to display a list of available key triggers;
TYPES   to display a list of available non-key triggers;
PREVIOUS   to display the name of the previous trigger;
NEXT   to display the name of the next trigger.

7.3.6.2 Trigger events and types

The *events* associated with triggers are grouped into five categories:

1. *entry event*—caused by the action of entering a form (PRE-FORM trigger), a block
   (PRE-BLOCK trigger), a record (PRE-RECORD trigger) or a field (PRE-FIELD
   trigger);
2. *query event*—caused by a retrieval operation (POST-QUERY and PRE-QUERY
   triggers);
3. *change event*—caused by an insert, delete or update operation (POST-CHANGE,
   PRE-DELETE, POST-DELETE, PRE-INSERT, POST-INSERT, PRE-UPDATE, and
   POST-UPDATE triggers);
4. *exit event*—caused by the action of leaving a form (POST-FORM trigger), a block
   (POST-BLOCK trigger), a record (POST-RECORD trigger) or a field (POST-FIELD
   trigger);
5. *keystroke event*—caused by a keystroke operation (e.g. the KEY-PRVBLK trigger that
   redefines the [Previous Block] function key).

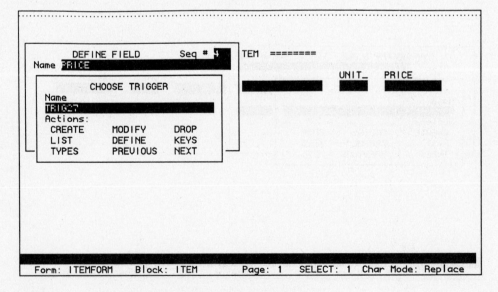

Figure 7.16   The CHOOSE TRIGGER window (field level)

One kind of trigger is not associated with any specific event. This is a *user-named trigger*, which can be called from another trigger and reused whenever needed.

At each trigger level, the available trigger types can be displayed by performing the LIST action in the CHOOSE TRIGGER window. This action results in a pop-up window called LIST TYPES (Figure 7.17). Because the lists of triggers are large, the LIST TYPES window is scrollable (using the PREVIOUS and NEXT actions).

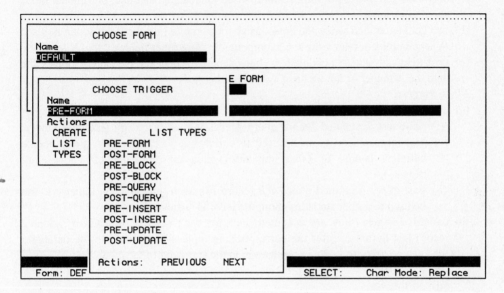

Figure 7.17 The LIST TYPES window

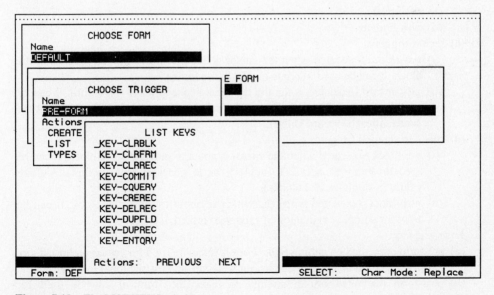

Figure 7.18 The LIST KEYS window

Key triggers, that is the triggers associated with keystroke events, can be displayed by performing the KEYS action in the CHOOSE TRIGGER window. The action brings up the LIST KEYS window (Figure 7.18). *Trigger types* can be classified into five groups:

1. *Field triggers*:
    (a) post-change (executed when the cursor is about to leave a field whose value has been changed and is not null, it can be used to change, calculate, or validate fields about to be left);
    (b) pre-field (executed when the cursor is about to move into the field, it can be used to set complex default values, e.g. computable from other fields);
    (c) post-field (similar to post-change, but executed whenever the cursor leaves the field, i.e. whether or not the field value has changed).
2. *Block triggers*:
    (a) query triggers:
        (i) pre-query (executed before query processing, activated by [Execute Query] key, takes place; it can be used to enrich search criteria of a query and to initialize counts or other statistics which are computed by post-query triggers),
        (ii) post-query (executed after *each* record has been retrieved by a query; it can be used to gather statistics about the records retrieved);
    (b) commit triggers (they are executed once for each deleted, inserted or updated record just before or after the corresponding tuple is committed to the database; they can be used for update propagation in the form and in the database):
        (i) pre-delete,
        (ii) post-delete,
        (iii) pre-insert,
        (iv) post-insert,
        (v) pre-update,
        (vi) post-update;
    (c) record triggers:
        (i) pre-record (executed when the cursor is about to move into any record in the block, it can be used to relate blocks in the form);
        (ii) post-record (executed when the cursor is about to leave the record, it can be used for cross-field validation and calculations and to refresh or reformat the screen after the record is left);
    (d) block navigation triggers:
        (i) pre-block (executed when the cursor is about to move into the block, it can be used to authorize access to a block or to generate more complex default values in single-record blocks);
        (ii) post-block (executed when the cursor is about to leave the block, it can be used for complex validation of groups of records).
3. *Form triggers*:
    (a) pre-form (executed on calling SQL*Forms; it can be used for access authorization, setting-up system defaults or displaying welcome and instructional messages);
    (b) post-form (executed on an attempt to leave the form; it can be used for housekeeping and statistics).

4. *Key triggers* (which redefine the function keys and can be used to disable keys or perform special multiple functions with a single keystroke).
5. *User-named triggers* (which are executed from within another trigger and can be used to define more general triggers to be invoked by other triggers).

7.3.6.3 Triggering SQL commands

Technically, a trigger is composed of one or more commands. Each command constitutes a trigger *step*. Three kinds of commands are allowed:

1. *SQL command* which operates on information in database relations or in a form (extensions to SQL syntax are provided to permit data transfers between relations and forms).
2. *SQL*Forms command* which redefines the action of a function key or reproduces another permissible operation.
3. *User exit* which calls a programmatic interface.

Figure 7.19 illustrates a PRE-FORM trigger step which contains a SQL command. The trigger is defined at the form level and its type is PRE-FORM. It restricts the access to the form to users stored in the AUTHORIZATION relation. The pseudo-column USER is a kind of system variable which contains the name of the user currently operating the form. This trigger does not need to retrieve data from the relation; rather it succeeds or fails depending on whether or not the user exists in the relation AUTHORIZATION. To this aim, the trigger selects a constant, 'x' by convention, from the relation instead of a column (this is a faster way of trigger use).

The TRIGGER STEP ATTRIBUTES window is used to control actions after the trigger step succeeds or fails and to allocate memory to the step (Figure 7.20). The

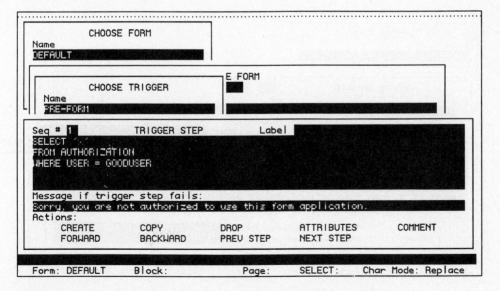

Figure 7.19 The TRIGGER STEP window (SQL command at form level)

SQL*Forms defaults to the first attribute shown on this window, that is "Abort trigger when step fails". This forces the user to correct the mistake before further operations can proceed (the only other alternative is to exit the form altogether). The normal criteria for success and failure can be reversed by selecting the attribute "Reverse return code". This can be used, for example, to make sure that a particular record does not exist in the database (i.e. SELECT fails) before a certain action (e.g. INSERT) is done.

The attribute "Return success when aborting trigger" is only meaningful if the first (default) attribute is deselected. It can be used to suppress the execution of a trigger if certain conditions are met. The attribute "Separate cursor data area", if selected, reserves memory space for, and speeds the processing of, the trigger step concerned (such a trigger should be executed frequently in the form to obtain desirable benefits).

At times, a SQL trigger does not need to access a database relation to return success or failure. This often happens if the SELECT statement is merely used for calculation based on values of the fields in the form. In such a case, the calculation is executed within the statement, but the FROM clause must still be present (it is required by SQL syntax). To make the whole exercise as painless as possible, ORACLE provides an "artificial" public relation called DUAL which contains only one column (named DUMMY) and one value ('X', by convention). Figure 7.21 illustrates a PRE-FIELD trigger step which calculates the value of AMOUNT in the INVOICE_LINE block (cp. Figure 7.6). The colon (:) is placed in front of field names to distinguish them from relation columns. Such a differentiation is not necessary in an INTO clause because the clause can only be used to select data into form fields (but the use of the colon enhances clarity).

7.3.6.4 Triggering SQL*Forms commands

A trigger step can contain a SQL*Forms command. As opposed to SQL commands which operate on information in database or in form, SQL*Forms commands perform control

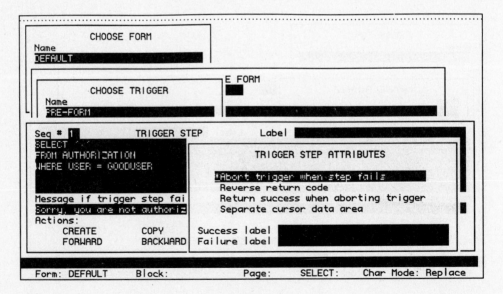

Figure 7.20 The TRIGGER STEP ATTRIBUTES window

actions such as redefining function keys, automatically performing actions which would normally require keyboard strokes, executing user-named triggers, calling other forms and running operating system commands.

SQL*Forms commands begin with a hash (#) character. The colon (:) is not used in SQL*Forms commands to reference form fields because these commands cannot refer to database columns. There are four SQL*Forms commands: #EXECMACRO, #COPY, #ERASE and #HOST.

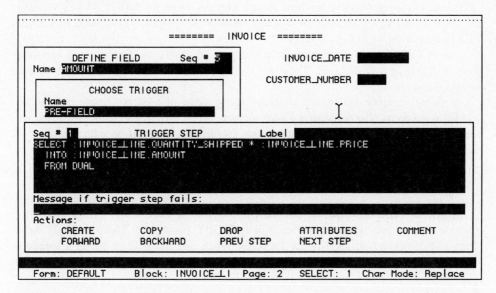

Figure 7.21   The TRIGGER STEP window (SQL command at field level)

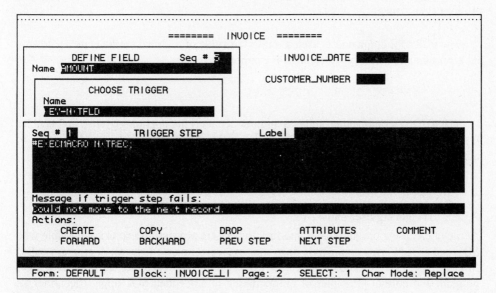

Figure 7.22   The TRIGGER STEP window (SQL*Forms command)

The #EXECMACRO command defines a *macro*, that is a series of actions to be performed by SQL*Forms. Following the #EXECMACRO keyword, a *function code* of each action together with its arguments (if any) is written. The semicolon (;) ends a macro command. The major use of macros is in defining the key triggers. Figure 7.22 shows a KEY-NXTFLD trigger with the step #EXECMACRO NXTREC;. The macro redefines the [Next Field] key in the field AMOUNT, that is in the last enterable field of the INVOICE_LINE block (cp. Figure 7.6). This is a multi-record block and the macro causes the cursor to move to the next record after the value for AMOUNT is given and the [Next Field] key is pressed (in fact, the value of AMOUNT is calculated by a PRE-FIELD trigger shown in Figure 7.21).

The #COPY command enables the copying of constants, field values and variables from a source to a destination. There are two kinds of variables: global variables and system variables.

A *global variable* can store a character string value of arbitrary length outside the blocks of the form. The name of a global variable is: GLOBAL.var_name; for example, the command to initialize the global variable GLOBAL.CUST_NUM with the value of the field CUSTOMER_NUMBER in the block INVOICE is:

```
#COPY INVOICE.CUSTOMER_NUMBER GLOBAL.CUST_NUM
```

A *system variable* identifies the current location of the cursor. It is a read-only variable (it can only serve as a source in a #COPY command). There are only three system variables which identify the form, the block and the field of cursor's location. These are:

- SYSTEM.CURRENT_FORM,
- SYSTEM.CURRENT_BLOCK, and
- SYSTEM.CURRENT_FIELD.

The #ERASE command is used to erase the value of a global variable and to destroy its definition and memory allocation, for example:

```
#ERASE GLOBAL.CUST_NUM
```

The #HOST command establishes an interface with the operating system and enables it to run operating system commands; for example, the following command connects to SQL*Plus and runs a command file called *salesreport*:

```
#HOST sqlplus.salesreport
```

7.3.6.5 Triggering user exits

A trigger can use a programmatic interface to perform processing that is not possible with SQL and SQL*Forms commands or to improve performance (speed). A program called from a trigger step is known as a user exit. A user exit resembles an embedded SQL program and normal principles of programming in embedded SQL apply (Section 7.2); however, a user exit needs to access not only the database relations (EXEC SQL statements), but also the form fields, global variables and system variables (EXEC IAF statements). The calling convention in a trigger step is:

```
#EXITNAME PARAMETERS
```

A user exit, as opposed to an embedded SQL program, does not include an EXEC SQL CONNECT statement. SQL*Forms connects to the database automatically. In SQL*Forms, the exit name must be in uppercase. Upon completion, a user exit returns a value to SQL*Forms indicating a:

- success:
  `return(IAPSUCC)` or
- failure:
  `return(IAPFAIL)` or
- fatal error:
  `return(IAPFTL)`.

In the following simple example of the user exit, a value of the date is obtained from the form field NEW_DATE and placed into the user exit variable *eff_date* (lines 18–19). This value is used to update the column DATE_EFFECTIVE in the relation NEW_PRICE_LIST (lines 20–21). The exit includes limited error handling (lines 17, 23–25). The entry *sqliem* specifies a message that SQL*Forms displays if the trigger step fails or if it causes a fatal error and the key [Display Error] is pressed.

```
1    /* User exit */
2    #include <stdio.h>
3    EXEC SQL INCLUDE SQLCA.H;
4
5    EXEC SQL BEGIN DECLARE SECTION;
6            char eff_date[9];
7    EXEC SQL END DECLARE SECTION;
8
9    int NEW_PRICE(cmd, cmdlen, msg, msglen, query)
10        char *cmd;
11        int  *cmdlen;
12        char *msg;
13        int  *msglen;
14        int  *query;
15
16   {
17        EXEC SQL WHENEVER SQLERROR GOTO exitfail;
18        EXEC IAF GET NEW_DATE
19                INTO :eff_date;
20        EXEC SQL UPDATE NEW_PRICE_LIST
21                SET DATE_EFFECTIVE = :eff_date;
22        return (IAPSUCC);
23      exitfail:
```

```
24              sqliem(msg, msglen);
25              return(IAPFAIL);
26    }
```

Line 2 in the user exit is customary in C environment, but it is not really needed by SQL*Forms. Line 3 includes SQL Communication Area. The DECLARE SECTION (lines 5–9) defines user exit variables referenced in EXEC SQL and EXEC IAF commands. The parameter *cmd* is a string containing the user exit name and parameter string in the trigger step that calls this exit. The parameter *msg* contains a failure message defined for the trigger step calling the user exit. The parameters *cmdlen* and *msglen* are pointers to the length of *cmd* and *msg*, respectively. The parameter *query* is a pointer to a status flag whose value is 1 if the calling trigger is POST-QUERY or 0 otherwise.

The EXEC SQL statements are discussed in Section 7.2. There are two EXEC IAF statements:

1. **EXEC IAF GET**   to read the value of SQL*Forms field into a user exit variable:

```
    EXEC IAF GET field1, field2, ... fieldn
             INTO :var1, var2, ... varn;
```

2. **EXEC IAF PUT**   to store a value (constant or a reference to a user exit variable) into a form field:

```
    EXEC IAF PUT field1, field2, ... fieldn
             VALUES(value1, value2, ... valuen);
```

7.4 CASE STUDY: PROGRAMMING

To illustrate the programming aspect of the case study development, a complete description of one form, CUS700, is given. This form produces the CUSTOMER SALES HISTORY (Figure 7.23) and is run whenever the list of previous sales to a customer is needed (e.g. to check whether an item on which an upgrade is requested was actually sold by the company to the customer). The form contains two blocks. In the first block, a customer is identified either by CUSTOMER ID or by SURNAME and FIRST NAME (a simplifying assumption is made that a combination of SURNAME and FIRST NAME provides the unique identification of a customer). In the second block, the application searches in the database for items purchased by the customer and displays those items in a multi-record block.

The triggers used in the form CUS700 refer to five database tables:

```
SQL> DESC SOLD_LIST_1
 Name                                      Null?       Type
 ----------------------------------        ---------   ---------
 CUST_REQ_NO                               NOT NULL    NUMBER(5)
 CUST_ID                                   NOT NULL    CHAR(8)
 DATE_PURCHASED                            NOT NULL    DATE
```

```
SQL> DESC SOLD_LIST_3
 Name                              Null?      Type
 --------------------------------  ---------  ---------
 CUST_REQ_NO                       NOT NULL   NUMBER(5)
 ITEM_NO                           NOT NULL   CHAR(10)
 SERIAL_NO                                    CHAR(10)
 DATE_PURCHASED                    NOT NULL   DATE
 TYPE_OF_WARRANTY                             CHAR(5)
 DATE_WARRANTY_EXPIRES                        DATE
 APPLECARE_NUMBER                  CHAR(10)

SQL> DESC CUSTOMER_DETAILS
 Name                              Null?      Type
 --------------------------------  ---------  ---------
 CUST_ID                           NOT NULL   CHAR(8)
 FIRSTNAME                         NOT NULL   CHAR(15)
 SURNAME                           NOT NULL   CHAR(15)
 CUST_ADDR                                    CHAR(30)
 POST_CODE                                    CHAR(4)
 CUST_PHONE                                   CHAR(15)
 CUST_TYPE                                    CHAR(3)
 COURSE_DEPT                                  CHAR(20)
 DATE_STARTED                      NOT NULL   DATE
 DATE_VALIDATED                    NOT NULL   DATE
```

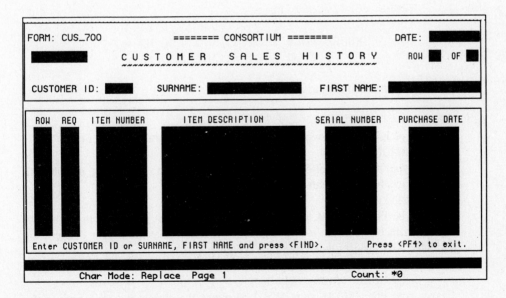

Figure 7.23   The CUSTOMER SALES HISTORY form

```
SQL> DESC ITEM_DESC
Name                                 Null?        Type
-------------------------------      ---------    ---------
ITEM_NO                              NOT NULL     CHAR(10)
CATEGORY                             NOT NULL     CHAR(2)
ITEM_DESCRIPTION                     NOT NULL     CHAR(40)
G_STORE_NO                                        CHAR(10)
FLAG_CURRENT                         NOT NULL     CHAR(1)
FLAG_PACKAGE                         NOT NULL     CHAR(1)
CODE_MARKUP                                       CHAR(1)


SQL> DESC MENU_SEL
Name                                 Null?        Type
-------------------------------      ---------    ---------
PID                                  NOT NULL     NUMBER(5)
PREV                                              NUMBER(3)
SELECTION                                         NUMBER(3)
USER_NAME                                         CHAR(10)
```

The list of items to be displayed in the second block is restricted by the SQL statement specified in the ORDERING item of the DEFINE BLOCK window (Figure 7.10):

```
SELECT CUST_REQ_NO, ITEM_NO,
       SERIAL_NO, DATE_PURCHASED
FROM SOLD_LIST_3
WHERE :BLK1.CUST_ID =
       (SELECT CUST_ID FROM SOLD_LIST_1
        WHERE SOLD_LIST_1.CUST_REQ_NO =
             SOLD_LIST_3.CUST_REQ_NO);
```

The form uses the following triggers:

At form level:
   Trigger type KEY-EXIT, step label 1 (performs [Exit/Cancel] key function):
   `#EXECMACRO EXIT;`
   Trigger type KEY-OTHERS, step label 1 (performs no operation; disables all function keys for the form except [Exit/Cancel]):
   `#EXECMACRO NULL;`
   Trigger type POST-FORM, step label 1 (calls a user exit that is discussed below; the comment between the << >> characters indicates that the trigger disables the attribute "Abort trigger when step fails" (Figure 7.20)):
   `#MENU_BACK`
   `<< CONTINUES WHEN FAILS >>`
   Trigger type PRE-FIELD, step label 1 (displays the current date and time in the field labeled DATE, but identified as DATE_NOW):

```
SELECT TO_CHAR ( SYSDATE, ' DD-MON-YY HH:MI:SS ')
           INTO :BLK1.DATE_NOW
           FROM DUAL
```

At the first block (BLK1) level:

Trigger type KEY-HELP, step label 1 (performs [Help] function; i.e. enables the [Help] key function after it was nullified in the KEY-OTHERS trigger at the form level):

```
#EXECMACRO HELP;
```

Trigger type KEY-NXTFLD, step label 1 (performs [Next Field] function); to allow searches on SURNAME, FIRST NAME if CUSTOMER ID is not known to the operator):

```
#EXECMACRO NXTFLD;
```

At the SURNAME field level:

Trigger type KEY-EXEQRY:

Step label 1 (displays a message to the user that the function is working; this message is displayed in an unlabeled field FUNCTION_STATE, in the top left corner of the screen, just below the form identification):

```
SELECT ' Function Working.. '
   INTO BLK1.FUNCTION_STATE
   FROM DUAL
```

Step label 2 (finds the CUSTOMER ID value on the basis of the values in the fields SURNAME and FIRST NAME):

```
SELECT CUST_ID
   INTO :BLK1.CUST_ID
   FROM CUSTOMER_DETAILS
   WHERE CUSTOMER_DETAILS.FIRSTNAME =
           :BLK1.FIRSTNAME
   AND CUSTOMER_DETAILS.SURNAME =
         :BLK1.SURNAME
```

Step label 3 (selects the count of the items purchased by the customer into the first block in the field labeled OF, but identified as ROW_TOT):

```
SELECT COUNT (ITEM_NO)
   INTO :BLK1.ROW_TOT
   FROM SOLD_LIST_3
   WHERE SOLD_LIST_3.CUST_REQ_NO =
         (SELECT CUST_REQ_NO FROM SOLD_LIST_1
             WHERE SOLD_LIST_1.CUST_ID =
                   :BLK1.CUST_ID)
```

Step level 4 (moves the cursor to the second block and performs [Execute Query] function):

```
#EXECMACRO GOBLK BLK2; EXEQRY;
```

At the CUST_ID field level:

Trigger type KEY-EXEQRY:

Step label 1 (displays a message to the user that the function is working;

this message in displayed in an unlabeled field FUNCTION_STATE, in the top left corner of the screen, just below the form identification):

```
SELECT ' Function Working.. '
  INTO BLK1.FUNCTION_STATE
  FROM DUAL
```

Step label 2 (selects the customer name into the first block; the comment informs about the message to be displayed if this trigger step fails (Figure 7.21)):

```
SELECT SURNAME, FIRSTNAME
  INTO :BLK1.SURNAME, :BLK1.FIRSTNAME
  FROM CUSTOMER_DETAILS
  WHERE CUSTOMER_DETAILS.CUST_ID =
        :BLK1.CUST_ID
<< MSG >> = Invalid CUSTOMER ID. Please check
           register.
```

Step label 3 (selects the count of the items purchased by the customer into the first block in the field labeled OF, but identified as ROW_TOT):

```
SELECT COUNT (ITEM_NO)
  INTO :BLK1.ROW_TOT
  FROM SOLD_LIST_3
  WHERE SOLD_LIST_3.CUST_REQ_NO =
        (SELECT CUST_REQ_NO FROM SOLD_LIST_1
           WHERE SOLD_LIST_1.CUST_ID =
                 :BLK1.CUST_ID)
```

Step label 4 (moves the cursor to the second block and performs [Execute Query] function):

```
#EXEMACRO GOBLK BLK2; EXEQRY;
```

Step label 5 (clears FUNCTION_STATE field):

```
SELECT ' '
  INTO :BLK1.FUNCTION_STATE
  FROM DUAL
```

At the second block (BLK2) level:

Trigger type KEY-NXTREC:

Step label 1 (discovers the last item record in the second block; the comment informs about the message to be displayed if this trigger step fails):

```
SELECT 'x'
  FROM DUAL
  WHERE :BLK2.ROWNUM != :BLK1.ROW_TOT
<< MSG >> = At last record.
```

Step label 2 (performs [Next Record] function, if not at the last record):

```
#EXECMACRO NXTREC;
```

Trigger type KEY-PRVREC, step label 1 (performs [Previous Record] function; there is no need to disable this step when the cursor is at the first record because SQL*Forms does it automatically and displays relevant message):

```
#EXECMACRO PRVREC;
```
At the ITEM NUMBER field level:

Trigger type POST-CHANGE, step label 1 (finds the value of ITEM DESCRIPTION corresponding to the ITEM NUMBER value):

```
SELECT ITEM_DESCRIPTION
   INTO :BLK2.ITEM_DESCRIPTION
FROM ITEM_DESC
WHERE ITEM_DESC.ITEM_NO =
          :BLK2.ITEM_NO
```
At the ROW field level:

Trigger type KEY-NXTFLD, step label 1 (moves the cursor to the first block):

```
#EXECMACRO GOBLK BLK1;
```
Trigger type PRE-FIELD, step label 1 (allows the user to see (in the top right-hand corner of the screen) what record of second block is currently processed):

```
SELECT :BLK2.ROWNUM
   INTO :BLK1.ROW_NOW
FROM DUAL
```

The MENU_BACK user exit, called from the form level trigger POST-FORM, is a generalized exit that supports a hierarchical menu-style processing of the entire application. The application consists of many integrated forms. The exit updates the user's tuple in the relation MENU_SEL and puts the user back to the original menu when the form CUS700 is exited (i.e. to the menu from which the form CUS700 was called).

```
1    /* The user exit MENU_BACK */
2    #include <stdio.h>
3    EXEC SQL INCLUDE SQLCA.H;
4
5    EXEC SQL BEGIN DECLARE SECTION;
6            VARCHAR userid[20];
7            VARCHAR passwd[20];
8            int prev;
9            int pid;
10           int sel;
11   EXEC SQL END DECLARE SECTION;
12
13   int MENU_BACK(cmd, cmdlen, msg, msglen, query)
14       char *cmd;
15       int  *cmdlen;
16       char *msg;
17       int  *msglen;
18       int  *query;
19
20   {
```

```
21          pid = getpgrp();
22      EXEC SQL  SELECT PREV
23                  INTO :prev
24                  FROM MENU_SEL
25                  WHERE PID = :pid;
26      EXEC SQL  UPDATE MENU_SEL
27                  SET SELECTION = :prev
28                      PREV = TRUNC(:prev/10)
29                  WHERE PID = :pid;
30      EXEC SQL  COMMIT;
31      return (IAPSUCC);
32      EXEC IAF GET BLK3.SEL INTO :sel;
33   }
```

FURTHER READING

Application programming interfaces to databases are discussed by Lacroix and Pirotte (1983) and in Procedure (1985). Logic programming interfaces to databases are a subject of intensive research; some interesting papers include Chang and Walker (1986), Ghosh *et al.* (1988), and Tsur (1988). Bancilhon and Ramakrishnan (1986) propose strategies to deal with recursive logic queries in relational databases. Types and persistence in programmatic database interfaces (specifically in native syntax interfaces) are addressed by Atkinson and Buneman (1987) and Buneman and Atkinson (1986). Features and limitations of conventional programming languages are very well presented in a popular textbook by Ghezzi and Jazayeri (1987). Each host language has its own programming literature. An introductory textbook on programming in Cobol by Grauer (1985) is recommended. Bates and Douglas (1975) wrote a valuable textbook on programming in PL/I.

Programming in embedded SQL according to the relational standard is discussed by Date (1987). Pro*C is documented in ORACLE (1987b). A basic C reference is presented by Kernighan and Ritchie (1978). More instructional treatment of C is offered by Miller and Quilici (1986). The description of the problem for which a Pro*C solution was given in Section 7.2.3 is borrowed from one of the exercises in Date (1986).

Generation of applications in SQL*Forms is described in ORACLE (1987c, 1987d and 1988). The operation of forms, including the run-time error messages and the specification of complex queries in SQL*Forms, is presented in ORACLE (1987e). The principles of good user interface design, in particular for human-computer interaction, are presented by Shneiderman (1987).

REFERENCES

ATKINSON, M. P. and BUNEMAN, O. P. (1987): Types and Persistence in Database Programming Languages, *Comp. Surv.*, 2, pp.105–90.

BANCILHON, F. and RAMAKRISHNAN, R. (1986): An Amateur's Introduction to Recursive Query Processing Strategies, in: *SIGMOD'86. SIGMOD Record*, 2, pp.16–52.

BATES, F. and DOUGLAS, M. L. (1975): *Programming Language/One. With Structured Programming*, 3rd ed., Prentice Hall, 336p.

BUNEMAN, P. and ATKINSON, M. (1986): Inheritance and Persistance in Database Programming Language, in: *SIGMOD'86. SIGMOD Record*, 2, pp.4–15.

CHANG, C. L. and WALKER, A. (1986): PROSQL: a Prolog Programming Interface with SQL/DS, in: *Expert Database Systems*, Proc. 1st Int. Workshop, ed. L. Kerschberg, The Benjamin/Cummings, pp.233–46.

DATE, C. J. (1986): *An Introduction to Database Systems*, Vol. I, Addison-Wesley, 4th ed., 639p.

DATE, C. J. (1987): *A Guide to the SQL Standard*, Addison-Wesley, 205p.

DRAFT (1985): *Draft Proposed American National Standard Database Language SQL*, Technical Committee X3H2 - Database, X3.135-1985, Project 363-D, 115p.

GHEZZI, C. and JAZAYERI, M. (1987): *Programming Language Concepts*, 2nd ed., John Wiley & Sons, 428p.

GHOSH, S., LIN, C. C. and SELLIS, T. (1988): Implementation of a Prolog-INGRES Interface, *SIGMOD Record*, 2, pp.77–88.

GRAUER, R. T. (1985): *Structured COBOL Programming*, Prentice Hall, 479p.

IBM (1986): *IBM DATABASE 2 Application Design and Tuning Guide*, Document Number GG24-3004-00, IBM, International Technical Support Center, Santa Teresa, 125p.

IBM (1987a): *IBM DATABASE 2, Data Base Planning and Administration Guide*, Program Number 5740-XYR, Order Number SC26-4077-3, Release 3, IBM, 226p.

IBM (1987b): *IBM DATABASE 2, System Planning and Administration Guide*, Program Number 5740-XYR, Order Number SC26-4085-3, Release 3, IBM, 319p.

KERNIGHAN, B. W. and RITCHIE, D. M. (1978): *The C Programming Language*, Prentice Hall, 228p.

LACROIX, M. and PIROTTE, A. (1983): Comparison of Database Interfaces for Application Programming, *Inf. Syst.*, 3, pp.217–29.

MILLER, L.H. and QUILICI, A.E. (1986): *Programming in C*, John Wiley & Sons, 431p.

ORACLE (1987a): *Database Administrator's Guide*, Version 5.1, The Relational Database Management System ORACLE, Oracle Corp., Part No. 3601-V5.1.

ORACLE (1987b): *Pro*C User's Guide*, Version 1.1, The Relational Database Management System ORACLE, Oracle Corp., Part No. 3504-V1.1.

ORACLE (1987c): *SQL*Forms Designer's Reference*, Version 2.0, The Relational Database Management System ORACLE, Oracle Corp., Part No. 3304-V2.0.

ORACLE (1987d): *SQL*Forms Designer's Tutorial*, Version 2.0, The Relational Database Management System ORACLE, Oracle Corp., Part No. 3302-V2.0.

ORACLE (1987e): *SQL*Forms Operator's Guide*, Version 2.0, The Relational Database Management System ORACLE, Oracle Corp., Part No. 3301-V2.0.

ORACLE (1988): *Introduction to SQL*Forms*, Version 2.3, The Relational Database Management System ORACLE, Oracle Corp., Part No. 19192-0288, 51p.

PROCEDURE (1985): *Procedure Language Access to Draft Proposed American National Standard Database Language SQL*, ANSC X3H2 - Database, 25p.

SHNEIDERMAN, B. (1987): *Designing the User Interface: Strategies for Effective Human-Computer Interaction*, Addison-Wesley, 448p.

TSUR, S. (1988): LDL—A Technology for the Realization of Tightly Coupled Expert Database Systems, *IEEE Expert*, Fall, pp.41–51.

8

Testing and Maintenance of Database System

Database development is an iterative process; in fact, it is a never-ending process (it ends only when the system ceases to exist altogether). As user requirements change or expand and as new software, hardware and software engineering methods become compelling, the existing design and implementation need to be monitored and improved. A prototyping approach to the design, facilitated by an open architecture of data dictionaries in the relational databases, is inherently transformational. New design objectives are often discovered even before the system is put into operation and the implemented system undergoes constant reviews by users and maintenance teams.

This chapter covers basic problems and techniques involved in testing and maintenance of a database system. The open architecture of relational technology is helpful in this task. ORACLE database administration and support utilities are used in examples.

8.1 DESIGN AND IMPLEMENTATION REVIEWS

Fundamental to the success of a database project are *reviews* conducted on each and every phase of the design and implementation process. Reviews are an organizational technique of the wider activity called *testing* which evaluates a system or its component to identify whether it satisfies specified requirements and whether it produces expected results under any conceivable condition. Testing applies to all phases of database development, not just to programs and applications which can be run on a computer system.

The database development process is nonhierarchical, that is, it is neither manifestly top-down nor bottom-up; hence, the testing process, which applies to completed bits and pieces of database development, cannot be strictly top-down or bottom-up. In general, when seen as a system-wide methodology, the testing process is usually top-down (earlier development phases and stages are tested first) but when applied to a particular system component, testing and review process can proceed in either bottom-up or top-down fashion or both (i.e. in a mixed fashion).

Testing of a system component (known as *unit* or *module testing*) must always be done within the framework of the overall system. All interfaces, that is all expected input from, and desired ouput to, surrounding components, must be clearly determined. Methods of achieving the system decomposition and specifying the interfaces have been developed within the discipline of structured analysis and design. One such method, extensively discussed in this book and best applicable to initial phases of database design, is *data flow diagramming*. The other method, applicable in the later design phases and (unfortunately) not discussed here, is structure charting. In brief, *structure charts* are an extension of DFDs in which DFD processes are transformed to so-called modules and enhanced by implementation details, such as control flows, error handling or communication mechanisms with external devices. They are widely used in the design of systems based on procedural languages, such as COBOL or Ada; however, the use of structure charts in modern database development, centered around declarative programming and application generators, is not established and would require some changes to the approach.

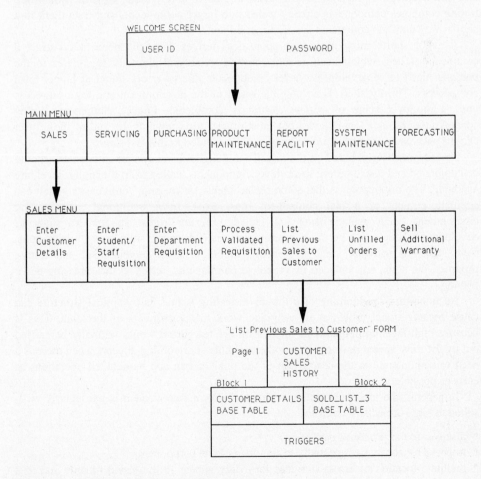

Figure 8.1   Modular structure of a database system

8.1.1   Bottom-up versus top-down testing

Data flow diagrams and structure charts, apart from providing graphical representations of the architecture of software systems, are by themselves complete analysis (data flow diagrams) and design (structure charts) methodologies. In testing the architecture is of primary interest. Figure 8.1 illustrates the architecture of a typical menu-driven database system. The application "List Previous Sales to Customer" is described in Section 7.4.

A question arises about how to review and test any particular component of a database system, such as the one illustrated in Figure 8.1. As already mentioned, this question cannot be separated from the approach taken to the database development.

Bottom-up testing is applicable whenever a developer wishes to complete the lower level components before the higher level components are fully developed. In order to guarantee that a component performs its tasks within the overall system, a software module, called *test bed* or *test harness*, needs to be written. The test bed calls the tested component in a way that verifies the role of this component in the overall system. Special test data need to be prepared for this task. If used in a systematic way, the bottom-up testing combines components already tested into larger components and tests them in a similar way until the completed system is assembled.

A major shortcoming of bottom-up testing derives from the need to construct a complex test bed, which itself requires testing. A second shortcoming relates to the potential need to re-develop low-level components due to errors found at higher-level components. Thirdly, there is no tangible result of the development and testing process until a top-level stage of *system testing* is completed. Finally, bottom-up testing concentrates resources and carries out most crucial tests towards the end of the project and the success or not of the project may well be decided in this last stage.

Top-down testing is based on the premise that higher level system components should be completed and tested before lower level components, called from the higher level, are available. The implication is that some replacements for missing components which can simulate outputs of a real component must exist. In a traditional programming environment, such replacements are called *program stubs*. In modern database development, they could be more appropriately named trigger stubs, screen page stubs, form stubs, or software stubs in general (Figure 8.1). As development and testing progress, the stubs are replaced by complete components, tested in the same top-down fashion.

An important shortcoming of a top-down testing is that its pyramidal structure can cause organizational problems in assigning work to all members of the team. This is because high-level components of the system are fewer and would normally be carried out by the most senior developers. Another possible shortcoming appears when there is a need to demonstrate to the user a part of the final system and its detailed operations as early as possible.

In general, the top-down testing seems to perform better and it is particularly well-suited to large projects. It tends to:

- discover major problems early;
- improve reliability by repeatedly testing lower level components;
- facilitate location of errors (because they only appear in the tested module and in a small subtree of stubs); and

- speed-up the testing process (software stubs are significantly easier to construct than test beds).

Top-down testing and software stubs should not be confused with so-called *black-box testing*. Black-box testing is a testing method whereby the test team makes no attempt to understand and analyze the internal structure and behavior of the tested component. Black-box testing concentrates on interfaces, that is on system inputs and outputs. Specific aspects of black-box testing are to feed the system with invalid data and to push the system to its operational limits.

Black-box testing is contrasted with *white-box testing* where the internal structure and behavior of the system are subject to scrutiny. A special aspect of white-box testing is to achieve adequate *coverage*, that is to ensure that all parts (e.g. program statements) of the tested component are activated during tests. In practice, the test coverage is also tested by seeding the software with known errors and observing whether the results are affected appropriately.

8.1.2 Structured walkthroughs and inspections

The structured walkthrough is a formal procedure to review the software. The procedure involves conducting a well-organized meeting (this justifies the word "structured") at which the reviewed system component is explained by its developer and put to the scrutiny of fellow developers on a step-by-step basis (this explains the word "walkthrough").

While the basic idea of structured walkthroughs may seem trivial, the evidence is, however, that the method works better than traditional review procedures. Special features of a structured walkthrough are:

- it can be used for any phase or stage of system development;
- the membership of the meeting is clearly defined;
- the tasks allocated to the participants are clearly specified;
- the duration of the meeting is short and fixed;
- the meeting pinpoints and documents the problems, but does not attempt to solve them;
- complete materials for the meeting are distributed and studied in advance;
- the number of meetings is not restricted but any meeting is set only when it guarantees to satisfy its objective.

The objective of a structured walkthrough is to attempt to show the presence of errors in the software and to do it in an effective and sociable manner. A typical membership of a walkthrough includes from three to six people. Project managers are excluded from the membership which consists of development team people, usually colleagues, who are given specific roles in the meeting. The team typically includes:

- the developer whose work is reviewed (this member can answer questions, if any, and may be expected to brief the meeting);
- a moderator to chair the meeting and to ensure its orderly and pleasant conduct, and perhaps to examine the conformance of the reviewed software with its specifications;

- a secretary to record decisions and actions;
- a member whose role is to examine whether the reviewed software and its documentation adhere to the standards of the organization;
- a member whose role is to examine the understandability and maintainability of the reviewed software;
- a member whose role is to examine the user friendliness and expandability of the reviewed software.

The duration of a walkthrough meeting should be from thirty to sixty minutes. The developer ought to take this into consideration when calling the meeting as the amount of work to be reviewed must correspond to the timing requirements of the meeting.

All participants must be allowed time prior to the meeting to study the materials. The meeting is supposed to take account of problems discovered during studying the materials, not to be a discovery forum by itself. Also, the meeting should not digress into a discussion of petty problems or into an attempt to find immediate solutions.

All identified problems, errors and omissions encountered during every walkthrough must be documented in a project notebook maintained by a project librarian or a secretary. The notes should include the schedule for the correction of identified drawbacks and for a follow-up review.

A structured walkthrough is purposely and inevitably informal, benevolent and subjective. Despite this, or rather because of this, the role of the walkthrough in system testing is quite special. The evidence is that structured walkthroughs contribute to:

- productivity, by making people feel a vital member of a team and not wanting to let the others down;
- software quality, by the collective effort of locating problems and constructing test data;
- meeting deadlines, by enforcing regular reviews;
- development of professional skills, by sharing ideas and learning from the experiences of colleagues.

While structured walkthroughs are informal and called relatively frequently, *inspections* are formal and normally take place only at two points during system development: after the design is completed and after the system is programmed. They are done under close management supervision, although managers do not normally attend the meetings. The membership of an inspection team consists of:

- the developer whose work is inspected;
- a chairperson to coordinate meetings and other activities;
- a tester who is formally responsible for testing the inspected software;
- a user (this will be a programmer if the inspection is carried out after the design phase).

The end point of structured walkthroughs and inspections is an α-*test*. The α-test is a subjective validation of the entire system at the end of the software development process to ensure compliance with software standards. It is done internally by the organization as a *quality control* activity. Software which has undergone a successful α-test is said to be quality controlled.

The α-test can be followed by a more objective test conducted by an independent software *quality assurance* organization. Such a test is called a β-*test*. After a successful β-test, the software is said to be quality assured. The ultimate in quality assurance is the *end-client acceptance test*, whereby the software is run on a client site for a specified period with no further commitments or obligations.

8.2   HOUSEKEEPING

Housekeeping encompasses routine maintenance tasks involved in keeping a database system operational and accessible. To this aim, a DBMS is equipped with housekeeping utilities, that is programs and procedures not involved in the main stream of database processing but specifically developed to conduct housekeeping tasks such as backup. (Starting from Version 6.0 of ORACLE, the housekeeping and other database administration utilities are integrated in a single product called SQL*DBA.)

8.2.1   Starting and stopping the system

A DBMS offers a utility to start and stop a database. In ORACLE such a utility has an acronym IOR (Initialize ORacle). It is used to start a database the very first time after installation and to start and stop it thereafter. The utility is very powerful and dangerous and misuse can destroy the content of a database. Preferably, only one person, the super-user, should be allowed to run this utility.

The IOR utility can be run with different arguments to produce different results. The initialize argument INIT is used to start the database the very first time. During such a start, called *cold start*, the database and before image files are restored to an empty state. Any existing user data is lost. (The *before image file* contains images of data before changes are made to it. It is used for rollback recovery, and to ensure the database consistency and concurrent processing (Section 8.2.3).)

The INIT option is used infrequently. It is required when migrating to a new version of ORACLE and when consolidating and reorganizing the database files. Prior to initializing ORACLE, the utility CCF (Create Contiguous File) needs to be run on most operating systems to allocate space for the database files and for the before image files (Section 6.2.2.2). Also, a full backup of the system (Section 8.2.3) has to be done before the IOR utility with INIT option is run.

A *warm start* of ORACLE is achieved by the IOR utility with the WARM argument. It re-starts the system and opens both existing database files and the before image file. Any outstanding transaction from the previous session is rolled back and the temporary files are dropped.

There are two ways of stopping ORACLE. A preferred way is to use the SHUT option in the IOR utility. This lets users who are currently logged on to complete their transactions and log off. Only when no users are active does the IOR SHUT proceed with the shutdown. The ORACLE processes are stopped and the files are closed.

The second way of stopping ORACLE is a bit brutal to the current users. It stops ORACLE processes immediately and logs current users off (with appropriate notification). Transactions in progress are lost and will be rolled back during the next warm start. This way of stopping ORACLE uses the argument CLEAR in the IOR utility.

Some housekeeping tasks, such as export/import (Section 8.2.3), require that the database administrator is the only user of the database. For this reason, the IOR utility allows for specification of the DBA option together with WARM or INIT arguments on the IOR command line so that only users with DBA authority can log on to the database. The database must be shut down and warm started again without the DBA option to allow all other users to access ORACLE.

Whenever ORACLE is started, a *parameter file*, which contains desired specifications of ORACLE operation, is read by the IOR utility. By default, this file is called INIT.ORA. The default can be overridden by using the argument PFILE=filename on the IOR command line. The parameters in the INIT.ORA file are used to:

- *provide labels* (such as names of the database and before image files);
- *indicate limits* (e.g. the maximum number of cursors that each user is allowed to open);
- *affect performance* (e.g. the parameter which specifies the maximum number of cached relation definitions can influence performance by reducing parse execution time for those definitions which are found in memory).

8.2.2 Enrolling and dropping users

Perhaps the most frequent housekeeping activity is enrolling and dropping users. It is also a very responsible activity. It grants users access to the database and assigns privileges to this access. The user is given a *username* and a modifiable *password*, which are independent from user identification and password needed at the operating system level.

The SQL standard uses the concept of an *authorization identifier* to identify the user of each schema and each module associated with an application program. The authorization identifier of a schema is the owner of all relations and views defined within that schema and must hold a necessary *privilege* to perform a given operation (SELECT, INSERT, UPDATE and DELETE) on a given relation or view. The owner of a relation or view holds all privileges on that relation or view; however, the standard makes the distinction between an updatable and not updatable (called *read-only*) view. The only applicable privilege on a read-only view is SELECT. The UPDATE privilege can be specified for individual columns of a relation or an updatable view.

A privilege on a relation or view is granted to a particular grantee (identified by an authorization identifier) with or without grant option. A privilege *with grant option* means that the recipient of the privilege can in turn grant privileges to other authorization identifiers; however, only the held privileges or a subset of held privileges can be granted to others.

In ORACLE, three kinds of privileges are distinguished. They are (in increasing order of importance):

- CONNECT
- RESOURCE
- DBA.

Any user enrolled in ORACLE has one or more privileges. A user is enrolled and the initial privileges are granted to that user by means of the SQL statement GRANT. For example, the following GRANT statement enrolls a new user (the CONNECT option) and grants the RESOURCE privilege to that user. The username is MAC and the password is LES.

```
GRANT CONNECT, RESOURCE TO MAC IDENTIFIED BY LES;
```

The password is required in the GRANT statement containing the CONNECT privilege. Additional privileges to an existing user can be granted without referring to the password (which, anyhow, could have been changed in the meantime by the user by using GRANT CONNECT TO), for example:

```
GRANT DBA TO MAC;
```

Normally, a user with the CONNECT privilege has to provide a username and password on any login to the database. Such a user needs to remember two sets of usernames and passwords (unless they are the same)—one set for the operating system and another for the DBMS. This may be irritating in some less stringent processing environments (such as in an educational institution) so ORACLE offers a so-called *automatic login option*. A user with an automatic login has identification-free access to the database upon being logged on to the operating system. The fixed prefix OPS$ on the ORACLE username in the enrolling GRANT statement signifies a user with the automatic login, for example:

```
GRANT CONNECT, RESOURCE TO OPS$G8825377
            IDENTIFIED BY GRAD_STUDENT;
```

In this example, a user with the operating system identification G8825377 is given an automatic login username OPS$G8825377. This automatic login username is stored in the data dictionary and enables the user, on attempting to access ORACLE, to ignore (by just pressing a [Return] key) the ORACLE prompt asking for a username.

Privileges to users with respect to relations and views are granted by means of another format of the GRANT statement, namely:

```
GRANT {privilege, privilege, ... | ALL}
    ON {relation | view}
    TO {user | PUBLIC}
    [WITH GRANT OPTION];
```

The privileges can be held on any combination of the operations ALTER, DELETE, INDEX, INSERT, SELECT and UPDATE. The privileges ALTER and INDEX are not permitted with views. ALL is assumed if the GRANT statement is not defined for a relation or view. The UPDATE privilege can be specified for individual columns by using a parenthesized list of columns, as shown:

```
GRANT UPDATE (column, column, ...) ...;
```

The special user PUBLIC represents all users enrolled in ORACLE. WITH GRANT OPTION authorizes the grantee to grant held privileges in turn to other users.

A user enrolled with only the CONNECT privilege can do more than the name of the privilege may indicate. Such a user may:

- access the database and ORACLE utilities;
- run SELECT statements on existing relations and views;
- perform data manipulation statements INSERT, UPDATE and DELETE on existing relations and views;
- create views and synonyms (the *synonym* (the CREATE SYNONYM statement) is an alternative name for a relation created to avoid the need to prefix another user's relation name with this user's name).

Additional entitlements are obtained if the RESOURCE privilege is granted. A user with both CONNECT and RESOURCE privileges may:

- create database relations, clusters and indexes;
- grant and revoke privileges on those created (i.e. owned) objects to/from other users;
- perform auditing (the AUDIT statement) on the objects owned.

The DBA privilege is superimposed on the CONNECT and RESOURCE privileges and enables the database administrator to:

- perform any operation on any object owned by any user;
- enroll and drop users and grant and revoke users database access privileges, that is authorities (but not access privileges to database objects owned by other users);
- create and alter partitions (i.e. database files);
- perform unrestricted monitoring and auditing;
- perform database exports and imports.

By default, ORACLE is installed with two users having the DBA privileges SYS and SYSTEM. The SYS user owns all the data dictionary relations and the SYSTEM user owns all the data dictionary views. The SYSTEM user also owns relations and views created and required by ORACLE products built on top of ORACLE DBMS (such as SQL*Forms or SQL*Menu). These relations and views can be considered an extension of the data dictionary. The data dictionary objects are critical for the database operation and they should never be altered under normal conditions. In fact, the SYS and SYSTEM accounts should be used rarely, if at all. A separate user with DBA privilege ought to be created to perform database administrator's tasks.

There is one more user automatically enrolled to ORACLE when the system is installed. This user is called PUBLIC. A special aspect of the user PUBLIC is that it is a *group user* and all other ORACLE users are also the PUBLIC user. This means that *all* ORACLE users can be given access privileges to database objects for which the owner of these objects runs the GRANT statement with the PUBLIC option, for example:

```
GRANT SELECT ON PRICE_LIST TO PUBLIC;
```

A user is *dropped* if the CONNECT privilege is revoked from that user (by a user with the DBA authority), for example:

```
REVOKE CONNECT TO OPS$G8825377
```

A dropped user can be reinstated at some later time and regain the relations and views originally owned. This implies that the relations and views belonging to a dropped user continue to exist in the database unless they are also dropped by using the DROP statement, for example:

```
DROP TABLE OPS$G8825377.PRICE_LIST;
```

If the relations and views which have to be dropped are numerous, and there is no immediate need to drop them, a more convenient way is to eliminate such relations and views by doing selective export/import (Section 8.2.3).

8.2.3 Database backup and recovery

The database backup is a routine housekeeping activity during which the entire database is copied (dumped) to an archive external storage medium. The backup of a database is necessary to restore the database to the original state if physical damage occurs (e.g. as a result of a disk head crash). In such a case, a *redo* (or *rollforward*) *recovery* is performed. The backup copy of the database is loaded and all transactions completed since the backup was taken are redone. To support the redo operation, a special *log file*, called *after image file*, is written during normal database activities to record transactions which have been committed to the database.

The second and more frequent recovery activity, which does not involve a database backup, is termed an *undo* (or *rollback*) *recovery*. Such a recovery is required if the database is put into an inconsistent state after some transaction terminates abnormally (e.g. as a result of computer system failure). Such transactions need to be undone during the next warm start of the database. To support the undo operation, a log file called *before image file* is maintained. This file contains images of data before changes are made to it. These images become outdated and can be overwritten only after a relevant transaction is committed to the database.

A database backup can be taken either by using an operating system utility or by using a DBMS utility (called *export/import*); however, the two methods are not fully equivalent. An operating system backup is basically the backup of a disk file and, therefore, preserves any corruptions made to the database, including internal database structures (such as indexes). The internal database structures are not easily recoverable through recovery procedures, but they can be restored from an export backup file obtained by running an export/import utility. The restoration takes place during the import activity (e.g. the indexes are recreated rather than copied).

If this difference between the backups taken on an operating system level and those taken on a DBMS level is not critical, then consideration must be given to other issues. A major advantage of the operating system backup is speed and convenience. Such backups are relatively quick and can be done at the same time as other backups, not related to the database, are taken. The export/import backup is slow and can require many hours for large databases. This by itself may be prohibitive unless the DBMS supports the *online backup* (which means performing an export during normal database processing) and the *incremental export* (i.e. the export of data changed since the last export). The online backup and the incremental export are available in ORACLE Version 6.0.

Apart from recovery, the export/import utility can be used to consolidate the space within the database files, which have been fragmented during the normal database operations of creating and dropping relations and other database objects. The utility can also be used for selective restoration of database objects, thus effectively dropping some of them. This is achieved by not exporting some objects and/or by not admitting some of them to the import operation. As well as these uses, the migration to a new version of the DBMS involves the export/import utility (to this aim, a higher version import operation is applied to a lower version export file).

8.3 ADAPTIVE MAINTENANCE

Maintenance has a couple of interpretations. In a wider sense, maintenance covers all activities discussed in this chapter, ranging from system testing (Section 8.1) via housekeeping (Section 8.2) and monitoring and auditing activities (Section 8.3) to system enhancements (Section 8.4). In a narrower sense, maintenance refers to housekeeping, monitoring and auditing activities.

Adaptive maintenance means monitoring and auditing of an operational system with the aim of making diagnoses and adapting the system in order to perform better. *Monitoring* is the act of observing on a terminal the ongoing use of a database system. An online display utility must be provided by the DBMS to make the monitoring possible. *Auditing* is an act of recording information about the use of a database over some period in a file (called an *audit-trail*). This information can be processed to provide statistics of database use for further consideration.

8.3.1 Monitoring

In ORACLE the monitoring utility is called ORACLE Display System (ODS). The ODS utility allows the selection of different screens from the main menu to monitor various ongoing activities. The main menu of ODS is shown in Figure 8.2.

A display type is chosen by entering the name of one of the options (the names can be abbreviated to the first one or two characters, indicated by capital letters) and an operating system's interrupt sequence needs to be used to return to the main menu. For any particular display type, the display cycle interval can be set with the *CYcle <n>* command, where n is a cycle time in seconds. ODS offers a limited auditing capability by allowing the displays to be directed to a file (*Open <filename>* and *CLose* commands).

The *Bi* command monitors the use of the before image file (Section 8.2.3). This file is organized in a circular fashion such that the data is written sequentially in the next available blocks. The blocks belonging to different transactions are interspersed. A block (or blocks) of a transaction can be reused after the transaction commits, but only if no blocks belonging to another uncommitted transaction exist before that block in the circular file. This means that long transactions which do not commit can potentially clog the entire file, thus putting the system into a virtual deadlock. To alleviate such a risk, a before image file needs to be large, preferably half the size of the database files.

The before image screen provides information about the current use of the before image file, in particular:

Used blocks	gives the amount of before image blocks in use by currently active transactions;
Low block	gives the number of the first block of the before image file;
High block	gives the number of the last block of the before image file;
Head block	gives the number of the last block allocated to a current transaction;
Tail block	gives the number of the first (i.e. the earliest) block allocated to a current transaction.

The *Io* command provides a graphical display of the current relative contribution of each ORACLE process to the global I/O activity. The display gives only coarse information. The processes are identified by their identification numbers (called PID). The first four processes in the display are always *ORACLE background processes*. These are:

- Asynchroneous Read Ahead (ARH) which reads blocks from the database files into the ORACLE area in memory (called the System Global Area or SGA); this is a read-ahead, that is anticipatory, activity done on behalf of SQL statements executing full relation scans.
- Before Image Writer (BIW) which writes before image blocks from an SGA buffer to the before image file.

```
                         ORACLE Display System

                 Choose display type:


    Commands: Help (or ?)        - this display
              Bi                 - Before Image file statistics
              CLose              - Close the log file
              CYcle <n>          - set the update interval to 'n' seconds
              Display <width><height> - tell ODS display dimensions
              Exit               - Exit from ODS
              Io                 - System I/O distribution on per user basis
              Locks (0)          - Lock and Enqueue lists (0=all locks)
              Open <filename>    - open the log file
              Summary            - Summary of ORACLE system activity
              Table (D)          - Tables accessed by each user (D=RBA in dec)
              User <first-pid> <last-pid> - Detailed user stats
```

Figure 8.2   Main menu of ORACLE Display System

- Buffer Writer (BWR) which writes blocks, other than before image blocks, from SGA buffers to the database files or to the after image file.
- Cleanup (CLN) which periodically identifies and logs off ORACLE processes which terminated abnormally but still reside in the SGA; it also assists in shutdowns of the database.

The *Locks* command displays information about the locks currently held or waited for by processes. Locks are used to control concurrent access to the database by multiple processes. They prevent destructive interaction between processes. There are many types of locks, some of them are referred to in the Locks screen, namely shared and exclusive locks, and the locks on a data dictionary level and on a user table/row level.

The *Summary* display provides statistics about total activities on the entire database during a set time interval. It reports on:

- the number of logical (i.e. memory-based) and physical (i.e. external storage related) reads and writes;
- the number of commits and rollbacks;
- the number of deadlocks.

The *Table* screen monitors relations currently cached in memory. It shows, for each relation, the Relative Block Address (RBA) where the relation begins and the number of retrieval (read) and update cursors acquired by the users on that relation.

The *User* displays statistics on a per user basis. It provides the same statistics as in the Summary display and a few additional statistics, such as the number of cursors currently opened by the user's process.

8.3.2 Auditing

Auditing, while being a very useful maintenance technique, adds to the overall system workload and is, therefore, disabled in the default ORACLE setting. It can be enabled at any warm start of the database by setting the parameter AUDIT_TRAIL in the file INIT.ORA (Section 8.2.1) to a non-zero integer value. Information from auditing is stored by ORACLE, as any other information, in relations. More precisely, it is stored in data dictionary relation SYS.AUDIT_TRAIL and is accessible through ten data dictionary views owned by the user SYSTEM.

Auditing is controlled by two formats of the SQL statement AUDIT:

```
(1)   AUDIT {option, option, ... | ALL}
          ON {table | DEFAULT}
          [BY {ACCESS | SESSION}]
          [WHENEVER [NOT] SUCCESSFUL];
(2)   AUDIT {soption, soption, ... | ALL}
          [WHENEVER [NOT] SUCCESSFUL];
```

The first format audits a relation, view or synonym. Any of these objects can be audited only by its owner or by the DBA. The option list specifies what SQL statements are to be audited when applied to the specified object. For relations, the available options are: ALTER, AUDIT, COMMENT, DELETE, GRANT, INDEX, INSERT, LOCK, RENAME, SELECT and UPDATE. For views, all these options except ALTER and INDEX, are applicable; for example:

```
AUDIT INSERT, UPDATE ON PRICE_LIST BY SESSION;
```

The ON clause specifies the object to be audited. The option DEFAULT in the clause refers to the data dictionary view DEFAULT_AUDIT and can only be specified by the DBA. This views contains eleven columns, one column for each possible audit option. The original settings of the DEFAULT_AUDIT view disallow all auditing options. The AUDIT statement with the DEFAULT option specifies which operations can be audited on newly created relations. If afterwards there is a need to disallow some auditing, the reverse statement NOAUDIT needs to be used.

The BY clause determines how detailed the auditing should be. The BY ACCESS option writes a tuple to the audit trail for each SQL operation on the audited relation. The BY SESSION option writes a tuple to the audit trail for each user session accessing the audited relation.

The WHENEVER clause makes ORACLE perform auditing whenever:

1. an access to an audited relation is successful (WHENEVER SUCCESSFUL); or
2. an access to an audited relation is unsuccessful (WHENEVER NOT SUCCESSFUL); or
3. always (if no WHENEVER clause is specified).

The second format of the AUDIT statement allows the auditing of the system level operations and the operations of the DBA. This format can only be used by the DBA. The option list identifies the classes of database operations to be audited, namely CONNECT, DBA, NOT EXISTS and RESOURCE, as in:

```
AUDIT CONNECT WHENEVER NOT SUCCESSFUL;
```

The CONNECT option audits ORACLE logons and logoffs. The DBA option audits SQL statements that require the DBA authority (GRANT, REVOKE, AUDIT, NOAUDIT, CREATE PARTITION, ALTER PARTITION, CREATE PUBLIC SYNONYM, DROP PUBLIC SYNONYM). The NOT EXISTS option audits SQL statements that produce a "... does not exist" error (excluding the security violation errors). The RESOURCE option audits the statements: CREATE TABLE, DROP TABLE, CREATE VIEW, DROP VIEW, CREATE SPACE, DROP SPACE, CREATE SYNONYM, DROP SYNONYM, CREATE CLUSTER, ALTER CLUSTER and DROP CLUSTER.

The auditing information, recorded in the audit trail over some period, provides invaluable insight into the ways the database operates and performs. If used for adaptive maintenance, it can help to uncover major system bottlenecks and to determine the database objects on which extreme workloads are applied. These areas can then be designated for performance tuning.

8.4   PERFECTIVE MAINTENANCE

Perfective maintenance means re-designing and modifying the database system in order to satisfy the additional or changing user requirements or in order to respond to the changing environment of hardware or software. In computer-assisted software engineering environments, perfective maintenance is known as *software re-engineering* or *design recovery*. In database design and implementation, perfective maintenance has been traditionally studied under three interrelated topics:

1. database restructuring (i.e. changing the logical database schema);
2. database reorganization (i.e. changing the physical database schema);
3. program conversion (i.e. changing the application software).

In relatively static pre-relational database systems, perfective maintenance has a quite different dimension and significance than it does in dynamic relational systems. In pre-relational systems, any changes to database structures have far-reaching and unwelcome consequences on existing application software; hence, the design and implementation of those systems is considered as a basically forward movement, with no retreats possible until such time as a major perfective maintenance is undertaken. Perfective maintenance is therefore an infrequent event; however, as it is also a major, difficult and critical event, special utilities are provided by a DBMS to tackle it (such as a reorganization and restructuring utilities).

In relational database systems, perfective maintenance is more of a contiguous activity. Relational systems are more dynamic and provide for a better logical and physical data independence. They can accommodate less revolutionary changes to logical or physical data structures without serious or unclear consequences to application software. As relational systems also have an open architecture, all information, including that about internal database structures, is stored in readily accessible relations. This open architecture facilitates the gathering of information about the system-wide consequences of changes in database structures and enables problems to be fixed on an internal data dictionary level, if necessary.

As a result, no perfective maintenance utilities of the category known in pre-relational systems are currently provided by relational DBMSs. The user of a relational database is expected to be able to determine and localize the consequences of changes to database structures and then perform perfective maintenance. This is relatively easy as long as the proposed changes do not go beyond the data modification facilities provided by SQL (such as adding a column to a relation or renaming a relation). If, however, the proposed changes to data structures are extensive and incorporate new elements in the database design, perfective maintenance becomes no easier or less critical than in any pre-relational database system.

While extensive changes to database structures have consequences on application software which are difficult to determine and are often treated on a case by case basis, some more elementary changes can be classified and their consequences can be deduced. These consequences can involve conversion of existing programs. *Program conversion* can be of a syntactic nature or of a semantic nature. The former merely involves the need to rename variables and recompile the program. The latter requires modification of the program's logic. As a rule, whenever a semantic conversion of programs is needed, the views (i.e. view queries) which exist in the database (and are affected by the change) need to be semantically modified as well. For syntactic conversion of programs, a corresponding modification of views will normally include dropping and recreating them (after syntactic modifications are made).

Elementary logical level changes (*database restructuring*) include:

1. Addition of an attribute to a relation
   This transformation is directly supported in SQL of ORACLE by means of an ALTER statement, such as:

   ```
   ALTER TABLE LOAN ADD (DUE_DATE DATE);
   ```

   The new attribute DUE_DATE will be initiated with null values in all tuples of the relation LOAN. By and large, the transformation does not affect existing programs but a syntactic program conversion may be needed in those applications which contain SELECT * FROM LOAN ... statements. This is because * refers to all columns in the relation and will now include the DUE_DATE column. Similarly, the views which select all columns will no longer work correctly. To rectify that problem, such views need to be dropped and recreated.

2. Deletion of an attribute in a relation
   This transformation is not supported in SQL. The programs which make use of the deleted attribute will require semantic conversion. The conversion can be quite sweeping if the deleted attribute is a key attribute.

3. Modification of an attribute in a relation
   A limited support of this transformation is provided by SQL of ORACLE, as in:

   ```
   ALTER TABLE LOAN MODIFY (LOAN_AMOUNT NUMBER(9,2));
   ```

   In ORACLE, the allowed modifications are to change the attribute type or to decrease the attribute size; however, the modification is permitted only on columns that contain exclusively null values. Depending on the way the application programs process modified attributes, the program conversion may be syntactic or semantic.

4. Renaming of an attribute
   This transformation is not supported in SQL. The programs which make use of the renamed attribute will require only syntactic conversion (as long as the designer ensures that the attribute is renamed in all relations in which it exists). Views which directly refer to the renamed attribute need to be dropped and recreated.

5. Addition of a relation, view or synonym
   These transformations are done in SQL by means of a relevant CREATE statement. No existing applications should be affected.

6. Deletion of a relation, view or synonym
   These transformations are realized by the DROP statements. All existing applications, which refer to the deleted objects, are likely to be treated as outdated and will be removed. If not removed, they will require extensive semantic changes.

7. Modification of a relation

This transformation can mean a vertical (decomposition) or horizontal (partitioning) splitting of a relation. Alternatively, it can mean a merging (join) of two or more relations. The transformation is achieved by a series of CREATE and DROP statements. On the data definitional level, the transformation leads to the same problems as addressed by the normalization theory and view integration and the programs will need far-reaching semantic conversions. (Modification of a view is a procedural rather than definitional activity. It is achieved by dropping and recreating operations and may cause semantic conversions of programs. Modification of a synonym is equivalent to the renaming operation.)

8. Renaming of a relation, view or synonym

These transformations are directly supported in SQL, for example:

```
RENAME LOAN TO MORTGAGE_LOAN;
```

All existing views and programs which make use of the renamed objects will require syntactic conversion. The views affected by the change will have to be dropped and recreated.

Elementary physical level changes (*database reorganization*) include:

1. Addition of a partition or file

In ORACLE these transformations are achieved by the statements CREATE PARTITION and ALTER PARTITION (Section 6.2.2.2). No changes to existing views or programs result.

2. Deletion of a partition or file

These transformations are realized by not running the relevant CREATE PARTITION and ALTER PARTITION statements immediately before importing database (Section 8.2.3). No changes to existing views or programs result.

3. Addition or modification of a space definition

In ORACLE, these transformations are achieved by the statements CREATE SPACE (Section 6.2.2.2) and ALTER SPACE. No changes to existing views or programs result.

4. Deletion of a space definition

This transformation is achieved by the statement DROP SPACE, for example:

```
DROP SPACE DEFINITION COURSE_USE_SPACE;
```

Relations created with a reference to that space definition are not affected. No changes to existing views or programs result.

5. Addition of a cluster

In ORACLE, this transformation is achieved by the statement CREATE CLUSTER (Section 6.2.2.2). No changes to existing views or programs result.

6. Deletion of a cluster

This transformation is achieved by the statement DROP CLUSTER, for example:

```
DROP CLUSTER PERSONNEL;
```

There are several restrictions imposed on this transformation. It is not possible to drop a cluster that contains relations or to remove an individual relation from a cluster; however, the latter can be achieved by a sequence of logical level transformations:

(a) CREATE a new relation with the same structure and contents as the one to be removed from the cluster;

(b) DROP the old relation; and

(c) RENAME the new relation.

No changes to existing views or programs result.

7. Addition of an index

In ORACLE, this transformation is achieved by the statement CREATE INDEX (Section 6.2.2.2). No changes to existing views or programs result.

8. Deletion of an index

This transformation is achieved by the statement DROP INDEX, for example:

```
DROP INDEX XEMPLOYEE;
```

No changes to existing views or programs result.

FURTHER READING

Reviews and testing principles in system development are discussed by Brill (1983) and Macro and Buxton (1987). A good reference on structure charts is provided by Page-Jones (1980) and Peters (1988) gives a modern evaluation of the use of structure charts. Basics of structured walkthroughs are well presented in Bell *et al.* (1987) and in Hawryszkiewycz (1988).

The housekeeping utilities of ORACLE are presented in ORACLE (1987a). Authorization and privileges in the SQL standard are described by Date (1987) and in Draft (1985). Backup and recovery utilities and procedures for an ORACLE database are discussed in ORACLE (1987b) and in appropriate ORACLE installation manuals, such as ORACLE (1986). A monographic treatment of database recovery is offered by Bernstein *et al.* (1987).

The distinction between adaptive and perfective maintenance is used in the software engineering literature (e.g. Simons 1987, Steward 1987). Maintenance and auditing in ORACLE is described in ORACLE (1987a).

Despite the fact that perfective maintenance accounts for the majority of maintenance activities, the literature on this topic is inadequate basically because there is nothing much that can be said. Perfective maintenance, in particular in a relational database context, is a practised art on shaky grounds. Two interesting readings are Navathe (1985) and Shneiderman and Thomas (1982). SQL statements of ORACLE to support database restructuring and reorganization are defined in ORACLE (1987c).

REFERENCES

BELL, D., MORREY, I. and PUGH, J. (1987): *Software Engineering. A Programming Approach*, Prentice Hall, 250p.

BERNSTEIN, P. A., HADZILACOS, V. and GOODMAN, N. (1987): *Concurrency Control and Recovery in Database Systems*, Addison-Wesley, 370p.

BRILL, A. E. (1983): *Building Controls into Structured Systems*, Yourdon Press, 149p.

DATE, C. J. (1987): *A Guide to the SQL Standard*, Addison-Wesley, 205p.

DRAFT (1985): *Draft Proposed American National Standard Database Language SQL*, Technical Committee X3H2 - Database, X3.135-1985, Project 363-D, 115p.

HAWRYSZKIEWYCZ, I. T. (1988): *Introduction to Systems Analysis and Design*, Prentice Hall, 373p.

MACRO, A. and BUXTON, J. (1987): *The Craft of Software Engineering*, Addison-Wesley, p.380.

NAVATHE, S. B. (1985): Schema Implementation and Restructuring, in: *Principles of Database Design, Volume I, Logical Organizations*, ed. S. B. Yao, Prentice Hall, pp.361–96.

ORACLE (1986): *ORACLE for Pyramid 90X Series/OSX, Installation and User's Guide*, Oracle Corp., Part No. 1037-V5.0, 82p.

ORACLE (1987a): *Database Administrator's Guide*, Version 5.1, The Relational Database Management System ORACLE, Oracle Corp., Part No. 3601-V5.1.

ORACLE (1987b): *ORACLE Utilities User's Guide*, Version 5.1, The Relational Database Management System ORACLE, Oracle Corp., Part No. 3602-V5.1.

ORACLE (1987c): *SQL*Plus Reference Guide*, Version 2.0, The Relational Database Management System ORACLE, Oracle Corp.

PAGE-JONES, M. (1980): *The Practical Guide to Structured Systems Design*, Prentice Hall, 354p.

PETERS, L. (1988): *Advanced Structured Analysis and Design*, Prentice Hall, 272p.

SHNEIDERMAN, B. and THOMAS, G. (1982): An Architecture for Automatic Relational Database System Conversion, *ACM Trans. Database Syst.*, 2, pp.235–57.

SIMONS, G. (1987): *Introducing Software Engineering*, NCC Publ., 209p.

STEWARD, D. V. (1987): *Software Engineering with Systems Analysis and Design*, Brooks/Cole, 414p.

Appendix

CASE Tools
for Database Development

Computer-assisted software engineering (CASE) environments enforce a methodological approach to system development. They increase the productivity and quality of the design and implementation. As a modern technology, they integrate the best features of knowledge-based approach, databases, object-oriented paradigm and graphical user interfaces into coherent and powerful meta-systems to develop other systems. The following list of CASE tools for database systems development is not complete, but it is representative. New CASE tools are constantly emerging to meet new user requirements, design methods and workstation possibilities. The list provides, in alphabetical order, the names and vendors of the tools and short descriptions of features.

ACPVision, ERVision (Andyne Computing, Ltd.)
Mascot method of real-time software design, entity-relationship diagrams.

ANATOOL (Advanced Logical Software)
Data flow diagrams, structured specifications.

AUTO-MATE PLUS (Consulit)
Systems analysis, logical design (including normalization), physical design, schema generation for ADABAS, DB2, IDMS, IDS II, ORACLE and others.

Bachman Product Set (Bachman Information Systems)
Graphical manipulation of database designs, forward and reverse engineering of DB2 and IDMS databases, file administrator, entity-relationship diagrams.

BLUE (Interprogram B.V.)
Precedence analysis (Blue/10), system flows (Blue/20), Nassi-Shneiderman diagrams (Blue/30), program flow (Blue/40), data flow diagrams (Blue/50), entity diagrams (Blue/60), print and screen layouts (Blue/70), procedure flow (Blue/80), Jackson structured design (Blue/90).

CASE 2000 DesignAid (Nastec Corporation)
Yourdon's structured analysis and design, Orr's data-structured systems development, multiuser support based on central development database (data dictionary).

CASE*Designer, CASE*Dictionary (Oracle Corp.)
Data flow diagrams, entity-relationship diagrams, function hierarchies.

Consoi (SystemOID Inc.)
Entity-relationship diagrams (Consoi-ERM), data flow diagrams (Consoi-DFD), logical schema generation (Consoi-LDM).

CorVision (Cortex Corp.)
Entity-relationship diagrams, data view diagrams, action diagrams, menu diagramming.

Costar (Softstar Systems)
Cost estimation based on the Boehm's Constructive Cost Model (COCOMO); reports on the cost, effort and staffing for lifecycle phases: requirements, detailed design, integration and test, product design, code and unit test, maintenance.

Data-Station (Charles River Development)
Data flow diagrams, entity-relationship diagrams, data definition and schema generation.

Deft (Disus, a division of TSB International, Inc.)
Data flow diagrams, entity-relationship diagrams, program structure diagrams, forms editing.

***design* (Meta Software Corporation)**
Flowcharts, top down system design, simulation and analysis diagrams, organizational diagrams, source code documentation.

DesignMachine (Optima, Inc., formerly Ken Orr & Associates, Inc.)
Requirements definition of the Data Structured Systems Development (DSSD) methodology, integrated design data base.

Excelerator (Index Technology Corp.)
Data flow diagrams, structure charts and diagrams, data model diagrams, entity-relationship diagrams, presentation graphs, documentation generator, matrix graphs, block diagrams.

Entity-Relationship Approach; Data Modeling Tools (Chen & Associates, Inc.)
Entity-relationship diagrams (ER-Designer), database schemas generation (SchemaGen), linkage to mainframe data dictionary system (DDS-Link), normalization of entity-relationship design (Normalizer), generation of entity-relationship diagrams from English-like description (ER-AutoDraw).

FOUNDATION (Arthur Andersen & Co.)
Project estimating, work planning, project control and management (METHOD/1), data flow diagrams, flowcharts, structure charts, Warnier-Orr diagrams, decomposition diagrams, screens and reports painting (DESIGN/1), code generation and maintenance (INSTALL/1), DB2-based data dictionary.

Foundation Vista (Menlo Business Systems, Inc.)
Data flow diagrams, entity-relationship diagrams, program structure charts, screen and form design.

HTPM (Software Publishing Corp.)
> Project management: work breakdown structure, PERT charts, GANTT charts, task lists.

I-CASE (KnowledgeWare, Inc.)
> Decomposition diagrams, data flow diagrams, entity-relationship diagrams, property and association matrices, action diagrams, structure charts, screen layouts, information analysis and strategic planning, normalization, translation to hierarchical, network and relational models, COBOL generator.

IDDK—Intelligent Database Design Kit (IDDK Software)
> Data flow diagrams and function specification (DFD-Edit), hypersemantic entity-relationship-attribute modeling and normalization (ERA-Edit), logical schema derivation (L-Derive).

IDE (Interactive Development Environments)
> Graphical editors (dataflow diagrams, Yourdon's structure charts, Jackson's data structures, entity-relationship, control flows, state transition diagrams), data dictionary, drawing and naming validation.

IDMS/ARCHITECT (Cullinet Software)
> Entity modeling, relational data analysis, schema generation for IDMS, the definition of applications (including transactions, flow of control, program dialogs and maps).

IEF—Information Engineering Facility (Texas Instruments)
> Business function/entity usage matrices, entity-relationship diagrams, entity hierarchy diagrams, process hierarchy diagrams, process dependency diagrams, process action diagrams, dialog flow diagrams, screen design diagrams, procedure action diagrams, data structure diagrams.

IEW—Information Engineering Workbench (KnowledgeWare Inc. and James Martin and Arthur Young)
> IEW Strategic Bench, IEW Analyst Bench, IEW Design Bench, decomposition diagrams, entity-relationship diagrams, data flow diagrams, action diagrams.

Interactive EasyFlow (HavenTree Software Ltd.)
> Flowcharts.

LDD Logical Database Design (Holland Systems Corp.)
> Data elements definition, user views development (bubble charts), generation of normalized logical structure, physical design for hierarchical, network and relational systems.

MacBubles (StarSys Inc.)
> Data flow diagrams, data dictionary, mini specifications.

MacDesigner (Excel Software)
> Structure charts, tree diagrams, module descriptions.

MacProject II, SmartForm Manager (Claris)
> Project management: tables, histograms, PERT charts, Gantt charts (MacProject II), form design (SmartForm Manager).

MAESTRO (Softlab, Inc.)
>Project management, forms generator, code and JCL generator, graphics generator, procedure/rule/object language, version control.

MAST-ER (InfoDyne International, Inc.)
>Application development based on entity-relationship model.

MANAGER Family of Products (Manager Software Products Pty. Ltd. (MSP))
>Logical and physical database design for hierarchical, network and relational systems (DESIGNMANAGER), data dictionary (DATAMANAGER), graphical information engineering (managerVIEW), affinity analysis, functional decomposition, entity modeling and normalization (METHODMANAGER), application development (SOURCEMANAGER), test data generation and program testing (TESTMANAGER), project resource management and budgetary control system (PROJECTMANAGER).

MULTI/CAM (AGS Management Systems)
>Data flow diagrams, project bar chart, network scheduling chart, progress comparison bar, documentation generator.

POSE (A.C.S. International (ACSI) Pty Ltd)
>Data Model Diagrammer, Automatic Normaliser, Logical Database Designer, Data Flow Diagrammer, Structure Chart Diagrammer, Decomposition Diagrammer, Screen Report Painter.

PowerTools (Iconix Software Engineering, Inc.)
>Structured analysis with real-time extensions using data flow diagrams and process specifications (FreeFlow), structure charts (SmartChart), state transition diagrams (FastTask), algorithm design using pseudocode (PowerPDL).

ProMod (Promod, Inc.)
>Requirements analysis (Yourdon's structured analysis and real time analysis), system design (Parnas' modular design), program design (pseudocodes), and implementation (program templates in Ada, C and Pascal).

QuickBuild WorkBench (International Computers Limited)
>Data flow diagrams, entity models, application generation, data dictionary.

SDD—Semantic Data Dictionary (BHA Computer Pty. Ltd.)
>NIAM (Nijssen Information Analysis Method) modeling, normalization, relational schema generation.

SMARTS, CAPBAK, EXDIFF, TCAT, S-TCAT, TDGEN (Software Research, Inc.)
>Regression testing tools, coverage analyzers and test data generator.

Software-Through-Pictures (Interactive Development Environments)
>Data flow diagrams, entity-relationship diagrams, Yourdon's structure charts, Jackson's data structures, control flows, state transition diagrams, real time modeling.

teamwork (Cadre Technologies Inc.)
>Information modeling using entity-relationship diagrams, data dictionary, normalization etc. (teamwork/IM), systems analysis using data flow diagrams etc. (teamwork/SA), real-time modeling using control/data flow diagrams, state

transition diagrams, state event matrices, decision tables etc. (team*work*/RT), systems design using structure charts, module specifications etc. (team*work*/SD), customization and code generation (team*work*/ACCESS), schema generation for hierarchical, network and relational systems (team*work*/IM combined with team*work*/ACCESS).

Tek/CASE (CASE Division of Tektronix)

Structured analysis (Analyst/RT) and design (Designer), traceability, real time modeling.

THE DBA ASSISTANT (tm) (Software Architecture and Engineering, Inc.,)

Expert system based tools for logical and physical database design and software evaluation and performance (available for IDMS/R, intended for DB2 and DMS-1100).

TIP (Technology Information Products Corp.)

Business and information modeling in terms of entity-relationship and relational data models (TIP PLAN and TIP DEFINE), program generation using Jackson's technique (TIP CREATE), data dictionary (TIP REPOSITORY), normalization (TIP RELATE).

USER: Expert Systems (Information Engineering Systems Ltd.)

Startegic planning, tactical planning, data modeling, project management, design of screens, forms, reports, schema generation.

Visible Analyst Workbench (Visible Systems Corp.)

Graphical editor: structure charts, flowcharts, etc. (Visible Analyst), data flow diagrams (Visible Rules), data dictionary (Visible Dictionary).

vsDESIGNER, vsOBJECT MAKER (Visual Software, Inc.)

Drawing editor, integral word processor, attribute system, report generator, support of Yourdon, Warnier-Orr and Ward-Mellor methodologies, entity-relationship diagramming.

YOURDON SOFTWARE ENGINEERING WORKBENCH (Yourdon, Inc.)

Project dictionary, entity-relationship diagrams, structure charts, state transition diagrams, data flow diagrams (ANALYST/DESIGNER TOOLKIT), document generator (COMPOSE), editor and compiler to create a customized methodology (RULE TOOL).

Index